Midnight Rambles

MIDNIGHT RAMBLES

H. P. Lovecraft in Gotham

David J. Goodwin

EMPIRE STATE EDITIONS

AN IMPRINT OF FORDHAM UNIVERSITY PRESS

NEW YORK 2024

Fordham University Press has no responsibility for the persistence or accuracy of URLs for external or third-party Internet websites referred to in this publication and does not guarantee that any content on such websites is, or will remain, accurate or appropriate.

Fordham University Press also publishes its books in a variety of electronic formats. Some content that appears in print may not be available in electronic books.

Visit us online at www.fordhampress.com/empire-state-editions.

Library of Congress Cataloging-in-Publication Data available online at https://catalog.loc .gov.

Printed in the United States of America

26 25 24   5 4 3 2 1

First edition

CONTENTS

Midnight Rambles

"Age Brings Reminiscences"

SITTING IN HIS PROVIDENCE, RHODE ISLAND, study cluttered with books and bric-a-brac in May 1936, fiction writer Howard Phillips Lovecraft penned a revealing, nostalgic letter to his friend of over two decades, the poet and New York native Rheinhart Kleiner. After a twelve-year pause, the two men recently had begun corresponding again. Lovecraft reflected upon his experiences living in New York City between 1924 and 1926 and his adventures there with Kleiner and other trusted associates during that period. He scratched away at his writing desk resting beneath a window, which he previously described to an acquaintance as affording a view of nearby "old-time roofs," the downtown skyline, and the "sunset hills" surrounding the city on its western edge.[1] His apartment building at 66 College Street (Figure 1) sat next to the John Hay Library of Brown University, and every hour he could listen to the chiming of the campus bell. "Age brings reminiscences," Lovecraft confided in the opening sentence of his letter.[2]

He was forty-five years old and a failure by almost every conventional societal measure of his time (and our own): he was an impoverished, solitary, and divorced high-school dropout. He was an obscure author virtually unknown even among Providence's intellectuals and literati.[3] He shared an apartment with his elderly aunt, and he relied upon her for the management of his domestic affairs. He possessed few social outlets in his native city, and he seldom ventured from his home during the winter months. As

Figure 1. When writing at his desk in his final Providence home at 66 College Street, H. P. Lovecraft savored the view of historic buildings and the city's skyline. This photograph taken at the corner of College Street might capture the scene he admired from his window. (Courtesy of the Rhode Island Collection, Providence Public Library)

Lovecraft dwelled upon his memories of New York and his relationship with it, what private thoughts that he never dared put to paper might have flitted through his mind? Did he view his short time in that city as a squandered opportunity? Did he wonder about the paths not taken?

The year 1936 marked a decade since Lovecraft had returned to Providence from New York—a date that he judged as key to his personal narrative. During that spring, he maintained a diary of his activities. The entry for April 17, 1936, noted the tenth anniversary of his homecoming.[4] For various reasons, New York City weighed on his mind.

In April 1922, Lovecraft first visited the city as a houseguest of Sonia H. Greene, a Brooklyn milliner and fashion industry professional whom he had met at a literary convention in Boston, Massachusetts, during the previous year. The two soon began exchanging letters, and then Greene traveled to Providence to see him in September 1921. Without notifying family or friends, the couple wed in March 1924. This was possibly his only realized romantic relationship. Lovecraft lived in Brooklyn for the next two years, attempting and largely failing to secure a niche for himself in the publishing and literary world of New York City. During that time, he found himself within a tight circle of friends, all immersed in the life of books, writing, and the mind. The group happily whiled away countless hours rummaging through bookstalls, nursing cups of coffee while chatting at Automats, and embarking upon midnight rambles in Manhattan. He would never again possess such a gift of constant companionship.

By the time of Lovecraft's arrival in Brooklyn in 1924, New York stood as the cultural dynamo of the United States, and Manhattan was its main generator. While the city's avant-garde movements pushed the perimeters of arts and letters, its creative industries established the national discourse. Tin Pan Alley songwriters composed the music for America's theaters, concert halls, and homes. New York magazines filled display racks in drugstores and newsstands in towns and cities across the country, documenting current affairs, setting taste standards, and sharing shopping tips. The city's book publishers dominated the trade, educating and entertaining the reading public. Broadway dazzled audiences with its plays, musicals, and performances ready for export to regional stages. Meanwhile, émigré and largely Jewish intellectuals argued about drama, philosophy, and politics in cafes and restaurants in the Lower East Side. Modernist poets and painters rubbed shoulders in Greenwich Village galleries and speakeasies. Black writers and thinkers nurtured a cultural outpouring in Harlem.[5] Art, music, and literature belonged to both big business and scrappy bohemia in New York City in the 1920s.

Although the historic figures and narratives of culture in Jazz Age New York continually fascinate scholars, captivate readers, and haunt creative individuals, Lovecraft intersected with them only minimally—if at all—during his two years in the city. As a committed Anglophile fascinated by the eighteenth century, experimental literature could not seduce him. As a teetotaler, hedonistically ignoring the bans of Prohibition held no attraction for him. As a chronically impoverished writer, sampling the glamour of stylish hotels and swank nightclubs never was even an option. That is, Lovecraft was not a participant in the storied bohemian scene. He was an outsider even among outsiders.

During the first decades of the twentieth century in New York, the more famed and dominant artistic circles and movements existed alongside closely intertwined and mutually exclusive counterparts.[6] (This dynamic likely can be observed in other eras and places.) Lovecraft and his friends' small coterie of scribblers, booksellers, and intellectuals stand as one such largely independent and overlooked group. While Dorothy Parker held court with the Algonquin Round Table, while F. Scott Fitzgerald drank at the Plaza Hotel, and while Gertrude Vanderbilt Whitney hosted artists in her Greenwich Village studio, Lovecraft's literary gang crowded into rented rooms in unfashionable Brooklyn neighborhoods to discuss genre fiction and pulp magazines well into the night. These men experienced a very different New York.

Lovecraft saw his cultural and intellectual identity inextricably linked with New England's colonial and early American heritage. While living in New York, he embarked on leisurely treasure hunts for buildings and structures dating from those favored historic periods throughout all the city's five boroughs and as far afield as New Jersey, Long Island, and the Hudson River Valley. He discovered a rich vein of such sites in Greenwich Village. The neighborhood's architecture, not its artists, lured him to its streets. Through these remainders in the city, he sought a physical and imaginative connection to a past and largely vanished New York.

Meanwhile, Greene, his wife, struggled with financial and health challenges, leaving to work in a Cincinnati, Ohio, department store in December 1924. Lovecraft moved into a rooming house in Brooklyn Heights, resumed a bachelor lifestyle, and ultimately crumpled beneath the pressure of fending for himself in the city. Failing to adjust to its modern urbanity, he described himself as "an unassimilated alien."[7] On April 17, 1926, he boarded a train in Grand Central Terminal and returned to Providence. Ecstatically, he joined the ranks of artists frustrated, exhausted, and broken by New York who have exclaimed, "Goodbye to all that."[8] Although Lovecraft still visited the city to see friends over the years, he typically expressed nothing but contempt and revulsion for it. The density, rush, and diversity filled him with dread. He remained in Providence for the rest of his life.

A compulsive and prolific letter writer, Lovecraft jotted brief postcards and fashioned lengthy epistles to geographically distant acquaintances and friends whenever he had a free moment. He maintained an exhaustive and far-flung correspondence with fellow authors and forged strong relationships through it. Over the course of his writing life, Lovecraft composed between an estimated 88,000 and 100,000 postcards and letters. Presently, roughly 10,000 of these documents sit in archives, libraries, and private collections.[9] Some run dozens of pages filled with tight, cramped handwriting. Almost no topic was off-limits, and Lovecraft demonstrated openness, humor, curiosity, and empathy in many of his exchanges. For him, letters— both written and received—were "the breath of life."[10] Maurice W. Moe, a Wisconsin English teacher and longtime epistolary friend, argued that any "survey to determine the greatest letter-writer in history" must consider Lovecraft for inclusion.[11]

While living in New York, Lovecraft constantly wrote to his two aunts, Lillian Clark and Annie Gamwell, leaving a detailed record of his adventures, mishaps, and discoveries, and a portrait of the rapidly developing built environment, urban fabric, and natural landscape of the city that he encountered. In obsessively seeking out historic buildings and wild pockets of nature, he chronicled an older and quickly fading metropolis, much like photographers Percy Loomis Sperr and Berenice Abbott accomplished with their respective surveys of New York City.[12] These letters comprise nearly 250,000 words. By reading Lovecraft's correspondence with his aunts, one might experience the sensation of listening to a long, friendly, and free-flowing conversation. The chatter is comfortable, familiar, and full of quotidian facts, keen observations, brilliant insights, and disturbing comments.[13]

Lovecraft's letters to his aunts painfully reveal his calcified and casual racism and xenophobia. When writing to his family, he exhibited little restraint in maligning people of color, religious minorities, immigrants, and new Americans—effectively any individual or group not fitting neatly into the White Anglo-Saxon Protestant demographic category. Occasionally, he set a passage in a mock Black dialect or sketched a racist caricature in a page's margins. Merely a cursory examination of these texts allows little room for minimizing or denying this ugly facet of his character and its influence on his fiction. A full and open discussion of Lovecraft as a writer and a biographical subject requires an acknowledgment and exploration of this component of his legacy. His own words and thoughts on race and ethnicity—often ugly and unsettling—present the most clear and indisputable evidence.

Race and antipathy directed toward "the other" shaped Lovecraft's imaginative formation and intellectual worldview from an early age. As a teenager in 1905, he composed "De Triumpho Naturae: The Triumph of Nature Over Northern Ignorance," a twenty-four-line poem lamenting the fall of the Confederate South and the liberation of enslaved Blacks in the American Civil War.[14] This stood as Lovecraft's first explicitly racist piece of writing. Unfortunately, it did not prove to be an adolescent poor decision, a mistake remembered with embarrassment and shame. While looking back on his experience in high school as a man in his mid-twenties, Lovecraft expressed pride in his youthful reputation as an anti-Semite, and he believed that his "ineradicable aversion" to Jewish immigrants and Jewish Americans originated while he was then a student.[15]

His first published poem, "Providence in 2000 A. D.," chronicles an Englishman's travels to the Rhode Island state capital and his shock at seeing the multiplicity of ethnic neighborhoods and street names. Before fleeing aboard a steamship returning to the British Isles, the narrator encounters "a lone unhappy man," the last American in the city.[16] This poem appeared in Providence's *Evening Bulletin* on March 4, 1912. During that same year, Lovecraft penned "On the Creation of Niggers," a patently racist origin story of Black people described therein as "semi-human" and filled "with vice."[17] The only surviving copy of this work is a hectograph, suggesting that he distributed it in some fashion or planned as much. This item bears an unattributed handwritten date clearly resembling Lovecraft's own penmanship.

During his heady early days in the amateur journalism world in 1915, Lovecraft engaged in a back-and-forth printed debate with fellow writer Charles D. Isaacson on a host of issues, notably discrimination and intolerance against Black and Jewish Americans. In his own journal the *Conservative*, Lovecraft argued that the "negro [was] fundamentally the biological inferior" of whites and that "[r]ace prejudice [was] a gift of Nature."[18] This spurred an energetic response from a committed proponent of civil rights and a veteran in amateur journalist circles, James F. Morton. Paradoxically, this incident would lead to a deep friendship between the two men.[19]

Throughout his life, Lovecraft verbalized a deep-set and visceral abhorrence—sometimes couched in pseudo-scientific thinking—for any group antithetical to his definition of a solidly white American. This reached a fever pitch during his time in New York City, and it informed several stories that he wrote while living there. French author Michel Houellebecq characterized this escalation as "the brutal hatred of a trapped animal who is forced to share his cage with other different and frightening creatures."[20] Lovecraft's obsessions and fears over race, ethnicity, and immigration can be detected throughout his canon. Sometimes these might appear as stereotypical imagery prevalent in popular culture in the 1920s and 1930s or as allegorical explorations of miscegenation.[21] Lovecraft's racist and xenophobic anxieties and hatreds articulated before, during, and after his New York experience would have been familiar, if not outright shared, by many of his contemporary Americans (and, regrettably enough, by many current Americans). No writer operates in a complete cultural and societal vacuum. To a degree, he reflected a certain set of values and beliefs from his own time.

Nativism coursed through New England's intellectual and patrician classes in Lovecraft's youth in the 1890s and his young adulthood in the earlier twentieth century. Harvard-educated lawyer Prescott F. Hall, Massachusetts Institute of Technology president Francis Amasa Walker, historian and Massachusetts United States senator Henry Cabot Lodge, and other influential figures promoted severely limiting immigration, specifically that of Eastern and Southern Europeans. The Immigration Restriction League was founded in Boston in 1894, and its leadership included several prominent New England scholars and educators. Labor unrest and the Red Scare following the First World War further fueled nativist sentiment in the United States. The touting of eugenics by scientists, physicians, and social reformers dovetailed with the anti-immigration movement. The scholarly, literary, and popular presses published articles and books supportive of both. Lovecraft's fear and loathing of new Americans echoed that of a national consensus, culminating in the Immigration Act of 1924.[22]

America in the late 1910s and the 1920s was a deeply bigoted and racist society and nation.[23] Legal segregation, voter disenfranchisement, and an all-white justice system enforced a rigid caste structure in the Southern states. Racial violence and riots wracked multiple cities, including Knoxville, Tennessee, Omaha, Nebraska, and Chicago, Illinois, throughout 1919. The 1921 Tulsa Race Massacre left thirty-five city blocks—scores of businesses and over a thousand buildings and homes—in ruins and three hundred residents dead in the thriving neighborhood of Greenwood, then known as Black Wall Street. (This episode entered the popular historical imagination thanks to two acclaimed television series, *The Watchmen* and, ironically, *Lovecraft Country*). More than an estimated one thousand Black Americans were lynched between 1910 and 1920. A resurrected Ku Klux Klan claimed a membership between four and six million individuals, and a plurality of Americans considered it be an "ordinary" and a "respectable" organization.[24] Most powerful in the Northern and Midwestern states, the KKK labeled immigrants, Catholics, and Jews as unwelcome and un-American populations. Suspicion of Catholics propelled individual states to attempt to eliminate parochial schools through public referendums. Henry Ford published the *Dearborn Independent*, a weekly newspaper nationally distributed through his company's automobile dealerships, and it printed articles detailing an international Jewish conspiracy with a goal of universal domination.[25] Intellectually, if not explicitly, Lovecraft aligned himself with these dark currents flowing through American public life.

As his fiction has grown in popularity and even skirted the boundaries of mainstream culture, Lovecraft's personal beliefs and their position in his writings have become impossible to ignore for artists and readers, especially those of color. After winning a World Fantasy Award in 2011 and learning about the unsettling depths of Lovecraft's racism, Nigerian American science fiction and fantasy novelist Nnedi Okorafor admitted to feeling "conflicted" displaying her trophy, a bust of Lovecraft nicknamed "The Howard," in her own home.[26] Following commentary and petitions from different authors and editors, the World Fantasy Convention began using a new statuette to honor its awardees in 2016. Entranced by Lovecraft as a young reader, Victor LaValle remembered later "notic[ing] all these ways that he would just outright say racist and anti-Semitic things."[27] Eventually, LaValle responded by retelling Lovecraft's most overtly xenophobic and "anti-everybody" short story, "The Horror at Red Hook," from the point of view of a Black protagonist in his own novel, *The Ballad of Black Tom*.[28] Brooklyn-based writer and MacArthur Fellow N. K. Jemisin incorporated elements of Lovecraft's fiction and references to his racist legacy in her well-received novel *The City We Became*.[29] The Jordan Peele and Misha Green adaption of Matt Ruff's novel *Lovecraft Country* into an HBO series introduced the writer to a much larger and diverse audience. Both the novel and the television show are centered around Black characters struggling simultaneously with otherworldly forces and Jim Crow America.[30]

In addition to interesting storytelling and innovative writing, such an ongoing engagement with the troubling elements of Lovecraft's biography and canon have helped foster a critical investigation of him and a more inclusive fanbase. NecronomiCon Providence, a biennial international conference of "weird fiction, art, and academia" anchored by Lovecraft scholarship, welcomed guests of different nationalities, colors, abilities, and gender identities to the author's native city for its first pandemic-era gathering in August 2022.[31] The organizers stressed the openness of the event and its zero-tolerance policy toward behavior threatening it. Many panels—including one moderated by this book's author—featured speakers from varied backgrounds and examined topics of race, gender, and sexuality. An honest and nuanced conversation on Lovecraft has not dampened the enthusiasm for his writing.

Although this will not be a study of Lovecraft and race, anti-Semitism, and xenophobia, his reactions to people of different colors, cultures, and national origins partially defined his life in New York. These will be documented and explored throughout the narrative, primarily utilizing Lovecraft's own words from his letters and other private writings. Likewise, several of his New York stories explicitly capture and dramatize his beliefs on these subjects, and they will be analyzed with attention to such elements.

While it may be tempting to dismiss Lovecraft's ideas as simply products of his upbringing or his own era, recent American history and events, such as the election of Donald Trump to the presidency in 2016, the Unite the Right march in Charlottesville, Virginia, in 2017, the attack on the United States Capitol on January 6, 2021, and the ongoing mainlining of bigoted thinking in conservative politics demonstrate that such deep hatred pervades much of our society, culture, and media. Reading Lovecraft's letters and reflecting on his life—if only his New York chapter—might contribute to the ongoing national discourse concerning the position of artists and thinkers demonstrating values purportedly antithetical to our contemporary national ideals and mores and how we might appreciate the creative and intellectual output of such figures.[32]

Melancholy obsession with the past often dominated Lovecraft's thoughts and imagination. He was born to Winfield Scott Lovecraft and Sarah Susan Phillips Lovecraft on August 20, 1890, at 194 (later 454) Angell Street in the Providence home of his affluent maternal grandparents, Whipple Van Buren Phillips and Robie Alzada Place Phillips. The city was then an industrial hub, exporting textiles, jewelry, machinery, and other commercial goods. Winfield Scott Lovecraft worked as a traveling salesman for Gorham Manufacturing Company, a silver flatware and serving ware producer and bronze foundry headquartered in Providence. He and his young family soon settled in the Boston region and purchased a plot to build a house in Auburndale, Massachusetts.

On April 21, 1893, before Lovecraft was even three years old, his father suffered a violent psychotic break while staying at a Chicago hotel during a business trip. He burst from his room, screaming that a maid had insulted him and that his wife was being "outrag[ed]" (i.e., sexually assaulted) by multiple men on a different floor. Winfield Scott Lovecraft was traveling alone and not with Sarah Susan.[33] The accusation directed at a maid might suggest that he unsuccessfully attempted to solicit sexual favors from a female hotel employee or that he argued with a prostitute whom he invited back to his room. Several days later, Winfield Scott Lovecraft was escorted to Providence under sedation, where he was committed to Butler Hospital, a well-regarded psychiatric institution on the city's eastern edge on April 25.[34] He died on July 19, 1898, of general paresis, a terminal neurological disease caused by late-stage syphilis, roughly a month before his son's eighth birthday.[35] Lovecraft likely never saw his father in the hospital, and he only held a "but vague" image of him.[36]

With her husband institutionalized, Sarah Susan Lovecraft and her young son returned to her parents' house, a sprawling, well-appointed mansion with manicured grounds, a horse stable, and a garden fountain in Providence's East Side, a residential neighborhood and a bastion of well-heeled, socially connected native New Englanders. Fields and woods lay within easy walking distance. A precocious reader, Lovecraft lost himself in his grandfather's library. The boy's mother, grandfather, and extended family members kindled his passion for Greek and Roman mythology, eighteenth-century British literature and architecture, and astronomy and the sciences. Although intellectually gifted, he suffered from periodic mental and physical health difficulties—possibly both genuine and psychosomatic—and only sporadically attended school. Following cascading business and real estate failures, Whipple Van Buren Phillips died in 1904. Lovecraft lost his "closest companion."[37]

Soon thereafter, he and his mother were forced to leave the family estate for a rented apartment several blocks away at 598 Angell Street, a two-unit house.[38] Having been raised until then in relative comfort and privilege, he suddenly found himself living in "a congested, servantless home."[39] In 1908, Lovecraft left high school after "a nervous collapse."[40] He never completed his secondary education. Throughout his life, he obfuscated and lied about his lack of a high school diploma, even claiming that he was preparing to enroll in Brown University before his breakdown.

Sinking into an identity as "a failure in life" and a physical invalid during his young adulthood, Lovecraft withdrew into his own solitary world and allowed his mother and, to a lesser extent, his aunts to fuss over all his needs.[41] Former classmates and neighbors recalled him skulking around Angell Street, always staring blanky ahead and shunning any contact with them.

After the pulp magazine *Argosy* published a series of his letters and poems critiquing and satirizing one of its popular authors, Fred Jackson, in 1913, Lovecraft become involved in amateur journalism, an international association of nonprofessional writers publishing, printing, and exchanging their own work and periodicals, not unlike the culture of zines during the 1980s and 1990s or of blogs in the 2000s and 2010s. The *United Amateur*, the official magazine of the United Amateur Press Association, published his short story "The Alchemist" in its November 1916 issue.[42] He wrote more original fiction and submitted it to various amateur periodicals. Finally, Lovecraft began to emerge from his gloom and isolation. He established a reputation and a social life for himself in this small world of letters.[43] For a professional name, he simply paired his first and middle initials alongside his surname: he became H. P. Lovecraft.

Figure 2. Lovecraft's father and mother both died as committed patients at Butler Hospital, a psychiatric institution in Providence. Photograph from *Providence: Illustrated* (Chicago: H. R. Page, 1891)

In January 1919, his mother departed their shared household to temporarily live with her older sister and his aunt Lillian Clark "for purposes of complete rest."[44] For an indeterminate number of years, Sarah Susan Lovecraft had exhibited symptoms of severe mental illness. Speculation exists that she might have contracted syphilis from her late husband.[45] A former neighbor, Clara Hess, recalled witnessing Sarah Susan Lovecraft experiencing a panic attack on a trolley car and drawing the attention of their fellow passengers. On another occasion, she confided in Hess about spotting "weird and fantastic creatures" hurriedly emerging from dark corners and buildings.[46] While conversing with Hess, she fearfully glanced about as if expecting a sudden attack from these imagined monsters. On March 13, 1919, Sarah Susan Lovecraft was admitted into Butler Hospital (Figure 2), the same institution where her husband and her son's father had died. Since there are no surviving medical records for Sarah Susan Lovecraft or full accounts from herself, her son, or other family members, the exact details or diagnoses of her condition remain unknown. Considering the dramatic and sad events shaping much of his existence, Lovecraft's looking backward to New York City and searching for a path not taken seems understandable.

Additionally, the full context of his mentality and life in 1936 hinted at far deeper motivations behind his letter to Rheinhart Kleiner than evaluating past choices. Lovecraft embraced the caricature of a thrifty New England Yankee combined with that of a starving artist. He wore clothing sometimes decades old, bragged about his barebones diet, and shared economizing tips with fellow and aspiring writers. However, he was entering an increasingly dire financial situation even by these standards. When the science fiction magazine *Astounding Stories* purchased two of his pieces, the novella "At the Mountains of Madness" and the short story "The Shadow Out of Time" in late 1935, Lovecraft admitted that he "was never closer to the bread-line."[47]

Struggling to survive on a dwindling inheritance and on scant funds earned from freelance editing and ghostwriting projects, he budgeted himself two or three dollars each week for food. A Providence bookseller suspected that Lovecraft would skip meals in order to afford magazines and books. If he could count on ten to fifteen dollars each week—maybe $500 per year—he determined that he would be able to satisfy all his material needs. (For comparison, newspaper book critics earned a median wage of $51.32 per week in 1934.)[48] He increasingly failed to generate even those miniscule sums. He was an aging man without a steady job amid the Great Depression. His financial prospects appeared bleak. Lovecraft himself predicted a "fatal day of reckoning" approaching.[49]

In March 1936, his nearly seventy-year-old aunt, housemate, and last close living relation, Annie Gamwell, underwent a mastectomy. Because of complications, this required a lengthy hospitalization followed by a stay at a convalescent home. Lovecraft withheld the full details of her health from his correspondents, referring to her cancer surgery and recovery as the "grippe."[50] By the time he sat down to write to Rheinhart Kleiner in May 1936, he was dealing with his own worrisome health issues. As early as October 1934, he began experiencing recurring indigestion, abdominal pain, constipation, and fatigue. Possibly because of a lifelong fear of doctors and hospitals and his strained finances, Lovecraft abstained from seeking medical care.[51] He collectively diagnosed his stubborn maladies as the "grippe," as well.

Most troubling for him as a man of letters, Lovecraft grew despondent over his inability to compose fiction commensurate with his own high standards for his art and craft. He claimed to have destroyed dozens of manuscripts without sharing them with friends or editors over the past several years. In a letter to his onetime short story collaborator E. Hoffmann Price, Lovecraft openly questioned if his life as a writer was over and lamented being "farther from doing what I want to do than I was 20 years ago."[52] He was suffering from the most painful, agonizing, and humiliating condition dreaded by any literary artist and practitioner: his imagination—his ability to spin tales—had fallen silent. He was no longer writing.

Lovecraft might have been exchanging memories of New York with Kleiner for another reason: His time there, albeit brief, shaped him as a writer and as a man far more than he would readily confess. Those years solidified the importance of place to his writing, imagination, and very outlook on life. After abandoning his New York dalliance for the security of Providence, Lovecraft imbued his fiction with a strong and unique sense of local color. New England—its architecture, landscape, and geography—became a character itself in his stories.

Whether softened by middle-aged brooding, acknowledgment of mortality, or recognition of the development and decline of his creative prowess, Lovecraft momentarily and uncharacteristically succumbed to nostalgia for New York. How he missed "the long informal sessions" discussing "burning issues" and "the tours of exploration" of a nighttime Gotham with Kleiner and their mutual friends.[53] The perspective granted by time and maturity allowed him to recognize these fleeting gifts:

> That age was the last of youth for our generation—the last years in which we could feel that curious sense of the importance of things, & that vague, heartening spur of adventurous expectancy, which distinguish the morning & noon from the afternoon of life.[54]

Because of his passionate relationship with his native Providence and the foundational position of the New England region in his most influential and arguably best fiction, this period, which Lovecraft himself marked as "the last years," when he keenly experienced a life brimming with "the importance of things" and "adventurous expectancy," has been overlooked in his biography and in the enjoyment of his works. To quote the narrator of his own short story "He," Lovecraft's New York chapter—the era of his life between 1924 and 1926—has largely been dismissed as "a mistake."[55]

Contrary to Lovecraft's insecurities regarding his own literary skills and his pessimism concerning the afterlife of his writings, today he comfortably sits in the pantheon of American genre fiction, the presumptive twentieth-century successor to his own "God of Fiction," Edgar Allan Poe.[56] His reputation rests on a loosely interlocking series of short stories and novellas, collectively known as "The Cthulhu Mythos." (The term was coined by enthusiasts and readers, not by Lovecraft himself.) In many of these works, the narrator or protagonist, often a scholar, librarian, scientist, or otherwise bookish and always male individual, stumbles upon knowledge of malevolent alien entities that once held dominion over the Earth and will do so again. A very glimpse of these beings drives a person temporarily or permanently mad. Cults worship them as dark gods, serving as their human agents and silencing anyone attempting to speak of their historical and contemporary existence. The presence of these creatures—Cthulhu being the most deeply ensconced in the current cultural lexicon—point to the absolute meaninglessness of mankind in relation to the greater universe. Upon learning of these malevolent forces, the protagonists begin to perceive connections and conspiracies laced within current events. Science, religion, art, history—all the fruits of civilization—are fated to be obliterated upon the return and the re-ascendance of these omni-powerful aliens. The entire human race is little more than a biological chance error. Hope does not exist.

Lovecraft's writings, with their vivid world-building and bleak cosmogony, have entranced readers ever since their original prewar publication in pulp magazines. Best-selling novelist Stephen King noted the continual importance of Lovecraft's canon in shaping storytelling in literature, film, and other mediums:

> HPL continues to remain not just *popular* with generation after generation of maturing readers but *viscerally important* to an imaginative core group that goes on to write that generation's fantasy and weird tales.[57]

A mere cursory glance at the cultural landscape supports King's assertion. References to Lovecraft's literary creations and visions can be heard in the music of the seminal heavy metal bands Mercyful Fate and Metallica. They can be seen in the films of Academy Award–winning director Guillermo del Toro and in episodes of the Netflix's hit *Stranger Things*. They can be read in the novels of acclaimed writers Michael Chabon and Neil Gaiman. Tenacle-faced and wing-backed Cthulhu can be found on shirts, mugs, keychains, and almost every conceivable tchotchke. Thousands of fans flock to Lovecraft's hometown every year, hoping to experience the aura described in his writings. The list could go on and on. Much like the nefarious activities of the globe-spanning cults and the perplexing archaeological artifacts of the Great Old Ones in his fiction, Lovecraft is everywhere. One only needs to begin looking.[58]

The deep importance of Lovecraft to artists and his abiding popularity among readers point to a need to better understand him as a biographical subject. In his survey of New York and cinema, architect, author, and film-maker James Sanders characterized the city as the "ideal place to track an individual's arc of social, economic, or personal success" or conversely one's downward trajectory in such categories.[59] That is, an extended encounter with a great city reveals and exaggerates the strengths, foibles, attributes, and flaws of a character in a film or a person in the flesh-and-blood world. This is certainly true of Lovecraft and his years in New York City.

This book will focus on a specific time and place in the life of H. P. Lovecraft. It will not serve as an encyclopedic or close study of his biography and literary output.[60] Instead, it will attempt to structure a thorough telling of his relationship with New York City. Readers will be invited to walk through its streets and neighborhoods with Lovecraft and experience them as they appeared in his thoughts and imagination. Primary sources—published and unpublished letters, memoirs, diaries, ephemera, and documents—serve as the foundation of the text. Sometimes, the interpretation of these might lead to a disruption of accepted details concerning the biography of Lovecraft or the mythology surrounding him. This may take the form of listing a different date for an important event or arguing against an element long-believed factual. All such instances will be accompanied by discussion and documentation. As with any work of scholarship, the hope is to belong to an ever-unfolding conversation and that any mistakes or omissions will be corrected or filled by future contributors to such an exchange. The original spelling and punctuation of quoted primary sources will be retained, including Lovecraft's fond and purposeful use of archaic and British English. Editorial changes will be made only for clarification. As can be determined, place names reflect those used during the time documented.

The narrative in Chapter 1 begins with the death of Lovecraft's mother, Sarah Susan, in the spring of 1921 and his meeting with Sonia H. Greene, his future wife, later that year. This pair of events arguably propelled him to envision a life beyond Providence. Chapter 2 chronicles Lovecraft's first trip to New York City in April 1922, and Chapter 3 recounts his successive trips there during that same year. Lovecraft relocated from his hometown to New York in March 1924, and he lived in the city until April 1926. His life and literary output during those two years will be examined between

Chapter 4 and Chapter 9. Additionally, Chapter 9 will discuss his return to Providence, where he lived and wrote until his death in 1937. The conclusion summarizes the remainder of Lovecraft's life and speculates on what could be learned from considering his New York experiences.

In 1944, several years after H. P. Lovecraft's passing, Rheinhart Kleiner composed a short memoir on his friend and their time together in New York, appropriately selecting a Brooklyn coffee shop as the setting. "Much more might be said of those vanished days," he hoped.[61] The following pages represent a humble attempt to satisfy that long-sought wish.

1

###

"A Person of the Most Admirable Qualities"

DEPRESSION AND GRIEF THREATENED to overwhelm H. P. Lovecraft in the late spring of 1921. After spending two years as a psychiatric patient at Butler Hospital in Providence, his mother, Sarah Susan Phillips Lovecraft, died on May 24. She was sixty-three years old. He described her as "the only person who thoroughly understood" him.[1]

Approximately a week beforehand, Sarah Susan Lovecraft underwent gallbladder surgery. The procedure appeared to have been routine and without incident. Then, five days later, an attendant nurse stated that the patient told her that "I will only live to suffer."[2] Sarah Susan Lovecraft died on the following day. The death certificate listed the cause as cholecystitis (inflammation of the gallbladder) and cholangitis (infection of the biliary system).[3]

No record exists of Lovecraft seeing his mother after the operation. In fact, he apparently never visited her inside Butler Hospital during her entire time there. Refusing to enter the complex, he instead would meet her on its grounds. Then, they would walk through a wooded section of the hospital property overlooking the Seekonk River. They even had a favorite spot—the grotto. None of Sarah Susan Lovecraft's fellow patients recalled ever witnessing her together with her son.[4]

Lovecraft had shared a complex relationship with his mother. She adored him, considering him to be a writer with a keen mind and deep talents, even speaking "constantly and pridefully" of him to other Butler residents during her final days.[5] Yet, she likely needled him about his physical appearance, leaving him overly self-conscious of his looks throughout his entire life. (Lovecraft's dominant facial features, his thin face and long jaw, resembled those of his mother.) She encouraged him to pursue his interests in science, literature, and history. However, she failed to prepare him for the adult world of work and responsibilities, cultivating a childlike dependence on her and permitting him to leave high school without a degree. She maintained a stable household for her son after her husband and his father's mental breakdown and institutionalization. Then, she and Lovecraft lived claustrophobically alone together at the peak of her own severe (and possibly hidden or undiagnosed) mental illness. Lovecraft seemed to have spoken little, if at all, to close friends on the subject of the domestic situation with his mother during those undoubtedly challenging and traumatic years. His purported physical and mental health issues of his childhood and young adulthood might have been products of his mother transferring her own anxieties and fears onto her son. What sadness and pain his mother had inflicted upon him and herself within their shared home remains unknown.

Scraps of information gathered decades after the death of Sarah Susan Lovecraft and second- and even third-hand accounts provide some insights into the depths of her illness and its impact in shaping her son.[6] Marian F. Bonner, a librarian at the Providence Public Library, a friend of his aunt Annie Gamwell, and a correspondent with Lovecraft himself in the 1930s, recalled former neighbors of the Lovecraft family telling her about the mother and son loudly and violently arguing with one another. When approached about this, Lovecraft told Bonner that he and his mother had enjoyed reading aloud Shakespeare plays, and that explained the source of those overheard verbal brawls. "The more cruel the part, the better he liked it, and would shout it out to be heard by the neighbors," Bonner remembered being told.[7] In the context of his mother's long struggle with mental illness and Lovecraft's own reticence to discuss personal subjects, it might be judicious to speculate upon the truth behind this anecdote, particularly the response to Bonner's questioning. Was Lovecraft dissimulating about the past happenings in his household? Were Lovecraft and his mother merely trying to scandalize the neighbors? Since his aunts and presumably his mother placed a heavy value on public appearance and social status, Lovecraft's explanation seems to be suspect. This attempt to dismiss such a report as little more than neighborhood gossip might be read as a defensive mechanism by an individual coping with the array of emotions—guilt, shame, anger—from living in a home captured by mental illness.[8]

The dearth of primary documents and sources dating from the life of Sarah Susan Lovecraft argues for a degree of caution in accepting as irrefutable facts the accounts by Bonner and others. Beyond a commonplace book abandoned after her marriage and motherhood, no known letters or diaries survive from Sarah Susan Lovecraft.[9] Her Butler Hospital medical records were destroyed in a fire. Nonetheless, Bonner's memories echo a grim refrain heard—if only subtly—in all recollections of Sarah Susan Lovecraft, including those from her own son: she was, indeed, a woman deeply suffering.

As early as 1906, the symptoms of his mother's condition might have become recognizable to Lovecraft and others. During that year, she fell in a trolley car, and the accident resulted in "a nervous shock," according to Lovecraft.[10] He believed its "effects never wholly left her."[11] In all likelihood, Sarah Susan Lovecraft's immediate family only admitted her to Butler Hospital in 1919 when they could no longer effectively manage her behavior or hide it from inquisitive outsiders.[12] Given the matriarchal hierarchy of the family (Lovecraft was its sole remaining male, and his aunts were educated women), it seems unlikely that this decision was reached without serious and pained deliberation. Throughout Lovecraft's career as a writer, several of his better (and some lesser) stories pulsed with themes of hereditary decline and inherited madness. Certain works depict characters permanently lost to asylums—a stock genre device of which he would have been sadly familiar.

Still, Lovecraft clearly loved his mother, and he remembered her as "a person of unusual charm and force of character, accomplished in literature and the fine arts; a French scholar, musician, and painter in oils."[13] Her passing left him shocked and mourning. Writing to a female literary acquaintance a little more than a week after Sarah Susan's death, he acknowledged that he lacked "the will and energy to do anything heavier" than penning a simple letter.[14]

Throughout his adult life, Lovecraft prided himself in presenting a cool, unemotional, and ultrarational face to others, even to his most trusted and dear friends. This experience of profound loss—the passing of his last remaining parent and the only one of whom he held any vivid and true memories—challenged his desire to plod along with his practiced sangfroid.[15] Although declining to "weep or indulge in any of the lugubrious demonstrations of the vulgar," Lovecraft was unmoored.[16] He could not sleep. He could not write. He could not concentrate. He thought of suicide.

Lovecraft believed Sarah Susan to be the only person who genuinely cared for him and his well-being.[17] Without his "nucleus," life seemed empty, lonely, and pointless.[18] Reflecting on his mother's death, he seemed to envy her and longed to join her in "complete oblivion" and "non-existence."[19] While she was alive, Lovecraft staved off his darkest thoughts, wanting to spare her the sorrow of witnessing her son's passing by his own hand. Now, that had changed:

> It is now possible for me to regulate the term of my existence with the assurance that my end would cause no one more than a passing annoyance—of course my aunts are infinitely considerate and solicitous, but the death of a nephew is seldom a momentous event.[20]

Only his insatiable curiosity restrained Lovecraft from following through on his grief-induced (and possibly long-nurtured) desire. He anticipated discovering "enough interesting things to read and study" to occupy his mind for some time.[21] In all likelihood, the recipients of his letters, literary acquaintances and friends, found some assurances in this and similar statements and attempted to console him through this difficult moment.

Sarah Susan Lovecraft's death also appeared to coincide with the denouement of a different and rather murky episode in her son's personal life. He broke the news of his mother's passing to Boston-area poet Winifred Virginia Jackson by telling her that she "lost a friend" and one of "the earliest and most enthusiastic admirers of [her] work."[22] She and Lovecraft served together as United Amateur Press Association officers and collaborated on two short stories, "The Green Meadow" and "The Crawling Chaos."[23] The former was inspired by similar dreams experienced by both Lovecraft and Jackson. He promoted her as a talented and original poet in amateur journalist publications, most effusively in his essay "Winifred Virginia Jackson: A 'Different' Poetess."[24] The pair were also romantically linked.[25]

After receiving a photograph (or even a miniature portrait) of Jackson, "[a] picture of so great beauty," as a Christmas gift from her in 1920, Lovecraft responded by composing a flirtatious letter and a poem celebrating the image and its subject, "On Receiving Ye Portraiture of Mrs. Berkeley, Ye Poetess."[26] Jackson was roughly fourteen years his senior, recently divorced, and remarkably attractive.[27] At an unknown date and location, he snapped a photograph of her sitting at the seaside.[28] While she was corresponding with and possibly pursuing Lovecraft, Jackson was simultaneously having an affair with the Black American poet and literary critic William Stanley Braithwaite.

In his letter sharing his mother's death with her, Lovecraft enclosed a somewhat intimate and revealing gift, a photograph of his mother taken during the last year of her life. Since Jackson had never met his mother, Lovecraft wanted her to possess a physical connection with his deceased parent. Strangely, he compared his mother's and Jackson's looks:

> Her appearance was as handsome as mine is homely, and her youthful pictures would form close rivals to your own in a contest for aesthetic supremacy. Her beauty was of the opposite type—a very fair complexion, but dark eyes and dark brown hair.[29]

Regardless of the full understanding and true nature of Lovecraft and Jackson's relationship, they appear to have ceased exchanging letters by the end of 1921.[30]

Watching him "stagnate in dressing-gown" and "slippers," in Lovecraft's words, and growing increasingly concerned for his emotional and physical well-being after his mother's death, his aunts encouraged him to get out of the house and to see other people.[31] By the early summer, Lovecraft began traveling to Massachusetts and New Hampshire to visit literary acquaintances. When he attended the annual convention of the National Amateur Press Association held in Boston between July 2 and July 5, Lovecraft seemed to have shed the most debilitating layers of his grief.[32]

A Fourth of July midday dinner at the Hotel Brunswick, a storied establishment on Boylston Street off Copley Square, a public park in the city's Back Bay neighborhood, was the keynote event.[33] Lovecraft documented it in an unpublished essay, "The Convention Banquet."[34] The assembled audience sang "America (My Country, 'Tis of Thee)" to celebrate Independence Day.[35] Various attendees entertained the crowd with poetry and music. Lovecraft applauded two female performers for "pleasing humorous recitations, some of them in [a] Hibernian dialect."[36] The main program consisted of a series of speeches with preassigned themes presented by different amateur journalists.

Lovecraft delivered the opening speech, entitled "Within the Gates." He peppered his talk with self-effacing humor and classical and literary references, and he mildly roasted several of his seated colleagues.[37] For an individual who considered himself preternaturally reserved with a past inclination to withdraw from social life, his growing accomplishment as a public speaker was nothing less than impressive. His fellow writers remarked upon his ability to work a crowd.[38] Among them was a woman Lovecraft had met on the prior afternoon.

On July 3, Lovecraft accompanied a group of attendees on a boat tour of Boston Harbor.[39] While mingling on the deck of the soon departing craft, his poet friend Rheinhart Kleiner introduced him to a figure in New York's amateur circles from Flatbush, Brooklyn, Sonia H. Greene (Figure 3).[40] She was a trained milliner and a production and sales executive at Ferle Heller, an upscale Manhattan women's hat and clothing shop advertising new fashions from Paris.[41] Tall, curvaceous, and brown-haired, she was appraised by various acquaintances as a "striking dark beauty" with a "Junoesque" figure.[42] Greene's life carried as much upheaval and sadness as Lovecraft's own.

She was born Sonia Haft Shafirkin in Ichnya, a village approximately one hundred miles east of Kyiv, the capital city of Ukraine (then part of the Russian Empire) on March 16, 1883, to Racille (née Haft) and Simyon Shafirkin, both Jewish. Several days after Sonia's birth, the family fled a pogrom. After being conscripted into the Imperial Russian Army, Shafirkin served a sentence at a prison camp for attacking a superior officer. Then, Racille's Orthodox Jewish family pressured the couple to divorce, accusing Shafirkin of being religiously unobservant. His military service troubles suggest that other reasons might have factored into this decision. Racille resumed using her maiden name. Shafirkin emigrated to Germany or Switzerland with the expressed intention of sending for his former wife and child. Greene never saw her father again. Racille Haft eventually followed her brothers to Liverpool, England, bringing her seven-year-old daughter. Not long thereafter, she boarded a ship for the United States to try her fortune across the Atlantic Ocean. Sonia was left behind in England. Meanwhile, her mother worked as a dressmaker in New York City and then married Solomon Moseson, a shopkeeper in Elmira, a small city in the state's Southern Tier region. In 1892, when Greene was nine years old, one of her Liverpool uncles scrawled her name and an Elmira address on a cardboard sign, hung it around her neck, and packed her onto a ship headed to New York Harbor. Shortly after her arrival in the United States, she was reunited with her mother in Elmira. At fourteen, Greene dropped out of school and was apprenticed to a local milliner.[43]

While working in a hat shop or women's clothing store in Passaic, New Jersey, at the age of fifteen in 1898, she met another Jewish émigré in the garment industry, twenty-two-year-old Samuel Seckendorff, ironically enough at a Christmas Eve dance.[44] Seckendorff adopted the surname

Figure 3. Sonia H. Greene was introduced to H. P. Lovecraft during a boat tour of Boston Harbor in July 1921. The two were attending an amateur journalism convention in the city. Photograph from the *Rainbow*, October 1921

"Greene" at an uncertain point, possibly desiring a more American-sounding name. After a tumultuous courtship and engagement, the couple wed in 1899. Sonia Haft Shafirkin was now Sonia Haft Greene.

The marriage was not a happy one. Greene described her husband as a "brutal character."[45] The couple fought constantly and viciously. Samuel Greene played cards, lost a series of jobs, and chased other women. She was forced to support the household and soon became pregnant. A son was born in October 1900, only to die three months later in January 1901. The boy was apparently unnamed. In March 1902, Greene gave birth to a daughter, Florence.[46] This child survived.

Greene's relationship with her husband continued to unravel. Exhausted by his antics and irresponsibility, she sent Florence to live with her own mother, Racille, in Elmira, and she slowly built a life fully independent from him. In 1908 or 1909, she brought her daughter back to New York and ultimately settled in Brooklyn. Samuel Greene reportedly died in 1916, possibly having committed suicide.[47] As she continued to scale upward in New York's garment industry, Greene enrolled in night classes to improve her English language skills and general education. Her ability to overcome potentially crippling circumstances and succeed in an era before American women earned the right to vote or to fully control their own finances demonstrates a fiercely determined and tough character.[48] Lovecraft had never met anyone quite like her.

Kleiner recalled Greene navigating him toward Lovecraft and unsubtly pushing past his friend's rumored paramour, Winifred Virginia Jackson, on that July afternoon. Just as he introduced the two to one another, a photographer took a picture of the three of them together.[49] Wearing a stylishly embroidered dress and a large, round hat, both possibly of her own design, Greene flashes a flirtatious, inviting grin and stares directly at the camera with half-closed eyes. She appears to be locking arms with both men. With his formal winged collar shirt and pocket watch charms, Lovecraft appears self-consciously foppish and offers a solemn visage to the photographer. Upon first meeting him, Greene "admired his personality but frankly, at first, not his person."[50] Lovecraft remembered being "bored" by the tour of Boston Harbor.[51]

Later during that same boat ride, George Julian Houtain, an attorney and a Brooklyn-based amateur journalist and publisher, encouraged Greene, the New York contingent's "official vamp," to sneak behind Lovecraft and "get a half-moon clutch on his august form."[52] Houtain then snapped a photograph of the two with his Kodak Brownie camera. Greene's arm rests around Lovecraft's shoulder, and their heads are close together. He appears to be restraining laughter; she looks rapturous with

Figure 4. Greene grew more intrigued by Lovecraft throughout the Boston convention. This marked the beginning of their relationship.

joy. Lovecraft jokingly accused his friends of attempted blackmail and Greene as being their willful accomplice. This photograph remains the only known existing one of the pair alone together (Figure 4). Recounting that moment, Greene claimed that was when she "stole HPL away from Winifred Jackson."[53]

After the Fourth of July banquet and Lovecraft's well-received speech, he and Greene continued to get to know one another. They joined several other amateur journalists for a stroll along the Charles River.[54] While traveling back to Brooklyn after the convention, Greene buttonholed Kleiner and Lovecraft's other friends.[55] She wanted to know everything about this strange gentleman from Providence. Kleiner himself might have harbored a slight disappointment. On the boat ride, he—an "unattached young bachelor"—conspicuously had "linger[ed] near Mrs. Greene for most of the time."[56]

Shortly after their meeting in Boston, Lovecraft began mentioning Greene in his letters. Writing to Kleiner later that July, he praised her intelligence, albeit in a strange, xenophobic manner. Although she had read two of his recently published pieces, the prose poem "Nyarlathotep" and the short story "Polaris," she deemed both "incomprehensible."[57] Lovecraft professed little surprise that his writings stumped her, remarking that "Teutonic mysticism is too subtle for Slavs."[58] However, he did declare Greene to be "a welcome addition" to the realm of amateur journalism.[59]

This exchange is notable for several reasons. Throughout his entire adult life, Lovecraft espoused—sometimes quite proudly and crudely—nativist, anti-Semitic, and racist beliefs. This was not some youthful mistake or a onetime late-night rant: this was part of his personality, character, and worldview. This was Lovecraft. Throughout his voluminous correspondence and personal writings, this bigoted mentality appears in the most incongruous and odd moments. Lovecraft would share a warm, even touching impression or memory of a friend, pet, landscape, or place only to follow that sentiment with a racist comment or aside. A reader might interpret such remarks as acts of compulsion or, at best, obliviousness. This letter to Kleiner adhered to that pattern. Lovecraft heaped praise upon Greene and then maligned her purportedly foreign mental capacities. This episode and his entire relationship with Greene and other close acquaintances and boon companions present one of the trickiest questions about him. Regardless of his vocal and reprehensible beliefs, Lovecraft made exceptions for individuals falling into his negative categories. Although he expressed loathing for immigrants, white ethnics, and Jews, he would correspond with, mentor, and befriend both select men and women belonging to those demographic groups.[60]

Nonetheless, his burgeoning familiarity with Greene existed as a feat of compartmentalization for Lovecraft. From the beginning of their relationship, he was aware of her Eastern European and Jewish lineage. His friends exoticized Greene, often comparing her to a tempestuous, volatile character from a novel by one of the great Russian authors Fyodor Dostoevsky or Leo Tolstoy. Since Greene arrived in the United States as a child and was raised in an immigrant household, she might have carried traces of an accent. Yiddish was her first language and that of her daughter, Florence. Being a foreigner, an outsider from another land, was part of her personal story and history. She clearly exuded an unusual air for a buttoned-down Yankee such as Lovecraft. Still, none of this seemed to bother him. If anything, it appeared to entice him.

Lovecraft and Greene began exchanging letters that summer. Eventually, they would write to one another on a daily basis. On August 1, 1921, Greene typed a letter to Lovecraft, beginning it by complimenting his unpublished short story "The Temple."[61] Less than a month after first meeting her, he was soliciting her input on his writing. For many authors, this is an intimate and trusting act. Greene confessed that his story gave her "a source of pleasure not often found in works produced for monetary compensation."[62] Referencing an earlier discussion on aesthetics and the primary position of originality in defining true art, she stated that "The Temple" fit this criterion: it was an innovative work, and it represented "a wonderful command of language."[63] Greene's laudatory comments concerning Lovecraft's writing and storytelling most likely flattered him. That may have been the intention. Lovecraft fancied himself a gentleman of letters, not a moneygrubbing hack. He considered himself an artist, distinguishing himself from his soon-to-be contemporaries in the pulp magazine world. The literary and creative value of all his writings was paramount.

Greene continued her letter by unveiling her philosophical worldview, a softened adaptation of Friedrich Nietzsche's conception of the Übermensch or superman. This lengthy discussion was interspersed with allusions to Russian writer and political radical Maxim Gorky and Anglo-Irish playwright George Bernard Shaw and her own recollection of seeing Leo Tolstoy's son Ilya lecture on his father's work and legacy at Carnegie Hall in New York City.[64] She belittled the great writer's scion as "mediocre" and failing to cast "one ray of light" upon Tolstoy père.[65] Everything communicated at the talk could have been easily gleaned from published biographies and Tolstoy's own books. This anecdote hinted at Greene's cosmopolitan pursuits and lifestyle. She was an independent, thinking woman attending cultural events in New York City, a magnet for American and international artists, writers, and creative individuals. This might have tantalized Lovecraft.

Their mutual friend Rheinhart Kleiner pressed Lovecraft on his continual kind words for Greene. He replied that her generous donations to the United Amateur Press Association fund stoked his "rhapsodical tendency."[66] His impression of the Brooklyn milliner continued to evolve:

> Beneath the exterior of romantic spoofing & rhetorical extravagance she has a mind of singular scope & activity, & an exceptional background of Continental cultivation.[67]

Throughout the summer and the rest of the year, Lovecraft would continue to discuss Greene in his letters to Kleiner. He may have been subtly approaching his friend for advice. Kleiner knew Greene, a fellow Brooklyn resident, from local New York amateur writing circles, and he might possess insights into her pastimes and personality. Unlike Lovecraft, he claimed to hold a history in courting the opposite gender. He and Lovecraft had conversed about women in the past. On those occasions, Lovecraft admitted to his inexperience with romance and his purported disinterest in sex.[68] He may have felt comfortable expressing his curiosity for Greene with Kleiner and anticipated a sympathetic audience from him.

In late August 1921, Lovecraft shared an intriguing snippet of personal news with his friend: Sonia H. Greene would be traveling to Providence to visit him in early September. He hoped that his native city's "archaic" and "provincial atmosphere" would not bore her, a woman accustomed to the excitement and sophistication afforded by life in New York City.[69] In a strange aside, he mentioned that Greene had begun corresponding with Alfred Galpin, his protege and a University of Wisconsin–Madison undergraduate student, and that she might "kidnap [Galpin] some day."[70] (This easily could be interpreted as carrying a sexual undertone.) As he had with Kleiner, Lovecraft may have been looking to another friend—Galpin, in this case—to offer impressions of his potential romantic partner.

Greene arrived in Providence on the afternoon of September 4. After settling into her room at the Crown Hotel, a downtown establishment known for comfortable accommodations and quality dining, she telephoned Lovecraft. She was ready for an introduction to his city.[71] He met Greene at her hotel at 3:15 P.M., noting the exact hour and minute. Before beginning their urban explorations, Lovecraft insisted on taking a photograph of her.

Although worried that Providence's "tame" and "uneventful scenic pedestrianism" would fail to impress his "effervescent" guest, Lovecraft proudly guided Greene on a self-designed tour of his most beloved spots.[72] The pair first ascended the streets to College Hill, a neighborhood overlooking the downtown. He wanted her to sample its remarkable collection of historic eighteenth- and nineteenth-century homes and structures. Pausing at Prospect Terrace Park, he showed Greene its panoramic view of the Providence skyline. During their wanderings, he pointed out several of his favorite buildings, including a Queen Anne–style mansion. This was likely the Dr. George Wheaton Carr House on the corner of Benefit and Waterman Streets, built in 1885 and owned by the Rhode Island School of Design.[73] Next, he directed her farther eastward to his own neighborhood along Angell Street. Greene's appreciation of Providence's historic urban fabric heartened him:

> Mme. G. appeared pleased with the aspect of this section with its detached residences, neat lawns, & abundant foliage, & even expressed admiration for the Colonial style of architecture.[74]

For Lovecraft, a man who placed such a high value on the built environment and defined himself in many ways through his deep attachment to place, Greene had passed an important first test: she appreciated Providence. His Providence. Still, he felt compelled to qualify her response. Greene's experience lacked the "intense admiration which can arise only from an unmixed Anglo-American heritage."[75] Being Eastern European and Jewish, she might admire the architectural beauty of Angell Street, but her "fervour" could never match his own "shaped by 1400 years of English heredity."[76]

Then, Greene faced—knowingly or unknowingly—a second test. Lovecraft brought her to 598 Angell Street, his home, to meet his elder aunt, housemate, and family matriarch, Lillian Clark. The introduction apparently went well. Long after Greene's stay, Clark commented to her nephew on his lady friend's "ideas, speech, manner, aspect," and "even attire."[77] Afterward, Greene offered to treat both her hosts to dinner. Clark declined, allowing Lovecraft to share another long, leisurely stroll with his new companion. He took this opportunity to point out more of his favorite architectural highlights. She did not complain of Lovecraft's circuitous routes through different neighborhoods; in fact, she enjoyed "the antique" and "solemn hush of the venerable streets" and "the Georgian dignity of the old mansions."[78]

Before escorting Greene back to her downtown hotel, Lovecraft insisted on walking her through the nearby Brown University campus at twilight. When the two descended College Hill, he observed that she felt "the sensation of anticlimax involved in the abrupt transition from the ancient to the garishly modern."[79] Presumably, he underwent a similar emotional and mental experience every time he left his own swath of the city. Was he surprised, relieved, or excited that he and Greene seemed to exhibit the same aesthetic disposition toward historic buildings and spaces? That she perceived "the soul of Providence"?[80]

After a long conversation-filled dinner at the Crown Hotel restaurant, Lovecraft suggested that they catch a band concert in Roger Williams Park, a 435-acre landscaped oasis in southeast Providence. Although he self-deprecatingly described his idea as trite and unoriginal, Greene apparently disagreed: she jumped at his invitation and even splurged on a taxicab ride to the park. Reluctant to say goodnight, the two lingered in the lobby of her hotel after the concert. He promised to meet her on the following afternoon.

The next day, Lovecraft and Clark joined Greene for lunch at her hotel. She insisted on picking up the tab, and he found her generosity to be "quite unbounded."[81] After their meal, Greene wanted to tour the Rhode Island School of Design Museum and the adjacent Charles Pendleton House. Lovecraft was likely happy to oblige. The Rhode Island School of Design Museum is an encyclopedic teaching institution with well-known collections. As a milliner and a fashion industry professional, Greene might have displayed a special interest in its costume and textile galleries. A Georgian-style building, the Pendleton House features the collection of early American decorative arts connoisseur Charles L. Pendleton, including furniture, ceramics, and other items of material culture. Many of the pieces date from the eighteenth and nineteenth centuries and originated from the hands of Rhode Island artisans and craftspeople.[82] Lovecraft very well may have swelled with pride as he accompanied his guest through the museum and highlighted a cabinet fashioned in eighteenth-century Newport or a chair of the same vintage from Boston. Likewise, knowing his admiration for all things colonial and New England, Greene might have added the Pendleton House to her wish list to demonstrate a mutual taste with him. Her desire to view such examples of decorative art would have deeply impressed him.

While spending the remainder of the afternoon at Lovecraft's Angell Street apartment, Greene lost track of time. She rushed downtown to catch her scheduled train. Ever the consummate host, he chaperoned her to the station and located an empty passenger car in which they could talk privately. They only said farewell when the train began its departure. Reflecting on the two-day visit and Greene herself, Lovecraft expressed nothing but compliments, peculiarly enough, still couched in xenophobia:

Mme. G. is certainly a person of the most admirable qualities, whose generous & kindly cast of mind is by no means feigned, & whose intelligence & devotion to art merit the sincerest approbation. The volatility incidental to a Continental & non-Aryan heritage should not blind the analytical observer to the solid work & genuine cultivation which underlie it.[83]

Although he explained his growing admiration for Greene by citing her potential financial support and creative contributions to amateur journalism, reading between the lines of his letters hints at something far more serious developing—certainly genuine affection and possibly romantic curiosity.

Lovecraft and Greene's conversation did not end when he bid her adieu on her train. It only paused. More letters—presumably increasing in length and frequency—passed between Brooklyn and Providence. Eventually, Greene floated a novel and exciting idea: Lovecraft should come and stay with her in New York City. She offered to reach out to mutual amateur journalism colleagues and organize a "convention of freaks" and "exotics" during the upcoming holiday season.[84] Potentially traveling to New York appeared to intimidate Lovecraft. His earlier New England trips that summer marked his farthest venture from the familiar streets and sights of his hometown. Nonetheless, meeting longstanding correspondents, several of whom he considered dear friends, might have stood as an irresistible draw. Although he voiced skepticism over Greene's New York proposed gathering becoming reality, he would remain open to the idea.

Within the course of several months, Lovecraft's life had changed markedly. The death of his mother seemed to liberate him from his family's suffocating expectations and cloistered domesticity and from his own isolation and insecurities. Lovecraft marked his thirty-first birthday on August 20, 1921, and he demonstrated a willingness to make up for lost time. He reveled in the big-city excitement and play of Boston. He hobnobbed with literary acquaintances and basked in their applause. He juggled the attentions of accomplished and attractive women. Now, he heard New York calling.

2

"An Eastern City of Wonder"

ON THE EVENING OF April 4, 1922, H. P. Lovecraft received an unexpected long-distance telephone call from Sonia Greene. Since the previous day, she had been hosting a male friend from Cleveland at her apartment at 259 Parkside Avenue in Flatbush, Brooklyn. Despondent over his failure to find to a job in New York, her guest intended to return to Ohio. After she attempted to persuade him not to give up on the city, he voiced a very specific request: to speak to Lovecraft. Greene's visitor was none other than the poet, translator, and bibliophile Samuel Loveman.[1]

Five years earlier, in 1917, Lovecraft wrote a letter to him praising his poetry published in amateur periodicals. Loveman recalled the mannered and intentionally obsolete style of Lovecraft's prose. While reading the "meticulously rounded sentences," he veered "between sheer envy and downright laughter."[2] Soon after meeting Greene in Boston in July 1921, Lovecraft encouraged her to begin writing to Loveman. She demurred, but she later met him during a business trip to Cleveland. Loveman surprised her with a party of local amateur journalists at the fashionable downtown Hotel Statler.[3]

When Greene put Loveman on the telephone, Lovecraft felt "ecstatic delight" in talking with his fellow writer for the very first time.[4] Loveman was a treasured correspondent and held a prominent position in Lovecraft's far-reaching network of friendships forged exclusively by letters. He had appeared in several of his vivid dreams, which Lovecraft later culled for different pieces of writing.[5] By the end of their conversation, Loveman committed to staying for another day and not abandoning his New York ambitions.

Lovecraft answered a second telephone call from Loveman on the following evening. This time, Loveman declared that he required his friend's presence in New York if he himself were to remain there. Greene and several other New York literary friends successively came on the line and echoed Loveman's demand. The "suddenness and unexpectedness" of this group petition "turned the trick" for Lovecraft.[6] He packed his suitcase and caught a New York, New Haven and Hartford Railroad train—Number 173, the Colonial Express—to Pennsylvania Station on the very next morning of April 6, 1922, at 10:06 A.M.[7] Given his passion for Georgian architecture, his choice of a departure was unlikely coincidental.

Ever since first visiting Providence in 1921, Greene had nurtured a desire to bring Lovecraft to New York. Oddly, the possibility of him or Loveman staying with her in the near future did not appear to have arisen when she traveled to Providence only several days earlier on April 1.[8] Loveman's sudden appearance in New York and his pleading telephone calls to Lovecraft might have all been part of a long-term plan by Greene to draw him to the city.

When his train crossed the Harlem River, the natural boundary separating Manhattan and the Bronx, Lovecraft marveled at "the Cyclopean outlines of New-York."[9] His reaction at seeing the iconic skyline resembled that of many first-time arrivals to the city—a heady combination of awe, elation, expectancy, and wonder:

> It was a mystical sight in the gold sun of late afternoon; a dream-thing of faint grey, outlined against a sky of faint grey smoke. City and sky were so alike that one could hardly be sure that there was a city—that the fancied towers and pinnacles were not the merest illusions.[10]

In 1922, New York City was a metropolis assuredly claiming its place on the world stage as an equal to the great European capitals of London, Paris, and Rome. It was home to street peddlers and stockbrokers, visual artists and garment makers, clergy and flappers, blue bloods and immigrants, and Tammany politicians and bootlegging gangsters. Department stores, hotels, theaters, and skyscrapers shaped commercial districts in Midtown Manhattan and Wall Street. Docks and factories ran up and down the Hudson and East Rivers. Bridges and tunnels opened the further reaches of the Bronx, Brooklyn, and Queens to development and migration. New York stood as the financial, literary, fashion, artistic, and media epicenter of the United States. The five boroughs of New York—Manhattan, Brooklyn, Queens, Staten Island, and the Bronx—were home to 5,620,048 people, and 1,991,547, or approximately 35 percent, of these residents were foreign-born. Another 2,303,082, or roughly 41 percent, of New Yorkers were the children of immigrants. New Americans and their sons and daughters numbered 4,294,629 individuals, and they collectively comprised just over 76 percent of the city's total population.[11] Art historian Jean Clair captured the spirit of the city at this moment:

> New York . . . had become a refuge for many a wanderer and had fulfilled many a dream. In Manhattan, the city imagined by the architects of two generations had finally become a concrete reality. It opened its heart to everyone and astonished all, from the discerning and cultivated ambassador . . . to the small-time doctor from the outskirts of Paris.[12]

This was the New York City that Lovecraft studied from his train seat. Possibly much to his own surprise, he seemed ready for it.

Stepping out of his train car, Lovecraft found himself amid the frenetic confusion of commuters, tourists, and red-capped rail porters of Pennsylvania Station. Designed by the firm of McKim, Mead & White and modeled after the Ancient Roman Baths of Caracalla, it held the capacity to carry a thousand trains each weekday. The monumental Beaux Arts interior of one of New York's finest public buildings must have left Lovecraft—a lover of art and architecture—gape-mouthed and silent. He was no longer in sleepy Providence. After wandering through "the mazes of the vast terminal," he spotted Greene scanning the busy crowd for her out-of-town guest.[13] He did not record what words passed between them in the main concourse beneath its towering steel arches and many vaulted windows filling the station with sunlight.[14] Instead, he appeared more excited to meet Loveman in Brooklyn and shake his hand.

After years of letters, sharing thoughts on literature and ideas, and offering feedback on each other's writing, Lovecraft and Loveman finally greeted one another on the front steps of Greene's Parkside Avenue apartment building in Flatbush. Lovecraft measured his longtime epistolary acquaintance to be "refined, cultivated, and aesthetic" and a man full of "kindness, delicacy, thoughtfulness, and innumerable kindred virtues."[15] Loveman was "gracefully proportioned" with a gentle face and dark receding hair.[16] Once settled in Greene's home, the two men read their current respective projects: Loveman's poem "The Hermaphrodite" and his one-act play *The Sphinx: A Conversation* and Lovecraft's "Hypnos," a short story about a sculptor traveling through dream worlds aided by drugs and with a companion whom he first met at an English railway station. The two men spent the remainder of the afternoon immersed in a "whirl of words."[17]

The longtime correspondence and later friendship between Lovecraft and Loveman highlight the contradictory nature of Lovecraft's character. Samuel Loveman was Jewish and the child of immigrants from the former Austria-Hungary. Shortly after the two began exchanging letters in 1917, Lovecraft sponsored his application to join the United Amateur Press Association, stating that he was honored to vouch for Loveman, "Jew or not."[18] In a purported letter to Greene written early in their own relationship and well before Lovecraft traveled to New York, he lauded Loveman with a very singular qualification. Greene quoted this letter (now lost) in her own memoir:

> Loveman is a poet and a literary genius. I have never met him in person, but his letters indicate him to be a man of great learning and cultural background. The only discrepancy I find in him is that he is of the Semitic race, a Jew.[19]

This may have been Greene's first true encounter with Lovecraft's deep-seated anti-Semitism. Being Jewish herself, she admitted to being shocked at this "petty fallacy" and worried that his prejudice could signal the end of their nascent friendship.[20] He eventually placated her and "curtailed his outbursts" on ethnicity and race.[21] Strangely enough, this jumpstarted their own letter-writing. Greene now hoped that meeting Loveman might temper this strain of Lovecraft's bigotry.

Like Greene, Loveman represented another exception made by Lovecraft. Aside from being Jewish, Loveman was a minority of a very different sort in 1920s America: he was gay. Lovecraft appears to have remained unaware of Loveman's sexual orientation throughout their long friendship, and Loveman might not have been out during this time.[22] Although never explicitly addressing Loveman's identity as a gay man, Greene and Loveman's writings hint that she was knowledgeable and possibly empathetic of it. Through her career in the fashion industry, Greene might have encountered and even worked alongside gay men. Others in Lovecraft and Loveman's social and literary circles were certainly aware of the latter's sexuality.²³ Loveman himself lauded Lovecraft's penchant for overlooking the "peccadilloes" of his friends.²⁴ That is, he may have simply ignored this facet of Loveman.

Arriving from his job as a bookkeeper in the Manhattan offices of the Fairbanks Scales Company, Rheinhart Kleiner joined the festivities at Greene's apartment later that evening.²⁵ The four friends chatted for hours. Since she had to work on the following morning, Greene slipped away at some point. Lovecraft joked that she was "turned out of her own house and home."²⁶ During Lovecraft and Loveman's stay, Greene slept at a neighbor's.²⁷ This might have been a result of her wanting to avoid gossip over the exact nature of her relationship with her nonfamilial male guests, or it might have been a practical decision based upon physical space (always an issue in a New York apartment). Greene later congratulated herself for displaying "boldness" and "daring" by inviting two men to stay with her, suggesting her modest embrace of the loosening social and sexual mores of the 1920s.²⁸ With their host absent, Lovecraft, Kleiner, and Loveman felt no need to be mindful of her schedule. Their night concluded at one in the morning. Lovecraft talked so much that he partially lost his voice.²⁹

His official initiation into New York City began on the very next day. He and Loveman made an expedition to a site requisite for any lover of fine culture in Gotham for the first time: they visited the Metropolitan Museum of Art. Although its holdings of Egyptian artifacts and old masters intrigued Lovecraft, he quickly became immersed in the museum's ancient Greek and Roman collection. As a child, he was fascinated by the classical world, going as far as to express belief in the demigods and gods of Mount Olympus. As an adult, he remained a devotee of ancient Rome, often categorizing it as his ideal time in human history. He swooned upon entering these galleries:

> But for me the supreme thrill—not only of the museums but of all New-York—came from the majestick memorials of mine own classical spirit-home—S. P. Q. R. Roma. I felt Rome at the moment I entered the Musaeum [sic].³⁰

While Lovecraft and Loveman were dining with Greene at her apartment later that evening, James F. Morton came knocking to drag the two men to a musical recital and salon at the home of another friend, Adeline E. Leiser, in Cypress Hills, Brooklyn. Born in 1870, Morton was a veteran public speaker, writer, political activist, and convert to the Baha'i faith living in Harlem. He was one of the more colorful characters in Lovecraft's burgeoning literary network, arguing for civil rights and Esperanto and railing against the postal system and Sunday baseball games. Stocky, mustached, and with graying red hair, Morton wore old-fashioned suits and derby hats. He held bachelor's and master's degrees from Harvard University, making him one of the better traditionally educated figures acquainted with Lovecraft. The two writers began sparring over politics in amateur publications in 1915. Morton expressed progressive, sometimes radical, politics; Lovecraft adhered to a conservatism mired in racism. Nonetheless, when finally meeting in Boston in September 1920, they immediately connected.[31] Their shared New York adventures would result in a lifetime friendship.

By April 1922, Lovecraft viewed Morton with degree of pity. He marked him as an aging and eccentric man "animated by a futile and quixotic idealism" and passed over by time.[32] His sole income was freelance work that Lovecraft himself—never an individual flush with cash—directed his way.[33] He lamented his friend's current low state:

There is much of the heroic in James Ferdinand Morton, Jr., and I would give anything to see his worth recognised and rewarded as it should be. Justice, however, is the most flimsy of illusions; and honesty and goodness bring rewards only when chance weaves extraordinary circumstances about their possessor.[34]

A public proponent of equal rights for Black Americans since the early 1900s, Morton was a further example of the complexity inherent in Lovecraft's choice of friends. Lovecraft believed Morton was squandering his intellectual talents on "radical nonsense" and "repellent ideas."[35] Undoubtedly, this referred to Morton's long and early advocacy against the discrimination of Black and Jewish Americans.[36] Holding diametrically opposed political and social views on an array of issues, especially on that of race, did not appear to impact Lovecraft and Morton's respect or affinity for each other.

Although expressing little interest in Morton's plan for the night, Lovecraft and Loveman were reluctant to disappoint him and agreed to accompany him to Cypress Hills. Tellingly, Greene was not invited to join their outing. Lovecraft found the musical performance at the salon to be a pedestrian and somnolent affair. He labeled it as "bourgeois Victorianism" and backhandedly complimented one musician for "warding off the ever-present peril of obvious nodding."[37] Morton entertained the small audience with his theatrical recital of passages from *The Captive*, a short play by Gothic novelist and man of letters Matthew Gregory Lewis.[38] After the gathering dispersed, the true joy began for Lovecraft—a meandering nighttime walk filled with animated conversation with his friends. When Lovecraft and Loveman returned to Greene's apartment, a somewhat angry note awaited them: she would not be coming by to cook for them in the morning. They were on their own. Lovecraft sent Loveman out for breakfast.[39]

The two companions traveled into Manhattan for a full and exhaustive Saturday of sightseeing on April 8. They began their day by scouring the sidewalk bookstalls on Vesey Street in Lower Manhattan. Lovecraft snatched up a compilation of short stories by his favorite American writer, Edgar Allan Poe. Committed readers, both men could never pass by a bookshop, library, or a sidewalk peddler without searching for an overlooked treasure. James F. Morton and Rheinhart Kleiner joined them in front of the Woolworth Building, then the tallest building in the world, and the four friends rode the elevator to its observation deck. The view astounded Lovecraft:

> All Manhattan, Brooklyn, and Jersey City lay below, outspread like a map—in fact, I told Mortonious that the city-planners had done an excellent job in making the place almost as good as the map in my Hammond Atlas at home.[40]

Next, the group rode the Interborough Rapid Transit Company's Ninth Avenue Line, popularly known as the Ninth Avenue Elevated or El, uptown to tour the studio of Jewish-Ukrainian sculptor Louis Keila, an acquaintance of Morton.[41] Throughout Lovecraft's first New York foray, his friends introduced him to the cultural possibilities of the city, hinting at the adventures and life awaiting a writer or a creative-minded individual. Keila worked in an aging building on East Fourteenth Street off Union Square Park. Lovecraft compared its dark interior to the Cretan labyrinth from Greek mythology, noting its design of "a thousand corridors and one or two rooms."[42]

Morton wanted to show Keila's recent work, a bust of Morton himself, to his friends. Being a writer, an artist of letters, Lovecraft took special interest in seeing together the model and the sculpture, the raw material and the finished product. Although he admired Keila's talent, he remarked that the sculptor possessed "no manners or refinement," clearly maligning Keila with an anti-Semitic stereotype.[43] He suspected that Morton was "trying to civilise" Keila.[44] In fact, Morton might have been subtly pushing Lovecraft to confront his own prejudices.

Because he had a speaking engagement, Morton bade his friends a temporary farewell and handed all tour responsibilities to Kleiner. After browsing through more bookstalls and enjoying refreshments at a drugstore lunch counter, Lovecraft, Kleiner, and Loveman ventured to Wall Street and the Financial District. Walking through some of the city's oldest streets and viewing "skyscraper vistas" seemed to enliven Lovecraft's imagination.[45] He began to grasp the affection held for New York by many of its natives and adopted residents.

At a subway station newsstand, he spied the April issue of *Home Brew*, his friend George Julian Houtain's small humor magazine, then publishing a series of "Grewsome Tales" penned by Lovecraft himself. This particular issue contained the third story, "Six Shots by Moonlight." The ongoing narrative involved grave-robbery, murder in the name of science, and the medical resurrection of corpses. (The series ultimately numbered six stories, and they would eventually be collected and renamed "Herbert West—Reanimator.")[46] He purchased a copy and proudly showed his name in print to his friends—a thrilling experience for every writer.

Lovecraft, Kleiner, and Loveman rode the subway to Brooklyn Heights, arguably New York's first suburb and once the most affluent and desirable area in the borough. The neighborhood's brownstone buildings, many constructed prior to the American Civil War, and low-rise streetscape reminded Lovecraft of the Back Bay section of Boston. Possibly unbeknownst to him, Brooklyn Heights was quickly sliding into decline. The subway reached the neighborhood in 1908, opening it to immigrants and less well-heeled residents. This resulted in the longtime gentry and merchant class fleeing and their regal homes being converted into apartments and boardinghouses. However, another demographic shift, one possibly less visible, yet arguably equally potent for the character and future of the neighborhood, began during this period as well: artists and writers started gravitating to it in the never-ending quest for affordable rent.[47]

While strolling through Brooklyn Heights, likely admiring the sandstone ornamentation of a Romanesque Revival mansion or the simple elegance of a Federal-style home, the three friends happened upon an abandoned garden. This forgotten spot might have been the neglected grounds of the James S. Rockwell House at 2 Montague Terrace (Figure 5). A contemporary 1922 photograph shows an overgrown and impenetrable garden of clustered bushes and greenery. A sickly, spindly tree lords over the space, easily standing several stories tall.[48] This garden fascinated Kleiner and Loveman, and the two waxed poetically about it. Lovecraft withheld his revelry until the trio crossed the Manhattan Bridge at nightfall:

Figure 5. While Lovecraft strolled through Brooklyn Heights one evening, a neglected garden arrested his attention. This might have been the grounds of the James S. Rockwell House at 2 Montague Terrace. (Courtesy of the Collection of the New-York Historical Society)

Right there I surrendered to Klei about the beauties of his home town. Out of the waters it rose at twilight; cold, proud, and beautiful; an Eastern city of wonder whose brothers the mountains are. It was not like any city of earth, for above purple mists rose towers, spires, and pyramids which one may only dream of in opiate lands beyond the Oxus; towers, spires and pyramids that no man could fashion, but that bloomed flower-like and delicate; the bridges up which fairies walk to the sky; the visions of giants that play with the clouds.[49]

This rhapsody lasted until they entered Manhattan and crossed the Lower East Side to reach a subway station. Lovecraft derided that neighborhood, then the densest in the world and the home to hundreds of thousands of Yiddish-speaking immigrants and Americans, as little more than a con-glomeration of "some filthy Jew slums."[50]

The three friends concluded their night with a dinner hosted by George Julian Houtain at his apartment at 1128 Bedford Avenue in Bedford-Stuyvesant, Brooklyn. Lovecraft described it as "an archaic dump over a shop."[51] At that time, Houtain's block consisted of two- and three-story wood frame and brick buildings with ground-floor retail.[52] Regardless of Lovecraft's snobbishness, the group shared a satisfying meal and stimu-lating conversation. Flouting Prohibition, Houtain poured wine for his guests. Although a teetotaler, Lovecraft admitted to making "the most noise."[53] Good company appeared to be the only intoxicant he needed.

On the morning of April 9, Lovecraft and Samuel Loveman spent the early hours observing a quiet Sunday ritual observed by many Brooklyn residents: they walked in Prospect Park, the crown jewel of the borough designed by Frederick Law Olmsted and Calvert Vaux, the landscape ar-chitects behind Central Park and many other elegant urban green spaces throughout the United States.[54] Lovecraft snapped some pictures of the scenery with his Kodak camera. While Loveman continued to explore the park, Lovecraft took advantage of a free moment to telephone an-other New York correspondent, Frank Belknap Long Jr., to announce his own presence in the city and to invite Long to visit him and Loveman at Greene's apartment.[55]

Long was a twenty-year-old Columbia University student and aspiring fiction writer. A Manhattan native, he lived with his upper-middle-class professional family in an apartment building at 823 West End Avenue in the Upper West Side. He and Lovecraft began writing to one another in early 1920, and Lovecraft soon became a literary mentor to him. In April 1922, Long was still recovering from having his appendix removed during the past winter, and he had taken a sabbatical from his studies.[56] Ultimately, he would never return to college, choosing to pursue a writing career.

The telephone call from Lovecraft was both a pleasant surprise and a tantalizing curiosity for Long. When Lovecraft mentioned that he was staying at Greene's apartment, he elaborated on his relationship with her.

Lovecraft never expected to cross paths with someone "*quite* so congenial" and with whom he shared so many interests.[57] He felt flattered that such "an attractive young lady" found his company entertaining.[58] Lovecraft's admission that he was staying at the home of an unattached women of only recent acquaintance set Long's "thoughts whirling."[59] He promised to be in Brooklyn within an hour.

Over fifty years later, Long could still vividly recall his first impressions of Lovecraft. As he approached Greene's Parkside Avenue building, he spotted a solitary figure in his line of sight—a man sitting on one of the two short brick walls running alongside each side of the entrance. Even from a distance, he was certain that this was Lovecraft. He appeared stouter and older than in photographs. Lovecraft did not bother to mask his enthusiasm in meeting Long:

> When he rose and grasped my hand in greeting . . . I realized there was still a certain boyishness about him that could not be concealed. It was particularly noticeable in the region of his eyes, and his voice was not that of a middle-aged man.[60]

Lovecraft judged Long to be a modest, intelligent, and gifted young writer. Slightly built and delicate-featured with a shock of dark hair, he was attempting to grow a mustache. This tonsorial experiment resulted in good-natured ribbing from Lovecraft.[61] After the two exchanged pleasantries and discussed Lovecraft's impressions of New York, they went inside. Long was excited to see Greene.

Lovecraft directed him into the living room, and the two sat down. While they chatted, Long heard someone clattering around in the kitchen. After several minutes, Lovecraft disappeared into the next room and fetched Greene. This introduction left an equally deep imprint in Long's memory:

> She was still wearing a sun-shielding straw hat and was attired in a simple print dress that set off her dark beauty in an extremely becoming way. She was far more attractive than I had thought she might be. . . . She came straight toward me across the room, smiling graciously.[62]

He felt self-conscious in the presence of this stylish and beautiful older woman. After observing only several minutes of the easy banter and familiarity flowing between Lovecraft and Greene, Long suspected that the pair were more than just friends. He was impressed by Lovecraft's unstated romantic ability.[63]

•

When Samuel Loveman returned to the apartment after his solitary excursion in Prospect Park, the entire group sat down for a leisurely multi-course lunch. A generous host, Greene always plied company with rich and bountiful meals. Joining the four friends was her twenty-year-old daughter, Florence (Figure 6). Long noticed her freckled nose, slim waist, and luxurious dark hair. He seemed smitten by both mother and daughter.

Although Florence was likely living at Parkside Avenue at this time, she appeared to be staying elsewhere during Lovecraft and Loveman's visit. Greene had a difficult and contentious relationship with her only surviving child. Lovecraft seemed to channel her frustration, describing Florence as a "flapper" and "a pert, spoiled, and ultra-independent infant rather more hard-boiled of visage."[64] "Appalled at the hatred" she demonstrated toward Greene, Loveman remembered Florence "scream[ing]" at the gathered guests, "attack[ing] her mother, and singl[ing]" out individuals "for her confidences."[65] This discord between mother and daughter ultimately concluded in a lifelong estrangement. The reasons behind this permanent falling-out remain unclear.[66] Lovecraft offered no further opinion or commentary on Florence Greene anywhere in his known letters.

Well after the lunch party had dispersed and tellingly near the dinner hour later that evening, James F. Morton stopped by Parkside Avenue—possibly and purposefully unannounced. Offended that his friend received "so haughty a reception," Lovecraft decided to "let the foreigners shift for themselves" for the remainder of the night.[67] These "foreigners" were Loveman and Greene, his fellow houseguest and host, both of Jewish ancestry. In all likelihood, Greene was far from thrilled with being tasked to prepare an extra and unplanned setting at the table.

Eventually, the quartet traveled into Manhattan, so that Lovecraft and Loveman could experience another must-see for many first-time tourists—Broadway blindingly illuminated at night, the Great White Way.[68] The commercialism-writ-large left Lovecraft underwhelmed. He disparaged the signage for plays and products as "neither superlatively impressive nor in any sense truly artistic."[69] His lifelong aristocratic disdain for business and hustle might have been appreciated by the city's vanishing Knickerbocker elites.[70] After their self-guided walk through the Theater District and Times Square, Morton departed for home. Lovecraft lamented that his "fellow Anglo-Saxon" lived in "the semi-African jungles of Harlem."[71] Before calling it a night and heading back to Brooklyn, Loveman and Greene insisted on sitting down for dessert in a restaurant. Lovecraft griped that their waiter hardly spoke English.

Figure 6. Lovecraft met Sonia H. Greene's twenty-year-old daughter in April 1922. Aghast by her behavior, he described Florence Greene as "a pert, spoiled, and ultra-independent infant." (Courtesy of the American Heritage Center, University of Wyoming)

The next afternoon, Long opened his family's Upper West Side household to Lovecraft and Loveman for lunch. The formality and order of the meal impressed Lovecraft, a staunch defender of etiquette. Each dish was served in its proper order. A feline obsessive, he notably enjoyed meeting the family cat, "a sumptuous creature with silky mane," a Maine Coon named Felis.[72] He always included the full details of his encounters with domestic and stray cats alike in his letters.

After the noonday repast, Morton arrived to partake in the day's main event—a pilgrimage to the Edgar Allan Poe Cottage in the Bronx. A job interview prevented Loveman from accompanying his friends to the literary shrine. Lovecraft expressed relief and jubilation: he found himself among "the first one hundred percent Aryan, Anglo-Saxon" party since the beginning of his New York trip.[73] While heading to the Poe Cottage, Lovecraft, Long, and Morton picked up another literary acquaintance, Paul Livingston Keil, who lived in an apartment with his parents and siblings in a nearby Bronx neighborhood.[74] Much to the quartet's disappointment, the house had already closed for the day. However, they still were able to wander through the building's grounds and study its exterior.

Edgar Allan Poe rented and lived on the property between 1846 and 1849, and it inspired his final short story, "Landor's Cottage." During those years, he befriended Jesuit professors at nearby St. John's College (today's Fordham University). Its church's bells purportedly inspired his poem "The Bells." Sadness and loss haunted the writer. Virginia (née Clemm), his young wife, died in the home in 1847. Originally at the intersection of Kingsbridge Road and Valentine Avenue, the building was moved approximately 450 feet north to Poe Park on the Grand Concourse and opened as a house museum in 1913.[75] The New-York Historical Society completed restoration of the building in February 1922. The surrounding property was landscaped to recreate the paths and greenery as they likely appeared during Poe's residency.[76]

While walking among the trees in the park and along the house's narrow veranda, Lovecraft imaginatively stripped away the layers of development and history from the neighborhood:

Today it is a thing to stir the pulses. Fordham is now hopelessly fused into the solid mass of elevateds, apartment-house cliffs, busses, and boulevards which is New-York. But in Poe's day it was a village of magical charm, with verdant arcades, purling brooks, and fragrant sylvan lanes leading to quaint and antique Highbridge.[77]

Figure 7. A pilgrimage to the former Bronx home of Edgar Allan Poe was a must-see for Lovecraft during his first visit to New York City. He would count Frank Belknap Long (left) and James F. Morton (right) as trusted, lifelong friends.

He lamented the industrialization, density, and speed of the modern city, longing for an urban pastoral.[78]

Before leaving the grounds of the Poe Cottage, Long, Morton, and Lovecraft posed for a photograph taken by Keil (Figure 7). The three friends stand before the house museum with Lovecraft at the center of the group portrait. A trolley car whisks by modern apartment buildings rising in the background. Dressed in dark suits and overcoats, they all look gravely serious. Lovecraft and Morton sport watchchains, and Long appears more dapper with a bowtie and leather gloves. Visiting the Poe Cottage stood as a milestone for these friends. They were all men of ideas and letters. Lovecraft considered himself as writing in the school of Poe. It seems fitting that a photograph memorialized their shared moment. After having their picture taken, Morton predicted that Lovecraft would one day "be recognized as Poe's peer."[79]

Later that same evening, Lovecraft, Long, and Morton met Rhein-hart Kleiner and Samuel Loveman outside the main branch of the New York Public Library, a revered institution in the minds of booklovers. (In fact, Loveman and Lovecraft had started the day there.) After a dilatory conversation on the library's steps, Long left for the subway and home. The remaining four friends grabbed a quick dinner at an Automat, and then Kleiner led everyone on a walking tour through several of Manhattan's more picturesque and unique neighborhoods.[80]

Since all four men identified themselves as writers and freethinkers in their own individualistic and strange ways, Greenwich Village was their logical first stop. In 1922, the neighborhood was the heart of New York and arguably American bohemian life. Painters, poets, playwrights, authors, and political activists lived and honed their crafts within its narrow streets, immigrant cafes, art studios, and avant-garde theaters. Although fully aware of contemporary artistic trends and an outsider by any normal societal definition, Lovecraft expressed little open affinity for the creatives and misfits of Greenwich Village. Still, he felt himself swayed by its physical charm when strolling through Washington Square Park, the neighborhood's symbolic center and long a place of street performance, political protest, and romantic rendezvous.

Passing beneath the park's arch, an imitation Roman triumphal monument designed by architect Stanford White and commemorating George Washington, Lovecraft swelled with the "pride of a patrician triumphator."[81] Honoring the tradition of many New York writers and creatively oriented individuals, the four friends found a bench and "discuss[ed] all manner of learned things."[82] After Morton bid goodnight to Lovecraft, Kleiner, and Loveman, the three remaining compatriots continued toward the primary destination on their ambulatory agenda—the Lower East Side and Chinatown.

By the 1920s, travel guides and publications included itineraries of Manhattan's ethnic enclaves, marking such neighborhoods as "safe" for middle-class and implicitly White Anglo-Saxon Protestant sightseers and consumers. The tea parlors and import stores of Chinatown and the espresso bars and pastry shops of Little Italy offered an "exotic," yet ultimately predicative experience for tourists from the "real" America—a description often deemed unapplicable to New York.[83] In taking his out-of-town friends to the Jewish Lower East Side and Chinatown, Kleiner might have wished to present them with such a view of an "authentic" city. Even today, these neighborhoods remain popular with many contemporary visitors. Aware of Loveman's Jewish background, Kleiner might have thought he would appreciate patronizing businesses and vendors advertising and peddling their wares in Yiddish. Today, second-, third-, and even fourth-generation Americans find comfort in returning to their families' old neighborhoods in New York and other cities.

Regardless of Kleiner's motivations, Lovecraft expressed outright disgust for the Lower East Side and its residents. He insisted on keeping to the middle of the street to avoid physical contact with "the heterogeneous sidewalk denizens."[84] The very sight of this dense, polyglot, immigrant neighborhood stood as a physical affront:

These swine have instinctive swarming movements, no doubt, which no ordinary biologist can fathom. Gawd knows what they are—Jew, Italian, separate or mixed, with possible touches of residual aboriginal Irish and exotic hints of the Far East—a bastard mess of stewing mongrel flesh without intellect, repellent to eye, nose and imagination—would to heaven a kindly gust of cyanogen could asphyxiate the whole gigantic abortion, end the misery, and clean out the place.[85]

Although using crude and ugly language, Lovecraft's general view of immigration and new Americans, especially those from Eastern and Southern Europe, differed little from that promulgated by many popular magazines, such as *Good Housekeeping*, and the leadership of scientific and cultural institutions, such as the American Museum of Natural History.[86] However, Lovecraft's xenophobia veered in directions and posited outcomes extreme for mainstream eugenic proponents and racial gatekeepers: he presented the idea of spraying the Lower East Side with poison gas to clear it of excess and undesirable populations. Such a statement would not prove to be an outlier or anomaly.

Chinatown appeared to be more appealing or less threatening to Lovecraft. He admired the clean sidewalks, mocked tourists gawking at fake opium dens, and found Doyers Street, a narrow, curving commercial strip, to be "fascinatingly Oriental."[87] He, Kleiner, and Loveman concluded their adventures by crossing the Manhattan Bridge and seeing the city's skyline blazing at night.

Lovecraft's final full day in New York was April 11, 1922; he held a focused desire for it—a return trip to the Poe Cottage. When he, Long, and Loveman ventured to the Bronx that afternoon, the museum thankfully was open. Stepping through its main entrance, Lovecraft felt as if he was entering "a small world of magic."[88] A few scraps of Poe's furniture—his rocking chair and his wife, Virginia's, wooden bedstead—remained in the building's modest rooms. The rest of the furnishings and household objects represented styles from the late 1840s.[89] Everything stirred Lovecraft's imagination:

The atmosphere grows on one and finally grips one—it is so terribly vivid—the 'forties recalled in every sombre detail. The pitiful poverty shows—something sombre broods over the place. I seemed to feel unseen bat-wings brush my cheek as I passed through a bare, cramped corridor . . . the house is so pathetically small. . . . Such was the home of the man to whom I probably owe every genuine artistic impulse and method I possess. My master—the great original whose titanic powers I can so feebly seek to copy . . . Edgar Allan Poe.[90]

At this early stage in his writing career—largely limited to amateur, nonpaying, and nonprofessional periodicals—Lovecraft already saw himself as following the tradition established by Poe. He perceived himself to be a literary writer, an artist, not a journeyman typing tired phrases and boilerplate stories for quick cash. The bare poverty of Poe's existence appeared to shake him. Did he worry that he would follow his idol down this path as well? At thirty-one, Lovecraft had never held a conventional job of any sort. He was living off a small and diminishing inheritance and money earned from freelance editing and ghostwriting assignments. Already, he was hovering near poverty.

After the Poe Cottage, the three friends returned to Manhattan to pick up Sonia Greene at Ferle Heller, just a few blocks south of Central Park on 36 West Fifty-Seventh Street between Fifth and Sixth Avenues.[91] Walking from the Upper East Side, they were caught in a sudden spring shower and huddled on "the porch of a magnificent mansion."[92] When they finally joined Greene outside her workplace, Long exchanged "a ceremonious farewell" with his friends and then left for his home on the Upper West Side.[93]

To celebrate her houseguests' final night in the city, Greene treated them to an Italian dinner—Lovecraft's introduction to the cuisine—and a Broadway show.[94] The three attended a performance of La Chauve-Souris at the 49th Street Theatre. The Russian-French touring revue performed dances, one-act plays, comedic sketches, and songs; it was best known for popularizing Leon Jessel's "The Parade of the Wooden Soldiers."[95] Much of the program was conducted in Russian. Possibly filled with a nostalgia for her native region, Greene took Lovecraft and Loveman to a nearby Russian restaurant for coffee and dessert after the show. Coincidentally, this night marked one of the few outings Lovecraft shared with her throughout his entire trip. As always, she picked up the tab.[96]

Early the next morning of April 12, 1922, Greene accompanied Lovecraft and Loveman to Grand Central Terminal and waited with them until leaving for work at Ferle Heller. Before their respective departures, the two men "discoursed in the manner of a Greek and a Roman about to part in brotherly amity."[97] For the past several days, Lovecraft had spent nearly every waking moment in the company of friends. He explored the streets and sites of New York, merely scratching the surface of its cultural riches. He discussed literature and art during walks and meals. He grew closer to a woman desirous of his attention. Simply put, he lived the life of a writer. Over a month later, after returning to Providence, he remained energized and exhausted from his flirtation with Gotham, openly declaring to a longtime correspondent, "I'm hardly over it yet!"[98]

3

⣿

"It Is a Myth; A Dream"

WHILE WORKING ON A TEMPORARY BASIS at Ferle Heller's shop in Magnolia, a coastal village and popular vacation spot in northeastern Massachusetts, Sonia Greene decided to travel to Providence to spend a Sunday with H. P. Lovecraft and his aunts, arriving on June 18, 1922. An easy conviviality emerged between his family and possible paramour. The warmth directed toward Greene by his younger aunt, Annie Gamwell, surprised him. He elaborated on this usual display, noting that she "likes [Greene] immensely despite a racial and social chasm which she doesn't often bridge."[1]

This admission suggests that Lovecraft's aunts shared many of his own racist and xenophobic beliefs. Throughout his adult life, his letters to them often contained his most vitriolic, outlandish, and hateful thoughts on immigrants and minorities. Were Lillian Clark and Gamwell making an exception to their racial and social codes for Greene, much like Lovecraft did for his own acquaintances and friends? Did they recognize a budding attraction between their nephew and her? Or were they merely wishing to present themselves as gracious and amiable hosts? Regardless, Greene appeared to achieve the goal of her day trip. By the time Lovecraft walked her to the train station that night, he promised to join her for several days in Magnolia during the following week.[2]

Lovecraft likely arrived by June 25, apparently not holding a fixed idea of the length of his holiday. In his first postcard from Magnolia, he mentioned that he might stay for a week. Later, he changed his plans and

51

remained there until July 5. The seaside landscape and village atmosphere transfixed Lovecraft. The "mystical" and "antique waterfront" allowed him to step backward to colonial New England in his imagination, "savoring of a century ago."[3] He strolled along the ocean cliffs "whilst pearl-grey mists surged out of the sky to mix with sea."[4] He walked to nearby Gloucester, a historic fishing center in the state. He rose early to watch the sunrise. He worked on his writing. During his entire stay, Lovecraft lodged at the same property—either a small hotel or rooming house—as Greene. She was traveling alone. He was traveling alone.[5]

While in Magnolia, Lovecraft and Greene enjoyed long evening walks along the oceanside. On the esplanade leading to Gloucester one full-moon night, she heard a strange sound in the distance, almost "a loud snorting and grunting," and watched "the shimmering light forming a moon-path on the water."[6] Suddenly, Greene realized that a combination of this imagery and landscape would form an inspired fictional setting. She excitedly shared her idea with Lovecraft, wanting him to incorporate it into one of his stories. Instead, he countered that she compose her own tale. Greene demurred, but he pressed her to articulate the exact impressions she drew from their surroundings. Motivated by his "enthusiastic and sincere" belief in her literary ability, she outlined a story that very night.[7] The plot centered upon a hypnotic sea monster lurking in the waters off the Massachusetts coast.[8]

Lovecraft continued to encourage her to write the story on the following day. Greene longed to show her appreciation for his support. "Right then and there," she kissed him.[9] Later, she playfully recounted his reaction to such an unequivocal romantic and physical declaration:

> He was so flustered that he blushed, then he turned pale. When I chaffed him about it he said that he had not been kissed since he was a very small child and that he was never kissed by any woman, not even by his mother or aunts, since he grew to manhood, and that he would probably never be kissed again. (But I fooled him.)[10]

This attempt at intimacy revealed the deep extent of emotional repression in Lovecraft. Minor physical affection—a peck on the cheek, a comforting embrace, a reassuring pat on the arm—was likely absent in his family's household, and he never grew comfortable expressing feelings of tenderness. Lovecraft's admitting that Greene was his first kiss also clarified his past relationship with Winifred Virginia Jackson. If it was romantic or pursued in the hope for such, it had remained physically platonic.[11]

Neither Lovecraft's correspondence from Magnolia nor Greene's own account provides the exact date when their friendship transformed into an amorous attachment.[12] He certainly would have refrained from divulging any such details to his aunts. Shortly thereafter, he and Greene visited Newport, Rhode Island, a port city rich in colonial and Gilded Age heritage and then only accessible from Providence by ferry, on July 16. When he sent his aunt Lillian Clark a postcard from there, Greene added her own signature to it.[13]

A mere ten days later, on July 26, Greene once again opened her Brooklyn home to Lovecraft.[14] This was his third trip including her in a single month. A man and woman spending time together alone and with such frequency would indicate serious interest and signal the heady infatuation stage of a relationship. Clearly, something was happening between the two. After sharing several days with Greene, Lovecraft boarded the New York Central Railroad's Lake Shore Limited at Grand Central Terminal at five-thirty in the evening on July 29.[15] Now, he was heading to Cleveland, Ohio, easily the furthest he had strayed from his Providence nest.

After a night in the sleeping car, Lovecraft watched the passing Pennsylvania and Ohio countryside washed in the morning light from his train seat. Compared to his beloved New England, the scenery was underwhelming, and he ranked the flat Midwestern landscape as "inferior" and the region's towns and villages as "insufferably dismal—like 'Main St.'"[16] This reference to Sinclair Lewis's 1920 novel *Main Street*, a critique of self-satisfied small-town American life, is telling. Lovecraft's distaste for "the real America" displayed another contradiction in his intellectual character. Although his nativist beliefs largely resembled those dominant in middle America, he did not align himself with its largely anti-urban, anti-intellectual, and moralistic values. Reflecting on his physical view from the train, Lovecraft declared, "I was glad that my destination was a large city!"[17]

When Lovecraft disembarked in Cleveland later that morning, Alfred Galpin, his college-age Wisconsin correspondent, was waiting on the station platform to greet him. He instantly recognized the tall and lanky young man and was overjoyed upon finally meeting him. Galpin was staying in Cleveland for the summer, boarding with a family living around the corner from Samuel Loveman. Lovecraft rented a room from Galpin's landlords and remained in the city through the middle of August.[18]

For the next two weeks, Galpin and Loveman introduced their friend to their individual and mutual creative circles. Lovecraft mingled with painter William Sommer, composer Gordon Hatfield, bookseller George

Kirk, architect William Lescaze, and poet Hart Crane. These encounters emotionally and intellectually energized him: he humbly described it as "a novel sensation to be 'lionised'" by such a group of artists and thinkers.[19] Galpin was impressed by Lovecraft's ease in fitting in with his Cleveland friends:

> All who met Howard, so far as I can tell, no matter how strange they may have found him at first, liked him spontaneously and cordially. He was certainly one of those persons whose unsociable ways . . . were due to a sense of isolation from people among whom he might find himself thrown by chance, without any sense of communion; but when he felt himself in congenial company, he had a boyish charm and enthusiasm.[20]

Galpin and Loveman brought him to concert recitals and the Cleveland Museum of Art. Loveman affectionately recalled "wonderful walks at night and a marvelously brilliant but solid exchange of conversations" with Lovecraft.[21] Hoping to improve his taste in music, Galpin insisted that he listen to records of avant-garde classical composers and performers.

Probably suffering from both genuine and psychosomatic maladies throughout his life, Lovecraft discovered that this recent series of trips markedly improved his health. He announced that he was "altogether free from melancholy" and "positively cheerful," and he attributed this positive mental bounce to "the constant company of youthful and congenial literary persons."[22] The presence of like-minded people pursuing lives dedicated to culture and the mind allowed him to experience the promise of camaraderie and friendship. Simply put, he felt less alone. Being away from home affected his physical health as well. While in Cleveland, he did not suffer from "headaches or depressed spells" and felt "really alive."[23] Based on these sudden and positive changes, he doubted that Providence acquaintances would even recognize him. The sickly, aimless, and reclusive Lovecraft was beginning to fade away.

Cleveland proved to be eye-opening for another reason: Lovecraft encountered openly gay people for the first time.[24] One such person was the composer Gordon Hatfield. His comments on meeting Hatfield revealed his own discomfort and hostility. Lovecraft later referred to him as "that precious sissy" and remembered that he "didn't know whether to kiss it or kill it."[25] His repeated usage of "it" dehumanized Hatfield, classifying the composer as a creature of sorts, something lesser than a man. He mocked the musician's wardrobe and appearance as effeminate, poking fun at his "little white sailor's cap" and "sport shirt open at the neck."[26] Lovecraft also met Hart Crane, another gay man, that summer. Samuel Loveman, who would hold long friendships with both men, recalled Lovecraft "sardonically and not without mimicry" decrying the poet's "morality" (clearly a codeword for sexuality).[27] Since Loveman himself was a gay man, yet likely not "out," Lovecraft's indictment of Crane must have pained him.

Lovecraft's derisive reaction to Hatfield and Crane, two men who appeared to temporarily welcome him into their small bohemian community, draws attention to his own sexuality. Nearing his thirty-second year, Lovecraft had experienced the first physically romantic encounter of his life with Sonia Greene earlier that summer when they kissed on the Massachusetts coast. This lack of intimate history with the opposite sex and an apparent disinterest in gaining it by a man approaching early middle age might raise suspicion. Literary critics have pointed out the near absence of female characters in the majority of Lovecraft's fiction as a possible insight into his thoughts on sex and gender. Much later in his own life and in correspondence not intended for publication, Loveman interpreted Lovecraft's view toward Hatfield, Crane, and gay men in general as a possible act of self-deflection over his own hidden insecurities:

> H. P. L., in his mockery of the tribe, had much more of this attribute in him than he would conceivably have cared to acknowledge—his vent about the virility of the Romans, his awkwardness before women, etc. No? Think it over. I admit that it was completely subconscious.[28]

Although discounting such claims, Alfred Galpin conceded that Lovecraft's "high-pitched voice" coupled with his "mincing manners" might have been misinterpreted by "any outsider."[29] Speculation aside, no strong evidence exists of Lovecraft himself doubting or testing his sexuality identity. This fact has yet to stymy conjecture or fictionalizations of the subject.[30]

Overall, Lovecraft found Cleveland to be a revelatory, successful, and uplifting adventure. Much as he had during his spring sojourn in Brooklyn, he experienced belonging to a true intellectual and literary circle. He began to gradually realize that this might be impossible in his native Providence, where he derided art and culture as "confined to artificial" and "quasi-Victorian society groups."[31] Maybe for the first time, Lovecraft desired a different life for himself, one away from his family and well-worn patterns. Traveling to Boston, New York, and now Cleveland to socialize with fellow creative individuals freed him to imagine the possibilities. When he finally left Ohio on the early morning of August 16, he did not board a train to Providence. Instead, he returned to New York and Sonia Greene.[32]

While his April trip to the city lasted less than a full week (six days, to be exact), Lovecraft lived in Greene's Brooklyn apartment for nearly two months during his second New York retreat. This residency lasted until an indeterminate date in the middle of October. No longer passively playing the tourist, Lovecraft began to display a comfort with the city. He grew familiar with its streets and spaces. He established favorite haunts and routines. He even introduced sites to longtime and native New Yorkers. Finding his days filled with a "ceaseless round of pleasant activity" and "intellectual encouragement," he fancied that he was living in an intoxicating dream.[33] Invigorated, Lovecraft exclaimed that it was wondrously "odd to welcome the next day instead of dreading it!"[34]

Several weeks into his lengthy stay, Lovecraft considered himself belonging to "a literary gang" and spent nearly every free hour traipsing through the city with Rheinhart Kleiner, Frank Belknap Long, and James F. Morton.[35] In the company of one or more of these friends, he regularly attended the cinema, scoured used bookstores, patronized museums, and lost himself in winding conversations in coffee shops. On many evenings, he dined with Greene in restaurants and sat beside her during plays. Seemingly every week, he joined a literary salon in a café or a private home. Such a lifestyle may sound familiar or, at the very least, desirable to many present-day creatively minded urban denizens. Indulging in the cultural pleasures of city life, Lovecraft postponed returning to Providence and cited Greene's desire for him to remain as the prevailing reason. Since she worked long hours and frequently completed piecework for clients at home in the evenings, Greene lamented that she "hardly had a visit from" him.[36] He appeared unable to withstand the charms of his hostess.

Meanwhile, Lovecraft continued to reevaluate Providence, finding it lacking when compared to New York and its abundant artistic and intellectual riches. The conservative Yankee now disparaged the cultural environment of his hometown:

> The only trouble with Providence is its *inhabitants*—backward & unimaginative bourgeois types who go to church, revere the gods of commerce & the commonplace, & find their utmost limit of aesthetic & intellectual expansion in mock art-clubs & tame lectures wherein gossip of the day & social pageantry form the real motive forces. Estimable Philistines—worthy folk—correct & solid citizenry—but still living in the anaesthetic [*sic*] eighties of the nineteenth century.[37]

Lovecraft's bilious commentary echoed that of scathing contemporaneous critics of American life, such as novelist Theodore Dreiser and journalist H. L. Mencken.

In contrast, the cultural circles of New York hinted at something much more active, vibrant, and thrilling. Greene hosted parties at her apartment frequented by Kleiner, Long, Morton, and other intellectuals, including feminist writer Winnifred Harper Cooley, author of *The New Woman-hood*.[38] Lovecraft was impressed by Cooley's literary taste and by the fact that she had met short story writer Ambrose Bierce, whom he considered to be a pioneer in American horror fiction. This chance meeting would have never happened in Providence.

Morton invited Lovecraft to be his guest at a September dinner of the Sunrise Club, an organization founded in 1889 by Edwin C. Walker, a sexual freedom advocate and political radical, and dedicated to public debate on a wide range of cultural, social, and political topics.[39] This four-course meal was held at Café Boulevard, a restaurant in the Hotel Continental at West Forty-First Street and Broadway, and it attracted over one hundred members, notably Alabama-born poet and writer Clement Wood and an unspecified member of the Ochs family from the *New York Times*, quite possibly the newspaper's owner and publisher Adolph Ochs himself. Lovecraft marveled at his friend's command of facts and language during the discourse with such august figures, proudly declaring that "intellectually Morton leads them all."[40]

Lovecraft's account of the event neglected to include a key tenet of the Sunrise Club: its membership was integrated and open to people from all backgrounds. Lectures advocating for civil rights for Black Americans or featuring Black activists and intellectuals were not uncommon. That is, Lovecraft might have seen men or women of color seated alongside whites at the table. Quite possibly, Morton could have introduced him to the organization to challenge his views on race.[41]

Early film writer Ernest Dench held regular meetings of the Blue Pencil Club, an amateur journalism group counting Greene, Kleiner, and Morton as members, at his home in Sheepshead Bay.[42] Lovecraft attended one of these gatherings on a late September evening. Demonstrating his increased familiarity with the city's streetscape and transit network, he ventured deep into south Brooklyn on his own. He attributed this personal feat to his "boasted geographical sense."[43]

At Dench's home, Lovecraft met Everett McNeil, "a quiet, pleasant," aging author.[44] McNeil was primarily a writer of adventure stories and novels for adolescent boys and was living in strained circumstances in Hell's

Kitchen, then a hardscrabble Manhattan neighborhood. The white-haired, stooped, and sixty-year-old McNeil forged a quick bond with Lovecraft.[45] They would remain friends until McNeil's death in 1929.

While rambling through New York, Lovecraft began to encounter sites, buildings, and museums sating his hunger for history. Providence and New England connected him to America's colonial past, and he adored his native region for providing him with this intellectual, physical, and daresay spiritual sustenance. He discovered that a similar linkage might lie both hidden and visible in New York. During the early autumn of 1922, he joyously realized that pockets of the city's early history, even "a lingering trace or two of the ancient countryside," survived amid its skyscrapers, bridges, and railroads.[46]

Twice in two days, on September 13 with James F. Morton and Frank Belknap Long and on September 14 alone with Long, Lovecraft traveled to Washington Heights in Manhattan to tour the Jumel Mansion (the present-day Morris-Jumel Mansion). Originally built in the Palladian style in 1765, the mansion later served as George Washington's New York headquarters during the early days of the American Revolution in the autumn of 1776. When the Continental Army retreated from the city later that year, Hessian and British forces occupied the house. In the late eighteenth century, it offered views of Connecticut, New Jersey, and the New York Harbor, explaining its strategic location for the combating armies.[47]

Lovecraft found the museum and its grounds to be "entrancing," yet he lamented the encroachment of development and industry:

> Now, the view is polluted by city edifices & unsightly railway yards—but once it consisted only of blue water, green fields & forests, occasional white houses & steeples, & gently rolling hills—a pastoral scene of ineffable beauty.[48]

During his second visit to the Jumel Mansion and in the company of Frank Belknap Long, he chatted with an elderly museum attendant. To Lovecraft's delight, this man shared his own memories of the neighborhood's rural past and suggested other colonial sites.

Later during that very same outing, Lovecraft and Long walked to the High Bridge, the oldest standing bridge in New York. The structure spans 1,450 feet across the Harlem River and connects Manhattan and the Bronx. It was completed in 1848 as part of the Croton Aqueduct to carry fresh drinking water to Manhattan from the Croton River in Westchester County.[49] While crossing the High Bridge, Lovecraft envisioned himself shadowing his literary idol, Edgar Allan Poe. The writer often utilized the bridge for fresh air and exercise during his three years living in the

Bronx.[50] He rhapsodized that Poe loved to traverse this "stately piece of antique masonry" at twilight and that the poet composed "Ulalume" while upon it.[51] (This was educated fantasizing on Lovecraft's part.) Glancing down at the banks of the Harlem River, Lovecraft detected elements of a preindustrial city. He spotted an "idyllic lane" and speculated that George Washington may have traveled it during the Revolution.[52]

In late September, Lovecraft postponed his return to Providence for a second time in order to continue investigating "cryptical urban arcana" with his friends.[53] One of Lovecraft's favorite companions, especially for long, often nighttime excursions, was Rheinhart Kleiner. On one particular evening, the two men studied the Flatbush Dutch Reformed Church and cemetery, a historic Dutch church complex roughly a half-mile walk from Greene's apartment. The congregation of the church formed in 1654 when Flatbush was a Dutch settlement on Long Island. The current structure was built between 1793 and 1798 in the Federal style, and its foundation consists of stones from an earlier church on the same site.[54] The cemetery tombstones bear Dutch and English birth inscriptions dating as far back as the seventeenth century.[55] While Lovecraft walked among the graves, the past came alive:

> As I viewed this village churchyard in the autumn twilight, the city seemed to fade from sight, & give place to the Netherland town of long ago. In fancy I saw the cottages of the simple Dutchmen, their small-paned windows lighted one by one as evening stole over the harvest-fields.[56]

Soon thereafter, Lovecraft and Kleiner made another pilgrimage to the church's cemetery. While birds busily flew about and pecked at the hallowed ground in the twilight, Lovecraft committed a surprising act of archaeological sacrilege for such a committed antiquarian: he chipped away a fragment of headstone with a 1747 birthdate to keep as a memento.[57] Like every writer, he was always on the lookout for raw materials for story ideas. An article in a newspaper, a snippet of overheard conversation, or, in this case, an act of morbid vandalism might be mined for his fiction. Later in 1922, he penned "The Hound," a short story about a pair of grave robbers inspired by this desecration.[58] Additionally, he later incorporated possible references to the Flatbush Dutch Reformed Church (Figure 8) and its cemetery into two other pieces of fiction, "The Lurking Fear" and "The Horror at Red Hook."[59]

While on an afternoon jaunt along Flatbush Avenue, Lovecraft and Kleiner discovered a modern-day re-creation of Brooklyn's colonial past. Amid the everyday storefronts and buildings of the street, the two friends

Figure 8. Brooklyn's Flatbush Dutch Reformed Church and its cemetery provided Lovecraft with fodder for several short stories. He chipped away a fragment from a centuries-old headstone as a keepsake. (Courtesy of the Brooklyn Public Library, Center for Brooklyn History)

espied "a low, arched opening" bearing the name "Albemarle Arcade."[60] After passing through the gateway, Lovecraft whimsically remarked that he and Kleiner stood before "the most delightful conceivable replica" of a quaint and quiet side-street of eighteenth-century London. In fact, they had stumbled upon Albemarle Terrace.[61]

Designed by the Brooklyn firm Slee & Bryson, this cul-de-sac was built in the Colonial Revival style and completed in 1917.[62] Lovecraft cataloged the exquisite architectural and landscape features of the development's homes—door knockers, iron railings, brick sidewalks, and lush trees—and declared the neighborhood to represent "the complete early Georgian scene faithfully reproduced for modernity."[63] Once again, he imaginatively stood in a New York of earlier centuries. What Lovecraft consistently longed for—a ready connection to history—could very well exist beyond his familiar New England. Indeed, he favorably compared Albemarle Terrace to Orchard Avenue, a street of striking homes in his own East Side neighborhood in Providence.[64]

During his nearly two months in New York, Lovecraft sought out the city's history with his every daytime and nighttime ramble. Every borough—save Queens, which he neglected to visit—held a special delight for him. In Staten Island, he marveled at the "sleepy villages, old houses, quaint streets," and "unpolluted countryside."[65] The "unpolluted" geography of Staten Island likely referred to a lack both of visible urban development and immigrants. (Contrary to Lovecraft's observations, the borough held a sizable immigrant population.)[66] In Port Richmond, on the island's North Shore, he and Kleiner surveyed a historic place of worship, the Reformed Protestant Dutch Church, and its unkept cemetery.[67] Lovecraft poetically described the latter as:

> lonely, neglected, & unseen from the outside world—hilly, darkened by the shade of trees, & overrun with weeds, tall grass, & climbing moss. The moss has almost obscured the inscriptions on most of the gravestones.[68]

As he strolled through the weedy cemetery with its lichen-covered graves, he heard an underground stream burbling beneath the church, "echoing spectrally in the masonry vaults."[69]

In the Bronx, Lovecraft gazed longingly at a brick-and-mortar remainder of the long-gone Dutch gentry and the oldest building in the borough, the Van Cortlandt Mansion. James Van Cortlandt inherited the nearly finished home after his father, Frederick, died in 1749. The family were prominent merchants and landowners in colonial New York, and the manor was built on their plantation. This land is now Van Cortlandt Park, and the mansion sits on its grounds.[70] At the time of Lovecraft's autumn stop at the museum, a secretary desk crafted in the 1760s in Rhode Island was on exhibit.[71] If properly labeled or pointed out by a guide, Lovecraft would have certainly gravitated toward this piece.

He became enamored with preserves of Manhattan's rural and even pre-settlement past in the northernmost point of the island. This "last scrap of genuine *countryside*" surviving within several miles of "the teeming region of skyscrapers" astounded him.[72] On a late September afternoon, Lovecraft, Frank Belknap Long, and James F. Morton embarked upon a thorough exploration of this section of Manhattan.

Their foray began at the Dyckman House on the corner of West 204th Street and Broadway in the Inwood neighborhood. When the Dyckman family built the home in the 1780s, it was surrounded by orchards and fields and served as the center of the family's 250-acre farm. Although Lovecraft admired the gambrel roof and fieldstone walls of Manhattan's last eighteenth-century Dutch Colonial farmhouse, he was absolutely smitten by its resident cat. He cradled the animal in his arms as he toured the building, even creating a fictional genealogy and ancestral history for the feline. While blissfully distracted by the cat, he lost his footing and fell down the cellar stairs.[73]

After the Dyckman House, the three men strolled through a strip of today's Inwood Hill Park bordering Spuyten Duyvil Creek, the waterway coursing between the northwestern tip of Manhattan and the Bronx. The natural landscape and scenery of the last remaining old-growth forest on the island created a masterful illusion of a rustic past. Indeed, Lovecraft imagined that he and his friends were stepping into the arcadian outskirts of New Netherland. His rhapsody began with a reference to Henry Wadsworth Longfellow's poem "Evangeline: A Tale of Acadie":

> Here is a forest primeval, with winding paths, gigantic trees, & not a mortal in sight. Suddenly, at a turn of the path, one sees far below in a valley the blue waters of Spuyten Duyvil, & of the Hudson beyond. On the banks are the huts & nets of fishers, & at small piers boats ride wistfully at anchor. . . . Another turn & we are in the ancient forest again. From the main path a byway leads . . . we come upon a small farm where poultry-guarding dogs bark warningly at us. The illusion is perfect. . . . As for the New-York of subways & skyscrapers—pouf! it is a myth; a dream![74]

When Lovecraft, Long, and Morton finally emerged from this gauzy world, the moon was rising. Its light shone upon nearby construction equipment and newly cleared ground. The city was coming to Inwood. Presaging the wish of contemporary preservations to save unique and beloved spaces in their own neighborhoods and localities, Lovecraft hoped that Inwood and its forestland (Figure 9) would not be "desecrated by the vandal hand of progress" and the "real-estate industry."[75]

While the living remnants of New York's early history mesmerized Lovecraft, he was far less enamored with the city's bursting immigrant and minority communities. In fact, he expressed a palpable contempt and disgust for them. Coincidentally, several of his literary acquaintances and friends resided in such neighborhoods. Much like many struggling artists and creative individuals in any era, these writers embraced impecunious and often unpredictable lifestyles. They were always scouting for cheap rents in cheap buildings—luxuries often impossible to find in "respectable" areas of New York or, for that matter, any desirable city.

James F. Morton, the graying radical, lived at 211 West 138th Street in Strivers' Row in Harlem. This neighborhood of elegant rowhomes housed many upwardly aspirational and professionally successful Black Americans,

Figure 9. When exploring New York City, Lovecraft sought pockets of nature largely unblemished by urban development. Today's Inwood Hill Park in Manhattan stood as such a space. (Courtesy of the Museum of the City of New York)

and Morton might have rented there in part because of his long dedication to civil rights. While Harlem was quickly transitioning to a majority Black population by 1922, it was simultaneously experiencing a flowering of the arts, music, and letters—collectively, the Harlem Renaissance.[76]

Lovecraft's reaction upon first visiting Morton's apartment was sadly predictable. While admiring the "decayed," yet "prepossessing" grandeur of the buildings, he was horrified that his friend dwelled on "a street now overrun by *niggers* of the cleaner" and "less offensive sort."[77] On the other hand, he qualified his distaste upon inspecting Morton's mineral and stamp collections and well-stocked library, prompting him to plan many future trips to Harlem. His bibliomania easily overpowered his racial animus. Lovecraft also took an instant liking to Morton's "eccentric" landlord, the Sunrise Club founder and septuagenarian Edwin C. Walker.[78]

A new acquaintance, the wizened Everett McNeil, rented a room in a tenement building in Hell's Kitchen, a congested Manhattan neighborhood between Eighth Avenue and the Hudson River from east to west and West Fifty-Ninth and Thirtieth-Fourth Streets from north to south. Irish criminal gangs maintained a dominant presence in its waterfront warehouses and on its piers, and the largely impoverished immigrant area held a seedy reputation well into the late twentieth century.[79] McNeil, a veteran writer, barely eked out a hand-to-mouth existence, even once subsisting on sugar packets pocketed at coffee shops. He spent most of his days at the New York Public Library in nearby Bryant Park, only a short walk from his West Forty-Ninth Street room.[80]

Lovecraft appeared to be equally perplexed, saddened, and unnerved by Hell's Kitchen's residents—white by his definition:

> Squalor is extreme, but not so odorous as in the foreign districts. Churches flourish—for all the natives are devout & violent Roman Catholics. It was odd to see slums in which the denizens are Nordic—with shapely faces, & often light hair & blue eyes. Nowadays we associate evil with dark foreign features.[81]

Although Lovecraft reported stories of Hell's Kitchen's "old toughs" dropping bricks on the heads of police officers or roving the streets in gangs, he ranked the largely Irish criminals and their violence as distinctly above those of the "slinking Dago or Jew" populating other crowded tenement districts.[82]

Sonia Greene's neighbors in her building even failed to escape Lovecraft's hostile judgment. When she threw a dinner party for him and a handful of literary friends in early September, she invited Harold Moran, a thirteen-year-old aspiring poet, and his mother, Lenore, a public school teacher. The family likely lived on the same floor as Greene. Lovecraft had met Harold a few days earlier when he wandered into Greene's apartment with his cat. He rated the adolescent and his mother to be "quite intelligent—at least, as much so as devout Roman Catholics can be."[83] However, he did offer kinder words for the Morans' cat, Fluffy, describing it as "the most fascinating jet-black" Maine Coon that he had ever seen.[84]

During this extended New York retreat, Lovecraft and Greene's relationship appeared to mature well beyond that of friendship. On multiple occasions, he delayed his inevitable return to Providence, presenting his friends and, to a greater extent, her pleading insistence that he dally longer in Flatbush as an excuse. She disliked any allusion to his inevitable departure.[85] In their separate accounts of his April visit, Lovecraft and Greene both underscored the detail that she slept at a neighbor's apartment.[86] No similar disclaimer was repeated this time.

His descriptions of his domestic episodes with Greene painted a portrait of a staid couple comfortable in the pleasures of hearth and home. He praised her as a cook, a housekeeper, and a hostess. As a fashion professional, she attempted to update his wardrobe and improve his sartorial style. In addition to furnishing Lovecraft with free room and board, Greene treated him to plays, movies, and restaurants. Like all his friends, she was familiar with his perpetually strained finances.[87]

Greene regularly introduced Lovecraft to novelties of the city that he may have overlooked or have been reluctant to experience amid his own pursuits of history and culture. An evening on the town on September 15 reveals the push-and-pull between them. The couple—presumably Greene paid—bought balcony seats for a screening of *The Hound of the Baskervilles* at the Capitol Theatre, a lush movie palace at West Fifty-First Street and Broadway replete with a resident orchestra. Afterward, she wanted to try a tea shop in Greenwich Village. Lovecraft griped about the customers, the waitstaff, and the service, but he conceded to enjoying the food. Regardless of his stubbornness, foibles, and faults, Greene relished his company. She was widowed, nearing forty, and with an adult child preparing to leave home or already having left. She might have been daydreaming about beginning a new chapter in her life, possibly with a partner at her side. And there was Howard Phillips Lovecraft.

Constantly, he voiced his pleasure with New York's "unceasing variety in amusements, excursions," and "conversations."[88] As Lovecraft spent more time cavorting with friends, savoring the company of Greene, and losing himself in the rhythms of the metropolis, he further viewed Providence in a less favorable and comparably negative light: its society was stuffy; its residents were narrow-minded, its culture was ossified, and even its bookshops were poorly curated.[89] He openly lamented his eventual departure, resigning himself to it "with stoical imperturbability."[90] Greene suggested that he make his visit permanent. Together, they could "bring 'Providence' to Parkside Ave."[91]

For reasons not altogether clear, this campaign hinged on Lovecraft's aunts traveling to New York. Possibly, he hoped to acquaint his family to the city; a positive experience on their part might facilitate an understanding or even approval of his still unspoken desire to relocate there. He might have wanted to showcase Greene's skills and qualities as a homemaker, professional, and a companion. He might have wished to reveal what life could be achievable for him as a writer in New York. After a series of entreaties, his younger aunt, Annie Gamwell, finally consented to come to Flatbush in early October.

Greene freshened up the apartment with new curtains and plants in anticipation of her special guest. Drawing from his newly acquired "metropolitan knowledge," Lovecraft drafted an exhaustive itinerary of historic sites, prominent buildings, and premier museums to best display the bountiful treasures and distractions of the city.[92] He introduced Gamwell to his friends, some of whom she knew from their own past sojourns in Providence, and the writers in the Brooklyn-based Blue Pencil Club. In particular, she appeared to relish the company of Frank Belknap Long and his family. (Considering Lovecraft's own fixation on ethnic pedigree, this is far from surprising. The Longs were, like he and Gamwell, "real" Americans.) Lovecraft shared a selection of his most beloved haunts and discoveries in different parts of Manhattan and even the Bronx. Judging by his letters to his elder aunt, Lillian Clark, Gamwell appeared to have appreciated Greene's effusive hospitality and Lovecraft's tireless enthusiasm as a guide.

Regardless, she could only stay away from home for so long. This was a trip, not a temporary residency. When Gamwell left for Providence in mid-October, she took Lovecraft with her. Greene's attempt at convincing him to move to New York or obtaining his aunt's imprimatur for such a decision appeared to have been futile. After months filled with culture and conversation and truly embracing the life of an urban intellectual, Lovecraft bade farewell to his adventure in Gotham and reluctantly returned to his "hibernation."[93] Greene confessed that her home felt empty without him. This gradually led to a serious understanding between the couple, and one resting on "perhaps dangerous ground."[94]

4

███

"Brigham Young Annexing His 27th"

HABITUALLY UNAWARE OF TIME, H. P. Lovecraft missed his train at Providence's Union Station on the morning of March 2, 1924. After buying a ticket for the 11:09 A.M. departure to Grand Central Terminal in midtown Manhattan, he found a telegraph office and cabled ahead that he would be arriving behind schedule and at a different destination.[1] The original plan was for him to take the earlier 10:09 A.M. New York, New Haven and Hartford Railroad train to Pennsylvania Station.[2]

As a lover of architecture and the built environment, Lovecraft might have allowed himself a moment to wander through the station and admire its design and ornamental flourishes. Since places, objects, and culture— far more than people—infused his worldview with meaning, he likely appreciated a public space crafted to instill a sense of awe and wonder in people going about their day.[3] Fashioned by the local firm Stone, Carpenter & Wilson, Union Station opened in 1898. It was built of yellow Roman brick and sandstone with a main entrance incorporating a triumphal arch.[4] This collective effect possibly appealed to Lovecraft, a devotee of the ancient world. Stone, Carpenter & Wilson created notable buildings throughout Providence and Rhode Island in the late nineteenth and early twentieth centuries, including the neoclassical Ladd Observatory at Brown University, a site beloved by Lovecraft with a fervor equaling his loathing for the firm's Arts-and-Crafts-inspired Fleur-de-Lys Studios in the College Hill neighborhood. He almost certainly knew of the station's position in the architectural heritage of the region.[5]

Lovecraft always traveled with a black leather valise holding writing material, papers, and books. On that morning, it contained the final draft of a short story with the working title "Under the Pyramids." He was ghostwriting it for the famous escape artist and magician Harry Houdini for publication in *Weird Tales*. Already having missed the magazine's March first deadline, Lovecraft might have rested on a waiting room seat to review his typed manuscript for last-minute edits.[6] Proud of his literary practice, he labored over every word, punctuation mark, and turn of phrase. Maybe he became absorbed in his work, or maybe he dawdled about the station. Regardless of how he had passed the time, he rushed to his train in such a frenzy that either he forgot the Houdini story on a bench or it slipped from his bag. A lost-and-found advertisement for the manuscript appeared in the classified section of the *Providence Journal* on the next day, March 3.[7]

Aside from his dash to the boarding train, Lovecraft enjoyed "a pleasing journey" and disembarked at Grand Central Terminal at 3:40 P.M.[8] Waiting for him was Sonia H. Greene. He had told no one—neither friends nor his aunts—the true motivation behind his leaving Providence. The reason and destination for his journey were one and the same—this woman, the fashionable and cosmopolitan milliner whom Lovecraft had met in Boston in 1921. He had come to New York to wed Greene.[9]

After their rendezvous, the couple left for Brooklyn. At Greene's Flatbush apartment, Lovecraft met Gertrude Tucker, another houseguest and presumably a chaperone to ensure proper etiquette prior to the wedding day. Originally from Baltimore, Tucker managed a literary agency, the Reading Lamp, with its own house magazine. Her Anglo-Saxon Protestant pedigree impressed Lovecraft. The three "zestfully discussed" the couple's wedding plans and their hope-filled future, and more "congenial and appropriate" conversation followed a "superb" chicken dinner prepared by Greene.[10]

The next morning, Lovecraft visited the Reading Lamp offices at 437 Fifth Avenue, near Bryant Park and across the street from the Lord & Taylor department store, to discuss the possibility of Tucker finding a position for him in a publishing house. She also graciously allowed him to use a typewriter to begin retranscribing the lost Houdini manuscript.[11] Afterward, he and Greene sat down for "a fine *spaghetti*" lunch at a nearby Midtown Manhattan restaurant. (Italian cuisine became his favorite after his sampling it during his first trip to New York two years earlier.)[12] His appreciation for the food failed to restrain him from referring to the business as "a Dago joint."[13] Then, Lovecraft and Greene rode the subway to Brooklyn Borough Hall. Their matrimonial moment had arrived:

We took out a marriage license with all the cool nonchalance and easy *savoir faire* of old campaigners . . . but you'd ought to have saw [*sic*] me! Brigham Young annexing his 27th, or King Solomon starting in on the second thousand, had nothing on me for languid fluency and casual conversation![14]

The municipal clerk expressed disbelief at the couple's respective ages: he thought Greene was the junior partner in the pending nuptials. In fact, she was a few days shy of forty-one, and Lovecraft was thirty-three.[15] Their age difference delighted Lovecraft: he compared their romance to the tempestuous one shared between Edgar Allan Poe and Sarah Helen Whitman, a Providence poet six years older than her famous suitor, in 1848 and near the end of Poe's own life.[16]

Through her professional connections, Greene received a bargain on their wedding bands from a small Brooklyn jeweler. Lovecraft selected a platinum ring "with twenty-four diamond chips" for his bride-to-be.[17] She wanted a simpler and more affordable one, but "he insisted that the future Mrs. Howard Phillips Lovecraft must have the finest."[18] This marked one of the few occasions when Lovecraft spent any of his meager earnings exclusively on Greene. He assured her that his payment from the Houdini story would easily cover the cost, and he joked that even more lucrative writing commissions lay in the future.[19] After a manicure for Greene and a haircut for Lovecraft, the two hopped into a taxicab. They were as ready as they ever would be.

Although an avowed materialist and atheist, Lovecraft placed a high value on tradition and history.[20] According to his philosophical worldview, they allowed mankind to bestow temporal order to an otherwise finite and meaningless existence. He approached his nuptials from this intellectual framework. Previously married and the mother of an adult child, and certainly more world-wise than her soon-to-be spouse, Greene wanted a civil marriage.[21] Lovecraft deemed such a notion to be impossible.

The couple were wed on March 3, 1924, at St. Paul's Chapel (Figure 10), an Episcopal church on Broadway between Fulton and Vesey Streets in the Financial District of Manhattan. Constructed between 1764 and 1766, St. Paul's stands as the oldest house of worship on the island and a fine specimen of Georgian church architecture. It should have come as little surprise to Greene that Lovecraft wanted to exchange their vows before its altar. He feigned comical incredulity that an alternative setting or ceremony could have been fathomed: "A hades of a question to ask an old British Colonial ever faithful to His Majesty, King George the Third!"[22]

Figure 10. H. P. Lovecraft and Sonia H. Greene were wed at St. Paul's Chapel in Lower Manhattan. Although an avowed atheist, Lovecraft found value in the history and tradition provided by the formal marriage rite. (Courtesy of the Museum of the City of New York)

St. Paul's embodied the eighteenth-century Anglo world that Lovecraft considered his imaginative home. His and Greene's wedding would enjoin them to a family tradition and a historical lineage. His own parents were wed in St. Paul's Church, an Episcopal parish in Boston. Admiral Richard Howe worshiped at St. Paul's Chapel during the British occupation of New York in the Revolutionary War.[23] With two church staff members serving as witnesses, curate Reverend George Benson Cox performed the marriage rite.[24]

Lovecraft honored the solemnity, if not the meaning and perceived immutability, of the sacrament:

> In the aesthetically histrionic spirit of one to whom elder custom, however intellectually empty, is sacred, I went through the various motions with a stately assurance which had the stamp of antiquarian appreciation if not of pious sanctity. S. H., needless to say, did the same—and with an additional grace.[25]

He found comfort in the religious ceremony and the cultural adherence surrounding a conventional marriage. The tradition—not the faith—demanded his reverence and awe.[26] As with many new husbands, he saw the "grace" and refinement of his bride and wanted others to, as well.

Only a single day ago, Lovecraft secreted himself out of sedate Providence. Only a single day ago, he was a solitary bachelor and an obscure writer. Now he was a proudly married man with a captivating wife. Now he pursued his literary career in the publishing capital of the United States. As Lovecraft and Greene left the chapel—maybe gushing, joyous, and lightheaded like most newlyweds—life seemed aglow and open to the gentleman from Rhode Island. Finally, he might be able to trade "his listless midnight mooning and helpless hermitage for a more active life."[27]

Late on the following afternoon, Lovecraft and Greene departed from Pennsylvania Station for their honeymoon in Philadelphia. He classified the legendary (and today long-mourned) McKim, Mead & White Beaux-Arts masterpiece as "magnificently Roman."[28] After arriving at Broad Street Station, the main Philadelphia hub for the Pennsylvania Railroad, in the early evening, they checked into the nearby Robert Morris Hotel.[29] Lovecraft confidently signed "Mr. and Mrs." for the very first time in the establishment's registry. The building matched his aesthetic preferences, accomplishing "the marvel of harmoniously combining a Gothic exterior with a Colonial interior" in his estimation.[30] (One wonders if Lovecraft and Greene, or maybe she alone, planned the entire getaway to satisfy his intellectual passions.)

Before celebrating their marriage too heartily, Lovecraft needed to file his Houdini short story. He had already missed the deadline by three days. Luckily, he had packed his handwritten manuscript. Lovecraft and Greene located a public stenographer's room at the Hotel Vendig (Figure 11) at North Thirteenth and Filbert Streets and only several blocks from their own accommodations.[31] At the cost of a single dollar, they rented a Royal typewriter for three hours. The couple quickly established a happy working routine. While Greene dictated, Lovecraft typed. He discovered this to be a much more efficient process than him transcribing his own drafts:

> A marvellous way of speeding up copying, and one which I shall constantly use in future, since my partner expresses a willingness amounting to eagerness so far as her share of the toil is concerned. She has the absolutely unique gift of being able to read the careless scrawl of my rough manuscripts—no matter how cryptically and involvedly intertwined![32]

Greene was proud of their first marital collaboration and her own ability to comprehend Lovecraft's work and decipher his cramped handwriting:

> It was I alone who was able to read these erased and crossed-out notes. I read them slowly to him while H. P. pounded them out on a borrowed typewriter, borrowed from the hotel in Philadelphia where we spent the first day and night copying that precious manuscript which had to meet the printer's dead-line [sic].[33]

The first night of their honeymoon may have been atypical—no exquisite meal or fine champagne—yet this scene seems rather touching: Greene reading aloud her husband's words, possibly adding a dash of theatrics and emotion. Lovecraft attentively listening to his wife, clacking at the typewriter keys. They might have believed that they were embarking on a mutual creative life fueled by literature and ideas.

Having spent the beginning of their honeymoon laboring over Lovecraft's ghostwriting assignment, the couple purchased tickets for a guided bus tour of the City of Brotherly Love. Initially unimpressed by the Victorian architecture dominating the downtown (known to Philadelphians as Center City), Lovecraft soon entered "an ancient town in negligee," a city "frayed at the edges" and "dimly lighted" yet "dignified by a sense of background and maturity" and commanding "respect and finally admiration."[34] Although a proud Anglophile who lamented America's separation from the United Kingdom, he could not resist the fine design of Independence Hall, the building in which America's founding fathers debated and signed both the Declaration of Independence and the Constitution.[35] Indeed, Lovecraft

Figure 11. Lovecraft and Greene traveled to Philadelphia for a short honeymoon. They spent much of their time preparing a typed manuscript of "Under the Pyramids" for *Weird Tales* magazine in the stenographer room at the Hotel Vendig. (Courtesy of the Library Company of Philadelphia)

gushed over the "noted edifice's magnificent colonial interior."[36] Studying various buildings near Independence Hall, he gained a vivid insight into eighteenth-century urban life and "the soul of the Colonial *city*"—quite a different set of experiences and images than those that he gleaned from visiting towns and villages.[37] The Betsy Ross House was "a pleasing type of modest colonial city residence."[38] Christ Church, a storied house of worship listing Benjamin Franklin, George Washington, and other prominent Revolutionary War figures as past congregants, stood as an example of "the utmost extreme of Georgian ecclesiastical magnificence."[39]

However, when the bus route passed through a Black neighborhood, Lovecraft's revelry was vexingly disrupted. He referred to the area as a "nigger quarter."[40] "Blot out the black faces," Lovecraft suggested, and one could imaginatively return to Philadelphia's colonial past.[41] This exercise willfully ignored the presence of enslaved and free Blacks living in the city during that very period in its history. By the conclusion of his and Greene's tour, Lovecraft pictured "fox-hunting squires" in "every rural shade" and "periwigg'd gentlemen" in "every urban doorway."[42]

Following their full day of sightseeing, Lovecraft and Greene again patronized the Hotel Vendig's stenographer room for a second round of typing and transcription. They returned to New York by train later that night. Overall, Philadelphia struck Lovecraft as "one of the most distinctive" and intriguing cities.[43] "View'd all too shortly," he hoped to return to it for a more leisurely and detailed exploration in the near future.[44] Lovecraft contently evaluated their Philadelphia getaway as a success—"most practical and industrious."[45] The newlyweds spent the remainder of their vacation finishing the manuscript for *Weird Tales* and easing into their shared life in Brooklyn.[46] Although happy to help her new husband, Greene couldn't completely hide her frustration. While focused on completing his story, they "were too tired and exhausted for honey-mooning or anything else."[47] Clearly, she had other hopes for their first days as man and wife.

Many biographers and commentators on Lovecraft depict him as largely uninterested in sex and devoid of physical desire. Presumably a virgin until his marriage, he availed himself of various publications on sex to prepare for his future role as a husband. Greene complained about his disinclination toward displays of affection and his hesitancy to speak of love. His own friends sometimes needled him about his squeamish in discussing women and sex.[48] However, an episode fondly—maybe even proudly— remembered by Greene might undercut this image of him as a cold and frigid individual: Lovecraft enjoyed watching her dance seductively to a recording of "Danse Macabre" by Camille Saint-Saëns:

I danced a very slow cake walk . . . at first slowly, lifting my legs, with bent knees in imitation of walking more slowly and quietly. . . . I [danced], slow or fast, as the music prompted. . . . At the end of the music and my dance, H. P. L. was enchanted.[49]

"Enchanted" may have alluded to other sensations—longing or lust—aroused in Lovecraft by his attractive spouse. Contrary to popular and scholarly conceptions of him, Lovecraft might have avoided avowals of passion and conversations about sex because they evoked feelings of discomfort and insecurity. That is, he simply could have wished to not air publicly such matters and to keep them within the private sphere of his life.

Since leaving Providence, Lovecraft had received at least one letter from his aunt Lillian Clark at his new Brooklyn home. This indicates that he had talked about his visiting New York for an extended period with his family and that he had provided Greene's Parkside Avenue apartment as a forwarding mailing address. On March 9, 1924, almost a full week after coming to the city under rather vague circumstances, Lovecraft sat down and wrote a long letter circuitously disclosing his and Greene's nuptials to his aunts, Lillian Clark and Annie Gamwell. Only after stoking anticipation for several pages did he finally break the news.[50]

Greene had asked Lovecraft to inform his aunts of their plans and invite them to the wedding. He refused, claiming that he wished to surprise them.[51] Less than a month earlier, Greene had written to Clark, stating that she saw Lovecraft's literary success as her own current life's goal.[52] During his and Greene's honeymoon, he mailed a series of postcards to Clark. His new wife signed several of them, even remarking on one that she hoped to soon see Clark in New York. Lovecraft's aunts, thus, might not have consumed his letter with the desired shock.

Why the insistence for secrecy? In the letter announcing his marriage, Lovecraft excused his reticence by pointing to his "hatred of sentimental spoofing, and of that agonisingly indecisive 'talking over' which radical steps always prompt among mortals."[53] He continued by expounding that someone of his temperament—"a sensitive personality"—would find the attention and resulting discussion "infinitely exhausting."[54] He could not understand why this "decisive and dramatic gesture" would leave anyone "even slightly hurt."[55] He concluded by stating that the marriage was a "well considered" and "individualistic" decision.[56]

His explanation could be interpreted in several ways. Never at ease in verbalizing emotions and feelings—he never once wrote that he loved his wife in this letter—Lovecraft might have simply wanted to keep the matter to himself and feared the normal effusiveness following an engagement or marriage announcement. However, the tone of his letter may be read as respectful, yet defensive. The choice to marry Greene was his alone and required no consultation from his aunts. Lovecraft likely suspected or outright knew that they would disapprove of his relationship with and marriage to Greene.[57]

Why might have they expressed such an opinion? Greene was an immigrant, a Jew, and a working woman—not to mention slightly older than Lovecraft. Such a personal background and history did not probably appeal to a family clinging—almost self-deludingly—to its identity as Yankee aristocracy. Knowing Lovecraft's own prejudicial beliefs, his aunts might have been mystified by his selection of a partner. Additionally, Clark and Gamwell may have harbored a practical and legitimate concern regarding Greene: her past and possibly unsettled romantic entanglements. When one of Lovecraft's aunts, presumably Gamwell, was staying with Greene in Brooklyn on an unspecified date, she returned to the apartment and discovered her talking animatedly with a strange man. The two had obviously been quarreling. After being introduced to Lovecraft's aunt, the man quickly left. Unbeknownst to Gamwell, this individual was a past suitor still infatuated with Greene. Lovecraft's aunt was not likely naïve enough to believe whatever story Greene manufactured after she had accidentally interrupted their argument.[58]

A different encounter involving Lovecraft's aunts hinted at his rationale and even justification for keeping his family in the dark. Not long after receiving an engraved marriage announcement from Lovecraft and Greene, his Providence friend Muriel Eddy and her husband, writer Clifford Martin (C. M.) Eddy Jr., were contacted by Annie Gamwell. She wrote to the couple and asked if they wanted some of Lovecraft's household items. Since her nephew was now married, she stated that he would no longer need them. The Eddys accepted the offer and visited Lillian Clark and Gamwell with their two young children and infant daughter. Muriel Eddy found both women to be friendly: they even indulged her older children with milk and cookies. Gamwell insisted on giving them a peculiar gift—a hundred or so postcards from Greene to Lovecraft.[59] Eddy described them:

> These all held loving, spirited messages to H. P. L. from his sweetheart in New York. Not knowing their possible value in the far-away future, I did not hold on to of any of these cards bearing Sonia's signature, written in her breezy, happy handwriting. It was plain to

be seen, from the messages on the cards, that this pretty woman of writing ability—among her other gifts—really liked our H. P. L.![60]

What ultimately happened to those missives, those love letters? After playing with them for a period of time, the Eddy brood soon lost interest. Then, Greene's postcards "went the way all children's toys go . . . in the ash-heap!"[61] No mention was given as to sending them to Lovecraft by Clark and Gamwell (and, oddly enough, by Eddy). His family appeared to view the postcards as little more than rubbish. This might have suggested their true feelings—anger, betrayal, abandonment—about his marriage and even Greene herself and their presumption that Lovecraft was gone from Providence for good.

Regardless of his aunts' reservations toward Greene and their possible displeasure at his going to New York, Lovecraft seemed to believe that he could convince them of the charms of his bride. He credited Greene for shattering his ennui and detachment from the larger world, melodramatically referencing long-standing suicidal thoughts:

> having no goal but a phial of cyanide when my money should give out . . . when suddenly, nearly three years ago, our benevolent angel S. H. G. stepped into my circle of consciousness and began to combat that idea with the opposite one of effort, and the enjoyment of life through the rewards which effort will bring.[62]

Lovecraft's praises continued. Greene's intelligence and conversation were captivating. Her cooking was "the last word in perfection as regards both palate and digestion."[63] She encouraged him to exercise and get fresh air.[64] Quite simply, she made him happy.

The suspicions regarding his family did little to explain Lovecraft and Greene's subterfuge with friends. On the very evening before his leaving Providence, he called upon the Eddys at their home and socialized with them well into the night. Muriel Eddy claimed that Lovecraft discussed moving to New York, yet he omitted a critical detail: "Never a word did he say about marriage, nor had he ever mentioned such a person as Sonia Greene."[65]

Although Lovecraft hid his relationship with Greene from family and friends, he confessed to Frank Belknap Long that his fascination for New York now rivaled that for his native Providence in early February. Roughly a month before his marriage, he alluded to relocating to the former city in his correspondence with his literary acquittance Clark Ashton Smith, and he cited a desire for the ready company of like-minded individuals as his motivation.[66] Amid a lengthy and detailed autobiographical letter to *Weird Tales* editor Edwin Baird, Lovecraft predicted that his own perilous finances would soon find him "in all probability in New York."[67]

Baird earlier had advised Lovecraft to introduce himself to Gertrude Tucker, the owner of the Reading Lamp agency. In his letter to him, Lovecraft noted that he communicated this recommendation to Greene, whom Baird knew as a fellow contributor to *Weird Tales*. Fully aware of Lovecraft's self-admitted "indolent habit of never getting around to anything," Greene took it upon herself to stop at the offices of the Reading Lamp with samples of his writing.[68] This anecdote revealed not only Greene's interest in promoting Lovecraft's career but her unsubtle campaign to persuade him to move to New York. Her comfort in serving as his surrogate with Tucker and her clear desire for his success evidenced a strong personal bond. Lovecraft's departure from Providence and betrothal to Greene may not have been as dreamy or spontaneous as first supposed.

In fact, the couple may have been engaged or seriously discussing marriage for an appreciable length of time. Greene penned a short article, "Amatory Aphorisms," for the second and final issue of her amateur periodical the *Rainbow*. This piece might be interpreted as a coded message in print to her secret paramour.[69] Lovecraft allegedly sent her an epistolary discourse on romance and matrimony, describing middle-aged individuals such as themselves "craving for another chance to find true love which maturity alone seems capable of fashioning."[70] Greene longed to marry him after reading that letter.[71] In both her published and unpublished autobiographical writings, she discusses an official proposal from Lovecraft and an engagement period of a year or more.

During their unorthodox courtship, Greene suffered through an anti-Semitic diatribe from Lovecraft on at least one occasion. In response, she reminded him of her own Jewish ancestry and even offered to release him from their engagement.[72] Unfortunately, similar episodes proved to be a regular ingredient of their relationship. "Always after such outbursts," Greene remembered, Lovecraft would embrace her and apologize.[73]

Regardless of the reasons guiding Lovecraft's silence concerning his relationship with Greene, he began sharing their newlywed status several days after informing his aunts. In a letter laced with self-effacing humor and inside jokes to James F. Morton, he boasted that he had discovered a novel way to shock and surprise his dear friend. Lovecraft stated that his letter's return Brooklyn address was now permanent, presuming that Morton could follow the verbal tracks to the truth: he and Greene, "the superior nine-tenths of the outfit," were married.[74] Wanting to collectively notify mutual friends with an official wedding announcement, Lovecraft requested that Morton refrain from spreading the news. In a follow-up letter to Morton, he justified his and Greene's Episcopal wedding ceremony, repeating his earlier explanation to his aunts that the aesthetic and ritualistic qualities of it—not the sacramental or religious—drove their decision.[75]

As word spread throughout Lovecraft and Greene's interlocking social circles, how did acquaintances and friends respond? Rheinhart Kleiner recalled *Home Brew* publisher George Julian Houtain and his wife telling him about the wedding during a taxicab ride:

> At once, I had a feeling of faintness at the pit of my stomach and became very pale. Houtain laughed uproariously at the effect of his announcement, but agreed that he felt as I did.[76]

Kleiner had introduced Lovecraft and Greene in Boston in 1921, and Houtain had cheekily snapped a photograph of the two at this consequential meeting. Pushing aside any private misgivings, Kleiner composed a poem celebrating the couple, "Epistle to Mr. and Mrs. Lovecraft." The *Brooklynite*, the Blue Pencil Club's periodical, published the piece in its April 1924 issue.[77]

Although Frank Belknap Long likely shared Kleiner and the Houtains' surprise, he responded with the good cheer expected by a friend and sent a congratulatory note.[78] Still, he later admitted to a long-standing belief that the marriage was "totally unexpected by [Lovecraft's] friends and correspondents" and that he perceived it as "incredibly impulsive" in hindsight.[79] Samuel Loveman even suspected that Greene might have coerced Lovecraft into matrimony. Morton seemed more shocked by Lovecraft's insistence on the religious ceremony than by the marriage itself.[80] The *United Amateur*, the newsletter of the United Amateur Press Association, celebrated the wedding and described the couple's three-year relationship as having "ripened by a marked community of tastes and parallelism of interests."[81] Several Brooklyn newspapers, including the borough's most popular daily, the *Brooklyn Daily Eagle*, carried the marriage announcement as well.[82]

Whatever the hidden and expressed sentiments of friends and family, Lovecraft and Greene were now officially man and wife in the most dynamic city in America. He had just finished a story for Harry Houdini, one of the more recognizable and popular performers of the day, and he anticipated consistent writing assignments and publications. Lovecraft and Greene's new life seemed wide open and their future bright.

5

▚

"The Somewhat Disastrous Collapse"

AFTER HIS PHILADELPHIA HONEYMOON with Sonia Greene, Lovecraft began establishing himself in his new Flatbush home. In the same letter announcing his wedding to his aunts, he asked them to ship his most essential possessions, such as clothes, a favorite dictionary, and unpublished manuscripts, to Brooklyn.[1] When Rheinhart Kleiner called upon the newlyweds, the volume of home goods (linens, silverware) and, of course, the indispensable tools of a writer (typewriter, desk accessories) arriving from Providence amazed him.[2] Parkside Avenue was now Lovecraft's domestic and literary nest. His books, art prints, and other material objects allowed him to re-create an environment and setting essential to his ability to think and write. Greene indulged her new husband, allowing him to convert a full room in the apartment into a study. He sketched detailed diagrams of the floor and wall arrangements of this literary sanctuary.[3]

Throughout March 1924, Lovecraft provided additional instructions to his aunts as to what he needed to seamlessly transfer his career and life to New York. Notably, he requested a box full of letters—presumably, his saved correspondence with professional acquaintances and close friends.[4] If this cache included his postcards from Greene, then his aunts appeared to have sifted through it, removed those items, and left them for the Eddy children to find when their parents appraised Lovecraft's purportedly unwanted possessions later that spring.

Regardless of his aunts' presumed disappointment, if not resentment, over his marriage, Lovecraft invited Lillian Clark and Annie Gamwell to

Flatbush and claimed that his wife lent "her urgent voice to the chorus of demand."[5] Later that month, Gamwell accepted her nephew and new niece-in-law's offer and visited while staying with a friend in Ho-Ho-Kus, an affluent commuter suburb in Bergen County, New Jersey.[6] This desire for Lovecraft's aunts to come to New York directly after his actual wedding—literally during the honeymoon phase of his marriage—does carry an odd ring. He revealed his elopement to his aunts in a letter dated March 9, 1924. Gamwell arrived in Ho-Ho-Kus by March 11 at the very latest, a mere two days after Lovecraft's marriage announcement and eight days after the wedding itself, and she likely lingered in New Jersey through March 30 and later for several days as a guest at Parkside Avenue (Figure 12).[7] During those first two weeks, she regularly commuted into New York. Lovecraft attested that her trip to New Jersey was "happily coincidental" to his own news.[8] Given the exact timing, this statement was dubious.

Why was it so critical for a member of Lovecraft's family to be in New York? Did he believe that seeing him happy with Greene might temper his aunts' negative expectations of his relationship with her? Did Gamwell hope that she could convince her nephew of the perceived error of his ways and lead him back to Providence, as she had in the autumn of 1922? Did Lovecraft simply pine for the approval of his family? Did Gamwell just need to understand why he hid his and Greene's romance and marital plans from her and her sister, Clark? Lovecraft was a thirty-three-year-old man living apart from his matriarchal family and attempting to forge an independent life for the very first time. Both he and his aunts appeared to have difficulty allowing old familial patterns to wither and new ones to bud.

Putting aside the motivations behind Gamwell's visit, Lovecraft solicited her assistance and advice for settling into Brooklyn, and, in turn, he happily served as her guide to New York. In fact, at the beginning of her stay, he sought out buildings and sites exemplifying the city's colonial history—the existence of which remained "unsuspected by the vulgar throng"—and enlisted Gamwell as his partner in this project.[9] Lovecraft's letters to both of his aunts testify to the family's shared interest in architecture and preservation in Providence and New England. Possibly, he wished to prove to Gamwell that a similar built environment and historic fabric miraculously survived in the booming metropolis of 1920s New York. He often required reassurance himself.

After lunch with Greene at a French restaurant in Midtown Manhattan on March 14, Lovecraft treated Gamwell to a tour of one of his favorite New York neighborhoods—Greenwich Village. The previous decade's flowering

Figure 12. Sonia H. Greene's Brooklyn apartment at 259 Parkside Avenue was Lovecraft's and her first home together as husband and wife. (Courtesy of the Municipal Archives, City of New York)

of art, literature, and radical politics had embedded it and its creative denizens in the public imagination. Although that movement had slowed by the time of Lovecraft's arrival, it imbued Greenwich Village with a cachet and desirability, drawing small-scale investment and rehabilitation to the neighborhood's historic and architecturally significant building stock.[10]

Lovecraft never visited Greenwich Village to socialize with its resident writers and painters, and he regularly derided bohemians and individuals pursuing countercultural lifestyles. Strangely enough, he never perceived himself as belonging to such a fraternity of outsiders as he fashioned an existence fully indifferent to conventional moneymaking and material success. Instead, he enjoyed wandering through the neighborhood's often narrow and sometimes curving streets to marvel at its eighteenth-century and nineteenth-century buildings. If he listened, he could hear the "rattle of coaches."[11] If he squinted, he could espy the "smoke of homely chimney-pots."[12] In Greenwich Village, he could sidestep his own modern age and glide into the past.

Lovecraft and Gamwell began their walk at Washington Square Park, the neighborhood's main public space popular with tourists and residents alike. Although he openly lamented the park's unofficial status as "the lurking-place" for bohemians and artistic poseurs, the careful restoration of mansions on Washington Square's north side cheered him.[13] He lovingly admired their "quiet brick facades and austere stone doorway-pillars" and how the buildings themselves "glowed mellowly in the afternoon sun."[14] With its former grandeur fully burnished, this row of nineteenth-century Greek Revival homes provided "the last touch of desirable background" to Washington Square and evoked a New York captured in the novels of Henry James and Edith Wharton.[15] The north side of the park would remain a site of preservation campaigns and competing visions for the urban fabric throughout the next several decades.[16] Unbeknownst to Lovecraft, the realist painter Edward Hopper, now famous for manifesting scenes of alienation and isolation in a dreamy, yet modern cityscape, lived at 3 Washington Square North. This is only one example of the fertile creative world thriving in New York at that moment. Lovecraft inhabited a sphere of that world—just not one shared by Hopper.

After Washington Square, Lovecraft and Gamwell strolled south along MacDougal Street. He complained about the graffiti and "bizarre signs" of "pseudo-artists" besmirching many of the "splendid Colonial" buildings, and he hoped that these structures would eventually be restored to a condition matching that of the nearby mansions along the park.[17] Such preservation efforts eventually would contribute to the displacement of artists, writers, and hangers-on and prompt their movement to other areas of Manhattan, the city, and the metropolitan region.[18] Through observation, news stories, or simply word-of-mouth, Lovecraft seemed to be cognizant of the accidental or intended consequences of the historic rehabilitation of urban property and, possibly, to welcome them.

Reaching Bleecker Street, he remarked that the neighborhood sank into "a tortuous Italian slum."[19] (Italian immigrants and Italian Americans stood as the dominant ethnic group in Greenwich Village by the 1910s.)[20] Ignoring "a distinctly squalid aspect" of Minetta Street, Lovecraft detected a "quaint loveliness" in the design and details of the thoroughfare's structures.[21] On Charlton Street, with its "gleaming white doorways, polish'd knockers, [and] jaunty dormer windows," Lovecraft pictured himself sauntering through New York of the late eighteenth century—a city decidedly constructed on a human scale, still existing alongside the natural world, and notably devoid of an appreciable number of non-English-speaking immigrants.[22] This city never existed beyond his imagination: New York always held a comparatively diverse and multilingual population since its founding as a Dutch colony. Nonetheless, while losing himself in "the labyrinthine ways" of Greenwich Village, he discovered that the city possessed a colonial architectural heritage distinct from Philadelphia and his native Providence.[23] Such a realization impressed and comforted Lovecraft; perhaps he wished for Gamwell to experience a similar sensation. This was his new home. This New York.

Lovecraft's relationship with the city evolved alongside his leisurely and minute exploration of it. That is, he discovered New York by walking through it. During his second and lengthy stay with Greene in the autumn of 1922, he began to establish a bond with the city. Traversing its streets, stumbling into its hidden pockets, he gradually comprehended its flow and appreciated its own richly layered history. This encounter with the city on foot, this immersion with its quotidian rhythms, was not unique. Lovecraft's incipient understanding and his vehicle toward it resembled that of an iconic urban figure: the flaneur.[24]

Commenting on his own nineteenth-century Paris, French poet Charles Baudelaire described this quintessential creature:

> For the perfect *flâneur*, for the passionate spectator, it is an immense joy to set up house in the heart of the multitude, amid the ebb and the flow of movement, in the midst of the fugitive and the infinite. To be away from home and yet to feel oneself everywhere at home; to see the world, to be at the centre of the world, and yet to remain hidden from the world. . . .[25]

While living in New York, Lovecraft relished nothing more than rambling through it, often at odd hours of the night. Nonetheless, he differed from the accepted characterization of the flaneur in a concrete and important feature: the crowd, the people of the city going about their adventures and routines, held little interest for him. The physical tissue of the city—its buildings, its parks, its places—drew his obsessive gaze. Signs and symbols of the urban past, not the intricate daily play of street life, fascinated him.

More mundane and pressing considerations prompted Lovecraft's mental mapping of the New York streetscape. When he and Greene first met in 1922, she held a comfortable position at the Midtown fashion emporium Ferle Heller with a purported annual salary of nearly $10,000.[26] (For comparison, the average household income was approximately $1,236 in 1920).[27] By their wedding day, however, Greene's finances were deteriorating.

In 1923, Greene left Ferle Heller to open a hat boutique in her own neighborhood of Flatbush. Shortly thereafter, she partnered with a high-end dressmaker and tailor to launch a women's clothier in Manhattan. This business was likely located at 25 West Fifty-Seventh Street, directly across the street from Ferle Heller's 36 West Fifty-Seventh Street location.[28] A former client underwrote the rent for the first three months, and the shop came fully furnished. Greene stocked imported Parisian hats and offered bespoke products. She even hired two assistants away from Ferle Heller. Unfortunately, this entrepreneurial venture proved to be a bust, closing after the initial three-month period. Attempting to recoup a percentage of her investment, Greene stocked her Brooklyn shop with expensive hats originally purchased for an affluent Manhattan clientele. Her Flatbush customers could not afford such pricey merchandise. By March 1924, this business itself was struggling.[29]

On February 9, less than a month before Lovecraft slipped off to New York, Greene wrote to his aunt Lillian Clark that she had fallen on hard luck and desperately needed a new professional position. Striking a cautiously optimistic note, Greene felt "sure there is one waiting for me somewhere."[30] This odd confession could have further contributed to Lovecraft's aunts' ambiguity over his seemingly sudden nuptials: they might have understood that their nephew—although a gifted writer—could never support a household, especially in a city as expensive and competitive as New York. Likely spurred into action by Greene's shaky business activity and personal finances and maybe even his own desire to contribute to the household coffers, Lovecraft met with Gertrude Tucker of the Reading Lamp agency almost immediately upon returning from his honeymoon.

Tucker interviewed him in her offices near Bryant Park on the afternoon of March 10. They discussed Lovecraft's interests and prospects as a working writer. She foresaw a market for a collection of travel essays focusing on his "antiquarian" adventures and chronicling historic buildings and "weird survivals," and she requested that he provide her with three sample pieces on these general subjects.[31] Judging from Lovecraft's vivid descriptions and well-researched histories of New England, Philadelphia, and New York in his correspondence, he might have excelled at such a project. Tucker asked to review all his unpublished manuscripts, and she hinted at the possibility of securing a contract for him to serve as a columnist for an unspecified magazine chain and even negotiating an agreement with a book publisher. He left the Reading Lamp feeling elated.

Unfortunately, Lovecraft's hopes (or Tucker's estimation of him) may have been misplaced. Later that same month, he complained about her insistence on seeing finished chapters of his book on American superstitions and her inability to comprehend the research required "to approach such a theme with even a shadow of the adequate background."[32] This was likely the proposed book that she believed might attract publishers. Lovecraft had difficulty honoring deadlines—a bane to any agent or editor. Being an unknown and untested writer, he should have attempted to demonstrate his work ethic and professionalism. This would have provided Tucker with the incentive to pitch his writings to magazines and publishers. Ultimately, his relationship with her literary agency resulted in only a single book review.[33]

While he was managing his prospects with the Reading Lamp, Lovecraft continued to build his relationship with *Weird Tales*. On the same day when he interviewed with Tucker, he reported that its founder and publisher, Jacob Clark (J. C.) Henneberger, approached him about relocating to Chicago, where the publication was partially based, and sitting in the editorial chair of "a *new* magazine of weirdness."[34] Henneberger intended to execute "a radical change" in *Weird Tales*.[35] This seems have been a possible rebranding or restructuring of its creative and literary scope. Lovecraft was his ideal candidate to lead this endeavor, and Henneberger planned to travel to New York to discuss the opportunity with him.[36]

Lovecraft wavered over the prospect of moving to Chicago and the Midwest so shortly after having left Providence. Greene urged her husband to accept Henneberger's offer if it proved to be legitimate, telling him that she would happily accompany him to the Windy City. However, place and a close identification with it mattered to Lovecraft. His wanderings through New York had allowed him to begin constructing an imaginative linkage with the city. Moving to Chicago would sever that nascent and tenuous bond. To Lovecraft, "such a break away from Colonial scenes would be little short of tragic," declaring that living among that era's history furnished him with the "very breath of life."[37] In 1924, Chicago was still a young and modern-facing metropolis—not even a hundred years old. Lovecraft would find no Dutch churchyards or Federal-style mansions in Illinois, the home of the Chicago and Prairie Schools of architecture.

Genuine practical concerns informed Lovecraft's skeptical view of Henneberger's proposition, as well. He questioned the financial health of *Weird Tales* and its owner's other publishing ventures. Henneberger had already lost tens of thousands of dollars on the magazine, and he was heavily in debt by February 1924.[38] If Lovecraft accepted the offer, he worried that the publication would fold after only a few issues, and then he would find himself unemployed and stranded "in ugly, modern, crassly repellent CHICAGO."[39] As he contemplated this tentative position, *Weird Tales* published several of his short stories: "The Rats in the Walls," "Facts Concerning the Late Arthur Jermyn and His Family," and "Hypnos."[40]

Meanwhile, Lovecraft found cautious assurance and hope in Harry Houdini's satisfaction with his ghostwriting of "Under the Pyramids." Houdini "took to it marvelously" and later sent Lovecraft an open invitation to his Harlem home at 278 West 113th Street, only blocks from Morningside Park.[41] Judging from Houdini's public persona and his own correspondence with him, Lovecraft estimated the famed magician to be a congenial and friendly person "in a mildly commonplace way."[42] He looked forward to finally meeting Houdini and browsing his private library—including its rare volumes on spiritualism, witchcraft, demonology, magic, and the supernatural.[43]

In his accounts of his professional exchanges with Houdini, Lovecraft made no mention of the escape artist's Jewish heritage, then publicly known and a primary reason for his appeal to immigrants and new Americans. Houdini was born Erik Weisz in Budapest, Hungary (then part of Austria-Hungary), and his father, Mayer Samuel Weisz, was a rabbi. Possibly, Lovecraft could mute his bigoted instincts in business matters, or he might simply have been ignorant of this part of his client's personal history. The two men would maintain an active professional relationship until Houdini's sudden death in 1926. At that time, Lovecraft and fellow Providence author C. M. Eddy were ghostwriting *The Cancer of Superstition* for him. This was conceived as a book-length project documenting the history of the phenomenon and ultimately debunking it. Work ended on the volume with Houdini's death.[44]

While Lovecraft and Greene attempted to pursue their respective careers, they continued to celebrate their marriage with friends, including many from local amateur journalist and literary circles. During Gamwell's March visit, the couple opened their apartment to members of the Blue

Pencil Club. The *Brooklynite* carried a front-page announcement congratulating them on their recent nuptials, noting that all the club's members shared "the heartiest good wishes."[45] Lovecraft shared the news with his far-flung correspondents, sometimes offering a self-deprecating and stereotypically male joke about his henpecked and subservient state.[46] These postcards and letters testify to his pride and happiness in calling himself a partner and husband to Greene. Several were written on stationery from the Robert Morris Hotel, where the couple stayed during their Philadelphia honeymoon, perhaps representing a conscious or subconscious memorializing of the event or a method of showcasing it.[47]

Lovecraft wasted little time in taking advantage of the possibilities for an author in New York. His lengthy activity in amateur journalism and his own reputation within it allowed him to quickly tap into a nexus of writers and intellectuals. Many arrivals to any new place often struggle for years to form genuine relationships. This was not the case with Lovecraft. In late March, he attended a meeting of the Writers' Club, an organization of literary professionals based in Manhattan or Brooklyn, at which muckraking journalist and author Will Irwin delivered a lecture on William Shakespeare.[48] When the guests were leaving the event, Irwin helped Lovecraft with his coat. Lovecraft seemed humbled by his brief encounter with such an accomplished man of letters.[49]

Close proximity to writers and thinkers and the chance for casual and unplanned interactions with them are what New York offered to Lovecraft, and they underscore a fundamental and continual importance of cities to the lives and work of creative individuals. An outing with friends may lead to an unexpected and cordial exchange with a notable author. Who could guess what chain of events this might ultimately set off? Cities present artists, writers, and such professionals with the geographic density and networks to interact, collaborate, connect with, and—hopefully—inspire one another.

A member of Brooklyn amateur journalist groups, Greene was prevented from enjoying many late nights because of her early and long hours at her Flatbush shop. When Lovecraft stayed out with his friends, she never retired before he returned home and subsequently felt "like hell the next day."[50] During the early days of their marriage, he attempted to be mindful of his wife's needs and appropriately limited his socializing.[51] However, he did insist on one exception to this marital compromise. Lovecraft began to meet several good friends, such as James F. Morton and Frank Belknap Long, for a weekly nighttime gathering that often ran deep into the dark morning hours.[52]

Although Greene was no longer earning a sizable salary and Lovecraft was experiencing little success in finding a remunerative position as a writer, the couple—much like many newlyweds—looked to their future with confidence and optimism. In May, they obtained a mortgage on two lots in Bryn Mawr Park, a neighborhood in Yonkers, New York, a midsize city in Westchester County bordering the northern Bronx and with a then industrial waterfront on the Hudson River. Lovecraft and Greene acquired the mortgage through the Homeland Company, a real estate firm with offices at 18–20 East Forty-First Street in Manhattan that was spearheading suburban development throughout Westchester County.[53]

The Homeland Company's standard product appeared to be a five-year mortgage with a 25 percent down payment. The company offered buyers an array of home models and retained the right of first refusal to build on undeveloped properties during the length of the loan. Such a vehicle toward homeownership was common in the United States prior to the creation of the Federal Housing Administration in 1934 and, eventually, the standard long-term mortgage. Real estate firms would market cleared lots in emerging neighborhoods or suburbs to aspiring homeowners. Individuals would secure a mortgage for a property or purchase it with the intention of building their own home or contracting with a developer to do so.[54]

Lovecraft saw Yonkers as offering access simultaneously to the culture of New York and the rusticity of the countryside. When informing his aunts of his and Greene's investment, he described Westchester County as "the most idyllic" and "Novanglian Colonial" landscape that he had ever encountered.[55] Considering his love for Providence, this statement suggested his intended commitment to living in the New York metropolitan region and his hope that it held a reservoir of history with a purity measurable to that of his native New England. Not surprisingly, Lovecraft fantasized about being a rural gentleman overseeing the construction of a manor house inspired by colonial architecture.[56]

In the context of Greene's business troubles and Lovecraft's sporadic freelancing, was their Yonkers real estate investment based on a sound financial understanding or a heady delusion over their ability to achieve the national dream of homeownership? The 1920s was a decade of rampant personal consumption and systemic financial speculation. An unsound decision on their part would be far from unusual. Noticeably, Lovecraft neglected to include a compelling and personal reason his wife might have desired to move to Westchester: her mother, Racille Moseson, and her half-sister, Anna Kopp, and her young family lived in New Rochelle, a growing city in the suburban county. In the entirety of his surviving correspondence with his aunts, he never composed a single word about Greene's history or family.[57] It was as if she appeared from the ether at their first meeting in 1921.

By the summer of 1924, the couple's economic situation was nearing free fall. Aside from payments from selling a handful of short stories to *Weird Tales* and from modest ghostwriting assignments, Lovecraft had earned little since arriving in New York.[58] More worrisome, Greene's millinery shop suffered a "somewhat disastrous collapse."[59] She was the household breadwinner, arguably its sole earner. Materially and financially, she supported Lovecraft throughout their marriage. They had already listed a piano, a dining room set, living room furniture, and art prints for sale in the classified section of the *Brooklyn Daily Eagle*.[60] These were all likely Greene's household possessions; Lovecraft would never have willingly parted with his own.

Now approaching the age of thirty-four, Lovecraft had never held gainful employment. While living in Providence, neither his mother nor later his aunts ever pushed him to find a job or maintain any measurable adult responsibilities. This left him ill-prepared for a sudden and necessary entry into the workforce. That July, his only notable foray was a probationary stint as a salesperson at a Newark, New Jersey, branch of a collection agency. After being introduced to the general manager, Lovecraft characterized him as "a crude but well-meaning fellow" with "traces of a Levantine heritage."[61] Only five days into the job, he was dismayed to learn that the lion's share of potential clients for the firm's services were "the most impossible sort of persons" operating and owning businesses in New York's garment trade.[62] There is no mistaking this reference: Jewish immigrants and Jewish Americans locally had dominated that industry since the Civil War.[63] Lovecraft resigned that same day. His career in sales did not last even a full week.

Lovecraft continued to sift through job advertisements in newspapers and answered relevant postings with a verbose and slightly bizarre business letter. (Years later, his close friends openly ridiculed its tone and content.)[64] He placed a listing for his freelance editorial and writing services in the *New York Times* and sent unsolicited letters to several newspapers, magazines, and publishers in the Boston and New York City regions.[65] Lovecraft never mentioned receiving any replies.

Greene fared little better than her husband. After permanently closing her Flatbush store, she found a salaried position at Bruck-Weiss Millinery on West Fifty-Seventh Street and just off Fifth Avenue, Manhattan's most exclusive high-end shopping district. Bruck-Weiss was promoted as "the largest exclusive millinery shop" in both the United States and Europe.[66]

Coincidentally, and most likely unknown to Lovecraft and Greene, it was partially owned by Sadie Weiss, the wife of Harry Houdini's estranged brother Leopold Weiss and the ex-wife of his other brother, Nathan.[67] Possibly referring to Sadie Weiss, Lovecraft maligned the head of the firm as "a dour, capricious, and uncultivated woman."[68] Early into her new job, Greene was asked for a list of her longtime clients and was instructed to convince them to shift their business to Bruck-Weiss. After being furloughed because of a purported lack of sales several weeks later, she suspected that she was hired solely to obtain her customer list and that she soon would be summarily dismissed.[69]

Early August saw Lovecraft and Greene already behind on the mortgage payments for their Yonkers properties—purchased only that May— and discussing the need to find more affordable housing. All the while, he assured his aunts that he and, by extension, Greene, were economizing. The tone of his letters hinted that his family attributed all difficulties faced by the couple to his wife and her failings alone. While grappling with these challenges, he confessed to missing Providence and longing to return there to distant acquaintances.[70] (As he had for select letters earlier that summer, Lovecraft wrote on Robert Morris Hotel stationery—a detail rich with symbolism and psychological insights.) Notably, he refrained from sharing such feelings with his family.

A meager household budget did not preclude Lovecraft from exploring his newly adopted hometown and, like many transplants to New York, claiming parts of it as his own. He strolled through Riverside Park, "delightful and many-path'd," on the Upper West Side.[71] He window-shopped at antique stores, "the choicest emporia of the rare and beautiful," on Madison Avenue.[72] He gazed longingly at the new townhouses, "a paradise of Georgian gardens and Londonesque facades," at Sutton Place near the Manhattan side of the Queensboro Bridge.[73] Greene maintained a normal nine-to-five schedule, but she still accompanied her husband on some of his urban adventures that summer. The couple toured museums and historic sites and treated themselves to the occasional dinner and movie. Lovecraft insisted that no Italian restaurant's red sauce could compare to his wife's "brand still more magical in its subtle appeal."[74] Although facing very real and difficult troubles—joblessness, lack of money, Lovecraft adjusting to a life independent from his family, and Greene's own estrangement from her daughter—they appeared to appreciate each other's company and to carve out moments and memories for themselves.

Greenwich Village continued to sate Lovecraft's aesthetic appetite for eighteenth-century architecture. On August 19, the evening prior to his thirty-fourth birthday, Lovecraft conducted an exhaustive survey of the neighborhood, visiting sites until then only familiar to him through books.[75] Greene joined him on this excursion, undoubtedly hoping to enjoy, if only vicariously, her husband's passion for old streets and old places. Whenever Lovecraft walked through Greenwich Village, he always altered his path to maximize his chance of encountering a building, alleyway, or even lamppost hitherto unknown to him. This August stroll through one of New York's most storied neighborhoods was a resounding success.

The "old spirit" of Greenwich Village "defied alike the forces of time, death, and decay."[76] While Lovecraft stopped to admire the small gated front garden of a mansion near the corner of Washington Square South and MacDougal Street, "a feline convention" of six or seven cats emerged from the shadows "to chat" with him.[77] On Grove Street, he approved of the "freshly painted classic doorways" and their "shining knockers," and he glanced lovingly at "the most delicious imaginable silhouette" of slanted roofs and dormer windows on the horizon.[78] "Endless rows of Colonial houses" lined Christopher Street.[79]

Gay Street (Figure 13) particularly touched his aesthetic imagination. When he and Greene "rounded into the quaint, curving little alley where city turmoil never reaches," he experienced a "delighted breathlessness."[80] While reviewing the restoration of many buildings' doors, windows, and facades, he commented upon the street's "unpleasing proximity of African habitations."[81] This casual racist remark—surprisingly muted for Lovecraft—suggested his understanding of the twin forces of segregation and disinvestment affecting certain urban neighborhoods. Historically, Gay Street housed Black servants working for Greenwich Village's well-to-do families; however, these Black residents were gradually leaving the neighborhood by this time.

Next was Patchin Place, a narrow residential cul-de-sac just off West Tenth Street and between Sixth and Greenwich Avenues. Jefferson Market Courthouse and the Interborough Rapid Transit Company's Sixth Avenue Elevated train overlooked this tiny pocket community. Lovecraft deemed the former structure (now a public library branch and a National Historic Landmark) as "ugly and Victorian."[82] The rowhouses, wrought iron fencing, and shade trees of Patchin Place entranced Lovecraft. In its alley, a single antique-looking streetlamp "cast alluring shadows of archaic things half of the imagination."[83] The collective environment was nothing less than magical: "It was the living Georgian past."[84] In the 1910s, Patchin Place housed an informal group of feminist intellectuals who regularly hosted salons featuring radical and primarily women speakers. By the time of Lovecraft

Figure 13. Lovecraft regularly wandered New York City's nighttime streets to discover buildings reflecting the architectural styles of colonial and early America. He described Greenwich Village's Gay Street as a "quaint, curving little alley." (Courtesy of the New York Transit Museum)

and Greene's visit, it was home to several writers, including man of letters John Cowper Powys and poet E. E. Cummings. Lovecraft seemed to be unaware of Patchin Place as a fixture in New York's avant-garde culture.[85]

Greene discovered the next target on her husband's itinerary—Milligan Place. This tiny community sits on Sixth Avenue between West Tenth and Eleventh Streets. Today, its nondescript gate is sandwiched between three-story buildings with ground-floor retail, and most passersby would never notice the passage leading to this "haven of antiquity."[86] An elderly man, "a neighbouring loafer of weatherbeaten face and incongruously good speech," discussed Milligan Place's history with Lovecraft and Greene and invited them to follow him through its entrance.[87] Then, Lovecraft found himself standing in a triangular courtyard, dumbstruck by the row of modest brick homes tucked away from the noise of the street and the nearby elevated train. The flagstone sidewalk, young trees, and the buildings' wooden shutters and iron railings appealed to his deepest sensibilities. To his wonderment, "the hush of centuries was on the place."[88]

Likely appreciating Lovecraft's delight, the wizened guide—presumably a resident or caretaker—offered to show the couple more of Milligan Place. He led them through a courtyard doorway, down a hallway, and out another door into an inner enclosed alleyway, possibly an airshaft, dimly lit by a pair of lamp poles. Buildings with "Colonial doorways" and "small-pan'd windows" stood at the south end of the alley.[89] Lovecraft reflected on this chance discovery by his wife:

> Buried deep in the entrails of nondescript commercial blocks, this little lost world of a century and a quarter ago sleeps unheeding of the throng. . . . Having seen this thing, one cannot look at an ordinary crowded street without wondering what surviving marvels may lurk unsuspected beneath the prim and monotonous blocks.[90]

Adding to his starry-eyed impression of Milligan Place was that many of its inhabitants were authors and artists. In his past Greenwich Village rambles, Lovecraft bemoaned the dominant presence of bohemians and immigrants. In his estimation, these creative residents of Milligan Place were genuine and admirable writers—not poetasters or poseurs. This small Manhattan courtyard haunted Lovecraft, evoking a different and lost New York City, one in which he believed that he might have thrived.

After departing Milligan Place, Lovecraft and Greene ambled along West Eleventh Street, lined with early nineteenth-century homes and buildings. There, Lovecraft noticed "a clump of pallid slabs and shafts" behind a spiked fence.[91] This was the Second Cemetery of Congregation Shearith Israel. Today, a brick pathway cuts through the small triangular plot, and ivy grows around the dozen or so gravestones bearing faded Hebrew carvings. A single obelisk looms over the sacred ground. The cemetery was consecrated in 1805 and operated until 1829; Shearith Israel was the city's only synagogue until 1825.[92] Spotting this small Jewish graveyard did not appear to dampen Lovecraft's enjoyment or incite his anti-Semitism. He tellingly observed that "most of the startlingly palaeogean quality of the elder one is absent."[93] The dearth of visible Hebrew inscriptions on the headstones might have pacified this dark instinct of his. Moreover, the age of the site and its belonging squarely to the past possibly made it safe and acceptable. This Jewish cemetery was both literally and figuratively a dead place.

Finally, Lovecraft and Greene walked to the subway and headed home to Brooklyn. Their evening tour of Greenwich Village and attendant discoveries left him elated and expectant:

It had been a great day, and gave me perhaps more of the ancient New-York than any other one of my numerous pilgrimages. The town is full of Colonial arcana, and in time I mean to unearth and revel in them all![94]

Throughout his years in New York, Lovecraft never ceased searching for such "Colonial arcana."[95] His letters overflow with vivid and detailed descriptions of buildings, streetscapes, gardens, and parks, providing a diary of his activities and a written record of a past city.

6

⁞⁞⁞

"A Maze of Poverty
& Uncertainty"

AS THE EARLY GLOW OF HIS MARRIAGE dimmed beneath mounting financial pressures, Lovecraft shifted his energy to the tending of his social life. Many of his friends with whom he bonded during his visits to New York in 1922 still worked and lived in the city. He likely spent an inordinate amount of time with Rheinhart Kleiner, Frank Belknap Long, and James F. Morton during his early months in Flatbush. Since meeting the boys' adventure author Everett McNeil at a Brooklyn literary salon in 1922, he grew to enjoy his company, as well. In fact, McNeil may have been the first individual to encourage Lovecraft to submit his stories to *Weird Tales* in 1923, initiating his long and impactful professional relationship with the magazine.[1]

Arthur Leeds, a forty-two-year-old Canadian expatriate, former carnival hand, and journeyman writer, became a regular fixture in the social circle of Lovecraft and his friends. He wrote screenplays for silent films in the 1910s and served in the Canadian military in Nova Scotia during the First World War. By 1924, Leeds's wife had left him and moved to Chicago with their three children. Bunking at a residential hotel in Hell's Kitchen, he barely earned a living penning a column for *Writer's Digest* and short stories for pulp magazines. Although he always was neatly groomed, Leeds's wardrobe of threadbare and ill-fitted clothes reflected his strained circumstances.[2] Since both he and McNeil lived in Hell's Kitchen, the latter presumably connected Leeds to the group.

Several Cleveland transplants found spots in this expanding literary bunch. George Kirk moved to New York to build a career as a bookseller in August 1924, leaving behind his fiancée, Lucile Dvorak, in Ohio. Tall, lean, dark-haired, and bespectacled, Kirk had experienced much of life for a young man in his mid-twenties. By the time he arrived in the city, he had dropped out of high school, married and divorced, and lived in California for a two-year stint.[3] Having befriended Kirk in Cleveland in 1922, Lovecraft introduced him to the other men.

Much to Lovecraft's delight, his longtime correspondent Samuel Loveman came to New York in early September 1924. Another former Clevelander, Hart Crane, lived in a de facto arts commune at 110 Columbia Heights near the Brooklyn waterfront, and he secured a temporary room for Loveman in the building. Philadelphia publisher Centaur Press recently had accepted his bibliographic study on the American aesthete writer Edgar Saltus.[4] When Loveman stepped off the train at Grand Central Terminal, he likely imagined a promising new life for himself.

These eight individuals—all aging or aspiring intellectuals and men of letters—formed a literary brotherhood that supported and sustained each member throughout their shared time in New York City. Although other figures cycled in and out of the group, its core remained the same: Rheinhart Kleiner, George Kirk, Arthur Leeds, Frank Belknap Long, Samuel Loveman, Everett McNeil, James F. Morton, and H. P. Lovecraft. By early 1925, they had christened themselves as the Kalem Club. The moniker was derived from the last names of the original and inaugural members, each of which began with the letter k, l, or m.[5] Lovecraft himself never used the name, always referring to the Kalem Club as "the boys" or "the gang."[6] Belying his historic—and somewhat false and self-generated—reputation as a recluse, he operated as the primary connector and mover of the circle. As with any network of colleagues, friends, or family, arguments, misunderstandings, and fallings-out occasionally disrupted its social harmony. Nonetheless, many of these men remained close throughout their respective lives, testifying to the depth and strength of their relationships and their ability to survive discord, distance, and time.[7]

In August 1924, the Kalem Club was amid its early days, with formative member Loveman still in Cleveland. The group began meeting on Thursday evenings with hosting duties rotating among the members. (This running date later changed to Wednesday.) The friends debated philosophy, politics, literature, science, and art. They presented their own stories, poems, and essays and solicited feedback, direction, and criticism.

They shared writing and job-hunting hints. Of course, they talked about books—always books. Rheinhart Kleiner remembered these meetings as:

> a congenial place for the completest and most untrammeled expression of opinion. Personal convictions, as well as the merest whimsies of thought, were here openly paraded and insisted upon, and there was no one too diffident to wage battle for the most astonishing paradox, if it happened to be his own.[8]

He believed that the chemistry, energy, and comradery of these gatherings "could never be effectively retold."[9] This did not prevent him from attempting to unspool the loose agenda of a normal evening with the Kalem Club:

> Our discussions and diversions were nothing if not spontaneous— and they were undoubtedly spontaneous. From some of our more serious sessions, the mind recalls a comprehensive appraisal of Walt Whitman's poetry, by James; a bit of amusing cynicism regarding Jane Austen's novels, from George; and a stout pronouncement that no woman over forty ever wrote a true lyric, on the part of Belknap. On one occasion, Sam read T. S. Eliot's poem, "The Waste Land," aloud, and those who did not succumb to torpor were aroused to torridity in the expression of opinion.[10]

This brief account reveals several truths about the Kalems. Although largely self-educated (only Morton held a college degree, and several members, including Lovecraft, were high school dropouts), they were incredibly well-versed in literature and fully aware of modernism and other cultural trends shaping American arts and letters.[11] Again, this contradicts Lovecraft's mythology as a man out of time. Evidenced by Frank Belknap Long's arguably agist and sexist remark on women and poetry, the Kalems were also an exclusively male circle. The opposite sex seldomly attended their meetings or partook in their social activities.

At the center of the group sat Lovecraft. Long warmly recalled him unofficially yet loquaciously presiding over the majority of their meetings:

> He never seemed to experience the slightest necessity to pause between words. There was no groping about for just the right term, no matter how recondite his conversation became. When the need for some metaphysical hair-splitting arose, it was easy to visualize scissors honed to a surgical sharpness snipping away in the recesses of his mind.[12]

When these meetings concluded—sometimes well past midnight—members with scant professional or personal responsibilities and not required to rise at an early hour often carried the conversations to diners or Automats. Then began the "long walks" and "nocturnal prowls."[13]

The late-night excursion following the meeting held on August 21, 1924, the day after Lovecraft's thirty-fourth birthday, provided a typical example. When the gathering disbanded at one-thirty in the morning at Kirk's Upper West Side apartment on West 106th Street, he accompanied his guests to their respective subway stations. Then, the remaining Kalem Club members, Lovecraft, Kirk, and Leeds, hiked down Broadway to an orange drink stand at Columbus Circle.[14] Next, Leeds broke away upon reaching his residential hotel at West Forty-Ninth Street. Since "the evening" was "yet young," Lovecraft "proposed to show off the local Georgian antiquities" to Kirk, still a newcomer to the city.[15] He was game.

Lovecraft's agenda would intimidate even the most intrepid and veteran flaneur. Already having traversed nearly seventy city blocks, the two friends now walked from Hell's Kitchen to Greenwich Village. During the small hours, Lovecraft pointed out colonial homes and doorways near Abington Square, a small triangular park edged by Hudson and West Twelfth Streets and Eighth Avenue, in the latter neighborhood. He ushered Kirk through the gate of Grove Court, a "delicious" alley off Grove Street between Bedford and Hudson Streets and showed him its "bits of garden" and "occasional restored doorways."[16] He led his companion through Gay Street and Patchin and Milligan Places. Kirk "went into raptures" at the sight of the last spot, and Lovecraft himself delighted in "their utter and poignant charm in the sinister hours before dawn, when only cats, criminals, astronomers, and poetic antiquarians roam the waking world."[17]

Strange men poking into the nooks and crannies of buildings and public spaces at a late hour always attracts suspicion. While Lovecraft and Kirk were strolling along Minetta Street, a police cruiser slowly trailed the pair and even stopped to monitor them for a moment. After the police resumed their patrol, the two friends ducked into a narrow alley and came upon a "cryptical" moonlit courtyard.[18] Evading the attention of authorities and Lovecraft's infectious enthusiasm emboldened Kirk. No dark alleyways, shadowy stairwells, or questionable characters would temper his desire to follow the man from Providence.

The emptiness and quiet of the night allowed Lovecraft to investigate and appreciate the city with an attention impossible in the daylight. The nocturnal atmosphere also enabled him to study its sites from an idealized and sanitized point of view. There were few people—especially those deemed the wrong sort of people by Lovecraft—to disrupt his flight of fancy. While tabulating the "thousand charms" of Minetta Street, he expressed relief that the neighborhood's "Italian squalor was faded into shadow."[19]

After fortifying themselves with coffee at a diner, Lovecraft and Kirk proceeded eastward along Charlton Street, the "best preserved of all the colonial thoroughfares."[20] They stopped in front of 63 Prince Street, a "pitifully decrepit" Federal-style building where former President James Monroe died on July 4, 1831.[21] On Cherry Street, they discovered a court-yard with a uniquely diamond-shaped streetlamp. Wanting to gain a fuller view of both, Lovecraft and Kirk entered one of the presumably inhab-ited buildings facing the space and climbed "curious, winding stairs" to its roof.[22] These intrepid urban explorers displayed no hesitation in trespass-ing. That is, breaking the law.

After inspecting old warehouses beneath the piers of the Brooklyn Bridge, Lovecraft and Kirk proceeded down Pearl Street to lower Man-hattan to seek out more antiquities. They "dr[ank] in the colonial houses" and watched the rising sun "gilding the steeples of the Brooklyn shore across the glittering water" of the East River.[23] While nearing city hall, they experienced the "climax" of their ramblings: "gaz[ing] at the sun-splendid pinnacles" of the Woolworth Building through the central arched vault at the base of the massive Municipal Building designed by McKim, Mead & White.[24] Satisfied by their adventures, the friends finally parted ways. Immediately upon returning home, Kirk penned a letter to his fiancée to capture "some of the charms of the last twelve hours."[25] Lovecraft saun-tered into his Brooklyn apartment a little before nine o'clock. He never mentioned if his wife had expected him at an earlier and more reasonable hour.

While Lovecraft began to regress to habits and schedules more befit-ting an untethered bachelor than a contently married man, outside forces continued to buffet him and Sonia Greene. Most of her savings were lost in poor investments.[26] The couple began selling their household items to pay for their daily needs. Between "genial smiles and puffs of unending cigars," Reverend George T. Baker, the rector of St. Gabriel's Protestant Episcopal Church, located on 331 Hawthorne Street and a few blocks from the couple's apartment, offered $350 for Greene's piano on August 24, 1924.[27] This was $150 less than the $500 price earlier advertised in the *Brooklyn Daily Eagle*.[28] Parting with the instrument must have pained Greene. For a self-made immigrant, the piano likely symbolized cultural and class aspirations and accomplishments. Lovecraft seemed to detect a predatory glee behind the pleasant face of the "round-collar'd rector."[29]

On the following morning, Greene stumbled and badly sprained her ankle on the subway. She resisted going to a physician for several days, possibly fearing losing time in her search for work or even worrying about paying for any treatment. Lovecraft collected a check for the piano from Baker and quickly cashed it to settle an outstanding forty-eight-dollar bill with their grocer. Later that same week, a desperate and still injured Greene insisted on journeying into Manhattan for an interview. She braced herself against her husband during the entire commute. Lovecraft desultorily looked for work, meeting with several advertising professionals. After one such "unsatisfactory conversation," he spent the remainder of his day on a "lone" tour "of colonial exploration" in Greenwich Village.[30] The "lost lanes of an elder city" proved to be preferable to the obligations of hearth and home, auguring his eventual approach to his marriage and his emotional commitment to his spouse.[31]

Shaking off the burdens of "undue domesticity" on August 31, Lovecraft traveled through Staten Island from tip to tip.[32] At Tottenville on the South Shore of the borough, he boarded a ferry crossing the Arthur Kill to Perth Amboy, New Jersey. He spent the day surveying that city's waterfront with its "quaint, dingy, huddle of eighteenth-century" buildings and the New Packer House, a historic downtown hotel with an original structure dating from before the American Revolution.[33] At twilight, he began the long trip back to Brooklyn.[34] While he enjoyed this outing, Greene remained home with her sprained ankle. This pattern continued throughout the summer and fall of 1924.

After several days cloistered in the apartment, Lovecraft received a telephone call from publisher J. C. Henneberger on September 7. He was visiting New York on business, and he invited Lovecraft to his hotel to discuss a "fine job."[35] Now a minority partner in *Weird Tales* after its financial restructuring, Henneberger hoped to publish a new humor magazine with Lovecraft as the editor. Lovecraft's letters reveal a sharp wit, unique comic sense, and surprising awareness of popular culture, suggesting that he could have mastered this genre with the right creative direction. Henneberger experienced his first publishing success with *College Humor*, and he might have hoped to repeat that accomplishment.

During the next two weeks, Lovecraft and Henneberger periodically met to discuss business plans for the magazine. Finally, after reviewing Lovecraft's sample jokes, Henneberger offered him the position with a starting weekly salary of forty dollars (and a guarantee of raising it to one hundred dollars) on September 18. Lovecraft understood that this opportunity would require his complete time and total creativity. He seemed prepared and eager for the challenge. To celebrate, Lovecraft patronized the Metropolitan Museum of Art, the American Museum of Natural History, and the Brooklyn Museum, proclaiming, "I darned near *live* at such places!"[36] Unfortunately, nothing ultimately arose from Henneberger's big promises and talk. In the end, he lacked sufficient funds or the drive to launch the periodical. Henneberger compensated Lovecraft for his preparatory writing with a sixty-dollar credit at the Charles Scribner's Sons bookstore. Cash-strapped, Lovecraft futilely attempted to convince the shop staff to convert it into hard money.[37]

Resigned to the collapse of his hopes of an editorship, Lovecraft resumed seeking out less desirable work. He obtained appointments with advertising agencies, an accounting firm, and even an electrical laboratory. The latter instilled the most optimism in him. After he interviewed for a position as a lamp tester, the hiring manager purportedly assured him that the job belonged to him unless a more experienced applicant appeared by the day's end. Steeling himself for the now seemingly inevitable disappointment, Lovecraft "bet such [a] one *will* apply!"[38] Apparently, one did. He never received an offer.

Harry Houdini arranged an introduction for Lovecraft with Brett Page, an executive at the Manhattan-based Newspaper Feature Service. A meeting took place with Page at his office at 241 West Fifty-Eighth Street near Columbus Circle on October 14, 1924. Although he had no freelance or full-time work to offer Lovecraft, Page advised him that he might make a good editor at a trade publication or as a reader or revisionist at a publishing house. His disappointment aside, Lovecraft appreciated the conversation and ranked the newsman to be "amazingly affable."[39] Meanwhile, Greene re-injured her ankle after "another stumble," and she suffered through her own discouraging interview at Saks & Company's brand-new flagship location on Fifth Avenue.[40] The couple found themselves lost "in a maze of poverty & uncertainty."[41]

Throughout this difficult period, Lovecraft continuously attempted to convince his aunts of the wisdom behind his relocating to New York. He regularly sent them books, newspaper clippings, and art prints discussing or portraying the history and architecture of the city. Since his aunts were already prejudiced against Greene, Lovecraft might have wished to downplay the severity of his and her economic situation in his letters to Providence. By this point, however, Greene likely had concluded that

Lovecraft's aunts were never going to support their marriage. A meager family inheritance continued to generate income, and Lovecraft was to receive fifteen dollars per week from those earnings. However, his aunts only sent him five dollars at sporadic intervals.[42] Lovecraft and Greene certainly could have benefited from his rightful share of the family assets. Given all this, his incessant and compulsive letter writing to his aunts seemed to aggravate his wife. She remarked that his letters contained nothing new and simply repeated "the same thing over and over again."[43] In a surprising display of self-awareness, he agreed.

Dwindling finances and domestic strife did not dampen Lovecraft's quest for neglected buildings and overlooked corners embodying the New York of past centuries. After reading a short *New York Times* article on the historic sites of Elizabeth, New Jersey, he began plotting a visit to the city. The feature's language describing "elm-shaded" mansions and "ancient streets" could have been written by Lovecraft himself.[44] Directly south of Newark, Elizabeth sits across the Newark Bay from Staten Island and peninsular Bayonne, New Jersey.

On October 10, 1924, Lovecraft rode a trolley through Staten Island to reach an Elizabeth-bound ferry. The "wealth of hideously decayed colonial houses" passed on the way to the Howland Hook Ferry terminal on the northwestern coast of the borough tickled his aesthetic and historical sensibilities.[45] When he later stepped onto "the dingy wharf" in Elizabeth, Lovecraft was repelled by finding himself amid "a Polish slum."[46] However, after taking a taxicab to the city's downtown and obtaining a historic guidebook, he was ready to wander through unknown streets.[47] Hoping to sense the aura hinted at in the newspaper piece and travel guide, he quickly lost track of time. At an underused and unpaved section of the original Essex and Middlesex Turnpike, he looked westward and watched a sunset over a relatively untouched expanse of fields and forests. A "riot of flame" and "glamour, paint[ed] the sky with a thousand streamers of weird" and "unimagined wildness."[48] Lovecraft swore that he would never forget that moment.

Determined to experience Elizabeth and its history at their fullest, he returned to the city early on the following day. From his seat on a trolley car, Lovecraft stared at a morning haze "akin to elfin magick" blanketing the downtown skyline.[49] The sight of "ancient gambrel roofs of the forefathers—good old English roofs" acted as a visual and emotional balm.[50] In his imagination, the colonial past was a time unadulterated by modernity and non-English peoples.

His itinerary began at the First Presbyterian Church of Elizabeth, a house of worship built between 1783 and 1793 after an earlier structure was burned by the British during the American Revolution in 1780.[51] Lovecraft studied its façade, steeple, and clock. The adjacent cemetery was filled with "crumbling brownstone slabs," some dating from as early as 1687 and bearing the surnames of a who's who—Ogden, Crane, Caldwell—of early New Jersey.[52] Throughout the day, Lovecraft encountered home after home, building after building from the eighteenth and nineteenth centuries all remarkably remaining in a region undergoing massive development. While atop a hill and looking toward the New Jersey countryside, he detected the gathering forces of suburbanization. "Most of this country is now doomed by prospective real-estate," he lamented.[53] In fact, many of the landmarks admired by Lovecraft that October are long gone. He documented the former homes of prominent founding families of Elizabeth—the Jouets, the De Harts, and the Hetfields—as still standing and exuding the spirit of a past era.[54] Although those buildings no longer exist, others noted by Lovecraft still remain, such as the Bonnell House, built in the late 1600s by Huguenot and Connecticut native Nathaniel Bonnell, and the Belcher-Ogden Mansion, the former home of both the royal governor of New Jersey Jonathan Belcher and later New Jersey governor Aaron Ogden.[55]

While ambling through downtown Elizabeth, a building just off the southeast corner of Scott Park, a rectangular green space named after Mexican-American War general, 1852 Whig presidential candidate, and former Elizabeth resident Winfield Scott drew Lovecraft's curiosity. As a writer, he was always searching for fodder for stories. This property at 1099 Elizabeth Avenue (Figure 14) struck him as "a terrible old house—a hellish place where night-black deeds must have been done in the early seventeen-hundreds."[56] Its unpainted façade, ivy-entangled second story, and steep roof exuded a sinister air. Lovecraft imagined that it was cursed, even "corpse-fed."[57]

This presumably derelict, if not abandoned, structure and his back-to-back visits to Elizabeth left an indelible impression. While riding the subway several days later, Lovecraft's thoughts returned to the "weird things" he had encountered in New Jersey.[58] Suddenly, a story began percolating in his mind. Upon returning home, Lovecraft immediately made notes and constructed an outline. Then, he spent several days focused on composing an initial draft. Over the next few months, he workshopped the piece with his aunt Lillian Clark and the Kalem Club. Lovecraft entitled it, "The Shunned House." The building in Elizabeth served as a model—the other one being in Providence—for the story's subject.

Figure 14. A "terrible old" building at 1099 Elizabeth Avenue in Elizabeth, New Jersey, served as a partial inspiration for Lovecraft's short story "The Shunned House." (Courtesy of the Local History Collection, Free Public Library of Elizabeth)

Sickness, madness, and early death afflicted occupants of "The Shunned House" for well over a hundred years. Selecting Providence as the story's geographic setting alluded to a homesickness on Lovecraft's part, to which he had already admitted in his correspondence with faraway literary acquaintances. The narrator and his uncle, Dr. Elihu Whipple, a kindly, bookish, bachelor—the eventual stock character type in Lovecraft's fiction and arguably a masque for himself—set out to uncover the dark, forbidding secrets of the home. Whipple was also the first name of Lovecraft's beloved paternal grandfather, Whipple Van Buren Phillips. "The Shunned House" remained unpublished during Lovecraft's lifetime.[59]

In Elizabeth, Lovecraft believed that he had stumbled upon a repository of colonial and early American architecture and history and a refuge from the ugliness and crassness he perceived in much of his contemporary world. This illusion was punctuated at several points during his leisurely explorations of the city. His interactions with the present day vividly revealed the more baleful aspects of his character. While fancying that he was walking in the eighteenth century, he stopped to read the cornerstone of a new building designed in the colonial style. Lovecraft was aghast to learn that it was a synagogue, Congregation B'nai Israel.[60] He complained that "low Poles" populated the city's industrial sections and that "niggers" were "thick in the byways."[61] Nonetheless, Lovecraft was reassured after seldomly passing members of such groups in Elizabeth's downtown and its middle-class and affluent residential neighborhoods.

In addition to its built environment, Elizabeth appealed to Lovecraft's belief in the superiority of Americans of Northern European and British descent. He approvingly observed that the city lacked the "taint of New York" and "its nasty cosmopolitanism."[62] This clearly referred to New York's large immigrant populations, specifically its Jewish demographic. According to Lovecraft, all Elizabeth's prominent and influential citizens were "native Yankees."[63] In reality, his overall impressions and accounts of the city were heavily blinkered. By 1924, Elizabeth was a multiethnic industrial city with a diverse population. Of its 95,783 inhabitants, 67,883, or approximately 70 percent, were immigrants or their children.[64]

While discovering the New York metropolitan region, Lovecraft also nurtured his social and artistic networks. Thanks to the efforts of his fellow Kalem Club members, he began to skim the orbit of other and sometimes more well-known and formative literary figures and circles. For instance, Samuel Loveman was good friends with poet Hart Crane, and he attempted to bridge the divide between the two writers. Following a Sunday dinner at Lovecraft and Greene's Parkside Avenue apartment on October 12, 1924, Loveman invited Lovecraft to join him in calling on Crane in his Columbia Heights building. There, the two friends found him recuperating from a multiday drinking spree, which concluded only when a fellow modernist poet E. E. Cummings came across a deeply intoxicated Crane in Greenwich Village and managed to get him home in a taxicab. Eventually, the three men, Lovecraft, Crane, and Loveman, headed toward the Brooklyn waterfront to revel in the nighttime vista of Manhattan. Standing along the East River shoreline, they stared at "the flaming arc of [the] Brooklyn Bridge," "the constellation of Manhattan lights," and "the glimmering beacons of slow-moving" ships.[65]

Although Lovecraft expressed disappointment with Crane's penchant for drunkenness and discomfort with his sexuality, he held nothing but high regard for his literary talent and artistic taste. Throughout their acquaintanceship—they certainly were never friends—Lovecraft displayed a surprising tolerance and sympathy toward Crane: he worried that the poet was squandering his natural gifts and drinking himself to an early grave. Crane voiced a much lower opinion of Lovecraft, referring to him as the "piping-voiced husband" of "Miss Sonia Green" [*sic*] and a "queer" individual.[66]

The incessant urban adventures and late-night escapades with his friends contributed to the worsening state of Lovecraft's domestic affairs. While his wife worked on and off, his failure or unwillingness to secure even minimal employment exacerbated the stress and instability in their household. On October 20, 1924, a shocking and unsettling event prevented Lovecraft from further evading his responsibilities. After spending the evening at his desk, he began preparing to retire around midnight. While taking a bath, he heard Greene scream from their bedroom. He soberly recounted dashing to his wife and finding her seized with "sudden gastric spasms."[67] Lovecraft called a taxicab and rushed her to Brooklyn Hospital. She did not leave until eleven days later, on October 31.[68]

Lovecraft visited Greene every day. He brought her small gifts and personal items to make her feel comfortable, buoy her spirits, and maybe even spoil her. Indulging his wife's interest in chess, he relearned it after not touching a piece for twenty years. (Lovecraft generally loathed games.) Her hospital room offered a pleasant view of Fort Greene Park, thirty acres redesigned by Frederick Law Olmsted and Calvert Vaux in 1867.[69] Lovecraft hoped that this visual amenity would speed his wife's recovery.

Greene was diagnosed with both a gastrointestinal and a nervous condition. An attending physician recommended an immediate removal of her gallbladder. Recalling his own mother's death from complications from a similar operation, Lovecraft demanded that they receive a second opinion. A female physician then examined Greene and offered a less dramatic course—a new diet and an extended period of rest. This must have come as a huge relief.[70]

With the couple's growing financial worries—a stunning reversal particularly for Greene—Lovecraft's inability to obtain any work, and likely other unsaid difficulties, Greene's mental health may have been fraying for some time. This might not have been her first episode of severe psychological distress. After learning about her hospitalization, George Kirk wrote to his fiancée that Greene had experienced "another breakdown."[71] Lovecraft witnessed his own mother's descent into mental illness and permanent institutionalization, and he possibly suffered horribly from living with a parent with such sickness. Although his letters present few hints, his wife's sudden collapse must have recalled this past personal trauma. He might have feared that he was about to live through it again. Consciously, he drew a clear parallel between Greene's gallbladder issues and his mother's. He did not wish to watch his spouse die in the same way.

Lovecraft's visits with his wife marked his first time inside a hospital in his own memory, and he reluctantly "acquired no little familiarity with the sights, sounds, and atmospheric touches" of it.[72] Medical facilities carried strong negative associations for him. Given that both his parents died in a mental hospital, this is not surprising. Throughout Greene's inpatient treatment, Lovecraft continued to attend the Kalem Club's weekly meetings and socialize with his fellow members. These were his friends: he likely confided in them and looked to them for advice and sympathy. Again, his correspondence says nothing on this, but one must assume that the Kalems provided him with emotional support and needed escape.

On Halloween, Greene returned to Parkside Avenue. While she was recovering in Brooklyn Hospital, Lovecraft kept their apartment tidy and attended to outstanding repairs. This resulted in his "first experience in lone housekeeping."[73] He wanted his wife to know "no difference from normal" upon her finally coming home.[74] When Greene walked through their apartment door, she entered a living room decorated with orange and black streamers and paper witches. Lovecraft had planned a small Halloween party with their neighbor and friend, Lenore Moran, as the sole attendee.[75]

Although presumably appreciative of her husband's attentiveness and her warm homecoming, Greene still required a period of convalescence. She read a newspaper listing for an affordable rest home on a farm just outside of Somerville, New Jersey, forty-odd miles from New York City. On November 9, 1924, Lovecraft and Greene rode the evening train to Somerville, where they were met by the son of the farm's owner. Lovecraft picturesquely described the automobile ride from the station as "whirling for moonlit miles" and "past fields where yellow farmhouse lights glittered."[76] The farm's proprietress and her dogs greeted the couple upon their arrival.[77] Then, she showed her guests their room and apprised them of the property's creature comforts. The farmhouse's book selection and its quiet environment impressed Lovecraft. Before retiring for the night, he and Greene strolled along the grounds.[78]

On the following morning, Lovecraft surveyed the surrounding landscape. "Distant purple hills" sat on the horizon.[79] The gables of nearby farmhouses peaked through the treetops. "Rows of golden sheaves" filled the fields.[80] He remarked that the countryside's demographics were "quite desirable," meaning that the visible local residents were native-born, nonethnic white Americans.[81] After lunch, he and Greene walked several miles into town. Much to his relief, his wife "gained a healthy colour which she ha[d] long lacked"—the result of just a single afternoon of fresh air and exercise.[82]

They spent the remainder of the day in Somerville, enjoying its village atmosphere and "quaint huddle" of architecture, specifically the Somerset County Courthouse, a white marble Beaux Arts structure built between 1907 and 1909.[83] As night began to fall, the couple went to the train station and parted ways. The rest home had arranged for a ride back for Greene. Lovecraft boarded a train to Bound Brook, New Jersey, and a connecting Reading Railroad line headed to Philadelphia. After several long months of intractable troubles, Lovecraft and Greene might have benefited from time alone and away from one another. Before bidding each other a temporary farewell, they had reached a critical and undoubtedly difficult decision: they would give up their home at Parkside Avenue in Brooklyn.[84]

Soon after checking into a room at the YMCA in downtown Philadelphia, Lovecraft began his "antiquarian exploration" of "Dr. Franklin's thriving town."[85] The night was always a welcoming time for his wanderings. He spent the next several days enraptured by the city's bounty of churchyards, parks, and "mazes of colonial brick alleys."[86] Never one to limit himself to the safe pathways cut for everyday tourists, he ventured to parts of Philadelphia well beyond its downtown and historic districts.

Lovecraft toured the house and gardens of John Bartram, the colonial-era botanist and horticulturist, in the southwest section of the city. He rose in the early morning hours to watch the sunrise over the Schuylkill River in Fairmount Park, a sprawling oasis beginning in the northwestern edge of downtown. He traveled to Germantown, the site of a Revolutionary War battle, in northwest Philadelphia, and as far as Chester, Pennsylvania, to seek out colonial-period homes and buildings.[87] He saw history unfurling everywhere before him. Originally intending to stay until November 13, he was so enchanted by this "piquant world of vanished yesterdays" that he decided to postpone his departure by another day.[88] Later reflecting upon his travels, Lovecraft wondered how he would ever forget such a place steeped in the past. He ranked this trip as his best and most memorable one to the City of Brotherly Love, seemingly forgetting his honeymoon there earlier that spring.[89]

This fascination did not rest solely on his passion for history and architecture. While visiting the city, Lovecraft was duly impressed by the color, cast, and pedigree of many of its residents. For him, Philadelphia differed from New York in a very specific way:

None of the crude, foreign hostility & underbreeding of New York—none of the vulgar trade spirit & plebeian hustle. A city of real American background—an integral & continuous outgrowth of a definite & aristocratic past instead of an Asiatic hell's huddle of the world's cowed, broken, inartistic, & unfit. What a poise—what a mellowness—what a character in the preponderantly Nordic faces![90]

Lovecraft believed that the "right" Americans predominantly populated and maintained structural control over Pennsylvania's largest city. Again, much like his perception of Elizabeth, New Jersey, this was completely erroneous. Philadelphia was an industrial powerhouse and shipping center with large Jewish, Italian, and Eastern European populations, of which many were immigrants or their direct descendants. Black Americans from the South had begun migrating to the city in large numbers, as well. Lovecraft uncharitably acknowledged this demographic fact, observing that "some of these ancient alleys have sunk to nigger slums."[91] Overall mesmerized by Philadelphia's rich colonial heritage, he chose to not to see the real city. The Philadelphia experienced by Lovecraft lay only in his imagination.[92]

When he finally returned to Brooklyn on November 14, 1924, Lovecraft was surprised to find Greene waiting for him. She had left Somerville earlier than initially planned. The farm had been a dreary place. The housekeeping was poor, and a fellow lodger, "a nervous woman" switching between "moroseness" and "loquacity," unnerved her.[93] Their apartment—which they recently determined to vacate as soon as possible to minimize expenses—would have to furnish Greene with her much-needed tranquility. Lovecraft's short vacation had ended.

After deciding to remain at Parkside Avenue until the end of the year, the couple began downsizing. Greene sold her books. An appraiser came to the apartment and offered far less money than anticipated for several relatively new pieces of furniture. These were hers, too. Meanwhile, Lovecraft insisted on retaining his antiques. (Greene preferred the term "dilapidated" to describe her husband's prized possessions.)[94] He counted on these items—a desk, a cabinet, a table—to recreate his Rhode Island scholar's cell. He had accomplished this feat in Flatbush, and he aimed to repeat it wherever he ultimately would reside. This was a conscious plan on Lovecraft's part. In a letter to Lillian Clark, he regretted that she would not see his "Providence-like study before it is broken up."[95]

Although Lovecraft prided himself on displaying a stoical acceptance of life's inevitable vagaries, and although he maintained an even tone in his correspondence with his family, the loss of his and Greene's home must have weighed heavily upon him. His choice of stationery—that from the Hotel Vendig in Philadelphia, where he and Greene retyped the Houdini story during their honeymoon—for several of his letters detailing the gradual dismantlement of their apartment might have suggested his true mental state and revealed an honest understanding that this chapter in his life was concluding.[96] Domesticity, a sense of rootedness, comfort, and familiarity, mattered dearly to Lovecraft. He never ceased longing for his beloved childhood home, his grandfather's Providence mansion. Now he was losing another home, the setting for hosting conversations with friends, the foundation for building a life with his spouse, and a place containing new warm memories.[97] Leaving Parkside Avenue must have painful. Greene had lived in the apartment since at least 1920. She might have felt as if she had lost everything—her daughter, her business, her savings, her health, now her home—since marrying Howard Phillips Lovecraft.

With a firm moving date of December 31, Lovecraft and Greene still did not have a new apartment leased or even a specific neighborhood targeted by late November. In New Jersey, Elizabeth promised more affordable rents and an "old American background" coupled with "the leisurely aura of good breeding" more harmonious to Lovecraft's personal sensitivities.[98] However, he realized that any job prospects and his literary life necessitated easy access to the subway and Manhattan. It was during this time that Lovecraft and Greene may have decided to live apart. His accounts of a housing search are largely in the first person, and he referred to wanting a small room alone for himself. Greene hoped to find a more comfortable rest home and return to the country, but insurance difficulties denied her the needed funds. Lovecraft believed that his wife's physical and mental health benefited from her staying in their own apartment and avoiding the "slithering human vermin" in the subway and the city at large.[99] A seventy-five-dollar check from his aunts was to last the couple until the end of the year.

Things were not entirely bleak. Thanks to the generosity of Samuel Loveman, Lovecraft received a lead (ultimately unsuccessful) for a position at a bookshop. An acquaintance visiting from Washington, D.C., beekeeper and author Edward Lloyd Sechrist, invited him to a literary salon at a Greenwich Village apartment. Although Lovecraft complained about the "quasi-intellectuals" in attendance, he enjoyed mingling with his fellow revelers and even picked up a tip about an opening at a publishing house.[100] Their neighbor, Lenore Moran, and James F. Morton helped Greene with her ongoing naturalization process. She and Lovecraft continued to enjoy movies, museums, and the occasional dinner out, with him even sampling ravioli for the first time.[101]

On Thanksgiving Day, the couple hosted George Kirk and Samuel Loveman. The dining table was tantalizingly cluttered with platters of turkey roasted with herbs and chestnuts, creamed cauliflower, sweet potatoes, "cranberry sauce with the soul of Rhode-Island bogs in it," "plum pudding such as [Washington] Irving never tasted," and other culinary delights.[102] To show their appreciation for such a delicious home-cooked meal, Kirk and Loveman promised to introduce Lovecraft to poet, critic, and contributor to the *Nation* Allen Tate later that holiday weekend.[103] After saying goodbye to their guests and settling down for the evening, Lovecraft and Greene were pleasantly surprised by the doorbell ringing. Rheinhart Kleiner, James F. Morton, and two other friends, Ernest Dench and his wife, Iva, had come calling. Still the consummate hosts, Lovecraft and Greene treated everyone to cake and tea and talked well past midnight with their friends. After several troubled months, Thanksgiving granted the pair a welcome respite, pleasant company, and a farewell of sorts to their early married life in Brooklyn.

On December 1, Lillian Clark arrived from Providence. She might have stayed with Lovecraft and Greene and later with friends in Mount Vernon, New York, a small city in southern Westchester County. Then, Greene received an unexpected job offer—her first real good news in some time— from a Cincinnati department store, Mabley & Carew, with a start date in the New Year. Now she would be leaving New York, and she wanted her husband to join her in Ohio. Lovecraft desired otherwise: he loathed the idea of living in the Midwest and preferred to stay near his friends. One can only speculate how this affected Greene as she prepared for a long-term, if not permanent, departure.[104]

Lovecraft began searching for new housing with assistance from his aunt, and he soon located a room at 169 Clinton Street in Brooklyn Heights. To him, the neighborhood was a "region of brick" and "brownstone, within sight of the sea" and "with an old-world air of musty stateliness."[105] Samuel Loveman residing nearby at 78 Columbia Heights provided the area with an added attraction. "The chimes" of a nearby Gothic church "seemed to sing a welcome."[106]

On December 31, 1924, Lovecraft and Greene left 259 Parkside Avenue, their first home together, for Clinton Street. The room at this new address was largely filled with Lovecraft's own furniture, household items, and bric-a-brac that had been shipped from Providence earlier that year. There, he would rebuild his writer's nook. Whatever Greene was not bringing to Cincinnati or had not been sold was placed in storage. Then, she boarded a train for Ohio at Grand Central Terminal, leaving a day earlier than originally scheduled. This was not likely an auspicious parting. After seeing his wife off, Lovecraft headed to the Upper West Side and George Kirk's apartment for a New Year's Eve party.[107] He was a bachelor again.

7

███

"A Pleasing Hermitage"

WHILE HIS WIFE WAS REBUILDING her career in Cincinnati, Lovecraft settled into his new quarters at 169 Clinton Street. Once a desirable and wealthy district, Brooklyn Heights was bleeding middle- and upper-class residents by 1925. Many of its formerly grand rowhouses and mansions were cut into small apartments and boarding and rooming houses. Parroting a perennial refrain of struggling writers, artists, and creative individuals, Lovecraft understood that "the leanness of [his] purse" required concessions regarding his choice of housing.[1]

Although admitting to a "general seediness of the neighbourhood," he found his second-floor room at the northwest corner of the building to carry a Victorian-era charm.[2] Equally important, the forty-dollar monthly rent fell within his limited budget.[3] Lovecraft's three-story rooming house, likely with garden-level and attic rooms, stood at the intersection of Clinton and State Streets and one block north of Atlantic Avenue, a shopping corridor transitioning into a hub for Arabic and Middle Eastern residents. The ornamental flourishes of the building's exterior windows and doorways embodied the area's vanishing grandeur. Approximately twenty-five people were lodging at 169 Clinton Street (Figure 15).[4] Most of Lovecraft's fellow tenants were natural-born citizens, but several were Canadian, English, Norwegian, and Syrian immigrants. An Irish landlady, Matilda Burns, lived on the premises and managed the entire household.

Lovecraft's room had a high ceiling, white molding, blue wallpaper, and paneled window seats. These interior details combined with his antique

Figure 15. Lovecraft began renting a room at 169 Clinton Street in Brooklyn Heights in late December 1924. He grew to loathe the building, his fellow tenants, and his landlady. (Courtesy of the Municipal Archives, City of New York)

furniture, treasured books, and writerly paraphernalia allowed him to design a "tasteful library-study effect."[5] A desk sat between two windows, granting him a "generous view" of the street and its "ancient brick houses" whenever he glanced up from his work.[6] Several freestanding bookcases lined the walls. Books and papers covered a large table in the center of the floor. A reclining Morris chair and a tall reading lamp faced the two corner windows. On the wall opposite, a sofa with a folding bed rested between a pair of alcoves. These compartments served as separate dressing and washing areas. Art and curios added warmth, color, and distraction. One or more paintings by his deceased mother hung in the room. Lovecraft's new home "admirably" matched his personal taste and evoked memories of his beloved grandfather's house at 454 Angell Street in Providence.[7] As a whole, this meticulously arranged environment formed "a pleasing hermitage" from the noise and clamor of New York City.[8] His fellow Kalem Club members concurred and applauded Lovecraft on his ability to create an "exceptionally classic" and "restful" living space exuding "a mellow sedateness."[9]

Upon moving to Brooklyn Heights, Lovecraft began keeping a diary of his activities. This primarily served as a record or checklist for his correspondence with his Providence family. The minutiae documented in these letters—meals eaten, people met, chores completed—often required postscripts scribbled on the backs of already sealed envelopes. Quickly increasing in volume and length, these letters showed a compulsive need to report his day-to-day existence to his aunts or a request by them for such dispatches. Meanwhile, a specific detail in his diary hinted at a possible mental distance growing alongside the geographical separation between Lovecraft and Sonia Greene: he listed his aunt Lillian Clark—not his wife—as his emergency contact.[10] This might imply that he carried the diary on his person as a form of identification, as well.

Less than two weeks after her departure for Cincinnati, Greene visited Lovecraft at Clinton Street for several days beginning on January 11, 1925. Revealingly, she secured her own room in the building for the length of her stay. (Lovecraft noted that it was the very same one occupied by his Aunt Lillian earlier that month.)[11] Although their sleeping arrangements suggested a discord or freeze in their marital relations, Greene appeared eager to spend time with her husband and help him establish his new writer's abode. The couple soon slipped into their former domestic patterns. They dined at Italian restaurants. They attended a Broadway musical. They explored Green-Wood Cemetery. Its beautifully landscaped grounds and historic memorials likely appealed to Lovecraft's appreciation for craft and a well-built urban space.[12]

Braving an evening ice storm, Lovecraft and Greene walked from Clinton Street to see their mutual friend Samuel Loveman's new room at nearby 78 Columbia Heights. Still recovering from her health scares of the previous year, Greene grew "fatigued" by such physical exertion during the inclement weather.[13] After chaperoning her home in a taxicab, Lovecraft ventured back into the night with his friends, Loveman and George Kirk. The three men crossed the Brooklyn Bridge into Chinatown and stayed out until dawn. When presented with the choice of sharing a quiet night with his long-distance spouse or embarking upon a nocturnal escapade with his literary companions, he invariably preferred the latter. This also could have explained Greene's "fatigue."

Still, Lovecraft tried to be a caring husband in his own way. When Greene enlisted his wordsmith skills in composing a lecture that she was to present to Mabley & Carew department store managers and executives, he strung a fresh ribbon into his typewriter and began polishing her draft. He always supported his wife's career, notably during its lower points. On January 15, the night before Greene was scheduled to take a train to Cincinnati, Lovecraft treated her to a performance by Harry Houdini at the Hippodrome Theatre, a 5,300-seat entertainment venue on Sixth Avenue between West Forty-Third and Forty-Fourth Streets.[14] Earlier in the week, Lovecraft called his client, the famous escape artist, about getting tickets. Houdini obliged his ghostwriter with a complimentary pair of choice seats.[15] He was in the middle of a six-week run at the Hippodrome with a program centered on debunking mediums and spiritualists.[16] A staunch rationalist, Lovecraft presumably relished this element of Houdini's act.

After accompanying his wife to Grand Central Terminal on January 16, Lovecraft began shopping for writing materials in Manhattan. Earlier in the week, he and other members of the Kalem Club had surprised Samuel Loveman with an antique bookcase and bric-a-brac to celebrate his new home and his thirty-eighth birthday. However, Lovecraft and Frank Belknap Long wanted to present Loveman with pens, stationery, ink blotters, and other sundries requisite for any bibliophile. While Loveman was at work that afternoon, Lovecraft sneaked into his home. He carefully arranged all the newly purchased items. Later that evening, Lovecraft hosted a Kalem Club meeting at Clinton Street. Afterward, the group asked Loveman to show them his room. When he turned on the light and welcomed his friends inside, he was startled to see his desk fully supplied. Loveman's "rapture was of appropriate magnitude," and it demonstrated the warmth and solidarity within this literary band.[17] Although all struggling to fashion lives of books and ideas in New York, Kalem Club members always exhibited cheer when one of their number encountered success and empathy when grappling with failure. Despite his own ingrained prejudices, Lovecraft held a deep and genuine fondness for Samuel Loveman.

Relocating to Ohio unfortunately failed to ameliorate Sonia Greene's stubborn health problems. After receiving treatment for a longstanding nasal cavity issue, she learned that surgery ultimately would be necessary.[18] When she briefly returned to New York between February 3 and February 6, she discovered—presumably not to her delight—that Lillian Clark would be sleeping overnight in another room at Clinton Street before returning to Providence on the following day. Lovecraft appeared to be simultaneously oblivious and attentive to his wife's struggles. After Greene asked him to dine with her in Manhattan, he proceeded to invite along his aunt and several Kalem Club members. However, he did skip the customary Wednesday meeting with his friends to spend the night with Greene, citing her health as the reason behind his absence.

On her last evening in Brooklyn, Greene began complaining of severe eye pain. Hoping to mitigate her agony, she lay on the edge of Lovecraft's foldout sofa bed with an electric heater blowing on her face throughout the night. When Lovecraft contacted Frank Belknap Long's father, a dentist, in the morning, he referred Greene to a Midtown Manhattan optical specialist. A cinder was found and extracted from her eye. Shortly thereafter, when Lovecraft and Greene arrived at Pennsylvania Station to catch her train to Cincinnati, her ill luck continued unabatedly: she discovered that her sleeping berth had been sold to another passenger.[19] Regardless of their true feelings concerning the couple's marriage, even Lovecraft's aunts themselves were moved by their niece-in-law's relentless misfortune. Annie Gamwell wrote a consolatory note to Greene, who, in turn, shared her gratefulness for such "solicitude" in that and "other communications" with Lovecraft.[20] Addressing Lillian Clark's own worries, he assured her that his wife had arrived safely in Cincinnati and that she was steadily recovering.[21]

While Lovecraft suffered hardships with Greene, he shared joys with the Kalem Club. In late January, George Kirk left his rental at West 106th Street in Manhattan and moved into a third-floor room directly above Lovecraft at 169 Clinton Street. The two men would see each other nearly every day while they both resided at that same address. When Lovecraft missed a weekly Kalem meeting during Greene's visit in early February, Kirk slipped a note beneath his door. James F. Morton had been named the first curator of the newly formed Paterson Museum in Paterson, an industrial city on the Passaic River in New Jersey. Morton first had learned about the civil service exam for the position through an acquaintance of a Blue Pencil Club member.[22] Lovecraft was thrilled for his friend. In his opinion, Morton finally earned for himself "just the intellectual, social," and "financial niche he should always have occupied."[23]

On many evenings and often well into the night, Lovecraft joined his fellow tenant Kirk, fellow Brooklyn Heights resident Loveman, or other Kalem Club confidants for winding conversations at diners or cafés. One mainstay of the group that winter was the Double R Coffee House at 112 West Forty-Fourth Street between Sixth Avenue and Broadway, an establishment owned by former President Theodore Roosevelt's sons, Theodore Jr., Archibald, and Kermit, his daughter Ethel and her husband Richard Derby, and Roosevelt's cousin Philip. The aroma of freshly roasted coffee beans wafted through the seating area of the Double R. House letterhead and envelopes sat in small caddies at each table, and a small library of dictionaries and encyclopedias was available for perusal by word-minded customers.[24] The Kalems, specifically Kirk, Kleiner, and Loveman, found the atmosphere "exceeding[ly] dear" to their aesthetic sense.[25] Inspired by the setting, the friends occasionally wrote poetry while sipping their coffee. Lovecraft penned two poems at the Double R's tables, including an untitled ode to the café itself.[26]

As a gay man, Samuel Loveman might have perceived the Double R to be welcoming and refreshing for a reason distinctly different than that of his friends. The coffeehouse reportedly offered a tolerant environment for queer men and women. George Kirk mentioned its reputation in a letter to his fiancée:

> If you had been longer in NYC you'd know that there are many boys and many girls both male and female. My dear Double R is claimed to be a hangout for these half and halfers.[27]

Throughout the 1920s, all-night coffee shops and eateries often presented queer men—conservatively dressed professionals and flamboyant drag queens alike—with safe third spaces. Since Lovecraft and his friends frequented such spots at late hours, they likely witnessed these men mingling, cruising, or simply chatting over coffee.[28] Needless to say, Lovecraft would have refrained from including such unexpected observations and encounters in his letters to his aunts.

Although Lovecraft appeared sanguine about his wife's prospects in Cincinnati even after her troubled stay with him in early February, Greene's situation there had quickly deteriorated by the end of that month. Since the beginning of the year, she had been hospitalized twice in Ohio.[29] She had failed to adjust to the work environment at the Mabley & Carew department store, finding it "hostile" and "exacting."[30] Finally, Greene was dismissed or quit. Absolving his wife of any culpability, Lovecraft blamed "quibbling executives" and "invidious inferiors."[31] Regardless of the true explanation behind his wife's departure, she was once again unemployed.

Greene retreated to Brooklyn on February 23, 1925, and remained at Clinton Street until March 19.[32] While Lovecraft expressed nothing but sympathy for his wife's travails, his letter announcing this unwelcome turn of events to his aunt Annie Gamwell suggests that his family might have posited a very different reason behind Greene's ongoing difficulties. Namely, all fault rested on her alone. Lovecraft emphasized that his wife's last communication to him before losing her position "sheds so much light on the hard conditions" suffered by her.[33] He even enclosed her letter with his own to his aunts. He stacked up details to present Greene in a positive light. She had obtained a short-term hat-design job to bring in badly needed money. She had honored his housekeeping routines, and she allowed him to maintain "the parlour-study atmosphere" of his "marvellous room."[34]

Unspoken in his correspondence with his aunts was that Lovecraft likely appreciated his wife's companionship. Greene stopped at the grocer for food when the couple dined at home, always wanting to ensure that he adhered to a proper diet. She shared in the errands and chores. When his friends dropped by, Greene acted as a hostess and brewed them tea. All the while, her presence seemed to place few limitations on Lovecraft's incessant socializing. Kalem Club members would call on each other at their respective homes throughout the week and hold their official meeting every Wednesday night. Lovecraft continued his daylong excursions and midnight rambles, often with George Kirk as his main partner.

Although buffeted by stressful circumstances—irregular employment, little money, tight quarters, and ill health—Lovecraft and Greene's marriage seemed stable during this brief period of renewed cohabitation. When she turned forty-two, Lovecraft presented his wife with a poem entitled, "To Xanthippe on Her Birthday—March 16, 1925." During their courtship, she often signed her letters with that sobriquet and addressed him as Socrates. Lovecraft's pet name for his wife might have alluded to a private joke about her temper: ancient sources and later cultural traditions held Xanthippe to be a tempestuous and combative woman focusing her ire on her long-suffering husband, Socrates. A poem continuing this private medley of flattery and flirtation was an intimate gift. Lovecraft still held a flame for Greene.[35]

Three days after her birthday, she once again quit Brooklyn, this time for Saratoga Springs, New York, a small resort city north of the state capital, Albany, famed for horse racing and therapeutic mineral spas. Following the previous autumn's medical advice, Greene hoped to rest in a far less dense and hectic environment. She rented a room in the home of a female physician, apparently carrying childcare duties as partial payment for her board.[36] The household was "refined" and "scholarly," and her landlady's young son was full of "intelligence" and "amiability."[37] However, this added expense and the lack of a predictable income diminished Lovecraft and Greene's already negligible finances. When their household was originally split in two, Greene promised to pay a percentage of the rent at Clinton Street. This proved to be increasingly impossible.[38]

With his wife largely absent, Lovecraft truly lived alone for the first time in his entire life. As a child and later a young man, he had shared a household with his mother, and she managed his affairs. After she was institutionalized, his aunts effectively took her place of "domestic control."[39] Then, Greene—perhaps both knowingly and unknowingly—succeeded into that role upon their marriage. Lovecraft had always expected women to take care of him, whether that be planning his meals or ensuring that his bills were paid.[40] When left to fend for himself in Brooklyn, what did he do? He looked to his aunts. In the stream of letters to Providence, he solicited their opinions and advice on the most simple and mundane decisions. Lacking an account at a local bank, he mailed them checks to deposit and cash. He shipped them shirts and shoes needing mending and repairs. Considering that he lived in New York with its high concentration of tailors and cobblers, this rather absurd exercise demonstrated the intensity of his reliance on his family.

A renewed bachelorhood and dwindling funds began to shape Lovecraft's diet. He bragged about his frugal and uniformly unhealthy food choices. He would stretch out a can of baked beans, a small loaf of bread, and "a goodly chunk of cheese" over his three daily meals, proudly stating that such "home dining" cost no more than thirty cents per day.[41] Lacking kitchen access in the rooming house, he would heat food over a Sterno stove, a portable burner fueled by canned heat, in his room and then keep any leftovers in a covered cup. Occasionally, he would substitute the beans with canned spaghetti or corned beef or treat himself to fresh fruit or cookies. Once or twice each week, he would eat at an Automat or a diner, assiduously limiting his bill to twenty-five cents. When he joined the

Kalems at a restaurant, they frequently insisted on picking up his tab. His friends were aware of his money troubles.

Such a barebones diet coupled with frequent long walks contributed to a sizable weight loss for Lovecraft. When he and Greene first married, she found her new husband to be "gaunt" and "hungry-looking," and she aimed to keep him well fed.[42] Naturally tall and lean, he had bulked up to two hundred pounds by the end of 1924. Rheinhart Kleiner remembered being "amazed at his girth" when climbing the stairs of a Brooklyn subway platform behind him.[43] By the spring of 1925, Lovecraft had slimmed down to a weight range of between 145 and 150 pounds.[44] He proudly related his need to have his pants brought in and to purchase narrower shirt collars.

His aunts seemed to voice justifiable concern about his dramatic weight change and his poor eating habits. He brushed off their worries as "scolding letters."[45] Greene "protested fearfully" at her husband's "alarming decline."[46] Even Frank Belknap Long's mother "lectured" him about his cadaverous appearance whenever he visited the family.[47] He claimed that he physically felt "twice as well" and that he no longer resembled an "old porpoise."[48] Lovecraft fixated on his weight for the remainder of his life, possibly struggling with a distorted body image.

Meanwhile, his outrage at New York's racial and ethnic diversity and its weakening effect on the de facto color line grew louder. While traveling to Florida by train, his aunt Annie Gamwell reported upon the strict racial segregation in the American South. Lovecraft delightfully approved of such government policy:

> The separation of people & niggers at the stations is an excellent idea—which ought to be practiced on the Harlem subway trains here—& it would please me always to alight at the quaint & picturesque town of WHITE.[49]

Ironically, he likely only ventured to Harlem to see James F. Morton, a committed advocate for civil rights for Black Americans. Lovecraft perceived his contemporary urban environment as marred, even polluted, by the presence of non-white residents, which he even further narrowly defined as individuals exclusively descended from Northern Europeans and British Islanders.

In a later letter to Gamwell, Lovecraft lauded white Southerners for enforcing racially divided public spaces, and he envied "the Jim Crow principle" for making "life endurable where blacks abound."[50] He bemoaned New York City's inability or unwillingness to import de jure segregation and extend it to other minorities:

I wish they'd apply it in N.Y. both to niggers & to the more Asiatic types of puffy, rat-faced Jew. Either stow 'em out of sight or kill 'em off—anything so that a white man may walk the streets without shuddering & nausea![51]

This remark was sandwiched between a paragraph about his search for freelance writing and editorial projects and a description of newspaper and magazine clippings exchanged between him and his aunt, intimating the disturbingly offhand and sadly everyday nature of such comments within their family.

Since his wife was convalescing in Saratoga Springs, Lovecraft's aunts proposed that he visit them in late March or early April. He brusquely swatted down this idea, melodramatically explaining that he could not endure returning to Providence unless it was permanent. If he even caught "a temporary glimpse" of his native city, he would resemble a sailor swept away "into the illimitable blackness of an alien sea" after being in "sight of his own harbour."[52] After slightly more than a year of marriage and life in New York, Lovecraft began admitting that he desired nothing more than to come home to Rhode Island. He just could not justify it yet.

A dearth of monetary resources failed to stymie his rich social life anchored by the Kalem Club. While literally wearing socks until they fell apart to avoid laundry bills, Lovecraft embarked upon a short, yet long-planned getaway to Washington, D.C., with George Kirk. An advertised five-dollar roundtrip fare proved to be far too tantalizing to pass up. After an overnight train ride, Kirk and Lovecraft arrived at the nation's capital in the early morning of April 12, 1925. Their friend, the apiary enthusiast and writer Edward Lloyd Sechrist, met them on the platform, looking "debonair" wearing a broad-brimmed hat and brandishing a walking stick.[53] While cutting through Union Station, Lovecraft marveled at its "noble and impressive waiting-room" with its vaulted ceilings based on the Baths of Diocletian in ancient Rome and designed by Chicago architect Daniel Burnham.[54] This was his first time in Washington.

After exploring the National Mall and the exteriors of the United States Capitol, Smithsonian Institution Building, and other grand public structures, the trio planned to meet another writing colleague, Anne Tillery Renshaw, and her female companion, at the Washington Monument. Renshaw owned a car and offered to serve as a chauffeur for her out-of-town guests. A whirlwind tour of the capital region commenced.[55] When the group passed through the historic neighborhood of Georgetown, Lovecraft found the natural flow of its streetscape to be a refreshing contrast to

Washington's meticulous design. Originally conceived by French engineer Pierre Charles L'Enfant and later adapted by surveyor Andrew Ellicott, the city's strict grid was bisected by diagonal grand avenues connecting a system of public squares and circles.[56] At the time of Lovecraft's jaunt, Georgetown's architecturally significant, yet aging buildings and homes were being gradually rediscovered and rehabilitated by federal employees, journalists, and white-collar professionals.[57]

Next, Lovecraft and his friends crossed into Virginia and visited the Fairfax County Courthouse, Mount Vernon, and other sites. He relished the landscape of the Old Dominion. Its "hill, valley, and forest scenery of the most striking magnificence" was a welcome change from New York.[58] The neoclassical style of the region's public buildings and monuments appealed to Lovecraft's aesthetic preferences. Standing before the Memorial Amphitheater in Arlington National Cemetery, he fancied that he was experiencing "a dream of the brightest scenes of classical antiquity suddenly crystallised into a glorious and titanick reality."[59] Lost in the excitement of sightseeing, he almost missed his return train that afternoon. (Kirk remained in the capital to conduct book-buying business). As the engine pulled away from Union Station, Lovecraft reflected upon the day and knew that Washington would become "a fragrant memory."[60]

Although his short trip provided him with a desired escape from New York, the city itself never lacked distractions. With George Kirk living directly above him and Samuel Loveman residing within easy walking distance, Lovecraft continued to be lured away from his desk by his friends. Nearly every diary entry that spring chronicles time dawdling at a bookstore, wandering through a museum, chatting at a diner, or lounging in one Kalem Club member or another's home. His day-to-day life—an overabundance of leisure time and the reliable presence of friends—more resembled that of a college student than a married man.

On the morning of May 16, 1925, Lovecraft was awoken by the radiator pipes banging loudly in his room.[61] This was a message from his upstairs neighbor, Kirk. Earlier into their shared time living at 169 Clinton Street, the two men developed a unique signal system by rattling the pipes in their respective rooms. Seemingly caring little for its effect on the peace and quiet of their fellow tenants, they regularly communicated with one another in this manner.

Kirk was enlisting Lovecraft in a book-hunting expedition. Shortly thereafter, Samuel Loveman arrived and joined the campaign, as well. Then, the three friends journeyed into Manhattan to an estate sale at 10 East Fortieth Street, a mansion practically kitty-corner to the New York Public

Library at Bryant Park.[62] Kirk desperately needed to stock the shelves of his new business, Martin's Book Shop. He and his partner, Martin Kamin, another Cleveland transplant, had just started their enterprise at 97 Fourth Avenue on Book Row. This was seven blocks of used and rare bookstores along Fourth Avenue, stretching south from just below Union Square to Astor Place.[63]

Browsing the wares being auctioned off—furniture, paintings, and objets d'art—left Lovecraft crestfallen. He inspected the recently deceased's private library with its oak wainscoting, paneled ceiling, and built-in shelves. Realizing that such a "shrine and retreat of taste" was likely to be dismantled by the mansion's eventual new owners, Lovecraft was reminded of his family's loss of his grandfather's home when he was a teenager of fourteen.[64] He saw "the fall of 454 all over again" and felt the anguish of that experience "still fresh after twenty-one years."[65] Breaking away from his melancholy reflection, Lovecraft helped his friends carry "armful after armful" of "splendid and tasteful" books to a pair of taxicabs idling at the curb.[66] After unloading the volumes at Kirk's store and elated by their successful outing, the three men rewarded themselves by patronizing his fellow Fourth Avenue booksellers. There might have been more printed treasures to find.

The tireless socializing began to erode Lovecraft's ability to concentrate on his writing. Hoping to recalibrate his energies to focus on his work—a purported primary driver behind his decision to remain in New York and apart from his spouse—he plotted to curtail the spontaneous "daily dropping-in and cafeteria loafing" shared between him and his friends.[67] He decried his convivial habits as the "death to any personal intellectual life or creative accomplishment."[68] Possibly still shaken by the estate sale and the memories it bestirred, Lovecraft embraced his resolution immediately on the following day of May 17.

Rising at noon—not an unusual hour for him—he gathered a stack of books and walked to Fort Greene Park for "a solitary open-air" afternoon.[69] The park sat roughly one mile further eastward into Brooklyn, minimizing any chance of Lovecraft running into friends and being roped into an adventure. Passing the day in a shady and isolated spot, he lost himself in his reading until twilight. Later, he treated himself to a pasta dinner at his favorite restaurant, John's Spaghetti House, and then stopped at a grocer to stock up food for several days. He was determined to remain in his room and work until the coming Wednesday's Kalem Club meeting.[70] Foreseeing unannounced guests, Lovecraft carried a chair and several books into one of his room's alcoves. This allowed him to keep the lamps off in its main quarter and present the appearance of him being out. The alcove's light was not visible from the hallway or street.

As predicted, Lovecraft heard a knock on his door that evening. Ensconced in his hiding space, he quietly ignored it. When Samuel Loveman called on the following night, Lovecraft answered wearing a dressing gown and slippers, and he made certain that his friend saw the papers and books scattered about the room. Loveman took the hint and departed without chatting "by the hour as usual."[71] This new regimen of self-imposed isolation did not last long. On that very same night, Lovecraft hosted Kirk—also "loafing about" in his sleepwear—to a dinner of canned pasta served on his "best blue china."[72] Throughout that week, he proceeded to fraternize with various members of the Kalem Club. Lovecraft could not resist the company of friends.

A dark event unsettled his literary sanctuary on May 26, 1925. After several days of shuffling about his room without getting properly dressed, Lovecraft realized that he had been robbed. While he had been sleeping, a burglar had forced open a door connecting his closet alcove with the adjoining rented room and stolen his best clothes (three suits and a new overcoat), his wife's suitcase, and an expensive radio set that he was storing for Samuel Loveman.[73] A suit airing out on a chair escaped the thieves, leaving him with a single set of clothes. Having not left his main room for three full days, he was uncertain of the exact time or even date of the crime. His pattern of sleeping through much of the day and working late into the night contributed to his confusion. It was now one-thirty in the morning.

Lovecraft dared not wake his landlady or rouse the other lodgers at such an ungodly hour. He wondered if he should even contact the police. But he needed to tell someone, so he settled down at his desk and gathered his thoughts. Then, he returned to a letter that he had begun composing earlier to his aunt Lillian Clark and immediately added all the known details. After sealing it in an envelope, he read until the household began to stir.[74]

At that point in the morning, Lovecraft informed his landlady, Matilda Burns, about the burglary, and the police were notified. Together, he and Burns were able to pinpoint the general time of the robbery. After a night spent writing, Lovecraft had retired at six or seven o'clock on the morning of May 24. Burns had learned that the tenants in the room adjacent to his had absconded without paying their rent around noon on that same day.[75] While awaiting the authorities, Lovecraft called Loveman. Although upset at the loss of the radio equipment (on which he still owed money), he was relieved to learn that the thieves neglected to steal a book collection that he also had entrusted to Lovecraft.[76] All other material concerns were incidental to the bibliophile.

Eventually, a police detective with a "brisk voice" and "steely-blue eyes" arrived at Clinton Street and took statements from Lovecraft and Burns.[77] He asked for a description of Lovecraft's clothes and the suspects, and he promised "his very best."[78] On the following day, Burns found the hangers for Lovecraft's stolen suits and the contents of his wife's suitcase in the vacant room. Her son examined the lock on the connecting door. Although the device itself was broken, Lovecraft had failed to deadbolt the door on his side. Sheepishly, he acknowledged that the shared entrance *ought* to have been" properly "barred" and secured.[79] The detective never had bothered to inspect the rooms, tacitly demonstrating the futility of recovering the property and the low priority of investigating such a crime.

Nonetheless, Lovecraft approached his misfortune with admirable equanimity. The robbery occurred just as he was attempting to readjust his attitude and lifestyle in relation to New York. After nearly five full months separated from his wife, socializing at the expense of his writing, and growing alienated from the city, he was finally "mustering up the forces of optimism, industry," and "reasserted individuality."[80] Undeterred, Lovecraft believed that he commanded the essential resources to continue to carve out a writer's life. With pen and paper and private time and space, he declared that "there's life left in the old man yet!"[81] He also understood that the entire episode could have concluded far worse. The thieves never entered his main room, leaving his art, books, and himself "unmolested" and unharmed.[82]

Lovecraft even poked fun at his temporary state in a letter to Lillian Clark, inking an illustration (Figure 16) of himself wearing only a belt, gloves, glasses, and a hat. Scraggly, knee-length hair and beard hid his nakedness. Supported by a cane, the cartoon Lovecraft walks past a storefront of Browning, King & Company, a national chain with locations in downtown Brooklyn and Providence. Alongside suit coats, the men's clothier's well-known advertisement—a crying infant paired with the caption "I Want My Clothes!"—stood in the display windows. This illustration was followed by lists cataloging Lovecraft's pilfered possessions and those remaining and with headings referencing a contemporary popular song, "Yes! We Have No Bananas."[83]

As to be expected, Lovecraft never recovered his clothing. He spent the next several months scouring Manhattan and Brooklyn for suits fitting both his exacting sartorial tastes (fabric with no patterns and jackets with three buttons) and his extremely tight budget. He documented his impressions of

Figure 16. Burglars stole most of Lovecraft's clothing in May 1925. He sketched a mock self-portrait in a letter, poking fun at his own poor luck. (Courtesy of the John Hay Library, Brown University)

the inventory and pricing of different haberdashers on the blank sides of their respective business cards. While Howard's Men's and Young Men's Clothes on Flatbush Avenue offered "really good stuff," Franklin Clothes sold suits befitting "prize-fight hangers-on" and "race track touts."[84]

Having a single suit only modestly impacted Lovecraft's busy calendar. In fact, on the very day when he discovered and reported the burglary, he rode the subway into Manhattan, dropped by George Kirk's bookstore on Fourth Avenue, joined Frank Belknap Long for lunch at his family's home, went to the movies, read in the New York Public Library, and lastly entertained Kirk and Samuel Loveman at 169 Clinton Street near midnight. Lovecraft proudly characterized this agenda as controlling his "old vacuously gregarious spirit."[85]

Needing to replenish his wardrobe also failed to prod him to look seriously for work. He had stopped pretending to pursue that exercise well before Sonia Greene left for Ohio. Aside from the random small checks from *Weird Tales*, he relied on continual support from his wife and to a much lesser degree his aunts.[86] Nonetheless, when the occasional easy opportunity came his way, Lovecraft mustered up the energy to capitalize upon it. At a Kalem Club meeting held during the same week of the burglary, Arthur Leeds spoke to him about writing freelance for a trade journal currently engaging Leeds himself.

This project essentially constituted a scheme: a writer would pen an advertisement for a business in the form of a short article—an advertorial in contemporary parlance—for the publisher. Next, a salesman would approach the particular business with the article. If the business agreed to order periodicals under the publisher's imprint, then the advertorial would be placed in said magazines. The original freelancer would receive a percentage of any sales. Leeds claimed that he was making his living from such an ethically questionable endeavor. Oddly enough, as someone who instinctively bristled at considering commercial demands regarding his own fiction, Lovecraft was instantly intrigued by Leeds's proposition, judging it to be "an excellent hack field for the pure writer."[87]

When the Kalem meeting broke up, Lovecraft and Leeds rode the subway downtown together and then discussed the freelance venture at length over coffee. Leeds promised to provide him with initial tips and guidance and to send him the first assignment within several weeks. Before even beginning this project, Lovecraft expressed dejection over its likelihood of materializing or resulting in a sizable payment. Thus far in New York, all his past "business vistas" had transformed into "mirages," resulting in him berating himself for "any naïve enthusiasm."[88]

Lovecraft would spend much of June and July drafting and tweaking the advertising articles for Leeds, even meeting him at his Columbus Circle office to review them. In the end, Leeds only placed a single piece by Lovecraft, one promoting the Alexander Hamilton Book Shop in Paterson, New Jersey. It does not appear to have been published. The entire scheme collapsed by late July. Lovecraft's pessimism proved to have been justified.[89]

8

⁞⁞⁞

"Circle of Aesthetic Dilettante"

IN EARLY JUNE 1925, Sonia Greene finally left Saratoga Springs for Brooklyn. Her lengthy convalescence accomplished the desired results of improving her mental and physical health. For nearly seven weeks between June 9 and July 24, she and Lovecraft would share a household. This would be their longest time together since their first year of marriage. The "turmoil" and "throngs" of the metropolis wore on them.[1] No longer experiencing a connection to New York's cityscape and built environment—the physical embodiment of history and culture for Lovecraft—he characterized the city as simply "a bore."[2]

While Greene was living in Upstate New York, the couple appeared to have discussed their future. Leaving the city became a real, if not the preferred, option. Before departing Saratoga Springs, Greene applied for a position at Filene's, a famed department store in Boston.[3] Likely guided by his wife's employment search, Lovecraft envisioned them first moving to Massachusetts before ultimately settling in Providence. In a letter to his friend Maurice W. Moe, he bluntly stated that he hoped to "get back to New England for the rest of my life."[4] "Getting away" from New York was becoming his "principal pastime."[5]

Throughout those several weeks that summer, Lovecraft better juggled his writing and his friends. He also dedicated more of his time to his spouse. George Kirk and Samuel Loveman decreased their unannounced visits. While both men were consumed with their respective bookstore jobs, they likely recognized Lovecraft and Greene's need for private time.

Kirk did not seem to care much for Greene, peppering his letters to his fiancée with snide remarks about her weight and age.[6] This might explain his minimal socializing with Lovecraft, as well. When he did embark upon the occasional outing with a friend, Lovecraft tried to include his wife.

Crammed together in a single room during a New York summer, Lovecraft and Greene escaped outdoors as much as their funds and schedules allowed. Shortly after his spouse's arrival from Saratoga Springs, Lovecraft introduced her to Elizabeth, New Jersey, which was fast becoming one of his favorite regional haunts.[7] Closer to home, they took advantage of Fort Greene and Prospect Parks in Brooklyn. Meanwhile, Greene traveled to Cleveland for an interview at Halle Brothers Company, popularly known as Halle's and that city's premier retailer. Lovecraft presumably ghostwrote her application letter.

When Greene returned from Ohio, she and Lovecraft traveled to Westchester County and appraised their building lots in the Bryn Mawr Park neighborhood of Yonkers. Remarkably, they—or possibly Greene by herself—somehow had held onto the property through their hard times. Lovecraft approvingly observed that the area still carried a "charm."[8] Greene's Cleveland interview could have buoyed the couple's spirits, allowing them to begin daydreaming again about owning their own home.[9] After months of misfortunate and financial woes, did they anticipate a more stable and prosperous future for themselves? A resumption of their early situation as a married couple?[10]

An unexpected professional opportunity for Lovecraft also might have increased this sense of optimism. Now living in Paterson, New Jersey, and building its museum in his new role as its first curator, James F. Morton became a less reliable fixture in the Kalem Club. However, he did attend the group's final June meeting, and he chatted at length with Lovecraft about a potential job. Morton anticipated a museum assistant position being created in the near future and presumed that this eventual employee would report to him. He thought that Lovecraft would be a perfect fit. Excited by this prospect, Lovecraft promised to "do my best to uphold my end" if the situation materialized.[11] Working at a museum could very well provide him with the economic foundation to build a middle-class life. He even joked in a letter to his aunt Lillian Clark that he would convince her to move to New Jersey if everything fell into place. (He neglected to reference his wife as belonging to this imagined domicile.) The Paterson Museum position would stand as a running possibility for the remainder of the year.[12]

Although Lovecraft now openly longed to leave New York, the variety of life found in the city continued to simultaneously intrigue and outrage him. On the evening of July 2, 1925, he and Greene rode a trolley car to Coney Island. The Brooklyn beach was arguably at its commercial peak, with multiple amusement parks, entertainment venues, and eateries on the boardwalk or within a short distance from it. The subway extended to Coney Island in 1920, and working-class New Yorkers fled their apartments for the sun, the surf, and the ocean breeze. Nearly a million visitors enjoyed swimming in the Atlantic Ocean, riding roller coasters, and eating Nathan's hot dogs on hot summer days.

On this particular night, Greene and Lovecraft were pleasantly surprised to find Coney Island sparsely crowded. Taking advantage of such a rare luxury, the couple patronized several of the sideshows (popularly known as "freak shows"), then a mainstay of the beach.[13] An aging performer dressed in a tuxedo and playing a violin and xylophone for the show's guests fascinated Lovecraft. This was "Zip, the Pinhead," otherwise known as "The What-Is-It."

A Black American born in New Jersey to formerly enslaved parents, William Henry Johnson, "Zip," suffered from microcephaly. He shaved off his hair except for a small tuft to draw attention to his extended jaw, tapered cranium, and small head. By 1925, he was a longtime veteran of circuses and sideshows, having performed at Barnum's American Museum and the Ringling Brothers Circus. While touring the United States between December 1867 and April 1868, novelist Charles Dickens purportedly saw Johnson at Barnum's and exclaimed, "What is it?" According to this legend, the author of *David Copperfield* and *Great Expectations* unknowingly had bestowed a permanent stage name upon Johnson.[14]

Given the range of acts at Coney Island, why did "Zip" draw Lovecraft's attention? In the margins of his letter chronicling his and Greene's night at the beach resort, he drew a sketch of the performer's head.[15] Lovecraft himself had a long face and high forehead. Prior to his marriage, he was deeply insecure about his facial features. When he was a child and later a young man, Lovecraft's mother may have tormented him about his looks. A neighbor recalled Sarah Susan Lovecraft describing her son as "awful" and "hideous" and her near obsession with his physical appearance.[16] She seemingly failed to observe that her son inherited her own facial characteristics. Greene herself remembered Lovecraft's acute complexes about his looks early in their relationship.[17] Subconsciously, might have the imprint of possible emotional abuse and trauma resulted in a quiet empathy for Zip on Lovecraft's part? As someone who instinctively disparaged ethnic and racial minorities, he refrained from making similar comments concerning this seriously disabled individual. He did not seem to be unnerved or disgusted by Zip's abnormalities or question the validity of his or his fellow (and presumably equally physically challenged) performers' social place on Coney Island and within the city beyond the beach.[18]

Back on the boardwalk, Lovecraft and Greene bought cotton candy and visited silhouette artist E. J. Perry.[19] She wanted to sit for him to obtain a memento of their night at Coney Island. Perry deftly cut his subject's profile from black paper with a pair of scissors and then matted his craftwork onto a white card stock. Although impressed by the portraitist's skill, Lovecraft unhesitatingly referred to him as "the smart nigger Perry."[20] Later, he mailed his wife's silhouette to his aunt for "permanent retention."[21] Lovecraft himself had posed for Perry in a Manhattan bookstore earlier in March 1925. Today, this silhouette stands as one of the better-known representations of Lovecraft and adorns a memorial plaque honoring him outside the John Hay Library at Brown University in Providence.

To celebrate the Fourth of July, Lovecraft and Greene decided to venture to Pelham Bay Park. Located in the far northeastern Bronx and a long subway ride from Brooklyn, Pelham Bay is New York City's largest public park at nearly 2,772 acres, or more than three times the size of Central Park, and its shorefront faces Long Island Sound. In 1925, the Pell House and other former manor homes dotted its grounds. (Now named the Bartow-Pell Mansion Museum, it alone survives into the present day.)[22] These aged and historic buildings likely enticed Lovecraft to this distant corner of the borough. Finding the subway relatively empty, Lovecraft expected to share a quiet day with Greene lost in the "rural solitudes" of the park.[23] As he had with many of his adventures in the city, he was searching for the urban bucolic—a New York frozen in a time before runaway industrialization and development.

When they reached the park after taking the train to the end of its line, the scene there shocked Lovecraft. It was crowded—a given on any summer holiday. As he scanned the people strolling the grounds, picnicking on the grass, or dipping into the water, his disappointment transformed into rage. Black people filled the park:

> I'll be shot if three out of every four persons—nay, full nine out of every ten—weren't flabby, pungent, grinning, chattering *niggers*! Help! It seems that the direct communication of this park with the ever thickening Harlem black belt has brought its inevitable result.[24]

In his view, people holding no claim to his ideal of a city befouled the pastoral landscape sought by him. He complained that this, "once lovely soundside park" had been taken over by "Georgia camp-meetings" and the African Methodist Episcopal Church.[25] With his day ruined, he insisted on going straight home after a perfunctory quick walk to the shore. Such a public outburst was not unusual. Greene recalled Lovecraft growing "livid with anger and rage" whenever crossing paths with groups of minorities in New York.[26] In his diary entry for that Fourth of July, Lovecraft followed the note on their Pelham Bay trip with a single word: "niggers."[27]

Later that July, concrete and long-needed financial relief came the couple's way. Greene met with a female representative from Halle's on several occasions, even joining her on purchasing appointments with millinery manufacturers and suppliers. On July 13, Lovecraft wrote that his wife believed that "she ha[d] the Cleveland position landed."[28] A week later, Greene was negotiating the details of her sales counter at the department store and finalizing her move to Ohio. She secured a decent room with a small kitchen for forty-five-dollars per month—five dollars less than Lovecraft's Brooklyn rent—and purchased a one-way train ticket to Cleveland for July 24. With all her possessions in storage, Greene essentially had been living out of suitcases in her husband's room.

On the night before her leaving for Ohio, Greene and Lovecraft sat down for a sumptuous meal at an Italian restaurant and then headed to Luna Park in Coney Island.[29] The park's Oriental-style buildings—towers, domes, and minarets—were brilliantly illuminated with a quarter million lights. They enjoyed "many unusual things," including an open-air circus.[30] Much to Greene's pride and delight, Lovecraft solved the mechanical trick behind a funhouse room that disrupted guests' sense of equilibrium and gravity with imperceptibly tilting walls and floors. Upon exiting the attraction, she could not resist bragging about her husband's deduction skills to the ticket-puncher and even showed him a quick sketch that Lovecraft had made to demonstrate the "ingenious riddle."[31]

Greene was scheduled to leave New York on a seven-thirty train at Grand Central Terminal on the following day. This would be her third occasion leaving New York for a new position that year. She and Lovecraft met in Midtown Manhattan that afternoon to enjoy several leisurely hours together, including a pleasant late lunch and browsing in a bookstore. When the time arrived for Greene to board her train, Lovecraft dutifully helped his wife with her bags and exchanged goodbyes with her. Then, he dashed to a nearby movie theater. While walking to Grand Central with his departing wife earlier that evening, he had spotted a cinema's marquee advertising *Down to the Sea in Ships*, a 1922 film about a Massachusetts whaling community. At that very moment, he had quietly decided on how he was going to enjoy his first night as a born-again bachelor. While Greene was sitting in a train car barreling toward Cleveland and likely fretting over starting another new job, Lovecraft eased into a plush movie seat and dreamed of his native New England.[32]

Slipping into his idealized memories of Rhode Island for solace and structure consumed more of Lovecraft's imaginative capacity following Greene's disappearance from 169 Clinton Street. Discussions of Providence history and figures and lamentations over the city's modern development and tepid appreciation of its architectural heritage filled pages of his correspondence with his family. He preferred reading Providence newspapers over those published in Manhattan and Brooklyn. At the New York Public Library, one of the world's richest collections of archival and printed matter, he pored over titles on Rhode Island history, often until closing time. Surrounded by his familiar furniture, books, and paintings in his Brooklyn Heights room, he attempted to conjure memories of "other" and "better days."[33] That past seemed simpler and purer. When not engrossed in his own writings centered upon "ancient things that never were," Lovecraft desired nothing more than to ponder "things that used to be in Rhode Island."[34]

During his ongoing survey of the city, he compared buildings, landscapes, and geographies of newly encountered places to those of New England. When picnicking on Hunter's Island in Pelham Bay Park with Rheinhart Kleiner, James F. Morton, and other acquaintances affiliated with the Blue Pencil Club, Lovecraft expressed satisfaction that the rocky coastline was "very palely suggestive" of New England and that the walk to the island cut through a "verdant countryside" of flowers and trees equally reminiscent of his native region.[35] By 1925, Hunter's Island had become a favorite camping ground for different immigrant groups. Although Lovecraft made no mention of such park patrons, he did note that Pelham Bay on this trip was "agreeably devoid of coons."[36]

In Brooklyn, he discovered an ethereal spot in Prospect Park. A brook-fed waterfall "tumbl[ed] down unnumbered cataracts betwixt rocky banks," and surrounding dense trees filtered the sunlight.[37] This was one of the park's several man-made waterfalls, possibly Fallkill Falls at the beginning of its watercourse. For Lovecraft, "this fantastic Eden" presented a "potent symbol of the wonder always lurking close to the surface of life."[38] After spending a whole day in Prospect Park, he rested on a bench at Concert

Grove, an outdoor venue and sculpture garden commemorating cultural figures in the park's southwest section, where he enjoyed a performance by the New York police band. While listening to the music, he fantasized that "Brooklyn faded swiftly away," and he imagined himself sitting by the lake in Roger Williams Park in Providence.[39]

These excursions revived Lovecraft. As long as he lived amid "the nightmare rookeries of this Babylonish metropolis," they were essential to his physical and mental health.[40] They oriented his imagination toward creativity and writing. Although he claimed to crave fields, forests, and "rural loveliness," city life made his access to open spaces possible.[41] Many of his favorite "agrestick" sites were public beaches, lands, and parks—open and free to all.[42] His poverty was no barrier to enjoying them. Not owning an automobile and likely having never learned to operate one, he relied upon public transportation to reach these places. Whether he would fully admit it or not, Lovecraft was an urban creature.

His rustic escapes had the desired effect: he hunkered down at his desk and completed a new short story between August 1 and August 2.[43] This tale blends elements from the hardboiled detective and horror genres. It also contains layers of xenophobic and racist imagery and stereotypes, outrightly jettisoning the ambiguity of metaphor and symbolism. Immediately after finishing this draft, Lovecraft described it in a letter to Frank Belknap Long as centered upon the "hideous cult-practices behind the gangs of noisy young loafers" in Brooklyn and as an experiment "to extract horror" from a setting lacking "any qualities save vulgar commonplaceness."[44] To accomplish that, he selected a Brooklyn waterfront neighborhood then primarily home to an Italian immigrant community and a small Black population, both working on the docks and in shipping-related industries.[45] The story was "The Horror at Red Hook."

The plot of "The Horror at Red Hook" hinges upon Irish-born New York police detective Thomas F. Malone uncovering the operations of a mysterious cult worshipping Lilith, a figure in Judaic and Mesopotamian mythology, and his attempt to outwit Robert Suydam, an eccentric descendant of an old Dutch family, leading the group from his "ill-preserved mansion" on Martense Street in Flatbush.[46] As the narrative progresses, Malone horrifyingly learns that the nameless "slant-eyed" cultists and "squinting Orientals," mainly Kurdish and Yazidi immigrants, are engaged in human-trafficking, bootlegging, smuggling, child-kidnapping, and human sacrifice.[47] Scarred by his experiences with this evil, the detective flees New York to convalesce on a Rhode Island dairy farm. His breakdown and retreat to an ethnically homogeneous and less industrial region might allude to Lovecraft's own desire to leave New York or his wife's psychological struggles and multiple attempts at a rustic recovery.

"The Horror at Red Hook" uniformly ranks as Lovecraft's most problematic piece of fiction, and it represents his raw reaction to a city becoming unpalatable to his sensibilities. He summarized it as "my brief hymn of hate."[48] Through this story, a reader sees New York through Lovecraft's eyes. It is a dismal, grim, and frightening place—a "polyglot abyss" and "a babel of sound and filth."[49] Vicious, swarthy foreigners speaking harsh, strange-sounding tongues prey upon blue-eyed, innocent children. Tunnels honeycombing the waterfront and adjacent neighborhoods provide a pathway for criminals, murderers, devil-worshipers, and illegal immigrants to invade and infect the city.

The nativist sentiment embroidered throughout "The Horror at Red Hook" would not necessarily have repulsed most readers in 1925. Anti-immigrant anxiety was a dominant current in American political and public life in the early decades of the twentieth century. A year before Lovecraft wrote this story, the Immigration Act of 1924 barred all immigrants from Asia and severely restricted those from Eastern and Southern Europe. The act's chief author, Washington Republican congressman and chairman of the House Committee on Immigration and Naturalization Albert Johnson, lauded the bill as saving America's "cherished institutions" from "a stream of alien blood."[50] The door to the United States had closed to the tired, the poor, and the huddled masses. Covers of pulp magazines, such as Lovecraft's main outlet *Weird Tales*, often showcased illustrations of white women threatened by creatures bearing stereotypical racial or ethnic features.[51] In F. Scott Fitzgerald's *The Great Gatsby*, the quintessential literary novel of America in the 1920s, the wealthy and boastful character Tom Buchanan openly fears the downfall of the white race and cites a pseudo-scientific monograph as evidence.[52]

Nonetheless, "The Horror at Red Hook" (Figure 17) is a New York story; it displays Lovecraft's intimate understanding of the city gained from his library research, long walks, and nighttime explorations.[53] References to local history and sites imbue the setting with color and authenticity. When introducing the antagonist Robert Suydam and his decayed mansion at Martense Street, Lovecraft situates the story of the character's family within the larger narrative of Flatbush. He chronicles how the city (and later borough) of Brooklyn encircled and eventually absorbed this former New Netherland village, including the Flatbush Dutch Reformed Church

and its cemetery, remainders of the early Dutch settlers and gentry. The latter is the resting place for multiple Martense and Suydam family members.

The choice of the surname "Suydam" for the story's central villain suggests a fine understanding of Brooklyn social history, as well. Hendrick Rycken emigrated from the Netherlands in 1663. For an unknown reason, his three adult sons adopted Suydam as a last name in 1710. (This ancestral mystery would fit perfectly in a Lovecraft story.) The family became prominent in farming and trade. Multiple buildings associated with different branches of the Suydams once stood in Brooklyn and Queens, including the former Suydam-Ditmas homestead on Flatbush Avenue.[54] Suydam Street runs through sections of those two boroughs, and Suydam Place, a one-block thoroughfare, sits in central Brooklyn. Both are geographic testaments to the extended family's historic position.

In "The Horror at Red Hook," the *Brooklyn Daily Eagle*, the borough's most popular newspaper, publishes the engagement announcement of Robert Suydam and Cornelia Gerritsen. The surname of the bride-to-be was likely a reference to Wolphert Gerritsen van Couwenhoven, a prominent seventeenth-century Dutch settler, or Gerritsen Beach, a remote Brooklyn neighborhood named after him and undergoing development when Lovecraft composed the story.[55] The fictional couple exchanged wedding vows at the Flatbush Dutch Reformed Church. The suspected cultists work in Greek coffee shops and corner newsstands, commercial mainstays of New York and businesses frequented by Lovecraft himself. Shopping along Atlantic Avenue, one block south of Clinton Street and even in his own rooming house, he would have overheard conversations in Arabic and other Middle Eastern languages. Various Red Hook church buildings, including several deconsecrated (Christ Chapel, 110 Wolcott Street), demolished (Sacred Hearts of Jesus and Mary Church, 35–39 President Street), or still operational (Visitation of the Blessed Virgin Mary Roman Catholic Church, 98 Richards Street), might have provided the fictional inspiration for the cult's base of operations.[56]

When discussing the genesis of "The Horror at Red Hook," Lovecraft attributed it to his own encounters with immigrant, working-class, and possibly criminal individuals in Brooklyn. He recalled sitting in a cafeteria late one night when plainclothes police searched "a party of young roughs" for illegal firearms.[57] In a coffee shop on a different occasion, he eavesdropped on taxicab drivers comparing anecdotes of their respective experiences as convicts at a notoriously violent prison on Blackwell's Island (today's Roosevelt Island) in the East River between Manhattan and

Queens and at Sing Sing prison in Ossining, New York.[58] Sonia Greene claimed that "The Horror at Red Hook" was inspired by Lovecraft's unpleasant observation of "rough, rowdyish men" at a Brooklyn restaurant where the couple was dining with friends.[59] Disgusted by the men's public behavior, he wove caricatures of them into his writing. The possibility of real danger seemed to lie just beneath the surface of Lovecraft's everyday life, underscoring the sometimes gritty and marginal nature of the buildings and neighborhoods affordable to him and his literary companions.

Well before composing this story, Lovecraft wanted to gain a first-hand impression of the waterfront and Red Hook, both within direct walking distance of his Clinton Street rooming house. He investigated the neighborhood on at least one occasion in March 1925, detecting "an evil hush" draped over "the entire sprawling fester" and "a hideous element" metastasizing throughout the area.[60] Always acutely aware of the built environment, he noted that this phenomenon spread across the varied architecture of the waterfront streets. Both "crumbling mansions" and "dingy frame tenements" were equally afflicted.[61] In his estimation, the rot of immigrants had poisoned much of this swath of Brooklyn. Nearby Gowanus presented a consoling contrast: it "resisted the foreigner" and thus retained a rugged "pride and self-respect."[62] Looking past Red Hook's "wild squalor," Lovecraft could not help but admire some of its modest brick homes.[63] A tarnished beauty managed to shine through the neighborhood's perceived decay.

After months of creative dormancy, Lovecraft was finally writing again. A second story flowed from his pen only several days after his finishing "The Horror at Red Hook." Feeling cooped up and uninspired, he left his room on the night of August 10, 1925, for "a nocturnal pilgrimage" of his favorite "colonial sights" in the city.[64] He began his wanderings in Manhattan's Chelsea neighborhood with its "curious houses" and "imagination-kindling streets."[65] Then, he strolled through Greenwich Village, "saturating" himself with its rich repository of historic homes and remainders of a Georgian New York.[66] Coming upon a litter of kittens, Lovecraft scooped up one of "irresistibly lovely little rascals."[67] He dropped the animal in his suitcoat pocket and carried it with him for nearly an hour. (He later returned the kitten to the spot where he originally met it.) Over the course of that night, he traversed much of lower Manhattan. Finally, in the early dawn hours of August 11—at five o'clock in the morning, to be precise—Lovecraft was ready to write.

With his creativity aflame from his interactions with architecture and history, Lovecraft continued onward with his "antique voyage."[68] He boarded the Staten Island Ferry with an ultimate destination in mind—Elizabeth, New Jersey. After crossing New York Harbor, he jumped onto a trolley to reach a ferry shuttling between Staten Island and Elizabeth. From his car seat, he watched the hills and coastline of the borough "turning pink" and "gold" with the rising sun.[69] While he rode the ferry to Elizabeth, the play of the sunlight on the water equally fascinated him.

The new morning soon saw Lovecraft walking through downtown Elizabeth and heading to Scott Park. "Pleasantly intoxicated" by the "unmetropolitan greenery" and the gambrel roof of the eighteenth-century General Scott House at the park's northern edge, he sat down and began to write.[70] "Ideas welled up unbidden," he remembered.[71] When he closed his notebook later that afternoon, it contained a finished draft of another new short story. This "hellish midnight tale" would be entitled "He."[72]

The story presents readers with a distillation of Lovecraft's own bitter disappointment with his life in New York and his bare disgust at a city seemingly overrun by immigrants unconnected with its Dutch and English colonial past. (Tellingly, he never shared the manuscript with his wife.)[73] The unnamed narrator of "He," a native New Englander and arguably an autobiographical stand-in for Lovecraft, unequivocally states that his "coming to New York had been a mistake."[74] The shame of his failure as a poet keeps him from returning to his home region. After his initial infatuation with the city passes, the narrator discerns what he believes to be its true, horrid nature. Seething crowds of "squat, swarthy strangers with hardened faces and narrow eyes" dominate its neighborhoods.[75] "Blackly Babylonian" modern apartment buildings and skyscrapers lord over the streetscape.[76] This is a corpse city wormed through with "queer animate things."[77] Only late-night searches for winding alleys, red brick homes, and Georgian fanlights—all relics of the now lost preindustrial, pastoral, and homogeneously Anglo-Dutch New York—preserve the narrator's identity.

Amid one of these rambles through Greenwich Village in the dark morning hours, a man dressed in eighteenth-century clothes and speaking with a similarly archaic English vocabulary approaches the narrator. This stranger offers to serve as his guide, promising to show him a treasure trove of colonial and early American sites in the neighborhood. The narrator's "quest for antique beauty and mystery" overwhelms all his reservations, and he follows the stranger through a maze of courtyards, passageways, and lanes.[78] Ultimately, the stranger invites the narrator into his ivy-covered mansion, where he shares his own dark history and reveals a kaleidoscopic vision of the past, present, and future of New York City.

Lovecraft injected "He" with both his affection for elements of the architecture and history of New York and his loathing for the forces of modernity and demographics reshaping it. The story's passages describing the hidden corridors and forgotten buildings of Greenwich Village evoke a mysterious, hypnotic metropolis. Ceaseless construction brutally threatens structures and spaces representing its past, and ever-spreading skyscrapers literally block out the sun. Meanwhile, the narrator's narrow, racial perceptions of his fellow New Yorkers—many of whom are transplants like himself—cast them as mindless, surging parasitic aliens devouring the city from within. The future unveiled by the stranger, one populated by "yellow, squint-eyed people," delivers even further menace, revulsion, and hopelessness.[79] The manor house of the stranger appears to be an interstitial portal or liminal zone physically linked with the colonial era romanticized by the narrator as a time far more elegant, artful, and humanistic than his own present age. Much to his shock, this supernatural bridge to the past unleashes just as much—if not greater—danger as the contemporary city that he has come to abhor. New York offers no safety or solace.

Much as he did in "The Horror at Red Hook," Lovecraft drew from his deep knowledge of the built environment of the city to create an impressionistic, yet realistic setting for "He." The narrative is situated in his favorite part of Manhattan, his own sanctuary from foreigners, modernity, and time itself, Greenwich Village. Much like the story's narrator, Lovecraft often wandered through this neighborhood to center himself psychologically, fantasize about a long-gone New York, and flee from the present-day world. Likewise, both he and his narrator were flaneurs, fascinated by places yet repelled by their people. The narrator's meeting of the eccentric stranger resembled Lovecraft's own interaction with a wizened and eloquent figure while exploring Milligan Place with Sonia Greene in August 1924. That elderly "gentleman of leisure" talked about the history of the courtyard community with the couple and cheerfully provided them with a private introduction to it.[80] Lovecraft likely recalled this winding tour of Milligan Place and its secret nooks when he described the narrator of "He" silently trailing the stranger through an "inexhaustible maze of unknown antiquity."[81]

The story's hidden Greenwich Village manor house might have been based upon the former Warren-Van Nest Mansion (Figure 18). Between today's Charles and Perry Streets and on Bleecker Street, this grand home was built by Sir Peter Warren, a British naval officer and colonial, in the 1740s. It was sold and demolished shortly after the death of its final owner,

Figure 18. The mysterious guide in "He" invites the story's narrator to his Greenwich Village manor house. This might have been modeled after the former Warren-Van Nest Mansion. Illustration from Frederick Clifton Pierce, *Field Genealogy* (Chicago: Hammond Press, 1901)

Abraham Van Nest, in 1864. Surrounded by trees, the mansion stood on the last scrap of farmland in this section of Manhattan.[82] Although he never referenced this specific site as a source for "He," Lovecraft knew that Warren owned an estate and lived in Greenwich Village during the 1740s.[83]

At the conclusion of "He," a passerby finds the narrator—bloodied and broken—lying at the entrance to a Perry Street courtyard. This passageway provided him with an escape from the ghastly events at the manor house, ironically into modern-day New York City. The *New York Evening Post* printed a story on this particular "little alley just off Perry Street," then colloquially known as Perry Court, on August 29, 1924.[84] Lovecraft began searching for it on the exact same day of the article's publication. Although Perry Court appeared to carry no visible street number, he experienced little trouble in discovering it.[85] Today, this is 93 Perry Street (Figure 19), and a backhouse or carriage house sits behind the main and street-facing property.[86]

On the evening of August 12, 1925, the very next night after he had drafted "He" in Elizabeth, Lovecraft attended a lively and invigorating meeting of the Kalem Club at the home of Rheinhart Kleiner in Bushwick, Brooklyn. The group discussed a raft of topics including "Paterson & poetry, evolution & Euripides, daemonology & the drama."[87] James F. Morton continued to allude to the Paterson Museum position, further

Little Sketches About Town

The Lost Lane

Figure 19. Lovecraft began searching for this "lost lane" at 93 Perry Street immediately after reading a *New York Evening Post* article featuring it. Illustration from the *New York Evening Post*, August 29, 1924

piquing Lovecraft's interest by describing that city's proximity to "deep, mysterious forests" and rural hinterlands.[88] When the gathering concluded at four o'clock in the morning, Lovecraft returned to Clinton Street and sat down at his desk.

Whether from the residual inspiration drawn from his roundabout trip to New Jersey, the energy tapped by penning a new story, or the excitement generated from a night well spent with friends, Lovecraft felt a new plot—possibly even a short novel—gestating in his "awakening faculties."[89] He labored over this sudden idea during the next several hours, jotting down the narrative details and a full outline. An earthquake that "rattled dishes, skewed pictures, rocked chandeliers, and produced a perceptible feeling of swaying" in his rooming house earlier that year partially enkindled the plot.[90] This was the Charlevoix–Kamouraska earthquake centered in the St. Lawrence River region in Quebec, Canada, and its tremors had reverberated throughout New York City and the Northeastern and Midwestern United States on February 28, 1925.[91] Although Lovecraft predicted that the writing would be a "simple matter," he did not attempt it until the following summer of 1926.[92] This story would become one of his most iconic and influential works, "The Call of Cthulhu."

In the wake of this encouraging spell of creativity, Lovecraft treated himself to "soul-saving all-night-&-day rambles through ancient" and "rural regions" as far afield as Union County, New Jersey.[93] Finally returning to Brooklyn on the evening of August 15, he learned that he had missed several telephone calls from Sonia Greene informing him that she would be arriving—apparently unannounced—later that very night. A letter from his Wisconsin friend, Alfred Galpin, awaited him as well. Galpin's own wife, Lillian, would be passing through New York on the following week, and he hoped that Lovecraft and the other Kalems might show her the city.[94] Alfred Galpin and his bride, Lillian Roche, had married in June 1924, and they now were living in Paris.[95] He only informed Lovecraft of their marriage two months later in August of that year. This seemed to follow the example of Lovecraft and Greene's own secret elopement and surprise marriage announcement.

The hosting prowess of Lovecraft and his "circle of aesthetic dilettante" proved to be rather comical.[96] Lillian Galpin reached the city by a transatlantic ship from Liverpool, England, on August 18, 1925. Instead of meeting his friend's wife at the pier, Lovecraft sent a letter to the cruise line to be delivered to her after debarkation. The message instructed Galpin to telephone him upon her landing. Having never received it, she wandered about New York for five hours before remembering Lovecraft's approximate address. Knowing the street name and the first and last numbers of his building, Galpin knocked on doors up and down Clinton Street until she happened upon his rooming house.

Lovecraft described Lillian Galpin as "no especial beauty" yet possessing "excellent taste" and "keen intelligence" and descending from Irish nobility.[97] In reality, she was born in the industrial city of Lowell, Massachusetts, into a large Irish immigrant family with a father from County Kerry.[98] (This fictional pedigree may have been created by Alfred or Lillian Galpin.) Hoping to assuage the young woman's worries about being in a new, strange city, Lovecraft rented a room for her at 169 Clinton Street. Unfortunately, it was infested with "an undesirable population of invertebrate organisms": bedbugs.[99]

Displaying more practicality than her husband and possibly embarrassed by their own living conditions, Sonia Greene acquired a room for Galpin at the nearby (and presumably pest-free) Hotel Bossert on Montague Street. The Brooklyn equivalent of the luxurious Waldorf-Astoria, the hotel was popular for its rooftop restaurant with impressive Manhattan views.[100] Although Greene graciously managed the finer hosting details to counter Lovecraft's obtuseness, the couple realistically lacked the financial resources to indulge Galpin with such a lavish gift. When Lovecraft offered to treat her to dinner, he expressed relief at the young woman's insistence on paying for her own meal.

Both Galpin and Greene attended that week's meeting of the Kalem Club, breaking the group's long-standing "men only" rule. Having briefly stayed in Paris some years past, James F. Morton cornered Galpin and droned on about his impressions of the City of Light. On the evening of her departure for Chicago on August 20, Lovecraft nearly caused his guest to miss her train as a result of his own inability to keep track of time.[101] He and his friends likely left Lillian Galpin with a strange impression of themselves and New York.

Although Greene was overshadowed by Galpin during the younger woman's stay, her own parallel visit to New York carried great symbolic and practical importance for her and Lovecraft and for any life that they hoped to build together. Thirty-three years after immigrating to the United States at the age of nine in 1892, she was becoming a naturalized citizen. Originally, Greene had filed for a declaration of intention on June 9, 1922, roughly two months after Lovecraft's initial trip to New York City.[102]

The naturalization ceremony occurred at the federal building in downtown Brooklyn on August 20. Lovecraft and their mutual friend Samuel Loveman served as witnesses. Greene was no longer an outsider or alien.

Finally, she was a genuine American. Throughout his correspondence with his aunts, Lovecraft seldom mentioned his wife's immigrant, ethnic, or religious background; however, he presented regular updates about her path toward citizenship. Was he doing this to keep his family abreast of household news? Or was he attempting to convince them that Greene was a worthy wife? That she was not just some grubby tradeswoman and dirty foreigner? The date of Greene's naturalization hardly seemed accidental: it was Lovecraft's thirty-fifth birthday.

Oddly, Lovecraft's account communicated no sense of pride, relief, or joy at his wife's momentous life change. After completing his duties as a witness, he deserted her at the federal building while she was still finalizing her paperwork. Instead of sharing a celebratory meal with Sonia Greene, he hurried to Clinton Street to chaperone Lillian Galpin through her final day in New York. Her husband's misplaced priority riled Greene. After an afternoon of sightseeing, Lovecraft came home to find a terse note from her. She reminded him that she, too, was leaving the city that day. Only for "a brief moment" would she be available to "any seers-off" at Grand Central Terminal before returning to Cleveland.[103] Although Lovecraft traveled into Manhattan to say goodbye to his wife, he immediately rushed back to Brooklyn to resume his role as a guide for Galpin. Lovecraft and Greene would only see each other on two more occasions that year, for a total of five days.

As the summer gave way to autumn, Lovecraft continually found comfort in his wanderings and his friends. James F. Morton invited him to join the Paterson Rambling Club for a Sunday morning hike in rural New Jersey in late August. Although he judged Paterson with its "hideous factory section" and "discouraging hordes of peasant foreigners" to be "one of the dreariest, shabbiest," and "most nondescript places" that he ever had the "misfortune to see," Lovecraft lost himself in the "woodland country" of rocky outcrops, quiet glens, mountain-top vistas, and lovely waterfalls just beyond its border.[104]

Walking beneath the Brooklyn Bridge in what is today's DUMBO (Down Under the Manhattan Bridge Overpass) neighborhood with Samuel Loveman on the night of September 8, Lovecraft saw moving lights and heard festive music emanating from a nearby street. When the two friends turned the corner, they came upon a "most delightful" and "unexpected scene," a procession of Italian immigrants and Italian Americans celebrating a feast day.[105] This was likely the Nativity of the Blessed Virgin Mary, the date commemorating the birth of Mary, mother of Jesus.[106] Lovecraft and Loveman enjoyed the "idyllic spectacle" of colorful flags, showering confetti, and theatrical mock-flagellations.[107]

On a September boat ride up the Hudson River with Samuel Loveman and Frank Belknap Long and his parents, Lovecraft grew intoxicated with the sublime natural scenery. The "lofty hills rose boldly" and "profusely" on both sides of the river and initiated him into the long tradition of painters, poets, and thinkers discovering inspiration and tranquility in the Hudson River Valley.[108] This journey left him with a single disappointment: he never caught a glimpse of Washington Irving's estate, Sunnyside, near the riverbank at Tarrytown, New York.

With Frank Belknap Long, Lovecraft watched cats "playing in the sun" and fiddler crabs scurrying about the Jamaica Bay shoreline in Old Mill, a waterfront section of East New York in Brooklyn.[109] At that time, the area still resembled a traditional fishing village with wooden sidewalks, make-shift huts, docked boats, and short bridges crossing inlets and salt marshes. He marveled at the ships' figureheads hanging above the cottage doorways and "each mark of quaintness" in this outer reach of Gotham.[110]

Knowing his friend's love for buildings embodying an earlier era, Rhe-inhart Kleiner showed Lovecraft the South Bushwick Reformed Church in Brooklyn. Kleiner was a longtime Bushwick resident and had attended services at the church. The Greek Revival style of the structure, such as the Ionic columns flanking its entrance, impressed Lovecraft, and he deemed it a "divine miracle" that it "mercifully escaped the taint" of the Victorian architectural schools dominant during its construction in the early 1850s.[111]

Lovecraft exerted far less energy in his perfunctory quest for employ-ment. In September, he made a big production about answering several advertisements for commercial writers, even mailing the newspaper clippings to his aunt Lillian Clark as proof of his efforts. When former *Weird Tales* publisher J. C. Henneberger passed through New York, he telephoned Lovecraft several times to schedule a lunch meeting. Lovecraft coughed up excuses to avoid him.

During this time, George Kirk had moved into Manhattan and was opening a new bookstore, the Chelsea Book Shop, on West Fourteenth Street between Eighth and Ninth Avenues.[112] Needing assistance in setting up the business, Kirk hired fellow Kalem Arthur Leeds as a clerk. Samuel Loveman started a new job managing an annex of bookseller Dauber & Pine. Both Kirk and Loveman could have been able to steer Lovecraft toward at least a part-time position in the book trade, but their knowledge of his personal and work habits likely gave them pause. While Kirk was establishing his store and clientele, however, he did enlist Lovecraft and other Kalems for envelope-labeling sessions lasting through the night and into the early morning. Ever ready to help a friend, Lovecraft was happy to oblige. At the same time, James F. Morton was organizing the transfer of the Paterson Museum from the public library to its own building, a retrofitted stable owned by a former mayor of the city, and he still anticipated the creation of an assistant position by the coming winter. Lovecraft's recent introduction to Paterson left him much less eager to relocate to New Jersey.

The adventures and bonds with the Kalem Club provided him with an anchor as other facets of his life steadily destabilized. After sleeping through Sonia Greene's departure after a one-day visit from her in mid-September, Lovecraft next saw his spouse when she traveled to the city for a three-day weekend in October. When he spotted Greene waiting at a table in a restaurant near Grand Central Terminal, he stopped to stare at her looking stylish and becoming in a new brown dress. His wife's ability to draw the attention of strangers with her fashion sense always excited Lovecraft. In fact, Greene recalled him being "so pleased whenever men—as well as women—used to admire" her.[113] As a husband and a man, Lovecraft was not entirely devoid of desire. During her stay, Greene asked him to read *If Winter Comes*, a novel by A. S. M. Hutchinson, hoping that they would discuss it. The plot of the 1922 bestseller involved emotional adultery, divorce, and suicide through a lens of moral and religious idealism.[114] The book "excellently sooth'd" Lovecraft "to sleep."[115]

Lovecraft and Greene's time together in October carried an elegiac air. Her future at Halle's appeared to be "unfortunately black" because of her rivalry with other employees working on commission and her own low sales during the slow shopping season.[116] Lovecraft worried that Greene would need to move back to New York and to live with him again at Clinton Street. He began forwarding his wife's letters discussing her travails to his aunts. Although he may have done this to furnish evidence on her behalf in the face of criticism, this did seem to violate the expected trust between spouses. Lovecraft told his aunts that the correspondence need not be returned. He confided to George Kirk—no dear friend of his wife—that he and Greene might be separating.[117] Their marriage appeared to have reached a critical point. Sonia Greene would make no further trips to see her husband that year. Before Greene returned to Cleveland, she and Lovecraft took snapshots of one another, as if desiring to create reminders to bestir feelings borne in their early days together.

Meanwhile, his tenancy at 169 Clinton Street grew contentious. After complaining for weeks about the chilly temperatures in the building, Lovecraft received notice of a raise in rent from forty dollars per month to ten dollars per week—an average increase of three dollars per month.[118] He suspected that his landlady was using a national coal shortage as a result of labor unrest at Pennsylvania mines as an excuse for keeping the heat low.[119] He absolutely hated the cold, believing that it physically impaired him.[120] After much dithering with hardware store clerks, Lovecraft bought a small oil stove to warm his room in the approaching winter months. He planned to use it to cook hot meals, later relishing canned beans and spaghetti that were "twice as good when hot."[121] When he asked his landlady to schedule a repair for a light fixture broken in his room for well over a month and for his own lamp that she had damaged, she brusquely informed him that he had "enough other lights for one room."[122] He confronted her about "spasmodic linen service, squalid bathrooms," and "transient" and "low-grade lodgers."[123] As the nights grew longer, his landlady interrogated him about his high electricity usage. Dismayed by the lack of hot water in mid-November, Lovecraft resorted to boiling water on his oil stove. Although his aunts and his wife advised him to search for a better living space, he resigned himself to remaining at Clinton Street. Moving was not a viable option: he simply could not afford it. Instead, Lovecraft plotted a writerly revenge, contemplating the inclusion of his rooming house with its shadowy tenants and skinflint proprietress in a future story.

Through the fall and early winter, he sought escape from the dreary realities of his decrepit lodgings, dwindling finances, and fracturing marriage by wandering through the metropolitan region. All he needed was mass transit fare and a solid pair of shoes. A November outing to Canarsie, Brooklyn, and its Jamaica Bay waterfront disappointed Lovecraft. A "few scattered" and "nondescript wooden houses" and the "shabby-looking" Golden City Amusement Park, shuttered for the season, failed to alight his historical imagination.[124] Determined not to squander the day, he investigated "vague rumours" trafficked by Rheinhart Kleiner of an eighteenth-century mansion in Jamaica, Queens.[125]

After a long subway ride, he was "rewarded by one of the major discoveries" of his "New-York explorations."[126] This was King Manor, the former estate of Rufus King, a signer of the United States Constitution on behalf of Massachusetts, a New York Federalist politician, and a minister to Great Britain under multiple presidents, beginning with George Washington and concluding with John Quincy Adams. Sections of the Dutch Colonial–style country home date from the 1730s, and King purchased the property in 1805.[127] Lovecraft believed that King Manor was the largest gambrel roof home that he had ever admired. Walking along its grounds, he surveyed the entire geographic context of the historic site. The "white-flagged walks," "green lawns," distant church spires, and "many another quaint old house" collectively created a "peaceful village effect."[128] Unfortunately, the nearby elevated train disrupted Lovecraft's fantasy.

From Jamaica, Lovecraft began a "quest" for a neighborhood with many buildings designed in the Tudor Revival style—Kew Gardens.[129] After he crested a hill on his walk from King Manor, Lovecraft suddenly gazed down upon "a Chaucerian village of dream" at sunset.[130] Although decidedly recent and suburban, Kew Gardens demonstrated an attractive urban planning model: it was constructed on a human scale, honoring the natural flow of the topography and producing a sense of history. Strolling through the neighborhood, Lovecraft admired the artificial weathering and discoloration of its buildings and its tight design restrictions. Together, they fashioned a uniform aesthetic sensation for residents and visitors.

Enchanted by the unanticipated delights of Queens, Lovecraft returned to the borough over the next two days. On Jamaica Avenue, he came across a seventeenth-century Dutch farmhouse fallen into "melancholy decay" in an overgrown lot.[131] He lamented the taming of Flushing Creek and its surrounding salt marshes by development and real estate interests. Lovecraft predicted that "this once lovely countryside" on the fringes of an ever-spreading metropolis would soon be lost.[132]

The holiday season brought both cheer and melancholy. Greene had managed to hold onto her department store position in Cleveland; in fact, she presented an article (written with Lovecraft's assistance) on salesmanship that was well received by Halle's staff and management. The peak shopping period prevented her from returning to New York for Christmas or New Year's. While cleaning his room in preparation for hosting Vrest Orton, a new literary acquaintance and a publicist for the *American Mercury* magazine, the poverty of his Brooklyn home and neighborhood became undeniably clear. Lovecraft wanted to go back to New England, his true intellectual and emotional home, and never "venture outside her confines."[133] Any career prospect would find him rushing there "with a haste almost comical to a spectator."[134] Greene purportedly planned to search for employment in Boston, as well. (However, a shipment of Greene's household goods in storage to Cleveland suggested that she actually foresaw herself remaining in Ohio for the immediate future.)[135]

Only the much-discussed possibility of a position at the Paterson Museum tethered Lovecraft to New York.

While reminiscing about Providence shop windows decorated for the holidays, he remembered "old homes at long-distance from the barren shades of a boarding-house room."[136] Lovecraft wished that his aunt and family matriarch Lillian Clark could preside over a proper holiday feast served by her Black housemaid "in proper uniform" and "apron" at his deceased grandfather's former mansion at 454 Angell Street.[137] His sentimental brooding aside, Lovecraft never lacked for company during the Yuletide season. At the final Kalem Club meeting before Christmas, James F. Morton surprised his gathered friends with small presents and personalized poems. He gave Lovecraft a snow globe encasing a fantastical castle. Touched that Morton picked a gift perfectly matching his taste, he included a sketch of it in a letter to his family.[138] Lovecraft slipped his own verses into cards mailed to the Kalems.

On Christmas Day, he joined Samuel Loveman and Everett McNeil at Frank Belknap Long's family's apartment for a sumptuous dinner, warm conversation, and parlor games. The home's bright decorations and tree lifted Lovecraft's spirits, and the family cat, Felis, entertained him with its sprightly antics. Although a committed atheist, he happily partook in the secular traditions—the food, the music, the lights, and the gift-giving—spun around the holiday. Much like his beloved eighteenth-century architecture, they linked him to a deep-rooted history and temporarily imbued life with a semblance of meaning.

9

"Long Live the State of Rhode-Island"

WITH HIS AVERSION TO COLD WEATHER, Lovecraft likely spent the early days of January 1926 shuffling about his room, fussing over his oil stove, and grumbling to himself about his fellow lodgers. The isolation wore on him. His wife was living in Cleveland. The constant calling of friends had dropped off. When he looked out his window at the gray winter street, he no longer saw a city ablaze with promise and adventure and neighborhoods full of stories and discoveries. Instead, he perceived New York to be a vile stew of physically, intellectually, and culturally degenerate immigrants and non-white peoples threatening to poison the scant remaining "proud, light-skinned" genuine Americans still confined within Gotham.[1]

In Lovecraft's eyes, an existential racial and ethnic conflict faced the country: it was potently distilled in the changing demographics of the city. He presented his full sentiments on the matter in a long and ugly passage in a letter to Lillian Clark, presumably a sympathetic recipient:

> The line is clearly drawn, & in New York may yet evolve into a new colour-line, for there the problem assumes its most hideous form as loathsome Asiatic hordes trail their dirty carcasses over streets where white men once moved, & air their odious presence & twisted visages & stunted forms till we shall be driven either to murder them or emigrate ourselves, or be carried shrieking to the madhouse. Indeed, the real problem may be said to exist nowhere but in New York, for only there is the displacement of regular people so hellishly marked.[2]

Lovecraft felt a hatred for the "squat, squint-eyed jabberers" in "his deepest cell-tissue," diagnosing this as a natural physical reaction for a full-blooded Anglo-American such as himself.[3] He viewed the non-Northern European immigrant as the antithesis and even enemy of his own biological and cultural lineage. While walking on the sidewalk, he attempted "to avoid personal contact with the intruding fabric."[4] That is, those that he deemed to be foreign, un-American, or "scum."[5] Lovecraft expressed a special hostility for the "Asiatic stock" and "Semitic types" populating New York, admitting a desire "to slaughter a score or two" when riding the subway.[6] However, he did concede that individual "superior Semites" might be absorbed into the preferential Anglo-Protestant culture if they cleanly cut all ties to their own history and language.[7] Soon, he predicted that New York would no longer be classifiable as a true American city: it would be the exclusive domain of immigrants and minorities.

Given Lovecraft's choice in friends and a spouse, his hardened and unapologetic anti-Semitism and xenophobia appear to be blind to his own reality, and they present a chilling insight into his own psychological state. When he talked with his cherished friend Samuel Loveman over coffee at an Automat or glanced at his wife Sonia Greene sitting beside him on a Brooklyn park bench, did he view them as nothing more than assimilated, Americanized progeny of an "alien mass"?[8] Did he judge himself guilty of betraying his own race and blood?

Lovecraft cataloged the ethnic and racial assaults on "the remnants of the American people" throughout the United States.[9] The towns and cities of his native New England were "flooded with scarcely less undesirable Latins."[10] The Irish were "the pest of Boston."[11] Both groups threatened to create a Catholic culture inimical to that of a rock-ribbed Yankee. "Hideous peasant Poles" weakened New Jersey and Pennsylvania, and Mexican and Native populations formed "a tough morsel" in the Southwest.[12] The worst offenders, Black Americans, necessitated "altogether different principles" and "methods."[13] Lovecraft concluded that the United States had created "a fine mess of its population" and that the country would "pay for it in tears amidst a premature rottenness unless something is done extremely soon."[14]

This bile was not only reserved for immigrants. The creative and intellectual mix of the city—its key draw for so many transplants and visitors—enraged him as well. He was "sick of Bohemians, odds" and "ends, freaks," and "plebeians."[15] People holding different ideas, views, and even memories unsettled him. Such individuals clashed with his self-image as "a regular conservative American" and as a man "well-born" and "comfortably nurtured in the old tradition."[16] Even his fellow Kalem Club members appeared to irritate Lovecraft that winter. He curtailed his interactions with his friends to nothing more than their standard weekly meetings.

The solitude and seclusion promised by his desk and his books were preferable to the "life of exile" in the "hateful chaos" just outside his door.[17] This loathing of New York's artistic and cultural class is just as confounding as Lovecraft's dark thoughts on race and immigrants. With his aspirations to earn a living as a writer and his keeping company exclusively with intellectuals, booksellers, and authors, he was a bohemian by any definition of the term. Although he was a married teetotaler disinterested in the experimental and modernist trends remaking American arts and letters in the 1920s, he lived anything but a conventional and predictable bourgeois life.

When Lovecraft did wander from his Clinton Street room during those first weeks of 1926, he often found sanctuary in the main New York Public Library in Manhattan and his neighborhood branch of the Brooklyn Public Library to conduct research for a new writing project.[18] In November 1925, Vermont-based printer and publisher W. Paul Cook solicited an article on the history of horror fiction from him for a new publication, the *Recluse*.[19] Although Lovecraft was working on the assignment gratis, reeducating himself in the genre invigorated his imagination. He discovered new authors and reevaluated familiar ones. The writing process itself was equally thrilling. He credited it with strengthening his prose and discipline. The scope and range of the piece expanded with Lovecraft's dedication to the subject. Finally finished in May 1927, the essay topped 28,000 words, presumably far beyond Cook's original conception.[20] "Supernatural Horror in Literature" was first published in August 1927 in the first and only issue of the *Recluse*. Today, it stands as a superb twentieth-century survey of the genre and its practitioners. Edgar Allan Poe scholar Thomas Ollive Mabbott cited the work as evidence that Lovecraft might have excelled as "a remarkable interpreter of literature," pointing to his analysis of the short story "The Fall of the House of Usher."[21]

Likely needing her own respite after the frantic holiday shopping season at Halle's, Greene left Cleveland for New York in mid-to-late January. Her presence may have punctured Lovecraft's winter gloom. As always, she tried her best to set her husband's domestic affairs in order. Listening to him complain for months about his broken alcove light, Greene decided upon the simplest solution: she hired an electrician. She served as hostess when Lovecraft held a Kalem meeting at Clinton Street, preparing "delectable" sandwiches and cake for their guests and plating both on blue china.[22] She ensured that her husband maintained a healthier diet, mended his clothes, and even stitched a new lampshade to add a splash of color to his room. Her fabric choice reminded Lovecraft of the front hall wallpaper in his grandfather's home in Providence. This highly personal and glorified past always rested in the forefront of his memory.

While in New York, Greene picked up piecemeal millinery work, inspected the wares at Manhattan boutiques, and met with former business acquaintances. Although Lovecraft wanted his wife to relax on her vacation, he understood her desire to earn a little extra money and return to Cleveland fluent in the latest fashion industry trends. Nonetheless, housekeeping and work did not fully consume Greene during her stay. She and Lovecraft dined at favorite Italian restaurants, bought tickets for a play at the Broadhurst Theatre in Manhattan, and watched Lon Chaney in *The Tower of Lies*, a film adaption of Nobel Laureate Selma Lagerlöf's novel *The Emperor of Portugallia*.

In early February, the couple ventured to the Bronx to tour the Hall of Fame for Great Americans on the north campus of New York University (today's Bronx Community College). Sixty-six bronze busts of prominent American politicians, inventors, activists, artists, and other figures then lined the open-air colonnade overlooking the Harlem River from a hilltop in the University Heights neighborhood.[23] Designed by architect Stanford White, the Hall of Fame was founded in 1900 and was officially dedicated in 1901. Lovecraft trudged through the snow-covered grounds and paid his respects to the sculptures representing portraitist and fellow Rhode Islander Gilbert Stuart and Lovecraft's own literary idol, Edgar Allan Poe. Before heading home to Brooklyn, he and Greene watched "the magick glow of a gold-&-crimson" sunset over northern Manhattan and the New Jersey Palisades.[24] Despite Lovecraft's loathing for the city, such moments in New York still delighted him.

Greene returned to Ohio on February 7. She had no plans to return to Brooklyn until the summer.[25] With her position in Cleveland seemingly secure and promising, she was physically and emotionally healthy—a welcome change from the previous two years. The latter improvement stood as a contrast to her husband's own mental state in early 1926.[26]

Whether energized by his immersion in horror literature, soothed by the fleeting companionship of his spouse, or simply tired of being cooped up in his room, Lovecraft broke his winter hermitage by mid-February and expanded his outings beyond the weekly Kalem meetings. One night that month, he visited Samuel Loveman working at the new Dauber & Pine bookshop at 66 Fifth Avenue between Twelfth and Thirteenth Streets. Lovecraft praised the "impeccable taste" of its main floor and the reading room with its "rugs, pictures," and "mahogany" in the used-book section in the store's lower level.[27] Later that same night, he and Loveman called upon George Kirk at the Chelsea Book Shop now at 365 West Fifteenth Street, joining an animated conversation among him and several other friends that lasted until the break of dawn.

Lovecraft traveled to Manhattan's Upper East Side to patronize the recently opened Museum of the City of New York in the Federal-style Gracie Mansion. (This became the official residence of the mayor of New York City in 1942.) He criticized the exhibits as being "very meagre" and "badly displayed" and the interior as feeling "cold" and "formal."[28] The museum's founder and first curator, historian and writer Henry Collins Brown, strove to present a more expansive and well-rounded interpretation of the city's past, focusing less on heroic narratives and more on daily life.[29] This pedagogy likely clashed with Lovecraft's own view of culture and history, especially as he refused to accept a changing city and nation. Seeing Brown at work revealed his own social insecurities and snobbery: the curator did not physically resemble a "courtly, white-bearded gentleman," but "a stocky, moustached person not yet very grey."[30] Lovecraft seemed to resent that a figure so visibly unlike a stereotypically refined and aged Yankee—that is, someone so unlike his aspirational self—managed a cultural institution.

In his own neighborhood of Brooklyn Heights, Lovecraft peeked into the Long Island Historical Society located in a Queen Anne–style building at 128 Pierrepont Street. Its red brick and terra cotta façade includes several ornamental busts of cultural and historic figures, such as Ludwig van Beethoven and Benjamin Franklin. Lovecraft was abashedly surprised that he had "never investigated" this organization "so near at hand" and touting both rich local history collections and an atmospheric reading room with stained-glass windows and ornately carved woodwork.[31] Today, this is the Center for Brooklyn History, now part of the Brooklyn Public Library.

That February, Lovecraft also penned his final tale written in New York City, "Cool Air."[32] Responding to a question about his fearful reaction to cold drafts and chilly weather, the unnamed narrator begins his story. In 1923, he comes to the city for "dreary and unprofitable magazine work."[33] Hampered by his own meager finances, he drifts through a series of boarding and rooming houses before settling into a building on West Fourteenth Street in Manhattan. One evening, he notices the smell of ammonia and a dripping wet stain growing on his ceiling. He informs his landlady, who believes that the upstairs tenant, Dr. Muñoz, a physician and scientist, must have spilled his chemicals on the floor. Afflicted by a mysterious ailment, the doctor never leaves his apartment. Regardless of the season, his heavy-duty air-conditioning system runs incessantly.

After suffering a heart attack while writing at his desk one afternoon, the narrator feebly knocks on his upstairs neighbor's door for help. Entering Muñoz's home, he is pleasantly surprised by its "rich and tasteful decoration" amid the "nest of squalor and seediness" of the building and the surrounding neighborhood.[34] The physician is clearly "a man of birth, cultivation, and discrimination," presumably much like the narrator.[35] While Muñoz attends to him, the narrator experiences a momentary sense of revulsion, which he attributes to the frigidness of the apartment and the doctor's physically cold touch. However, once the two men begin talking, both find comfort and camaraderie in "the society of a well-born man."[36] He begins calling on Muñoz on a regular basis, learning more about his experiments and discerning that his newfound acquaintance dabbles in scientific necromancy—an obsession to literally defeat death. As the doctor's health declines, the narrator becomes embroiled in his questionable activities and gradually comprehends the gruesome explanation behind the ever-decreasing temperature in the apartment.

"Cool Air" drew from Lovecraft's own New York experiences in both direct and subtle ways. The setting was modeled after George Kirk's rooming house at 317 West Fourteenth Street (Figure 20), where he rented between August and October 1925. Kirk operated his business, the Chelsea Book Shop, in the street-facing front room and lived in the back one. Collectively, they served as an epicenter of books and letters and as the headquarters for regular meetings and impromptu rendezvous of the Kalem Club. When Lovecraft first visited his friend at Fourteenth Street, he marveled at the building's interior: "a pair of immense Victorian rooms" on the ground floor of a house from "New York's 'Age of Innocence,'" with tiled hall, carved marble mantels," and "incredibly high ceilings covered with stucco ornamentation."[37] Although somewhat weather-beaten and run-down, Kirk's lodgings evoked an era of "vast wealth" and "impossible taste."[38] Just outside the front room's windows lay the noise and traffic of Fourteenth Street—the present-day city, which Lovecraft increasingly wished to imaginatively wall off.

When the narrator of "Cool Air" first entered Muñoz's abode, his initial impression matched that of Lovecraft for Kirk's new home. The narrator believed that he had stepped into "a gentleman's study rather than a boarding-house bedroom."[39] The "stained and sullied splendour" of the building in general attested to its "descent from high levels of tasteful

Figure 20. Today, a small hotel operates at 317 West Fourteenth Street, the building that inspired the setting for "Cool Air," Lovecraft's final New York story. (Photograph by author)

opulence."[40] In his letters, Lovecraft explicitly and repeatedly stated that the story's setting was based on his friend's former dwelling.[41] Kirk himself was flattered by Lovecraft's creative choice.[42]

Although less veined with racism and xenophobia than "The Horror at Red Hook" or "He," "Cool Air" still pulses with its author's unshakeable prejudices. The boardinghouse's landlady is "a slatternly, almost bearded Spanish woman named Herrero."[43] The narrator's fellow residents were "mostly Spaniards a little above the coarsest and crudest grade."[44] Odors of "obscure cookery" wafted through the halls and stairway.[45] In October 1925, Lovecraft snidely commented that Kirk's West Fourteenth Street building was becoming "Hotel Hispano-Americano."[46] Such an observation likely informed the composition of "Cool Air."

The story's two central characters, the unnamed narrator and Dr. Muñoz, present dual images of Lovecraft's conception of himself, specifically during his latter time in New York. The narrator is a man of letters, failing to earn a viable income as a magazine writer in the city and forced to inhabit quarters much below his self-declared social standing. He views his period in the building as a stasis or hibernation "till one might really live again."[47] While writing "Cool Air," Lovecraft held a similar estimation of his relationship with New York and his own life.

The high-born, cultivated, and educated Muñoz, a man of "striking intelligence and superior blood and breeding," resembled Lovecraft's own carefully crafted identity as the scion of shabby Yankee gentry once destined for far greater things.[48] With his keen attention to furnishings and art, Muñoz constructed a sanctuary from the rabble and commotion of the modern city. Lovecraft created a similar physical and mental refuge in his Brooklyn Heights room.[49] He even inserted a telling feature of his own home into his description of that of Muñoz: both men slept on a folding couch to maximize space and maintain the aura of "a gentleman's study."[50] Muñoz's bodily need for low and eventually freezing temperatures conversely mirrored Lovecraft's own dislike of the cold and his insistence on high heat.

When first conversing with the story's narrator, Muñoz began sharing "memories of better days."[51] In his letters, Lovecraft openly admitted to longing for Providence and missing its sites and scenery. He fixated on his preadolescent life in his grandfather's mansion, nostalgically remembering it as a stable and happy period and the social and financial apex of his family. For both Muñoz and Lovecraft, such "better days" lay irretrievably in an increasingly distant past.[52]

Shortly after finishing the draft of "Cool Air," Lovecraft received a limited, yet much-needed job proposition from Samuel Loveman in early

March. His employer, Dauber & Pine, needed a temporary employee to address envelopes for its catalogs. The bookstore offered Lovecraft $17.50 each week to prepare a total of 10,000 mailings, and the position was expected to last for several weeks. He jumped at this *"money-making scheme,"* believing that the routine work would leave his mind fresh and unencumbered for his own reading and writing and that it might even furnish him with funds for a trip.[53] Thanks to this unforeseen windfall, Lovecraft mused about traveling to Philadelphia and Washington, D.C. However, the early hours—a start-time of nine in the morning—vexed him. Since he never maintained anything close to a regular schedule, he didn't even own a functioning alarm clock.

While sorting his mail in late March, Lovecraft opened several letters that initiated a long-desired change. Both his aunts, Lillian Clark and Annie Gamwell, formally invited their nephew to permanently leave New York and to return to his beloved native New England. In a response dated March 27, presumably the same day he had read his aunts' letters, he gushed over the premise:

> Well!!! All your epistles arrived & received a grateful welcome, but the third one was the climax that relegates everything else to the distance!! Whoop! Bang! I had to go on a celebration forthwith . . . & have now returned to gloat & reply. . . . And now about your invitation. Hooray!! Long live the State of Rhode-Island & Providence-Plantations!!![54]

Anticipating his homecoming as imminent, Lovecraft began planning to ship his possessions from Brooklyn and to reintegrate into Providence. He discussed selecting furnishings for his still theoretical quarters, renewing his library card, hoarding transit tokens, and changing his address at the post office. He no longer saw a reason to mask his deep longing for Rhode Island and his bitter distaste for New York. Once he finally and officially returned to his real home, the previous two years would be nothing more than "a sort of vague nightmare."[55]

When surrounded by the familiar sights and sounds and buildings and streetscapes of Providence, Lovecraft predicted that he would resemble "the same tough nut at heart" and, more importantly, that he would be "ready for writing."[56] Often blocked in New York, his imagination and creativity would overflow with a renewed fertility in their proper New England environment. Concerning the more practical questions of the sudden proposal, Lovecraft left those matters to his family. Mundane, yet crucial details such as selecting a date, finding an apartment, or hiring movers existed beyond his capabilities. He was ready for his aunts to manage his life again.

What might have motivated Clark and Gamwell to announce to their nephew that Providence was waiting with open gates? For well over a year, Lovecraft had been ensconced at Clinton Street and living on-and-off with Sonia Greene. His poor finances and nonexistent work situation had trailed him from Rhode Island to New York. However, his rants against immigrants, minorities, and new Americans had grown more insistent and vocal. Although possibly concurring with Lovecraft's antipathy toward such groups and even sharing in his mean-spirited and racist humor, his aunts may have become concerned about his more visible and debilitating rage. Lovecraft's letters indicate that they cautioned him to temper his more extreme language—at least publicly. He assured them that he understood "when" and "where to discuss questions with a social or ethnic cast."[57] That is, he knew his audience.

Lovecraft was a regular dinner guest at the Long household, and he considered Frank Belknap Long to be the only member of his New York circle possessing "a peculiarly similar combination" of interests and background.[58] Simply put, he was a WASP and, therefore, avoided irritating Lovecraft's racial animus. Long observed that Lovecraft was becoming "increasingly miserable," and he worried that he would "go off the deep end."[59] His tired, haggard, and emaciated physical appearance disturbed Long, and Long's mother believed that Lovecraft risked his very "sanity" if he remained in New York "without a prospect of rescue."[60] According to Long—his recollection slightly differed over time—either he or his mother wrote to Lillian Clark and voiced fears concerning her nephew and urged that "arrangements be set in motion to restore him to Providence."[61] He doubted that Sonia Greene, Lovecraft's own wife, ever learned about this concerted campaign to extract him from Brooklyn.

Over the next several days, a series of letters flowed between Lovecraft and his aunts in which the three of them quickly hashed out a plan of action. In a remarkable display of practicality and attentiveness toward their nephew's limp writing career, Clark and Gamwell briefly suggested that he relocate to Boston or Cambridge to take advantage of the neighboring cities' joint role as the cultural, literary, and publishing center of New England. Although acknowledging the soundness of this advice, Lovecraft advocated for his primary choice of Providence. His argument rested upon his intellectual, creative, and physical bond with the city—one forged by the virtue of his lineage and steeled by his explorations into its traditions, lore, and history. His native geography was essential to his very being:

My life lies not among *people* but among *scenes*—my local affec-
tions are not personal, but topographical & architectural. No one in
Providence—family aside—has any especial bond of interest with
me, but for that matter no one in Cambridge or anywhere else has,
either. The question is that of which roofs & chimneys & doorways
& trees & street vistas I love the best; which hills & woods, which
roads & meadows, which farmhouses & views of distant white steeples in green valleys. I am always an outsider—to all scenes & all
people—but outsiders have their sentimental preferences in visual
environment . . . Providence is part of me—I *am* Providence.[62]

An unsettling coldness courses through this strange paean. Living
people or remembrances of past acquaintances played no role in Lovecraft's affinity for Providence or his relationship with any locale, including
his then home in New York. His literary friends, their winding conversations, their mutual support, and their shared adventures did nothing to
mold his emotional attachment to the city. Presumably, his wife exerted a
similarly infinitesimal pull on his thoughts and feelings. The natural landscape and the architectural environment of his native Rhode Island were
all that mattered.

This statement by Lovecraft contained a deal of mythmaking, as well.
He painted himself as an artistic recluse, toiling in seclusion and unaware
of his neighbors, fellow citizens, and mankind overall. Earlier in this same
letter, he compared himself to Nathaniel Hawthorne, a fellow New England author, who nurtured a mystique as a loner and a stranger in his own
land. Lovecraft wanted to belong in such a tradition of intellectuals and
writers. This creative temperament and melodramatic posturing did not
solely drive his insistence on reestablishing himself in Providence. Disgust
at the multicultural and diverse population of New York City also fueled
his desire: seeing "normal American faces in the streets" would assure
Lovecraft that he was again residing in "a white man's country."[63]

On April 1, 1926, a mere five days after replying to his aunts' invitation,
the most important question concerning Lovecraft's move was resolved.
Lillian Clark notified him of a ground-floor room with a kitchen alcove at
10 Barnes Street directly north of Brown University and in the College
Hill neighborhood.[64] Her nephew's response rivaled his enthusiasm upon
receiving the initial invitation to return to Providence:

Whoopee!! Bang!! 'Rah!! For God's sake jump at that room without a
second's delay!! I can't believe it—too good to be true! . . . Somebody
wake me up before the dream becomes so poignant I can't bear to
be waked up!!![65]

With an absolute exit from New York in the fast-approaching future, Lovecraft eagerly awaited the "deep breaths" he could take after fleeing the "infernal squalor" of Brooklyn Heights and the entire metropolitan region.[66] A home on "Barnes near Brown" represented a veritable paradise.[67] Mentally already in Providence, Lovecraft listed 10 Barnes Street as the return address on his reply to Lillian Clark.[68]

But, what of his wife, Sonia Greene? Was she included in this conversation? Did her needs, preferences, or desires shape Lovecraft's thinking on his impending departure from New York—the site of their marriage and their only shared home? The pair had begun discussing moving to Boston or another New England city as early as 1925, but Greene's success at Halle's in Cleveland seemed to have postponed that plan. Thus, the proposal for Lovecraft to move back to Providence might not have come as a completely unwelcome surprise for her; indeed, it could have dovetailed with Greene's own long-term hopes for them as a married couple. Regardless, Lovecraft informed his aunts that his wife supported "the move most thoroughly" in "a marvellously magnanimous letter."[69] Recounting this decision over twenty years later, Greene claimed—possibly erroneously or spuriously—that she, in fact, originally floated the idea of him returning to Providence with herself joining him after finding employment there.[70]

Despite his wife's professed sentiments, Lovecraft worried that she would view his leaving "in too melancholy a light" and as an affront against "the standpoint of loyalty" and "good taste" after the immutable reality of the situation had settled in.[71] Although he was retreating from New York and giving up his own dreams of breaking into its literary and publishing world, Lovecraft still held regard and affection for Greene. He did not want her to feel insulted or wronged. Additionally, he might have possessed genuine concerns about his spouse's mental health after her past psychological struggles. Nevertheless, any nagging marital responsibilities would not scuttle his Providence restoration.

On April 11, 1926, Greene arrived in Brooklyn to help Lovecraft pack and tidy up his affairs. They sifted through their items in storage and divided up their household goods. Any hope she held for resurrecting a life with him in New York City was gone. Still, she spent as much time as possible with her husband during their final shared days.

Maybe wanting them to play the role of a happy, content, and somewhat conventional married couple for one evening, Greene treated Lovecraft to dinner at a high-end restaurant in Midtown Manhattan on April 12. Uncharitably, he interpreted his wife's generosity as an attempt "to remove to some extent [his] extreme disgust" with New York and leave him with "more favourable parting impressions" of it.[72] Nonetheless, he admired the restaurant's "atmosphere of genuine taste" and "repose" and relaxed among its "fastidious clientele of regular people."[73] These customers were not "the beastly scum" that often surrounded him in all-night coffee-shops and Automats.[74] Lovecraft gorged on a multicourse meal including fruit, soup, French fries, and lamb, and he even ordered a second helping of dessert, "an utterly superlative cherry tart."[75] The establishment succeeded in cheering him up and making him "feel comfortably at home."[76]

Finished with the moving preparations on the evening of April 13, Lovecraft and Greene enjoyed "a long sunset walk" along Flatbush Avenue in their old neighborhood.[77] There, Lovecraft had stayed during his initial visits to New York City in the spring and summer of 1922. There, he and Greene likely had realized the serious nature of their courtship. There, they had first lived as man and wife. On that night—their last one in a place rich with intimate memories and associations—they dined at a neighborhood restaurant and bought tickets for a film at the Farragut Theatre.[78]

Was Greene hoping that Lovecraft would acknowledge the dreams of their early days together? That he might see past his frustration, bitterness, and disgust at New York and instead appreciate the companionship, marriage, and daresay love that he had found there? Was she nurturing a far-fetched, romantic desire that he would abandon his return to Providence and remain with her? If she was hoping to bestir Lovecraft's emotions, he appeared to be absolutely unreceptive to her efforts. He expressed no sentimentality or nostalgia for his two years in the city.

On the following night, Lovecraft rode the subway to the Long family's Upper West Side apartment for a final meeting with the Kalem Club. Nearly every core member of the circle, George Kirk, Rheinhart Kleiner, Arthur Leeds, Samuel Loveman, James F. Morton, and, of course, their host Frank Belknap Long, gathered together to say farewell to their conversational sparring partner, exploration companion, and treasured friend. Writer Vrest Orton attended the convening, as well; only Everett McNeil was absent. After small talk, Long ushered everyone into the dining room for a candlelit meal. As the guest of honor, Lovecraft was invited to sit at the head of the table. Following coffee and dessert, the friends handed around books and discussed literature and philosophy. As the hours passed, members began drifting away one by one. Morton left for the long trip back to Paterson. Orton rushed out to catch the last train to Yonkers. Exhausted from a day of bookselling, Loveman bid everyone goodbye. By one thirty in the morning, the last remaining attendees—Kirk, Kleiner, Leeds,

Figure 21. During his last midnight ramble in New York, Lovecraft stopped outside the Planters Hotel. He subscribed to the urban legend that Edgar Allan Poe briefly resided there during his own early days in the city. (Courtesy of the Milstein Division, The New York Public Library)

and Lovecraft himself—thanked Long for such a special night and began the journey to their respective subway stations. Kleiner broke off from the group at West Eighty-Sixth Street, and Leeds continued with them until West Seventy-Second Street. Then, Kirk and Lovecraft embarked upon a final all-night ramble.

The pair wandered through Greenwich Village, pausing at Lovecraft's favorite buildings. As if intuiting his coming departure, "many a friendly kitty-cat" greeted the two men along their leisurely hunt for remnants of Federal-style architecture.[79] Seeing past the layers of "squalor" and "decrepitude," Lovecraft espied two "fine Georgian specimens" on Hudson Street.[80] These houses' doorways with their stone arches and fanlights combined elements from similar buildings surveyed by him in New England, Philadelphia, and, of course, New York. Continuing their tour farther southward, Lovecraft and Kirk stopped in front of the Planters Hotel (Figure 21) on the corner of Albany and Greenwich Streets. Originally founded in 1833, it had been popular with Southern businessmen and politicians before closing at the beginning of the Civil War. In 1922, Planters had reopened as a restaurant. Lovecraft erroneously believed that Edgar Allan Poe had lodged there during his first days living in New York City in April 1844.[81] As the dawn was "swiftly turning pink," the two friends sipped coffee and gazed at the waters of the New York Harbor from the Battery in Lower Manhattan.[82] After nearly two years of adventures, Lovecraft and Kirk shared an "effusive" and "courtly adieux."[83] Then, they went their separate ways in the early morning light.

Dressed in his best gray suit and a winter overcoat, Lovecraft bounced through Grand Central Terminal, with its main concourse's stunning celestial ceiling, on the morning of April 17, 1926.[84] His wife might have accompanied him to help in establishing his new home—one without her.[85] Four years earlier, he had visited New York City for the first time to feast on its bountiful cultural offerings, meet trusted literary correspondents, and become better acquainted with the stylish and impressive Sonia H. Greene. After that exhilarating trip in April 1922, he returned to Providence on the 8:33 A.M. New York, New Haven and Hartford Railroad train. Lovecraft wished to ride a similarly scheduled departure for his "homecoming," symbolically acknowledging that this period in his life was concluding.[86]

Although he would always fondly remember watching sunsets over Central Park, relaxing beside the Japanese pond in the Brooklyn Botanic Garden, and talking with the Kalem Club for endless hours, Lovecraft judged his two years in New York to have been "a nightmare."[87] After possibly taking a last look at the architectural splendors of the station and shuddering at the urban chaos swirling beyond its walls, he boarded his train. H. P. Lovecraft was heading home. Finally.

CONCLUSION

"The Merest Vague Dream"

AS HIS TRAIN CROSSED INTO NEW ENGLAND on the morning of April 17, 1926, H. P. Lovecraft stared rapturously at the passing scenery of crumbling stone walls, rolling green hills, and village church steeples. Throughout his entire journey, he experienced a disorienting sensation of renewal: he envisioned himself as "a corpse" exhibiting the first "signs of a resurrection."[1] Time even seemed to flow differently. Although he had lost the past two years to the "nightmare" of New York and its "mongrels," Lovecraft pictured himself traveling backward to 1923 and then effortlessly skipping ahead into "the dawn of vernal 1926."[2] It was as if New York City had never happened. With each station stop, his beloved Providence drew closer.

When Lovecraft spied the neoclassical marble dome of the Rhode Island State House and heard the conductor shout the train's arrival, an initial rush of "ecstasy" surged through his body.[3] Then, a calmness and clarity replaced his sense of "excitement" and "strangeness" as he stood on the "holy ground" of his native city for the first time since March 1924.[4] Almost immediately after moving to New York, Lovecraft began dreaming of "his ancestral environment" with its Georgian buildings, leafy streets, and colonial vistas. Providence still resembled the city of his dreams and memories, exactly "line for line, detail for detail, proportion for proportion."[5] He felt as if he had never left it, declaiming:

> Simply, I was home—& home was just as it had always been since I was born there thirty-six years ago. There *is* no other place for me. My world is Providence.[6]

Although Sonia Greene either accompanied her husband or followed him several days later, Lovecraft's account of his homecoming never directly mentions her. He appeared to be already excising her from his own history. In New York, he was a married man. In Providence, he was a bookish bachelor. He intended to forget his experiment with the former city and its "slums, seediness," and "cheap cafeterias."[7] Unbeknownst to Greene and maybe Lovecraft himself, this would come to include her. She could never belong to his Providence. In the end, this mattered little to him. Back home, "the world [was] right side up again."[8]

As Lovecraft settled into his rented room at 10 Barnes Street and the picturesque College Hill neighborhood, he reacquainted himself with Providence and the surrounding region with explorations into areas previously unknown to him. Occasionally, these rambles threatened to disrupt his sentimental image of his hometown. While wandering into an industrial neighborhood pressed against a railway line, Lovecraft was horrified to enter "one of the most hellish slums" populated by "quasi-human forms of life" and "slug-like beings (half Jew and half Negro, apparently)."[9]

Ultimately, such accidental forays could not dilute his enthusiasm and passion for the city upon the early days of his return. On his "great residential hill," Lovecraft perceived "the Yankee stock" bravely holding back the "polyglot invasion" transforming other regions of New England and even sections of Providence.[10] This belief willfully ignored demographic reality: 168,028, or roughly 70 percent, of the city's 237,595 residents were immigrants or first-generation Americans by 1920.[11] Instead of recognizing it as a manufacturing and immigrant center, he selectively viewed Providence as exclusively defined by "reposeful colonial doorways" and "piquant little winding alleys" and geographically limited to the streets and neighborhoods in College Hill and the East Side.[12] Histrionically, Lovecraft designated this Providence to be "the most beautiful city in the world!"[13] He lived there for the remainder of his life.

Once more amid his "native scenes," Lovecraft found his mind growing lucid and strong.[14] His felicity with reading and writing increased in tandem with the reemergence of his "antique Providence fluency" previously stymied by his exile in "dreary New York" and the "Brooklyn desert of brick" and "brownstone."[15] After just several weeks immersed in his natural urban environment, Lovecraft's New York experiences—his struggles with Gotham's density, speed, and diversity, and presumably his intimate exchanges with his wife and colorful adventures with his friends—became nothing more than "the merest vague dream."[16] Soon, he dusted off his notes for a story pushed aside during the previous August. Ensconced in his Barnes Street rooming house, he completed a full draft by the summer's end. This tale, "The Call of Cthulhu," would eventually stand as one of his most popular works and his first to bend, if not break, the established parameters of the horror and science fiction genres.

Lovecraft defined his intellectual and creative bonds with his city as indissoluble and even symbiotic, grandiosely declaring, "I *am* Providence," before and after his homecoming.[17] Proximity and access to his favorite buildings, streets, parks, and scenery provided him with the elixir to stimulate his imagination. After finishing "The Call of Cthulhu," Lovecraft would write incessantly through the spring of 1927. During his two years in New York, he wrote a mere five short stories. Within his first eleven months back in Providence, he would compose an equal number ("The Call of Cthulhu," "Pickman's Model," "The Silver Key," "The Strange High House in the Mist," and "The Colour Out of Space") and two novel-length pieces ("The Dream-Quest of Unknown Kadath" and "The Case of Charles Dexter Ward"). All these works share a common and significant fictional element: they are set partially or fully in New England.[18] Only by leaving Providence was Lovecraft able to discern the region's centrality to his writing. His two long years in New York City revealed his "dependence on these things" and his "essential attachment to them."[19]

As his career progressed, Lovecraft mined New England's history, architecture, and geography to forge a vivid, detailed, and realistic landscape in his fiction. Regardless of his distaste for New York and his dissatisfaction living there, it provided him with the physical separation and mental distance necessary for him to mature as a writer. If he had not boarded a Manhattan-bound train in March 1924, he might never have fashioned his unique and disturbing literary vision.[20] Lovecraft enjoyed his most prolific creative period after returning to Providence, authoring all his "great texts" between 1926 and 1935.[21]

Printer and publisher W. Paul Cook believed that New York "thoroughly humanized" Lovecraft, transforming him from a sheltered, self-centered, and opiniated man into an experienced, considerate, and open-minded individual.[22] It exposed him to almost daily contact with "cultured, clever," and "sophisticated" fellow authors, thinkers, and—although he loathed the appellation—bohemians.[23] While residing in New York, Lovecraft relished a social and literary life no longer constrained by letters. If he wanted to discuss ancient philosophy, cultural anthropology, or Elizabethan tragedies, he only needed to step outside his front door and call upon a fellow Kalem Club member. His friends were always waiting to resume an earlier conversation or initiate a new debate. Many of these New York relationships would last until the end of Lovecraft's life. The cultural treasures of the city—its world-class museums, well-stocked public libraries, and artfully landscaped parks—allowed him, a high-school dropout, to enhance his endless self-education and savor high civilization on a minimal budget. Although nurturing little interest in the contemporary modernist trends in art and literature, his social and professional circles occasionally intersected with those of the city's avant-garde and grassroots cultural scenes.

Conversely, the challenges and indignities besetting transitory and life-long New Yorkers alike, in Cook's words, "tried" Lovecraft "in the fire."[24] He fumbled with searching for employment. He helplessly watched as his first and only home with his wife was lost. He lived in a drafty rooming house with questionable tenants and a cheap landlady. He was robbed of nearly all his clothes. He often relied on friends for food and meals. When Cook visited Lovecraft shortly after his return to Providence, he deemed the writer to be "the happiest man I ever saw" and judged that those experiences had transformed him into "pure gold."[25]

Lovecraft certainly left New York with greater exposure to different ideas and people. Throughout his life, he allowed many of his personal views to be moderated or altered by persuasion or facts. He presented himself as an analytical thinker, a man of science and reason. He shifted politically from a hidebound conservative to an ardent New Dealer in the 1930s.[26] The one notable and lamentable exception: Lovecraft's inflexible stance on ethnicity and race. His years in New York—its friendships and encounters—did not chip at these hardened and unpleasant core beliefs.[27] Subconsciously, his xenophobia was likely intertwined with a private sense of insecurity and failure amid a rapidly changing society and nation. These sentiments were ingrained in him long before his arrival in New York.

Instead of tempering Lovecraft's prejudices, sharing subway cars with Jewish immigrants, seeing Black Americans picnic at the beach, and hearing Middle Eastern languages spoken in his own Brooklyn neighborhood exacerbated them. A diverse and multicultural New York City did not stand as a model to be celebrated and adopted by other American localities: it literally served as a cultural and physical warning of the rot and degeneracy threatening to spread to Providence and New England. His scant fictional output while living in New York, primarily "The Horror at Red Hook" and "He," illustrated this terror and disgust. These feelings never truly diminished.

Lovecraft voiced support for Adolf Hitler during the rise of Nazi Germany in the early 1930s, even fantasizing about the dictator "wip[ing] Greater New York clean with poison gas."[28] He attacked classifying racial discrimination as antithetical to American ideals as "simply goddamned bull-shit!"[29] This language underscored his visceral hostility to expanding equality in American public life. Habitually well-mannered and courteous, Lovecraft seldom cursed. He advocated for an impermeable color line as "the only one sound attitude" for preventing any "admixture" between Black and white Americans.[30] In his later years, Lovecraft slightly softened his views on ethnicity and race, shifting to a framework based on cultural purity and chauvinism. However, he vehemently excluded Black Americans and Aboriginal Australians from this model: he would always contend that such races were "biologically inferior" and even less than fully human.[31] This hatred stood as a central component of his personal philosophy, sadly informing it just as potently as literature, architecture, and place. There is no separating Lovecraft as a man or as a writer from it, and this will always bedevil and disturb scholars and readers.

What might be most disappointing and damaging about Lovecraft's bigotry is that he was an author. Artists, musicians, scholars, and writers are often presumed to be open-minded and tolerant of other cultures, identities, and peoples and to serve as the vanguard for expanding rights and equality for those standing at the margins of mainstream society. Lovecraft proves this to be fallacious thinking. Past, present, and undoubtedly future members of the intellectual and creative classes have, do, and will carry their own unerasable flaws and inconvenient truths.

In Lovecraft's case, he chose to ignore or reject arguments and evidence pushing against his ideology on ethnicity and race. During his years in New York City, some of his contemporaries in the larger cultural world attempted to honestly challenge the dominant societal norms in these areas and to consider much different stances. Critic Gilbert Seldes promoted jazz music written and performed by Black musicians. Ernest Hemingway wrote his novel *The Torrents of Spring* as a partial satire on the construction of race in America. Eugene O'Neill explored discrimination and racism in his plays through Black characters and actors. (Lovecraft attended and even praised a staging of the playwright's *All God's Chillun Got Wings* in Greenwich Village in 1924.) Anthropologist Franz Boas was assiduously dismantling the concept of scientific racism itself with his pioneering ethnographic work. Within the Kalem Club, Lovecraft's own immediate circle, James F. Morton operated as a political and intellectual counterfoil with his long involvement in civil rights.[32]

After securing his Rhode Island refuge, Lovecraft was content to maintain his long-distance marriage with Sonia Greene. The relationship would be nourished solely by letters and the occasional visit. At a certain point,

Greene proposed that they rent a spacious house in Providence and invite both of his aunts to live with them. Then, she would open a women's clothing store and support the entire extended household. Upon learning of this idea, Lillian Clark and Annie Gamwell "firmly informed" Greene that their and Lovecraft's self-perceived social standing as Yankee urban gentry disallowed his spouse to work for a living.[33] The family's reputation could not "afford" such a blatant impropriety.[34] Possibly unspoken was a concern over their acquaintances and friends learning that their nephew had married a Jewish immigrant. Lovecraft himself appeared to contribute nothing to the discussion or to voice any support for his wife.

In 1926, Greene relocated to Chicago for an unspecified, yet "too good to renounce" position.[35] Hope of reconciliation with her estranged daughter may have guided this decision, as well. She believed that Florence was living in that city and attempted to establish contact with her. Failing to locate her sole surviving child, Greene returned to Brooklyn in 1927.[36]

By late April 1928, she was renting an apartment in Flatbush at 395 East Sixteenth Street and starting a hat shop nearby at 368 East Seventeenth Street.[37] Greene asked Lovecraft to come to Brooklyn and assist her in the initial busy days of her new business. In all likelihood, she hoped to convince him to rejoin her permanently as a proper husband. Lovecraft quickly made it clear that their sharing a household would be nothing beyond a short-term arrangement. New York would never be his home again. After living apart from her husband for over three years and only seeing him on a handful of occasions since he resettled in Providence, Greene welcomed even "that crumb of his nearness" as "better than nothing."[38] Lovecraft did not appear to hunger for his wife's company after such a long absence, choosing to spend the majority of his time with his friends and the Kalem Club.

The official opening day of Greene's store was April 28. Instead of helping his spouse arrange stock, chatting with her customers, or simply providing a supportive presence during an equally exciting and stressful experience, Lovecraft visited the American Museum of Natural History and the New York Public Library with Frank Belknap Long and writer Wilfred Blanch Talman.[39] He informed Greene "not to bother" preparing dinner for him and elected to eat a solitary meal at an Automat.[40] This seemed to pass for being considerate on his part.

Although Lovecraft expressed pride at his wife's shop, a "modestly tasteful establishment," and her selection of its wares, "naturally of the best" and "most piquant possible order," he shared his loathing for New York and his displeasure in having to be there again in his letters.[41] Greene complained about his endless socializing, wondering why she only saw him for a few hours each morning. The couple did share a day trip to Yonkers to inspect the two properties purchased during the early days of their marriage. Greene had recently sold one lot to settle the outstanding mortgage balance on the remaining parcel, an "artistic triangle" near Tibbetts Brook, a stream flowing through Yonkers and into the Bronx.[42] Lovecraft referred to the land as his wife's "piece of real estate."[43] This admission suggested a full separation of finances between the two of them by that time. Lovecraft remained in Brooklyn for six weeks, leaving on June 8 to travel through Vermont and Massachusetts and later down the eastern seaboard with stops in Philadelphia, Baltimore, and Washington, D.C. Greene underwrote the entire trip. Lovecraft even borrowed her suitcase.[44]

By the end of 1928, Greene began pressing her distant husband for a divorce. Unfortunately, the conservative and restrictive divorce laws of New York State only permitted one on the grounds of adultery.[45] Therefore, a mutually agreed-upon fiction needed to be created to initiate legal proceedings. Following the pattern of other New York residents hoping to end unhappy marriages, Lovecraft and Greene looked to a state with a more flexible environment.[46]

A petition for divorce was filed on Lovecraft's behalf in the Rhode Island Superior Court in Providence on January 24, 1929. Sonia Greene was accused of deserting him "for a period of more than three years."[47] A citation was issued notifying her of a hearing of the petition scheduled for March 4 and inviting her to present testimony. She received the citation and a certified copy of the petition on January 26.[48] On February 6, Lovecraft stated in a sworn deposition with his attorney that his wife had deserted him on December 31, 1924: the precise date when she had left for Cincinnati and when he had moved into 169 Clinton Street in Brooklyn Heights. His aunt Annie Gamwell stood as one of his two witnesses. One might surmise that she took some quiet delight in her role. A judge heard the deposition read by Lovecraft's attorney and summarily granted his client's petition for a divorce on March 25. Neither Lovecraft nor Greene seemed to have appeared in court.

The exact status of their divorce remains murky. A final decree is absent in the extant court records. Without this key document, the divorce cannot be declared closed with absolute legal certainty. Muriel Eddy claimed her husband, writer C. M. Eddy Jr., accompanied Lovecraft to his attorney's office and served as a legal witness to Lovecraft signing the final decree on March 25. According to her, Lovecraft "could safely say that he was a divorced man" on that date.[49] The lack of inclusion of this document in the public case file might be attributed to past record-keeping practices. During a certain period, final judgements were filed separately from main cases in Rhode Island court records. Eventually, the material pertaining to judgments and cases were interfiled, but some items were undoubtedly misplaced or simply lost.[50]

The other possibility: Lovecraft neglected or refused to affix his signature to the document. For several decades, this has been accepted as a biographical certainty. Regardless of his many failings, such a duplicitous and cruel act would have been out of character.[51] He appeared to bear Greene no ill will regarding the cessation of their marriage, citing its reason as "98% financial."[52] In March 1933, he even traveled to Hartford, Connecticut, to assist her with research at the Wadsworth Atheneum.[53] Additionally, he personally viewed his divorce as binding and complete, casting doubt on the assumption that he failed to sign the final decree. In fact, he bemoaned the "mediaeval lack of liberal statutes" and difficulty in obtaining a divorce in New York State.[54] Although Lovecraft seldom mentioned his failed marriage in letters to correspondents, he referred to himself as a divorced man and to Greene as his ex-wife on the rare occasion when the subject arose. In fact, he listed himself as divorced on the 1930 United States census and the 1935 Rhode Island state census, further questioning the allegation that he never completed the legal paperwork to formerly dissolve his marriage.[55]

In her published memoirs and private letters, Greene wrote respectfully, sometimes affectionately, concerning Lovecraft. Although she openly discussed his personal flaws and unsavory character traits, specifically his racism and anti-Semitism, she still admired his literary abilities and accomplishments, and she warmly recalled the dreams and life that she briefly had shared with him. Greene stated that she would "always remember" Lovecraft as she "would any good friend."[56] When evaluating their marriage, she believed that "he loved [her] as much as it was possible for a temperament like his to love."[57]

While vacationing in California in January 1934, Greene decided to stay and reinvent herself in the state.[58] She burned all her letters from Lovecraft—more than four hundred—before or after leaving Brooklyn, likely forever shrouding the range, language, and "the wonderfully beautiful thoughts" of their epistolary courtship in mystery and speculation.[59] Two years later, in 1936, she married her third husband, Nathaniel Abraham Davis, a Brazilian-Jewish immigrant and a former physician engaged in peace and justice nonprofit organizations. They enjoyed a happy and devoted relationship until his death in 1945. At an uncertain point in

the 1960s—decades after losing Davis and much later in her own life—
Greene was informed about the divorce decree missing from the Rhode
Island court records. This resulted in conjecture that her marriage to Davis
had been accidentally bigamous on their wedding day. Almost penniless,
she died in a Los Angeles nursing home at the age of eighty-nine in 1972.[60]

After the end of his marriage, Lovecraft (Figure 22) would travel to
New York once or twice most years. He conceded to finding the city "not
so hateful" as long as he was "not chained to it."[61] Between December
1932 and January 1936, he spent a part of each Christmas and New Year's
holiday season with Frank Belknap Long and his family, and he recon-
nected with members of the Kalem Club. During these sojourns, he would
patronize museums and historic sites and bewail the development chewing
up old buildings and wild spaces.

Ultimately, no amount of socializing or cultural consumption could
assuage Lovecraft's alienation and disgust with New York. Through the
remainder of his life, he never overlooked an opportunity to malign it and,
more tellingly, its people. When he first arrived in the city in April 1922,
he experienced "a sense of new, exotic worlds opening up."[62] After it had
become familiar to him, he saw nothing but "garishness" and "squalor"
and "dead-sea fruit."[63] In Lovecraft's mind, New York City no longer func-
tioned as a center of American culture and urbanity: it had "moved past
the zone of civilisation into that of definite decadence."[64] An entity "rotten,
as it were, before it is ripe."[65]

In January 1937, Lovecraft began a diary documenting an alarming
decline in his health. He noted swollen feet, digestive trouble, restless
sleep, and a constant weakness, attributing the collective symptoms to a
stubborn bout of the "grippe."[66] Finally, the family physician, Cecil Calvert
Dustin, was contacted, and a house call was made on February 16. Dustin
examined Lovecraft, wrote several prescriptions, and reached a quick
diagnosis—cancer of the small intestine. On the following day, Lovecraft
rued in a letter that his health would force him "to curtail all activities dras-
tically" throughout the winter.[67] He began having difficulty keeping down
food, and he needed to be supported by pillows to read or write. In late
February, he learned that his cancer was terminal. An internist checked on
Lovecraft on March 6, finding him sitting in a hot bath and with a grossly
distended abdomen. The heat and pressure from the water lessened the
"hideous pain" racking him.[68]

Four days later, on March 10, an ambulance carried Lovecraft to the
Jane Brown Memorial Hospital. He had barely slept in two weeks.[69] His
diary contains no entries after March 11. A Providence friend, Harry K.

Figure 22. After returning to his native Providence, H. P. Lovecraft never ceased viewing New York with revulsion. He occasionally visited the city to see friends, as documented in this photograph from 1931. (Courtesy of the John Hay Library, Brown University)

Brobst, visited Lovecraft in his room, grimly observing that he resembled "a cadaver" lying beneath its sheets.[70] "The pain," he told Brobst, "is unbearable."[71] On the morning of March 15, 1937, Howard Phillips Lovecraft died. He was forty-six years old.[72]

An unfinished letter to his old friend, intellectual debating partner, fellow Kalem Club member, and museum curator James F. Morton was found among Lovecraft's papers on his desk after his death. Characteristically discursive and conversational, Lovecraft wrote to Morton about attending astronomy lectures, playing with kittens in the woods, seeing President Franklin Delano Roosevelt at an election rally, decorating his and his aunt's apartment for Christmas, and critiquing Salvador Dalí and surrealist art. Twice in his letter to Morton—his last letter—he referenced New York City. Never by its name. Lovecraft called it "the pest zone."[73]

ACKNOWLEDGMENTS

WRITING A BOOK IS A thrilling, humbling, gratifying, and nerve-racking experience—even more so when attempting to chronicle and unpack the life and legacy of an endlessly fascinating, yet profoundly flawed individual such as Howard Phillips Lovecraft. Generations of readers cherish his genre-bending fiction and marvel at his complex world-building. Scholars have dedicated careers to documenting every facet of his existence and disseminating every scrap of his writing. His dark literary vision forms a bedrock of popular culture and fuels the imagination of artists in every medium. Not surprisingly, this first-time biographer awoke on many a night terrified that he might have included an erroneous date in the narrative of Lovecraft's life, overlooked a critical fact in his New York years, or misread a key passage in one of his copious letters. Whenever I found myself floundering, colleagues, friends, and family offered insight, encouragement, and advice.

Throughout the research, writing, and revision of this book, a band of archival, library, and museum professionals provided resources, direction, and answers. This entire undertaking would have been impossible without them. In institutional order, I would like to express a heartfelt thanks to: Alison McKay, Bartow-Pell Mansion Museum; Remo Cosentino, Bronx Community College; Cynthia Tobar, Archives and Special Collections, Bronx Community College; Liza Katz and Deborah Tint, Center for Brooklyn History, Brooklyn Public Library; Heather Cole, Genesis Barrera, Ann Morgan Dodge, Andrew Majcher, Nadine McAllister, Jasmine

Sykes-Kunk, and Robin Ness, John Hay Library, Brown University; Terry Metter, Center for Local and Global History, Cleveland Public Library; Thomas X. Casey, East Bronx History Forum; Aimee Fernandez-Puente, Local History and Special Collections, Elizabeth Public Library; John D'Angelo and Hannah Herrlich, Walsh Library, Fordham University; Gail McDonald, Maloney Library, Fordham University School of Law; Marija Gudauskas, Social Science and History Department, Free Library of Philadelphia; Kenneth Cobb, New York City Department of Records and Information Services; Joseph Van Nostrand, New York County Clerk; Eleanor Gillers, New-York Historical Society; Daniel Brenner, New York Transit Museum; Ann Poulos, Providence Public Library; Andrew Smith, Rhode Island Supreme Court Judicial Records Center; Lynne Farrington, Kislak Center for Special Collections, Rare Books and Manuscripts, University of Pennsylvania; Vicki Glantz and Renah Miller, American Heritage Center, University of Wyoming; John Carini and Nick Dembowski, Van Cortlandt House Museum; and Diane Mignault, Yonkers Public Library.

Since 2018, I have been privileged to be a fellow at the Wertheim Study and later the Frederick Lewis Allen Room at the Center for Research in the Humanities at the New York Public Library. Being a part of this community of scholars and writers at such a storied institution challenged and inspired me. Melanie Locay, Associate Manager for the Center, deserves high praise for creating opportunities for researchers to continue their work and share it with colleagues during the darker days of the pandemic. My own writing would have withered and perished without such conversations. A huge thank you to all the New York Public Library staff, specifically Rebecca Federman and Paul Friedman, and Michelle McCarthy-Behler and Kyle Triplett in the Manuscripts, Archives and Rare Books Division.

Midnight Rambles marks my second round working with the great team at Fordham University Press. Thank you for another wonderful publishing experience, Fredric Nachbaur, Will Cerbone, Aldene Fredenburg, Eric Newman, Kathleen O'Brien-Nicholson, and Katie Sweeney Parmiter.

Kevin Joel Berland and his feline assistants at Starfish House Editorial Services fashioned the index.

John Cecero, SJ, Vice President for Mission Integration and Ministry, Fordham University, and David Gibson, Director of the Center on Religion and Culture, Fordham University, furnished institutional support and writerly advice.

Publishing veteran Robert Farren reviewed a very early and rough draft and spotted cringe-inducing factual inaccuracies and writing errors.

My Cthulhu crew, Kirk Howle, Ralph Santiago, and Christopher Soprano, indulged the workshopping of my initial manuscript, and their feedback helped shape its ultimate narrative.

Sam Addeo invited me to join the Urban Archive network, allowing me to benefit from its amazing resources and to connect with fellow contributors.

Katie Uva offered me a forum to synthesize my early findings at *Gotham: A Blog for Scholars of New York City History*.

Kelsey Brow and Abigail Waldron hosted my first public talk on the complicated relationship between H. P. Lovecraft and New York City at the King Manor Museum, appropriately during the Halloween season.

The far-reaching, diverse, and supportive community at NecronomiCon Providence, including Niels-Viggo Hobbs, Sean Branney, Kenneth Heard, Andrew Leman, and Donovan K. Loucks, initiated me into the rewarding and entertaining world of weird fiction and Lovecraft studies.

Richard Upton Pickman assisted in the selection of historical photographs, and Leo Sorel ensured that all were ready for submission.

Fellow writers and scholars Henry L. P. Beckwith, Bobby Derie, W. Scott Poole, and Eric K. Washington, and Monica Wasserman generously shared their discoveries and insights.

Rick Easton and the staff at Bread and Salt literally cooked the meals that sustained me through many long days and nights of writing and editing.

Christine Garvey and Sarah Lohman nourished my creativity with their superb classes at the Brooklyn Brainery.

Finally, my wife, the talented, stylish, and lovely Jessica Murphy, understood my need to spend countless hours with H. P. Lovecraft and erstwhile members of the Kalem Club. I'm so grateful that we're sharing this writing life.

NOTES

Introduction: "Age Brings Reminiscences"

1. H. P. Lovecraft to F. Lee Baldwin, January 31, 1934, in Lovecraft, *Selected Letters*, ed. August Derleth and James Turner, vol. 4, *1932–1934* (Sauk City, Wisc.: Arkham House, 1976), 349.

2. H. P. Lovecraft to Rheinhart Kleiner, May 29, 1936, in Lovecraft, *Letters to Rheinhart Kleiner and Others*, ed. S. T. Joshi and David E. Schultz (New York: Hippocampus Press, 2020), 206; Kenneth Faig Jr., "Can You Direct Me to Ely Court?: Some Notes on 66 College Street," *Lovecraft Annual*, no. 9 (2015): 54–69; David E. Schultz, "66 College Street," *Lovecraft Annual*, no. 9 (2015): 70–80; Winfield Townley Scott, "His Most Fantastic Creation: Howard Phillips Lovecraft," in *Lovecraft Remembered*, ed. Peter Cannon (Sauk City, Wisc.: Arkham House, 1998), 21; S. T. Joshi and David E. Schultz, introduction to *Letters to Kleiner*, 14.

3. Scott, "His Most Fantastic Creation," 8. The *Providence Journal* book critic and editor Winfield Townley Scott lived only blocks away from Lovecraft for years, yet Scott had never met or heard of him.

4. H. P. Lovecraft to Annie E. P. Gamwell, March 17, 1936–April 21, 1936, in *Letters to Family and Family Friends*, ed. S. T. Joshi and David E. Schultz, vol. 2, *1926–1936* (New York: Hippocampus Press, 2020), 1,001.

5. Ann Douglas, *Terrible Honesty: Mongrel Manhattan in the 1920s* (New York: Farrar, Straus and Giroux, 1995), 13–21; Ethan Mordden, *The Guest List: How Manhattan Defined American Sophistication—from the Algonquin Round Table to Truman Capote's Ball* (New York: St. Martin's Press, 2010), 21; Christine Stansell, *American Moderns: Bohemian New York and the Creation of a New Century* (New York: Metropolitan Books, 2000), 20–26; Ross Wetzsteon, *Republic of Dreams: Greenwich Village; The American Bohemia, 1910–1960* (New York: Simon & Schuster, 2002), ix–xv, 10–14.

6. Steven Watson, *Strange Bedfellows: The First American Avant-Garde* (New York:

Abbeville Press, 1991). In his cultural history of the American scene in the 1910s prior to the First World War, Watson diagrams the different artistic and creative circles and their connections or lack thereof in New York City and other locales.

7. Lovecraft to Clark Ashton Smith, October 15, 1927, *Selected Letters*, 2:176.

8. Joan Didion, "Goodbye to All That," in *Slouching Towards Bethlehem: Essays* (New York: Picador Modern Classics, 2017), 331–51; Sari Botton, ed., *Goodbye to All That: Writers on Loving and Leaving New York* (Berkely, Calif.: Seal Press, 2013).

9. S. T. Joshi, "A Look at Lovecraft's Letters," in *Lovecraft and a World in Transition: Collected Essays on H. P. Lovecraft* (New York: Hippocampus Press, 2014), 441.

10. Fritz Leiber, "My Correspondence with Lovecraft," in Cannon, *Lovecraft Remembered*, 300.

11. Maurice W. Moe, "Howard Phillips Lovecraft: The Sage of Providence," in Cannon, *Lovecraft Remembered*, 90.

12. Susan Smith-Peter, "To See a City: Percy Loomis Sperr and the Total Photographic Documentation of New York City, 1924–45," *Gotham: A Blog for Scholars of New York City History*, October 7, 2021, https://www.gothamcenter.org/blog/lg4t4th8v fvm6xrzgefg5jjje3vovm.

13. S. T. Joshi and David E. Schultz, introduction to *Letters to Family*, 1:13; S. T. Joshi and David E. Schultz, introduction to *Lord of a Visible World: An Autobiography in Letters*, by H. P. Lovecraft, ed. S. T. Joshi and David E. Schultz (Athens: Ohio University Press, 2000), viii; S. T. Joshi and David E. Schultz, "Letters, Lovecraft's," in *An H. P. Lovecraft Encyclopedia* (Westport, Conn.: Greenwood Press, 2001), 144–47; Arthur S. Koki, "H. P. Lovecraft: An Introduction to His Life and Writings" (master's thesis, Columbia University, 1962), iii.

14. Phillip A. Ellis offers a study of Lovecraft's racial poetry, arguing that such an exercise presents "an example of how a racist thinks, how they create their mental image of race"; Ellis, "The Construction of Race in the Early Poetry of H. P. Lovecraft," *Lovecraft Annual*, no. 4 (2010): 124; H. P. Lovecraft, "De Triumpho Naturae: The Triumph of Nature Over Northern Ignorance—Lines Dedicated to William Benjamin Smith, Tulane University, La.," 1905, Howard P. Lovecraft Collection, Brown Digital Repository, Brown University Library, https://repository.library.brown.edu/studio/item/bdr:730818/; S. T. Joshi, *I Am Providence: The Life and Times of H. P. Lovecraft* (New York: Hippocampus Press, 2013), 1:110–11, 114; Ellis, "Construction of Race," 124–35.

15. Lovecraft to Kleiner, November 16, 1916, *Letters to Kleiner*, 72. Notably absent from this short discussion of Lovecraft and race is any mention or examination of his infamously named childhood cat, Nigger-Man. Since it is unknown if Lovecraft himself or an adult in his family named the pet, it seems injudicious to categorize this biographical detail as evidence of his deeply embedded racism. The pejorative and loaded term ("Nigger") was not an uncommon name for a pet during the time of Lovecraft's childhood and adolescence. Lovecraft frequently and fondly remembered his deceased cat in his letters and memorialized him by name as a nonhuman character in his short story "The Rats in the Walls"; Jason Colavito, "W. Scott Poole on Lovecraft's Relationship to Poe and His Racist Cat," Blog, February 28, 2017, https://www.jasoncolavito.com/blog/w-scott -poole-on-lovecrafts-relationship-to-poe-and-his-racist-cat; H. P. Lovecraft, "The Rats in the Walls," in *Tales* (New York: Library of America, 2005), 77–96.

16. H. P. Lovecraft, "Providence in 2000 A. D.," *Evening Bulletin* (Providence), March 4, 1912, Lovecraft Collection, https://repository.library.brown.edu/studio/item/bdr:925075/.

17. H. P. Lovecraft, "On the Creation of Niggers," 1912, Lovecraft Collection, https://repository.library.brown.edu/studio/item/bdr:925304/; Matt Ruff, *Lovecraft Country: A Novel* (New York: HarperPerennial, 2016), 14–15. A brief discussion of this poem and Lovecraft himself appears in the novel *Lovecraft Country*, by Matt Ruff, and later in the HBO series based upon it.

18. H. P. Lovecraft, "In a Major Key," in *Collected Essays*, vol. 1, *Amateur Journalism*, ed. S. T. Joshi (New York: Hippocampus Press, 2004), 57.

19. Bobby Derie, "'Concerning the Conservative' (1915) by Charles D. Isaacson," *Deep Cuts in a Lovecraftian Vein*, February 5, 2020, https://deepcuts.blog/2020/02/05/concerning-the-conservative-1915-by-charles-d-isaacson/; James F. Morton, "'Conservatism' Gone Mad," in *Letters to James F. Morton*, by H. P. Lovecraft, ed. David E. Schultz and S. T. Joshi (New York: Hippocampus Press, 2011), 407–10.

20. Michel Houellebecq, *H. P. Lovecraft: Against the World, Against Life*, intro. Stephen King, trans. Dorna Khazeni (New York: Cernunnos, 2019), 124.

21. Bobby Derie, *Sex and the Cthulhu Mythos* (New York: Hippocampus Press, 2014), 48–53; Carl H. Sederholm and Jeffrey Andrew Weinstock, "Lovecraft Rising," introduction to *The Age of Lovecraft*, ed. Carl H. Sederholm and Jeffrey Andrew Weinstock, foreword by Ramsey Campbell, commentary by China Miéville (Minneapolis: University of Minnesota Press, 2016), 25–28. In his broader examination on the author, his legacy, and sex, Derie briefly analyzes Lovecraft's unswerving thoughts on miscegenation. Sederholm and Weinstock cogently summarize the relationship between Lovecraft and race and establish a starting point to further investigate the subject.

22. Bluford Adams, *Old & New New Englanders: Immigration & Regional Identity in the Gilded Age* (Ann Arbor: University of Michigan Press, 2014), 5–7, 15; Joseph A. Conforti, *Imagining New England: Explorations of Regional Identity from the Pilgrims to the Mid-Twentieth Century* (Chapel Hill: University of North Carolina Press, 2001), 209–11; Lynn Dumenil, *The Modern Temper: American Culture and Society in the 1920s* (New York: Hill and Wang, 1995), 5, 201–7; Thomas F. Gossett, *Race: The History of an Idea in America*, new ed. (New York: Oxford University Press, 1997), 299–307; John Higham, *Strangers in the Land: Patterns of American Nativism, 1860–1925*, 2nd ed. (New Brunswick, N.J.: Rutgers University Press, 1988), 139–40, 274–77; Matthew Frye Jacobson, *Whiteness of a Different Color: European Immigrants and the Alchemy of Race* (Cambridge, Mass.: Harvard University Press, 1998), 76–78; Phillipa Levine, *Eugenics: A Very Short Introduction* (New York: Oxford University Press, 2017), 1–24, 62–71, 92–96; Geoffrey Perrett, *America in the Twenties: A History* (New York: Simon & Schuster, 1982), 78–83, 101.

23. Dumenil, *Modern Temper*, 207.

24. Linda Gordon, *The Second Coming of the KKK: The Ku Klux Klan of the 1920s and the American Tradition* (New York: Liveright, 2017), 3.

25. Dumenil, *Modern Temper*, 201–49; Ben Fenwick, "The Massacre That Destroyed Tulsa's 'Black Wall Street,'" *New York Times*, July 13, 2020; Gordon, *Second Coming of the KKK*, 2–7; Gossett, *Race*, 370–408; Andrew R. Heinze, "The Critical Period: Ethnic Emergence and Reaction, 1901–1929," in *The Columbia Documentary History of Race and Ethnicity in America*, ed. Ronald H. Bayor (New York: Columbia University Press, 2004), 413–598; Yuliya Parshina-Kottas, "What the Tulsa Race Massacre Destroyed," *New York Times*, May 24, 2021; "1921 Tulsa Race Massacre," Tulsa Historical Society and Museum, accessed December 29, 2022,

https://www.tulsahistory.org/exhibit/1921-tulsa-race-massacre/#flexible-content; Perrett, *America in the Twenties*, 78–88.

26. Nnedi Okorafor, "Lovecraft's Racism & the World Fantasy Award Statuette, with Comments from China Miéville," *Nnedi's Wahala Zone Blog*, December 14, 2011, https://nnedi.blogspot.com/2011/12/lovecrafts-racism-world-fantasy-award.html?q=lovecraft; Alison Flood, "World Fantasy Award Drops HP Lovecraft as Prize Image," *Guardian* (Manchester), November 9, 2015, https://www.theguardian.com/books/2015/nov/09/world-fantasy-award-drops-hp-lovecraft-as-prize-image.

27. "New Generation of Writers of Color Reckon with H. P. Lovecraft's Racism," *Takeaway*, August 12, 2020, https://www.wnycstudios.org/podcasts/takeaway/segments/lovecraft-country-reckons-hp-lovecrafts-racism.

28. "New Generation of Writers," *Takeaway*, August 12, 2020, https://www.wnycstudios.org/podcasts/takeaway/segments/lovecraft-country-reckons-hp-lovecrafts-racism; Victor LaValle, *The Ballad of Black Tom* (New York: Tom Doherty, 2016). *The Ballad of Black Tom* won both a British Fantasy Award and a Shirley Jackson Award.

29. N. K. Jemisin, *The City We Became* (New York: Orbit, 2020), 148–49, 341, 391; "N. K. Jemisin on H. P. Lovecraft," *New Yorker Radio Hour*, September 4, 2020, https://www.wnycstudios.org/podcasts/tnyradiohour/segments/n-k-jemisin-h-p-lovecraft-rerun.

30. David J. Goodwin, "Trapped in Lovecraft Country," *Sapientia*, September 3, 2020, https://crc.blog.fordham.edu/arts-culture/trapped-in-lovecraft-country/; Ruff, *Lovecraft Country*.

31. Sean Branney, David J. Goodwin, and Andrew Leman, "Men of Their Time: The Correspondence and Relationship of H. P. Lovecraft and James F. Morton (panel, NecronomiCon Providence, Providence, Rhode Island, August 20, 2022); David J. Goodwin, "The Odd, the Free, and the Dissenting," *Sapientia*, September 1, 2022, https://crc.blog.fordham.edu/arts-culture/the-odd-the-free-and-the-dissenting/; NecronomiCon Providence (website), accessed December 20, 2022, https://necronomicon-providence.com/welcome/; Elisabeth Vincentelli, "A Festival That Conjures the Magic of H. P. Lovecraft and Beyond," *New York Times*, August 28, 2022. The author moderated a panel at NecronomiCon Providence dedicated to the friendship of Lovecraft and James F. Morton on August 20, 2022. This conversation partially focused on their markedly different views on race and society.

32. Chinua Achebe, "An Image of Africa: Racism in Conrad's 'Heart of Darkness,'" *Massachusetts Review* 57, no. 1 (Spring 2016): 14–27; Lennard J. Davis, "The Value of Teaching from a Racist Classic," *Chronicle of Higher Education*, May 19, 2006; Bill Freind, "'Why Do You Want to Put Your Ideas in Order?' Re-Thinking the Politics of Ezra Pound," *Journal of Modern Literature* 23, no. 3–4 (Summer 2000): 545–63; John R. Harrison, *The Reactionaries*, preface by William Empson (London: Gollancz, 1966); Patricia Owens, "*Racism in the Theory Canon: Hannah Arendt and 'The One Great Crime in Which America Was Never Involved*,'" *Millennium* 45, no. 3 (2017): 403–24; Christopher Prendergast, "Representing (Forgetting the Past): Paul de Man, Fascism, and Deconstruction," in *The Triangle of Representation* (New York: Columbia University Press, 2000), 63–81. The cited writings collectively introduce the value in studying, teaching, and writing about foundational authors or works with problematic issues.

33. M. Eileen McNamara, annotator, "Medical Record of Winfield Scott Lovecraft," *Lovecraft Studies* 24 (Spring 1991): 15.

34. "Butler Hospital Has a World-Wide Reputation," *Providence Sunday Journal*, February 3, 1924. Although the Gothic Revival buildings comprising its original complex might conjure stereotypical images of horrific nineteenth-century asylums, Butler Hospital carried a reputation as a humane and progressive facility during the time of Lovecraft's parents' respective hospitalizations.

35. It is likely, although uncertain, if Lovecraft later learned the full facts regarding his father's health, hospitalization, and death. Some critics perceive a fear of the body and of a "physical inheritance" in Lovecraft's depictions of creatures in his fiction. Nevertheless, Lovecraft never revealed any knowledge of his father's syphilitic condition in his letters. Victoria Nelson, *The Secret Life of Puppets* (Cambridge, Mass.: Harvard University Press, 2001), 118; "General Paresis," MedlinePlus, accessed December 22, 2022, https:// medlineplus.gov/ency/article/000748.htm; M. Eileen McNamara, "Winfield Scott Lovecraft's Final Illness," *Lovecraft Studies* 24 (Spring 1991): 14; McNamara, "Medical Record," 15–17; Kenneth W. Faig Jr. "The Parents of Howard Phillips Lovecraft," in *An Epicure in the Terrible: A Centennial Anthology of Essays in Honor of H. P. Lovecraft*, ed. David E. Schultz and S. T. Joshi (Rutherford, N.J.: Farleigh Dickinson University Press, 1991), 49–52; Joshi, *I Am Providence*, 1:21–26.

36. H. P. Lovecraft to Maurice W. Moe, January 1, 1915, in *Letters to Maurice W. Moe and Others*, ed. David E. Schultz and S. T. Joshi (New York: Hippocampus Press, 2018), 44.

37. Lovecraft to Kleiner, November 16, 1916, *Letters to Kleiner*, 73.

38. Lovecraft to Kleiner, November 16, 1916, *Letters to Kleiner*, 73.

39. Lovecraft to J. Vernon Shea, February 4, 1934, *Selected Letters*, 4:357.

40. Lovecraft to Bernard Austin Dwyer, March 3, 1927, *Letters to Moe*, 432.

41. Lovecraft to Kleiner, November 16, 1916, *Letters to Kleiner*, 74.

42. H. P. Lovecraft, "The Alchemist," *United Amateur*, November 1916. Lovecraft originally wrote "The Alchemist" in 1908.

43. Lovecraft, "What Amateurdom and I Have Done for Each Other," in Joshi, *Collected Essays*, 1:271–74. Lovecraft penned a touching and honest reflection on how amateur journalism injected him with a needed dose of vitality and introduced him to a greater intellectual world.

44. Lovecraft to Kleiner, January 18, 1919, *Letters to Kleiner*, 129.

45. Derie, *Sex and the Cthulhu Mythos*, 37.

46. August Derleth, "Lovecraft's Sensitivity," in Cannon, *Lovecraft Remembered*, 35; Winfield Townley Scott, Bookman's Galley, *Providence Sunday Journal*, September 19, 1948; Winfield Townley Scott, Bookman's Galley, *Providence Sunday Journal*, October 3, 1948. Clara Hess shared her memories of Sarah Susan Phillips Lovecraft and H. P. Lovecraft with *Providence Journal* literary editor Winfield Townley Scott in 1948, nearly thirty years after Sarah Susan's institutionalization in 1919 and eleven years after Lovecraft's death in 1937. Although this suggests that Hess's memories might merit a degree of scrutiny, her recollections resemble other individuals' impressions of the Lovecraft family dynamics.

47. Lovecraft to J. Vernon Shea, December 5, 1935, *Selected Letters*, 5:210.

48. United States Department of Labor, Bureau of Labor Statistics, *Handbook of Labor Statistics*, 1936 ed. (Washington, D.C.: G. P. O., 1936), 988, https://fraser.stlouisfed.org /files/docs/publications/bls/bls_0616_1936.pdf; Lovecraft to Willis Conover, September 23,

1936, *Selected Letters*, 5:307–8; Lovecraft to Mrs. Fritz Leiber [née Jonquil Stephens], November 29, 1936, *Selected Letters*, 5:363–64; Mary V. Dana, "A Glimpse of H. P. L.," in Cannon, *Lovecraft Remembered*, 30–31.

49. Lovecraft to Mrs. Fritz Leiber [née Jonquil Stephens], November 29, 1936, *Selected Letters*, 5:364.

50. Lovecraft to Elizabeth Toldridge, March 15, 1936, *Selected Letters*, 5:229.

51. Joshi, *I Am Providence*, 2:1,002–6; H. P. Lovecraft to Duane W. Rimel, October 8, 1934, in *Letters to F. Lee Baldwin, Duane W. Rimel, and Nils Frome*, ed. David E. Schultz and S. T. Joshi (New York: Hippocampus Press, 2016), 220.

52. Lovecraft to E. Hoffman Price, February 12, 1936, *Selected Letters*, 5:224.

53. Lovecraft to Kleiner, May 29, 1936, *Letters to Kleiner*, 206.

54. Lovecraft to Kleiner, May 29, 1936, *Letters to Kleiner*, 206.

55. H. P. Lovecraft, "He," in *Tales*, 147.

56. Lovecraft to Kleiner, February 2, 1916, *Letters to Kleiner*, 51.

57. Stephen King, "Lovecraft's Pillow," introduction to Houellebecq, *H. P. Lovecraft: Against the World, Against Life*, 17. All italicized words throughout the text were originally italicized or underscored in cited sources.

58. W. Scott Poole, *In the Mountains of Madness: The Life and Extraordinary Afterlife of H. P. Lovecraft* (Berkeley, Calif.: Soft Skull Press, 2016); Sederholm and Weinstock, "Lovecraft Rising," in Sederholm and Weinstock, *Age of Lovecraft*, 8–25. Poole's biography-cum-cultural history thoroughly examines the long tail of Lovecraft's influence on popular and high culture. Sederholm and Weinstock present a short, focused look on the topic.

59. James Sanders, *Celluloid Skyline: New York and the Movies* (New York: Alfred A. Knopf, 2002), 20.

60. L. Sprague de Camp, *Lovecraft: A Biography* (Garden City, N.Y.: Doubleday, 1975); Joshi, *I Am Providence*; Poole, *In the Mountains of Madness*. The three cited biographies may allow readers to gain a fuller understanding of Lovecraft's life. Although highly readable and narratively compelling, de Camp's work contains factual gaps and leans heavily on a now dated Freudian analysis. A culmination of decades of reading and scholarship, Joshi's two-volume opus is the most exhaustive and wide-ranging work on Lovecraft. However, its density might dissuade the casual reader. Poole presents a discursive, intelligent, and enjoyable reflection on Lovecraft and popular culture. In my opinion as a lifelong fan of Lovecraft, the most revealing, challenging, and gripping introduction to him are his letters. Hippocampus Press continues to publish editions of Lovecraft's letters to individual correspondents, many of whom were accomplished writers or thinkers in their own right. Most instructive and delightful is reading Lovecraft's original letters and deciphering the lines and loops of his actual handwriting. Thankfully, many of these documents are now digitally available from the John Hay Library at Brown University.

61. Rheinhart Kleiner, "Bards and Bibliophiles," in Cannon, *Lovecraft Remembered*, 194.

1. "A Person of the Most Admirable Qualities"

1. H. P. Lovecraft to Anne Tillery Renshaw, June 1, 1921, in *Selected Letters*, ed. August Derleth and Donald Wandrei, vol. 1, *1911–1924* (Sauk City, Wisc.: Arkham House,

1965), 134; S. T. Joshi, *I Am Providence: The Life and Times of H. P. Lovecraft* (New York: Hippocampus Press, 2013), 1:390–91.

2. Winfield Townley Scott, "His Own Most Fantastic Creation: Howard Phillips Lovecraft," in *Lovecraft Remembered*, ed. Peter Cannon (Sauk City, Wisc.: Arkham House, 1998), 17; Joshi, *I Am Providence*, 1:390. Winfield Townley Scott had access to Sarah Susan Phillips Lovecraft's medical records from her commitment to Butler Hospital until her death, noting a Dr. F. J. Farnell as her psychiatrist. This was Frederic J. Farnell, M.D. He served in various positions as a psychiatrist and pathologist at Providence City Hospital, the Providence public school system, and Butler Hospital; published in medical journals; and sat on government commissions in Rhode Island. For his research, Scott interviewed the Lovecrafts' family attorney, as well. His account of both this conversation and the medical records carry a tinge of paternalism and sexism. The later destruction of these records effectively limits an accurate account of Sarah Susan Lovecraft's mental health and treatment. A study on psychiatric care and hospitalization and the management and practices at Butler Hospital between the 1890s and 1920s might help develop a better understanding of the respective experiences of Lovecraft's parents as permanently committed patients.

3. S. T. Joshi, *I Am Providence*, 1:390; "Rhode Island, U.S., Historical Cemetery Commission Index, 1647–2008," s.v. "Sarah Susan Lovecraft," Ancestry.com; "Cholecystitis," Mayo Clinic, accessed December 23, 2022, https://www.mayoclinic.org/diseases-conditions/cholecystitis/symptoms-causes/syc-20364867; Sarah Carle, "Cholecystitis and Cholangitis," in *Infectious Diseases Emergencies*, ed. Arjun S. Chanmugam et al. (New York: Oxford University Press, 2016), 181–86, Oxford Academic.

4. Lovecraft stated that he first entered a mental hospital ("a madhouse") in 1932. His friend Harry K. Brobst was then working as a nurse at Butler Hospital and provided Lovecraft with a tour of the facilities. Lovecraft referenced the "Butler Hospital Grotto" in a letter, comparing it to the then-rustic and largely undeveloped landscape of the Riverdale neighborhood in Bronx, New York. The grotto remained a favorite spot long after his mother's passing. Lovecraft to J. Vernon Shea, May 29, 1933, *Selected Letters*, 4:191; H. P. Lovecraft to Lillian D. Clark, May 7, 1928, in H. P. Lovecraft, *Letters to Family and Family Friends*, ed. S. T. Joshi and David E. Schultz, vol. 2, *1926–1936* (New York: Hippocampus Press, 2020), 649; Scott, "His Own Most Fantastic Creation," 16; Arthur S. Koki, "H. P. Lovecraft: An Introduction to His Life and Writings" (master's thesis, Columbia University, 1962), 70.

5. Scott, "His Own Most Fantastic Creation," 16.

6. Marian F. Bonner, "Miscellaneous Impressions of H. P. L.," in Cannon, *Lovecraft Remembered*, 29; Sonia H. Davis, "Memories of Lovecraft: I," in Cannon, *Lovecraft Remembered*, 275–76; Sonia H. Davis, *The Private Life of H. P. Lovecraft*, ed. S. T. Joshi (West Warwick, R.I.: Necronomicon Press, 1985), Winfield Townley Scott, Bookman's Galley, *Providence Sunday Journal*, September 19, 1948; Winfield Townley Scott, Bookman's Galley, *Providence Sunday Journal*, October 3, 1948; Scott, "His Own Most Fantastic Creation," 15–17. Aside from Lovecraft's personal letters, the published accounts alluding to Sarah Susan Lovecraft's mental illness are drawn from interviews with or writings by individuals who had known her personally, were acquainted with other members of the family, or were associated with Lovecraft himself. However, these were all documented long after the original chain of events, thus, the passage of time and the reputation of Lovecraft as a writer might have affected them.

7. Bonner, "Miscellaneous Impressions of H. P. L.," 29.

8. For an alternative and thoughtful analysis of the accounts of Sarah Susan Lovecraft and the possible manifestations of her mental illness, see W. Scott Poole, *In the Mountains of Madness: The Life and Extraordinary Afterlife of H. P. Lovecraft* (Berkeley, Calif.: Soft Skull Press, 2016), 28–85, 96–97.

9. Sarah Susan Phillips Lovecraft, "Commonplace Book," 1889, John Hay Library, Brown University. As an adolescent and young woman, Sarah Susan Lovecraft maintained a commonplace book, a collection of quotes, reading lists, family genealogy, and short reflections on literary, intellectual, and historical figures. This book demonstrates that she was an educated and culturally aspiring young woman and that her son partially inherited his love of literature from her. Her musings suggest a vibrant inner life and a possible frustration with the limited avenues available to Victorian women of her class. The commonplace book effectively ends with her marriage and the birth of her son. A page entitled "S. Susie Phillips Married Winfield S. Lovecraft" is left entirely blank.

10. H. P. Lovecraft to Maurice W. Moe, July 10, 1928, in Lovecraft, *Letters to Maurice W. Moe and Others*, ed. David E. Schultz and S. T. Joshi (New York: Hippocampus Press, 2018), 191.

11. Lovecraft to Moe, July 10, 1928, *Letters to Moe*, 191.

12. Cheryl Krasnick Warsh, "The First Mrs. Rochester: Wrongful Confinement, Social Redundancy, and Commitment to the Private Asylum, 1883–1923," *Historical Papers/ Communications historiques* 23, no. 1 (1988): 148.

13. Lovecraft to Renshaw, June 1, 1921, *Selected Letters*, 1:134; Lovecraft to Frank Belknap Long, June 4, 1921, *Selected Letters*, 1:135.

14. Lovecraft to Renshaw, June 1, 1921, *Selected Letters*, 1:133.

15. "My father died when I was very young—so that he is only the vaguest of memories to me"; Lovecraft to Frank Belknap Long, July 17, 1921, *Selected Letters*, 1:141. "'Of course he was genuinely heart-broken,' said [Frank Belknap] Long, 'but it was part of his pose not to show it. He played the role of [the] stoic right to the end.'" Arthur Koki quoted an interview with Long conducted during his graduate research (January 25, 1961), in Koki, "H. P. Lovecraft," 71.

16. Lovecraft to Renshaw, June 1, 1921, *Selected Letters*, 1:133.

17. Lovecraft to Rheinhart Kleiner, June 12, 1921, in H. P. Lovecraft, *Letters to Rheinhart Kleiner and Others*, ed. S. T. Joshi and David E. Schultz (New York: Hippocampus Press, 2020), 181.

18. Lovecraft to Kleiner, June 12, 1921, *Letters to Kleiner*, 181.

19. Lovecraft to Kleiner, June 12, 1921, *Letters to Kleiner*, 181.

20. Lovecraft to Renshaw, June 1, 1921, *Selected Letters*, 1:133–34.

21. Lovecraft to Renshaw, June 1, 1921, *Selected Letters*, 1:134.

22. Lovecraft to Winifred Virginia Jackson, June 7, 1921, *Letters to Kleiner*, 330; Charles Tromblee, "Lovecraft Collaborator—Winifred Jackson," June 24, 2017, https://winifredvjackson.blogspot.com/2017/06/lovecraft-collaborator-winifred.html. Winifred Virginia Jackson (1876–1959) was born in Maine and moved to Boston in her late teens. By 1921, she was twice divorced and worked as a secretary or stenographer to supplement her writing and publishing career. Tromblee presents a full and detailed analysis of Jackson.

23. Winifred Virginia Jackson and H. P. Lovecraft, "The Crawling Chaos," *United Co-Operative*, April 1, 1921; Winifred Virginia Jackson and H. P. Lovecraft, "The Green

Meadow," *Vagrant*, Spring 1927. Both stories were originally published under Jackson and Lovecraft's pen names, Elizabeth Neville Berkeley and Lewis Theobald Jr.

24. H. P. Lovecraft, "Winifred Virginia Jackson: A 'Different' Poetess," *United Amateur*, March 1921.

25. Joshi, *I Am Providence*, 1:311–13; George T. Wetzel and R. Alain Everts, *Winifred Virginia Jackson, Lovecraft's Lost Romance* (Madison, Wisc.: Strange Co., 197?), 1–3; S. T. Joshi and David E. Schultz, introduction to *Letters to Kleiner*, 16–19.

26. Lovecraft to Winifred Jackson, [c. December 25, 1920], *Letters to Kleiner*, 329–30; Joshi and Schultz, introduction to *Letters to Kleiner*, 18; H. P. Lovecraft, "On Receiving Ye Portraiture of Mrs. Berkeley, Ye Poetess," 1920, Howard P. Lovecraft Collection, Brown Digital Repository, Brown University Library, https://repository.library.brown.edu/studio/item/bdr:425393/. Not all of Lovecraft's original letters included a full date. In these instances, archivists, editors, or compilers determined approximate dates and included such citations within brackets. This style will be honored throughout the text.

27. Winifred Virginia Jackson's birthdate and age vary slightly depending on documents and sources.

28. Wetzel and Everts, *Winifred Virginia Jackson*, 6; Joshi and Schultz, introduction to *Letters to Kleiner*, 18. A reproduction of this photograph published in Wetzel and Evert's volume lists the image's date as 1918. In actuality, this photograph was likely taken in the Boston area in the summer of 1920 or in early 1921. Jackson was recently divorced in 1919, and Lovecraft was in Boston for amateur journalist meetings during those periods.

29. Lovecraft to Jackson, June 7, 1921, *Letters to Kleiner*, 331.

30. Joshi, *I Am Providence*, 1:311–13, 402–3, 424–25.

31. Lovecraft to Kleiner, June 12, 1921, *Letters to Kleiner*, 181.

32. George Julian Houtain, "Three—Oh!—Three: Veni! Vidi! Vici!," *National Tribune*, August 1921. Houtain chronicles the entire happenings of the convention, including specific dates. The exact time and date of Lovecraft's arrival and departure are uncertain. Several members lingered in Boston for several days after the official convention proceedings.

33. Built in the Romanesque Revival style, the Hotel Brunswick was a "charming" hotel touting "New England hospitality" and dining. It was later known as the Brunswick Hotel, or simply the Brunswick, and it was demolished in 1957. A photograph captures a small group gathering for tea in the hotel as the demolition work was ongoing. *The Brunswick Hotel, Copley Square, Boston, Mass.*, [c. 1930–1945], postcard, Digital Commonwealth, https://www.digitalcommonwealth.org/search/commonwealth:wh246s837; Verner Reed, *Brunswick Hotel, Boston, 1957*, 1957, photograph, Verner Reed Photographic Collection, Historic New England, https://www.historicnewengland.org/explore/collections-access/capobject/?refd=PC044.TMP.084.

34. Joshi, *I Am Providence*, 1:399–400; Lovecraft and Rheinhart Kleiner to Lillian Clark, July 6, 1921, *Letters to Family*, 1:37; H. P. Lovecraft, "The Convention Banquet," 1921, Lovecraft Collection, https://repository.library.brown.edu/studio/item/bdr:425486/; "All Star Boxing Bouts on Today," *Boston Post*, July 4, 1921, Newspapers.com; Houtain, "Three—Oh!—Three," *National Tribune*, August 1921. Lovecraft notes the event as occurring at eight at night in his essay. This is incorrect. The published account in the *National Tribune* reports the banquet as a lunchtime event and includes later activities (Charles River walk and a baseball game at Braves Field). A contemporaneous newspaper article corroborates the *National Tribune* account of the baseball game.

35. O. Ivan Lee, "Memorial of James F. Morton," *American Mineralogist* 27, no. 3 (March 1942): 200. The song's lyricist, Samuel Francis Smith, was the grandfather of one guest at the dinner, James F. Morton.

36. Lovecraft, "Convention Banquet," Lovecraft Collection, https://repository.library .brown.edu/studio/item/bdr:425486/.

37. H. P. Lovecraft, "Within the Gates, by 'One Sent by Providence,'" 1921, Lovecraft Collection, https://repository.library.brown.edu/studio/item/bdr:425545/; Edith Miniter, "Amateur Writings," in Cannon, *Lovecraft Remembered*, 83–84.

38. "Make something as good of it as was made of yours at the conference and you cover yourself with glory"; Edith Miniter to Lovecraft, July 4, 1921, Lovecraft Collection, https://repository.library.brown.edu/studio/item/bdr:418362/.

39. Houtain, "Three—Oh!—Three," *National Tribute*, August 1921, 18.

40. Miniter, "Amateur Writings," 83; Rheinhart Kleiner, "A Memoir of Lovecraft," in Cannon, *Lovecraft Remembered*, 197; Rheinhart Kleiner, "Discourse on H. P. Lovecraft," in Cannon, *Lovecraft Remembered*, 161; James Warren Thomas, "Howard Phillips Lovecraft: A Self-Portrait" (master's thesis, Brown University, 1950), 33; R. Alain Everts, "Mrs. Howard Phillips Lovecraft," *Nyctalops*, April 1973, 45; Davis, *Private Life*, 10; Davis, "Lovecraft as I Knew Him," in Cannon, *Lovecraft Remembered*, 253; Frank Belknap Long, *Howard Phillips Lovecraft: Dreamer on the Nightside* (Sauk City, Wisc.: Arkham House, 1975), 35. In a memoir on Lovecraft, Greene claimed that James F. Morton introduced her to Lovecraft, but she offered no elaborating context. Much later in her life, Greene recalled first meeting Lovecraft at an earlier and different event in Boston in 1921, contradicting the facts presented in her memoir. George Julian Houtain, Edith Miniter, and Rheinhart Kleiner's separate accounts of the Boston convention share matching details, providing evidence that Greene and Lovecraft did first meet on the boat in Boston Harbor on July 3, 1921. Frank Belknap Long wrote that Lovecraft himself told him that he and Greene met at the July Boston convention.

41. Invitation, 1910–1930, Landauer Collection of Business and Advertising Ephemera, New-York Historical Society, https://emuseum.nyhistory.org/objects/48417 /invitation?ctx=c12e48e2679649a60d448245da6c83b2af01dc17&idx=0; "Ferle Heller, 82, Former Milliner," *New York Times*, January 13, 1964; Herbert C. Heller [Reference Letter for Sonia H. Davis], November 14, 1942, Sonia H. and Nathaniel Davis Papers, John Hay Library, Brown University.

42. Long, *Howard Phillips Lovecraft*, 48; Kleiner, "A Memoir of Lovecraft," 198.

43. Sonia H. Davis, Autobiographical Writings, August 19, 1964, box 9, folder 1, Davis Papers; Davis, Autobiographical Writings, August 25, 1964, box 9, folder 1, Davis Papers; Davis, Autobiographical Writings, "In a small village on the outskirts of the town Konotop . . . ," undated, box 9, folder 4, Davis Papers; Davis, *Private Life*, 8; Joshi, *I Am Providence*, 1:401. Many of the dates pertinent to Greene's early biography conflict, depending on the source. Unless demonstrably inaccurate, her unpublished writings will be presumed to be correct.

44. 1900 United States Census, Manhattan, New York County, New York, digital image s.v. "Samuel Greene," Ancestry.com. Samuel Greene's age is often cited as having been a decade older than Sonia Greene. The 1900 United States Census lists his birthdate as falling in May 1876 and his age as twenty-four.

45. Alfred Galpin, "Memories of a Friendship," in Cannon, *Lovecraft Remembered*, 171.

46. 1905 New York State Census, Manhattan, New York County, New York, digital

image s.v. "Florence Greene," Ancestry.com; 1915 New York State Census, Brooklyn, Kings County, New York, digital image s.v. "Florence Greene," Ancestry.com; 1920 United States Census, Brooklyn, Kings County, New York, digital image s.v. "Sonia Greene," Ancestry.com; 1940 United States Census, Brooklyn, Kings County, New York, digital image s.v. "Carol Weld," Ancestry.com. The birthyear of Florence Greene has also been listed as both 1902 and 1903. A lack of an official birth certificate further complicates determining the correct date. The absence of this vital record suggests that Greene was a homebirth and not registered, a common practice among immigrants in New York City in the early twentieth century. Early available public records support assertions that 1902 was her correct birthyear. Florence Greene obfuscated personal details throughout her life, listing her birthyear as 1903 and 1904 in different documents.

47. Sonia Greene's account of the end of her relationship with Samuel Greene and of his death changed across her different memoirs and conversations. In her unpublished autobiographical writings, she writes that Samuel Greene was a "mental case" and possibly died in an institution in Chicago. Additionally, she hinted that she divorced Greene upon returning to New York in 1908 in these unpublished writings. Considering the conservative divorce laws in New York State at that time, this seems highly unlikely. Additionally, no divorce listing Samuel and Sonia Greene as parties was recorded in New York County during this period. In her published autobiography, she identifies herself as a widow. The 1920 census supports this statement. Near the end of her life, she reportedly stated in an interview with R. Alain Everts that Samuel Greene committed suicide; Davis, Autobiographical Writings, August 19, 1964, box 9, folder 1, Davis Papers; Davis, Autobiographical Writings, "In a small village on the outskirts of the town Konotop . . . ," undated, box 9, folder 4, Davis Papers; Davis, *Private Life*, 19; R. Alain Everts, "Lovecraft's Daughter III," in *Cry of the Cricket*, Candlemas 1983, 1; 1920 United States Census, Brooklyn, Kings County, New York, digital image s.v. "Sonia Greene," Ancestry .com; Joseph Van Nostrand, New York County Clerk, email to author, April 28, 2023.

48. Joshi, *I Am Providence*, 1:401–2; Davis, *Private Life*, 8–9; Galpin, "Memories of a Friendship," 170–71; Long, *Howard Phillips Lovecraft*, 48; "The Mysterious Love of Sonia H. Greene for H. P. Lovecraft," *Wired*, February 5, 2007, https://www.wired .com/2007/02/the-mysterious-2-2/; Scott, "His Own Most Fantastic Creation," 17; Davis, Autobiographical Writings, August 19, 1964, box 9, folder 1, Davis Papers; Davis, Autobiographical Writings, "In a small village on the outskirts of the town Konotop . . . ," undated, box 9, folder 4, Davis Papers.

49. Kleiner, "Discourse on H. P. Lovecraft," 161.

50. Davis, *Private Life*, 10.

51. H. P. Lovecraft to Moe, July 10, 1923, *Letters to Moe*, 115.

52. George Julian Houtain, "Amateur Writings," in Cannon, *Lovecraft Remembered*, 88; Houtain, "Three—Oh!—Three," *National Tribune*, August 1921, 18, 29. The photographs of Greene, Kleiner, and Lovecraft and of Greene and Lovecraft on the boat tour often have been cited as taken on July 5, 1921. The report on the July convention published in the *National Tribune* clearly states that the photograph of Greene and Lovecraft was taken on July 3, 1921. Greene also posed for a group photograph with two other female amateur journalists on that date. She is wearing the same outfit in all three photographs. As a fashion industry professional, she would have been highly conscious of her dress and appearance. It is almost impossible that she would have traveled without several different outfits.

53. Wetzel and Everts, *Winifred Virginia Jackson*, 3.

54. Houtain, "Three—Oh!—Three," *National Tribute*, August 1921, 23.

55. Miniter, "Amateur Writings," 83; Kleiner, "A Memoir of Lovecraft," 197; Houtain, "Amateur Writings," 88–89.

56. Kleiner, "Discourse on H. P. Lovecraft," 161.

57. Lovecraft to Kleiner, July 30, 1921, *Letters to Kleiner*, 183; H. P. Lovecraft, "Nyarlathotep," *United Amateur*, November 1920; H. P. Lovecraft, "Polaris," *Philosopher*, December 1920.

58. Lovecraft to Kleiner, July 30, 1921, *Letters to Kleiner*, 183.

59. Lovecraft to Kleiner, July 30, 1921, *Letters to Kleiner*, 183.

60. Lovecraft's friend Alfred Galpin emphasized this point in his exchanges with author and biographer, L. Sprague de Camp, noting "when it came to personal contacts there was little or no animosity"; Alfred Galpin to L. Sprague de Camp, April 29, 1971, Alfred Galpin Papers, John Hay Library, Brown University.

61. H. P. Lovecraft, "The Temple," *Weird Tales*, September 1925. "The Temple" was published several years after its original composition in 1920.

62. Sonia Davis to Lovecraft, August 1, 1921, Lovecraft Collection, https://repository .library.brown.edu/studio/item/bdr:417589/.

63. Davis to Lovecraft, August 1, 1921, Lovecraft Collection, https://repository.library .brown.edu/studio/item/bdr:417589/.

64. "Son Sees Prophecy in Tolstoy's Work," *New York Times*, January 20, 1917. Greene likely attended Ilya Tolstoy's appearance at Carnegie Hall in New York City on January 19, 1917.

65. Davis to Lovecraft, August 1, 1921, Lovecraft Collection, https://repository.library .brown.edu/studio/item/bdr:417589/.

66. Lovecraft to Kleiner, August 11, 1921, *Letters to Kleiner*, 184.

67. Lovecraft to Kleiner, August 11, 1921, *Letters to Kleiner*, 185.

68. Lovecraft to Kleiner, September 27, 1919, *Letters to Kleiner*, 142–44; Lovecraft to Kleiner, January 23, 1920, *Letters to Kleiner*, 152–53.

69. Lovecraft to Kleiner, August 30, 1921, *Letters to Kleiner*, 186. Lovecraft often used the plus sign (+) in place of the conjunction "and" in his letters. Published editions of these archival materials replace the plus sign with an ampersand (&). Unless included in a block quote or detracting from the meaning of the original writing, ampersands will be replaced by "and" and not placed within quotation marks.

70. Lovecraft to Kleiner, August 30, 1921, *Letters to Kleiner*, 187. Alfred Galpin recalled Sonia H. Greene visiting him in his college dormitory sometime between 1921 and 1922. He "felt like an English sparrow transfixed by a cobra"; Galpin, "Memories of a Friendship," 170.

71. The Crown Hotel building was purchased by Johnson & Wales University in 1966 and later demolished in 1992; "Jr. College Buys Hotel," *Newport Daily News*, August 11, 1966, Newspapers.com; Louis Azar II, *Downtown Providence* (Charlestown, S.C.: Arcadia, 2022), 84.

72. Lovecraft to Kleiner, September 21, 1921, *Letters to Kleiner*, 189.

73. William McKensie Woodward, *PPS/AIAri Guide to Providence Architecture*, photography by Warren Jagger Photography, foreword by William Morgan (Providence: Providence Preservation Society; American Institute of Architects, Rhode Island Chapter, 2003), 238.

74. Lovecraft to Kleiner, September 21, 1921, *Letters to Kleiner*, 190.

75. Lovecraft to Kleiner, September 21, 1921, *Letters to Kleiner*, 190.

76. Lovecraft to Kleiner, September 21, 1921, *Letters to Kleiner*, 190.

77. Lovecraft to Kleiner, September 21, 1921, *Letters to Kleiner*, 190.

78. Lovecraft to Kleiner, September 21, 1921, *Letters to Kleiner*, 190.

79. Lovecraft to Kleiner, September 21, 1921, *Letters to Kleiner*, 191.

80. Lovecraft to Kleiner, September 21, 1921, *Letters to Kleiner*, 191.

81. Lovecraft to Kleiner, September 21, 1921, *Letters to Kleiner*, 191.

82. "Charles Pendleton House," *RISD Museum*, accessed December 23, 2022, https://risdmuseum.org/exhibitions-events/exhibitions/charles-pendleton-house#content__section-introduction-977266.

83. Lovecraft to Kleiner, September 21, 1921, *Letters to Kleiner*, 191–92.

84. Lovecraft to Kleiner, September 21, 1921, *Letters to Kleiner*, 192.

2. "An Eastern City of Wonder"

1. H. P. Lovecraft to Maurice W. Moe, May 18, 1922, in Lovecraft, *Letters to Maurice W. Moe and Others*, ed. David E. Schultz and S. T. Joshi (New York: Hippocampus Press, 2018), 84.

2. Samuel Loveman, "Howard Phillips Lovecraft," in *Lovecraft Remembered*, ed. Peter Cannon (Sauk City, Wisc.: Arkham House, 1998), 204. Thirty-odd years after receiving Lovecraft's introductory letter, Samuel Loveman (1887–1976) warmly remembered his correspondence with him: "They were wonderful letters—marvelously readable, astonishingly erudite, incredibly human. Their range of subjects was monumental: Astronomy, Sorcery, Witchcraft, Archaeology, English Literature, Cabalism, Dutch New York, Eighteenth-Century Poetry, Alexander Pope, Roman Sculpture, Greek Vases, Decadence of the Alexandrian Period, Baths of Caracalla, T. S. Elliot, Hart Crane—heaven alone could enumerate their infinite range and breath-taking variety!"; Loveman, "Howard Phillips Lovecraft," 204–5.

3. Sonia H. Davis, *The Private Life of H. P. Lovecraft*, ed. S. T. Joshi (West Warwick, R.I.: Necronomicon Press, 1985), 10–11; Laura DeMarco, "A Visual History of Cleveland's Fascinating Hotel Statler," *Cleveland Plain Dealer*, February 15, 2018. The former Hotel Statler (also known as the Statler Hotel) is now a luxury apartment building in Cleveland.

4. Lovecraft to Moe, May 18, 1922, *Letters to Moe*, 84.

5. H. P. Lovecraft to Gallamo [Alfred Galpin and Maurice W. Moe], December 11, 1919, in *Selected Letters*, ed. August Derleth and Donald Wandrei, vol. 1, *1911–1924* (Sauk City, Wisc.: Arkham House, 1965), 94–97; H. P. Lovecraft to Rheinhart Kleiner, December 14, 1920, in *Letters to Rheinhart Kleiner and Others*, ed. S. T. Joshi and David E. Schultz (New York: Hippocampus Press, 2020), 174–75; H. P. Lovecraft, "The Statement of Randolph Carter," *Vagrant*, May 1920; H. P. Lovecraft, "Nyarlathotep," *United Amateur*, November 1920. The short story "The Statement of Randolph Carter" follows the narrative of a dream related to Alfred Galpin and Maurice W. Moe in December 1919. The story's titular character is a recurring fictional stand-in for Lovecraft, and its other character, Harvey Warren, represents Samuel Loveman. "Nyarlathotep" drew inspiration from a dream in which Lovecraft opened a letter from Loveman urging him to see the dark godlike entity and the prose poem's namesake upon its appearance in Providence.

6. Lovecraft to Moe, May 18, 1922, *Letters to Moe*, 84.

7. *The Official Guide of the Railways and Steam Navigation Lines of the United States, Puerto Rico, Canada, Mexico and Cuba*, April 1922, microfilm, p. 52–53, April–May 1922.

8. Lovecraft to Moe, May 18, 1922, *Letters to Moe*, 84.

9. Lovecraft to Moe, May 18, 1922, *Letters to Moe*, 84.

10. Lovecraft to Moe, May 18, 1922, *Letters to Moe*, 84.

11. Department of Commerce, *Statistical Abstract of the United States*, 1921 ed., comp. Edward Whitney (Washington, D.C.: G. P. O., 1922), 56, 59, https://www2.census .gov/prod2/statcomp/documents/1921-02.pdf#[33,{%22name%22:%22FitH%22},621].

12. Jean Clair, "Red October, Black October," in *The 1920s: Age of the Metropolis*, ed. Jean Clair (Montreal: Montreal Museum of Fine Arts, 1991), 37, 40.

13. Lovecraft to Moe, May 18, 1922, *Letters to Moe*, 84.

14. Pete Hamill, *Downtown: My Manhattan* (New York, Little, Brown, 2004), 101–2.

15. Lovecraft to Moe, May 18, 1922, *Letters to Moe*, 85.

16. Lovecraft to Moe, May 18, 1922, *Letters to Moe*, 85.

17. Lovecraft to Moe, May 18, 1922, *Letters to Moe*, 85.

18. Lovecraft to Kleiner, November 8, 1917, *Letters to Kleiner*, 93.

19. Davis, *Private Life*, 21. This quote is entirely from Greene's recollection. Unfortunately, the original letter no longer appears to exist. Her account of Lovecraft's impressions of Loveman matches those of others.

20. Davis, *Private Life*, 21.

21. Davis, *Private Life*, 21.

22. Loveman claimed to have been "unsophisticated . . . on the subject of homosexuality" in the early 1920s, remembering that he "lived in a world of [his] own"; Samuel Loveman to Alfred Galpin, March 19, 1971, Alfred Maurice Galpin Papers, Rare Book and Manuscript Library, Columbia University Library; S. T. Joshi, *I Am Providence: The Life and Times of H. P. Lovecraft* (New York: Hippocampus Press, 2013), 2:930.

23. "Last evening I sat at table thinking of you, only entering conversation when forced to. I missed little, however, since chaps were merely airing their usually absurd ideas about your sex. One was a homo. . . ."; George Kirk to Lucile Dvorak, October 11, 1924, in *Lovecraft's New York Circle: The Kalem Club, 1924–1927*, ed. Mara Kirk Hart and S. T. Joshi (New York: Hippocampus Press, 2006), 28.

24. Samuel Loveman, "Lovecraft as a Conversationalist," in Cannon, *Lovecraft Remembered*, 210.

25. Mara Kirk Hart and S. T. Joshi, "Rheinhart Kleiner," in Hart and Joshi, *Lovecraft's New York Circle*, 125.

26. Lovecraft to Moe, May 18, 1922, *Letters to Moe*, 86.

27. [H. P. Lovecraft], "News Notes," *United Amateur*, March 1922; Davis, *Private Life*, 11. When recounting this visit and the sleeping arrangements, Greene indicated that Lovecraft and Loveman stayed during the Christmas and New Year's holiday season. This was not the case. Greene's account conflicts at points with Lovecraft's. His dates from May 1922, a little more than a month after his stay; Greene's account originally was written in two versions, in 1948 and 1949. That is twenty-six and twenty-seven years after the event. Credence will be given to Lovecraft's account because of its contemporaneousness. A summary of the entire trip was printed in the *United Amateur* as well.

28. Davis, *Private Life*, 11; Lynn Dumenil, *The Modern Temper: American Culture and Society in the 1920s* (New York: Hill and Wang, 1995), 98–145.

29. Lovecraft to Moe, May 18, 1922, *Letters to Moe*, 93.

30. Lovecraft to Moe, May 18, 1922, *Letters to Moe*, 86.

31. Lovecraft commented upon first meeting Morton in September 1920: "Never have I met so thoroughly erudite a conversationalist before, & I was quite surprised by the geniality & friendliness which overlay his unusual attainments"; Lovecraft to Kleiner, September 10, 1920, *Letters to Kleiner*, 171–72; Joshi, *I Am Providence*, 1:216–19, 308.

32. Lovecraft to Moe, May 18, 1922, *Letters to Moe*, 88.

33. Lovecraft to Moe, May 18, 1922, *Letters to Moe*, 89.

34. Lovecraft to Moe, May 18, 1922, *Letters to Moe*, 89.

35. Lovecraft to Moe, May 18, 1922, *Letters to Moe*, 88.

36. "Dangers of Race Prejudice," *New York Times*, January 22, 1906; James F. Morton Jr., *The Curse of Race Prejudice* (New York: self-published, 1906); Masthead, *The Crisis*, December 1910, [3], https://repository.library.brown.edu/studio/item/bdr:507810/PDF/. Morton began speaking on the issues of racism and civil rights in the early 1900s. The *New York Times* covered his lecture "The Curse of Race Prejudice" at the Alhambra Theatre in Harlem on January 21, 1906. Morton wrote and self-published a book based on his speech later that same year. He served on various committees of the National Association for the Advancement of Colored People (NAACP), beginning at its founding in 1909.

37. Lovecraft to Moe, May 18, 1922, *Letters to Moe*, 89, 90. Lovecraft described his ambivalence in far more humorous language: ". . . good ol' woollybean [Morton] blew in to bear us off to a stupid musicale on which his honest heart was set. . . . It didn't sound very inviting . . . but we'd do near damn anything for good old Jim"; Lovecraft to Moe, May 18, 1922, *Letters to Moe*, 88.

38. Richard Davenport-Hines, *Gothic: Four Hundred Years of Excess, Horror, Evil and Ruin* (New York: North Point Press, 1998), 180–85. Matthew Gregory Lewis (1775–1818) is best known for his novel *The Monk*, a seminal, yet oft-mocked example of Gothic literature. The book continues to inform culture and inspire adaptations in various genres and media.

39. Lovecraft to Moe, May 18, 1922, *Letters to Moe*, 90.

40. Lovecraft to Moe, May 18, 1922, *Letters to Moe*, 90; James Flatness, "Mapping the World: Library Receives Hammond Archives," *Library of Congress Information Bulletin* 62, no. 5 (May 2003), https://www.loc.gov/loc/lcib/0305/hammond.html. Coincidentally, C. S. Hammond & Company, then the second-largest map and atlas publisher in the world, was headquartered in New York City.

41. Louis Keila was a Jewish-Ukrainian immigrant. Before his career as a visual artist, he "sold matches around Rivington St." in New York's Lower East Side. Keila sculpted a bust of President Warren G. Harding during his 1920 presidential campaign. He was an instructor at the City College of New York. In 1931, a studio fire consumed much of his work, including sketches and casts. Keila later taught his niece, Dorothy Block (1904–84). Block worked as an artist for the Federal Art Project, a New Deal program during the Great Depression; "Harding Family Portraits," *American Art News*, February 26, 1921, http://www.jstor.org/stable/25589769; "Boro Man's Work of a Lifetime Lost," *Brooklyn Daily Times*, February 7, 1931, Brooklyn Newsstand, Brooklyn Public Library.

42. Lovecraft to Moe, May 18, 1922, *Letters to Moe*, 91.

43. Lovecraft to Moe, May 18, 1922, *Letters to Moe*, 91.

44. Lovecraft to Moe, May 18, 1922, *Letters to Moe*, 91.

45. Lovecraft to Moe, May 18, 1922, *Letters to Moe*, 91.

46. The original title of the series was "Grewsome Tales," and it was published in *Home Brew*, February 1922– July 1922. The April 1922 issue of *Home Brew* was consulted.

47. John B. Manbeck, ed., *The Neighborhoods of Brooklyn*, intro. Kenneth T. Jackson, 2nd ed. (New York: Citizens Committee for New York City; New Haven: Yale University Press, 2004), 37; Federal Writers' Project, *The WPA Guide to New York City: The Federal Writers' Project Guide to 1930s New York*, intro. William H. Whyte (New York: New Press, 1992), 442.

48. "Miss MacLaughlin Weds," marriage announcement, *New York Times*, September 3, 1921.

49. Lovecraft to Moe, May 18, 1922, *Letters to Moe*, 91–92.

50. Lovecraft to Moe, May 18, 1922, *Letters to Moe*, 92.

51. Lovecraft to Moe, May 18, 1922, *Letters to Moe*, 92.

52. Percy Loomis Sperr, *Brooklyn: Bedford Avenue—Gates Avenue*, 1941, photograph, New York Public Library Digital Collections, https://digitalcollections.nypl.org/items/39b 1ca40-c533-012f-efa5-58d385a7bc34.

53. Lovecraft to Moe, May 18, 1922, *Letters to Moe*, 92.

54. Witold Rybczynski, *A Clearing in the Distance: Frederick Law Olmsted and America in the 19th Century* (New York: Scribner, 1999), 259–61, 269–77, 279–84. Rybczynski's biography on Olmsted succinctly chronicles Olmsted, Vaux & Company's involvement in the planning and construction of Prospect Park.

55. Frank Belknap Long, *Howard Phillips Lovecraft: Dreamer on the Nightside* (Sauk City, Wisc.: Arkham House: 1975), 35–40. The conversation lodged itself firmly in Long's imagination and memory. Over fifty years later, he re-created it for inclusion in his memoir on his friendship with Lovecraft.

56. Joshi, *I Am Providence*, 1:308–9; Lovecraft to Moe, May 18, 1922, *Letters to Moe*, 93.

57. Long, *Howard Phillips Lovecraft*, 36.

58. Long, *Howard Phillips Lovecraft*, 36.

59. Long, *Howard Phillips Lovecraft*, 36.

60. Long, *Howard Phillips Lovecraft*, 41.

61. Joshi, *I Am Providence*, 1:308–9; Lovecraft to Moe, May 18, 1922, *Letters to Moe*, 93.

62. Long, *Howard Phillips Lovecraft*, 45–46.

63. Long, *Howard Phillips Lovecraft*, 45–48.

64. Lovecraft to Moe, May 18, 1922, *Letters to Moe*, 93–94.

65. Loveman to Galpin, March 30, 1971, Galpin Papers, Columbia University Library.

66. Long, *Howard Phillips Lovecraft*, 50; Joshi, *I Am Providence*, 1:504–5; "Carol Weld," obituary, *New York Times*, April 1, 1979; John Weld to Randal Kirsch, October 27, 1967, Sonia H. and Nathaniel Davis Papers, John Hay Library, Brown University; R. Alain Everts, "Lovecraft's Daughter III," in *Cry of the Cricket*, Candlemas 1983, [1]; Sidney Moseson and Florence Stone, marriage certificate, March 25, 1923, file no. 0009587, New York City Municipal Archives, https://a860-historicalvitalrecords.nyc.gov /view/9396416; John Weld and Carol Greene, marriage certificate, September 13, 1927, file no. 0029357, New York City Municipal Archives, https://a860-historicalvitalrecords .nyc.gov/view/9509816; Loveman to Galpin, March 30, 1971, Galpin Papers, Columbia University Library. Florence Greene (1902–79) reportedly left her mother's household sometime after her twenty-first birthday in 1923. She would marry screenwriter and

journalist John Weld (1905–2003) in 1927 and adopt the name Carol Weld, a combination of her middle name and married name. She listed her mother's name as Sara Hart on hers and Weld's marriage license. The couple divorced in 1932. Carol Weld embarked on her own career as a reporter and worked as a foreign correspondent in the 1930s. She and Greene never reconciled. Greene mentioned her daughter only once in her memoir. Carol Weld died in 1979, only seven years after her mother's passing in 1972. Greene offered various reasons for this fractured relationship over the years: Florence's anger over her chaotic earlier life; Greene's refusal to send to her to a private university attended by a friend; and Florence's infatuation with Greene's half-brother and Florence's own uncle, Sidney Moseson. The last two merit skepticism. Florence never completed high school, and she was working as a stenographer for a chemical company by 1920. The later claim originates from a conversation between Moseson and R. Alain Everts (a.k.a. Randal Kirsch). Sidney Moseson did, in fact, marry a woman name Florence Stone in 1923. This might also explain the cloudiness and confusion surrounding his relationship with his niece. Greene and Sidney Moseson maintained a happy relationship throughout their lives, with Sidney partially supporting Greene in her later years. Samuel Loveman believed the broken relationship resulted from Greene's marriage to Lovecraft. John Weld, Florence's ex-husband, claimed not to know the source behind the estrangement.

67. Lovecraft to Moe, May 18, 1922, *Letters to Moe*, 94–95.

68. Robert Rorke, "How Broadway Got the Nickname 'The Great White Way' in 1880," *New York Post*, July 16, 2018; Fran Leadon, *Broadway: A History of New York in Thirteen Miles* (New York: W. W. Norton, 2018), 175.

69. Lovecraft to Moe, May 18, 1922, *Letters to Moe*, 95.

70. Hamill, *Downtown*, 164–68.

71. Lovecraft to Moe, May 18, 1922, *Letters to Moe*, 95.

72. Lovecraft to Moe, May 18, 1922, *Letters to Moe*, 96; Frank Belknap Long, "Felis: A Prose Poem," *Conservative*, July 1923. Lovecraft would publish a piece by Long about the cat in his own amateur journal, the *Conservative*.

73. Lovecraft to Moe, May 18, 1922, *Letters to Moe*, 96.

74. "Paul L. Keil of Lily Dale Died in Hospital," *Grape Belt and Chautauqua Farmer* (Dunkirk, N.Y.), July 3, 1953, Newspapers.com. Paul Livingston Keil (1900–53) was another peculiar, albeit minor figure in Lovecraft's literary circle. He traveled as a ship's printer in the 1930s and served in the Army Air Force during the Second World War. He later settled in Western New York State and worked as a printer and compositor for two local newspapers, the *Dunkirk Evening Observer* and the *Fredonia Censor*. While living in Western New York, he became involved in spiritualism and resided in Lily Dale, a community associated with spiritualists, and joined the Lily Dale Spiritualist Assembly.

75. "Poe Park," New York City Department of Parks & Recreation, accessed December 23, 2022, https://www.nycgovparks.org/parks/poe-park.

76. "Restoring Poe Cottage," *New York Times*, February 19, 1922; Kenneth Silverman, *Edgar A. Poe: Mournful and Never-Ending Remembrance* (New York: HarperPerennial, 1992), 301–2, 323–26; Scott Peeples, *The Man of the Crowd: Edgar Allan Poe and the City*, photographs by Michelle Van Parys (Princeton: Princeton University Press, 2020), 150–52; Reginald Pelham Bolton, "The Poe Cottage at Fordham," *Transactions of the Bronx Society of Arts, Sciences and History* 1, pt. 5 (1922): 1–14; Gary D. Hermalyn, "Poe Cottage," in *The Encyclopedia of New York City*, ed. Kenneth T. Jackson, 2nd ed. (New Haven: Yale University Press; New York: New-York Historical Society, 2010), 1,005.

77. Lovecraft to Moe, May 18, 1922, *Letters to Moe*, 96.

78. David Ley, *The New Middle Class and the Remaking of the Central City* (Oxford: Oxford University Press, 1996); Suleiman Osman, *The Invention of Brownstone Brooklyn: Gentrification and the Search for Authenticity in Postwar New York* (New York: Oxford University Press, 2011). This conception of the city—the luxuries of culture alongside the bounties of nature—might resemble the aspirations of a certain subset of contemporary gentrifiers.

79. Long, *Howard Phillips Lovecraft*, 237; H. P. Lovecraft, "Homes and Shrines of Poe," in *Collected Essays*, ed. S. T. Joshi, vol. 4, *Travel* (New York: Hippocampus Press, 2005), 255–59. Lovecraft himself would later write a short essay detailing the various homes of Edgar Allan Poe.

80. Lovecraft to Moe, May 18, 1922, *Letters to Moe*, 97–98.

81. Lovecraft to Moe, May 18, 1922, *Letters to Moe*, 97; Ross Wetzsteon, *Republic of Dreams: Greenwich Village; The American Bohemia, 1910–1960* (New York: Simon & Schuster, 2002); John Strausbaugh, *The Village: 400 Years of Beats and Bohemians, Radicals, and Rogues; A History of Greenwich Village* (New York: Ecco, 2013); Luther S. Harris, *Around Washington Square: An Illustrated History of Greenwich Village* (Baltimore: Johns Hopkins University Press, 2003). Many volumes chronicle Greenwich Village's artistic and creative contributions and history—unfortunately now increasingly in its past.

82. Lovecraft to Moe, May 18, 1922, *Letters to Moe*, 97.

83. Angela M. Blake, "New York Is Not America: Immigrants and Tourists in New York After World War I," in *How New York Become American, 1890–1924* (Baltimore: Johns Hopkins University Press, 2006), 111–38. Fremont Rider and Frederic Taber Cooper, comp., *Rider's New York City: A Guide-Book for Travelers, with 13 Maps and 20 Plans*, 2nd ed. (New York: Henry Holt, 1923), 122, 197–200. Blake provides a superb analysis of the incorporation of white ethnics and other minorities into New York City tourist literature and the remapping of the city to attract "real" Americans.

84. Lovecraft to Moe, May 18, 1922, *Letters to Moe*, 97; Lovecraft to Frank Belknap Long, March 21, [1924], *Selected Letters*, 1:333–34. Nearly two years later, Lovecraft still recalled his visit to the Lower East Side with unvarnished disgust.

85. Lovecraft to Moe, May 18, 1922, *Letters to Moe*, 97.

86. Blake, "New York Is Not America," 122–23, 127–28; John Higham, *Strangers in the Land: Patterns of American Nativism, 1860–1925*, 2nd ed. (New Brunswick, N.J.: Rutgers University Press, 1988), 270–77.

87. Lovecraft to Moe, May 18, 1922, *Letters to Moe*, 97.

88. Lovecraft to Moe, May 18, 1922, *Letters to Moe*, 98.

89. Bolton, "Poe Cottage at Fordham," 8.

90. Lovecraft to Moe, May 18, 1922, *Letters to Moe*, 98–99.

91. *New York City Telephone Directories*, October 1923, microfilm, p. 306, reel 170.

92. Lovecraft to Moe, May 18, 1922, *Letters to Moe*, 99.

93. Lovecraft to Moe, May 18, 1922, *Letters to Moe*, 99.

94. Davis, *Private Life*, 11.

95. Alma Law, "Nikita Balieff and the Chauve-Souris," in *Wandering Stars: Russian Emigré Theatre: 1905–1940*, ed. Laurence Senelick (Iowa City: University of Iowa Press, 1992), 16–31.

96. Lovecraft to Moe, May 18, 1922, *Letters to Moe*, 99–100; Davis, *Private Life*, 11.

97. Lovecraft to Moe, May 18, 1922, *Letters to Moe*, 100.

98. Lovecraft to Moe, May 18, 1922, *Letters to Moe*, 100.

3. "It Is a Myth; A Dream"

1. H. P. Lovecraft to Maurice W. Moe, June 21, 1922, in *Letters to Maurice W. Moe and Others*, ed. David E. Schultz and S. T. Joshi (New York: Hippocampus Press, 2018), 102–3.

2. S. T. Joshi, *I Am Providence: The Life and Times of H. P. Lovecraft* (New York: Hippocampus Press, 2013), 1:422–23; Lovecraft to Moe, June 21, 1922, *Letters to Moe*, 102–4.

3. Lovecraft to Lillian D. Clark, July 1922, Howard P. Lovecraft Collection, Brown Digital Repository, Brown University Library, https://repository.library.brown.edu/studio /item/bdr:425583/.

4. H. P. Lovecraft to Lillian D. Clark, June 29, 1922, in *Letters to Family and Family Friends*, ed. S. T. Joshi and David E. Schultz, vol. 1, *1911–1925* (New York: Hippocampus Press, 2020), 47.

5. Joshi, *I Am Providence*, 1:422, 425; Lovecraft to Clark, June 26, 1922, *Letters to Family*, 1:47; Lovecraft to Clark, June 29, 1922, *Letters to Family*, 1:47; Lovecraft to Clark, July 1922, Lovecraft Collection, https://repository.library.brown.edu/studio/item /bdr:425583/; Lovecraft to Clark, July 1, 1922, *Letters to Family*, 1:48. On June 26, 1922, Lovecraft wrote to Clark that he spent the previous day exploring the seaside, suggesting that he arrived on June 25 or earlier.

6. Sonia H. Davis, *The Private Life of H. P. Lovecraft*, ed. S. T. Joshi (West Warwick, R.I.: Necronomicon Press, 1985), 14.

7. Davis, *Private Life*, 14.

8. Sonia H. Greene, "The Invisible Monster," *Weird Tales*, November 1923; Sonia H. Greene and H. P. Lovecraft, "The Horror at Martin's Beach," in Lovecraft, *The Horror in the Museum and Other Revisions*, ed. S. T. Joshi, intro. August Derleth (Sauk City, Wisc.: Arkham House, 1989), 325–30; Joshi, *I Am Providence*, 1:422–24; H. P. Lovecraft to James F. Morton, December 5, 1923, in *Letters to James F. Morton*, ed. David E. Schultz and S. T. Joshi (New York: Hippocampus Press, 2011), 60–61; Lovecraft to Alfred Galpin, June 30, 1922–July 4, 1922, Lovecraft Collection, https://repository.library.brown .edu/studio/item/bdr:425619/. Lovecraft ultimately revised the story for Greene, and she submitted it to *Weird Tales*. The magazine published the story as "The Invisible Monster" in 1923. Its original title was "The Horror at Martin's Beach." This is now the canonical title.

9. Davis, *Private Life*, 14.

10. Davis, *Private Life*, 14.

11. Joshi, *I Am Providence*, 1:424–25.

12. Lovecraft to Galpin, June 30–July 4, 1922, Lovecraft Collection, https://repository .library.brown.edu/studio/item/bdr:425619/. In a letter to Alfred Galpin written over several days, Lovecraft noted that he was composing a passage on July 3, 1922, and then mentioned Greene's story idea. He offered no insight into the nature of his and Greene's relationship or its possible romantic turn. The first two pages of this letter are missing.

13. Ann Poulos, Providence Public Library, email to author, February 12, 2022; Sonia H. Greene and H. P. Lovecraft to Lillian Clark, July 16, 1922, *Letters to Family*, 1:48–49.

14. Lovecraft to Clark, July 26, 1922, *Letters to Family*, 1:49.

15. *The Official Guide of the Railways and Steam Navigation Lines of the United States, Puerto Rico, Canada, Mexico and Cuba*, July 1922, 157; Lovecraft to Clark, August 4, 1922, *Letters to Family*, 1:49. The Lake Shore Limited was a New York Central Railroad route running between New York and Chicago and operating from 1897 until 1956. A Boston section ran along certain schedules. Amtrak resurrected the line as an overnight route in 1975. In his letter to Clark, Lovecraft states his departure time as six-thirty in the evening. The published schedule lists it as five-thirty in the evening.

16. Lovecraft to Clark, August 4, 1922, *Letters to Family*, 1:50.

17. Lovecraft to Clark, August 4, 1922, *Letters to Family*, 1:50.

18. Samuel Loveman to Alfred Galpin, March 9, 1971, Alfred Maurice Galpin Papers, Rare Book and Manuscript Library, Columbia University Library; Galpin to Brom Weber, September 21, 1953, Galpin Papers, Columbia University Library. His summer in Cleveland in 1921 and Lovecraft's visit during it became a treasured memory for Alfred Galpin. At different points in his life, he considered writing a memoir capturing his adventures and encounters from that time.

19. Lovecraft to Clark, August 9, 1922, *Letters to Family*, 1:54.

20. Alfred Galpin, "Memories of a Friendship," in *Lovecraft Remembered*, ed. Peter Cannon (Sauk City, Wisc.: Arkham House, 1998), 166.

21. Samuel Loveman, "Howard Phillips Lovecraft," in Cannon, *Lovecraft Remembered*, 205.

22. Lovecraft to Clark, August 4, 1922, *Letters to Family*, 1:52.

23. Lovecraft to Clark, August 9, 1922, *Letters to Family*, 1:54.

24. "I had never heard of homosexuality as an actual instinct until I was over thirty"; H. P. Lovecraft to J. Vernon Shea, August 14, 1933, in *Selected Letters*, ed. August Derleth and James Turner, vol. 4, *1932–1934* (Sauk City, Wisc.: Arkham House, 1976), 234; Joshi, *I Am Providence*, 1:427.

25. Lovecraft to Morton, January 8, 1924, *Letters to Morton*, 63; George Chauncey, *Gay New York: Gender, Urban Culture, and the Making of the Gay Male World, 1890–1940* (New York: Basic Books, 1994), 15, 114–15. "Sissy," a pejorative term, signified that a man—likely gay—demonstrated an effeminate and decidedly unmasculine appearance and behavior.

26. Lovecraft to Frank Belknap Long, January 8, 1924, *Selected Letters*, 1:281.

27. Loveman, "Howard Phillips Lovecraft," in Cannon, *Lovecraft Remembered*, 205. Alfred Galpin confirmed that Lovecraft was aware of Hart Crane's sexuality in letters to early Lovecraft biographer L. Sprague de Camp. In fact, Loveman warned Galpin about Crane's habit of "trying to seduce his [male] friends"; Galpin to de Camp, June 6, 1972, Alfred Galpin Papers, John Hay Library, Brown University; Galpin to de Camp, May 8, 1971, Galpin Papers, Brown University; Galpin, "Memories of a Friendship," in Cannon, *Lovecraft Remembered*, 167.

28. Loveman to Galpin, March 27, 1971, Galpin Papers, Columbia University Library; Davis to Loveman, January 4, 1948, Lovecraft Collection, https://repository.library.brown.edu/studio/item/bdr:417603/; Loveman to Galpin, March 22, 1971, Galpin Papers, Columbia University Library; Loveman to Galpin, February 14, 1971, Galpin Papers,

Columbia University Library; Samuel Loveman, "Of Gold and Sawdust," in *The Occult Lovecraft*, by H. P. Lovecraft, additional material and interpretations by Anthony Raven, illustrations by Stephen E. Fabian (Saddle River, N.J.: Gerry de la Ree, 1975), 21–22. Samuel Loveman disowned his friendship with Lovecraft in a 1975 essay, "Of Gold and Sawdust," citing Lovecraft's anti-Semitism and bigoted remarks about Loveman himself. He claimed to be ignorant of his friend's varied prejudices until being informed of them by Sonia Greene. However, this reason and rationale warrant deep skepticism. Greene wrote to Loveman on the topic by 1948, and his two laudatory memoirs on Lovecraft were published respectively in 1949 and 1958. During the early days of the two men's friendship, Lovecraft wrote about such beliefs in amateur journalism articles. Also, Lovecraft's penchant for windy conversation likely brought every conceivable topic up for debate among his friends, including Loveman. In his letters with Alfred Galpin in the early to mid-1970s, Loveman expressed real bitterness that his poetry would be forgotten while Lovecraft's literary reputation appeared to be on the rise. This might explain his sudden disavowal of his old friend and his insinuations regarding his sexuality. Loveman asked Galpin to keep the contents of their letters private.

29. Galpin to de Camp, May 8, 1971, Galpin Papers, Brown University.

30. Bobby Derie, *Sex and the Cthulhu Mythos* (New York: Hippocampus Press, 2014), 38–48; Paul La Farge, "The Complicated Friendship of H. P. Lovecraft and Robert Barlow, One of His Biggest Fans," *New Yorker*, March 9, 2017, https://www.newyorker.com/books/page-turner/the-complicated-friendship-of-h-p-lovecraft-and-robert-barlow-one-of-his-biggest-fans; Paul La Farge, *The Night Ocean* (New York: Penguin, 2017); W. Scott Poole, *In the Mountains of Madness: The Life and Extraordinary Afterlife of H. P. Lovecraft* (Berkeley, Calif.: Soft Skull Press, 2016), 131–34. Bobby Derie's book is an exhaustive study of sex and its relationship to Lovecraft's biography, fiction, and creative legacy. Paul La Farge's novel *The Night Ocean* partly centers around a writer discovering "Erotonomicon," purportedly a diary kept by Lovecraft of his gay sexual liaisons.

31. Lovecraft to Clark, August 9, 1922, *Letters to Family*, 1:55.

32. Lovecraft noted that he would return to New York City from Cleveland on either "Wednesday" (August 16, 1922) or "Thursday" (August 17, 1922), depending on if he visited Niagara Falls. He did not appear to make that side trip, thus, he likely traveled to New York on August 16. Presumably, he rode the Lake Shore Limited. This train daily departed from Cleveland at 3:05 A.M. and arrived at Grand Central Terminal at 5:25 P.M., making a long, yet single-day journey; Lovecraft to Clark, August 9, 1922, *Letters to Family*, 1:55; *Official Guide of Railways*, July 1922, 157.

33. Lovecraft to Clark, September 13–16, 1922, *Letters to Family*, 1:63.

34. Lovecraft to Clark, September 13–16, 1922, *Letters to Family*, 1:63.

35. Lovecraft to Annie E. P. Gamwell, September 9–11, 1922, *Letters to Family*, 1:58.

36. Lovecraft to Gamwell, September 9–11, 1922, *Letters to Family*, 1:61.

37. Lovecraft to Gamwell, September 9–11, 1922, *Letters to Family*, 1:59.

38. Lovecraft to Gamwell, September 9–11, 1922, *Letters to Family*, 1:59; Lisa Tuttle, *Encyclopedia of Feminism* (Harlow, UK: Longman, 1986), 71. Winnifred Harper Cooley (1874–1967) was the daughter of suffragist, journalist, and author Ida Husted Harper. Cooley belonged to the first generation of self-identified feminists in the United States. Her most-read work was *The New Womanhood* (New York: Broadway, 1904).

39. Jeffrey B. Perry, *Hubert Harrison: The Voice of Harlem Radicalism, 1883–1918* (New York: Columbia University Press, 2009), 116–17, EBSCOhost; W. Stewart Wallace,

comp., *A Dictionary of North American Authors Deceased before 1950* (Toronto: Ryerson Press, 1951), 481. Notably, Edwin C. Walker inveighed against Postal Inspector Anthony Comstock and his censorship campaign in a 1903 publication, *Who Is the Enemy: Anthony Comstock or You?* (New York: E. C. Walker, 1903).

40. Lovecraft to Clark, September 29, 1922, *Letters to Family*, 1:83.

41. Lovecraft to Clark, September 26, 1922, *Letters to Family*, 1:75; Jeffrey B. Perry, *Hubert Harrison: The Struggle for Equality, 1918–1927* (New York: Columbia University Press, 2021), 130, 497, 522–23, EBSCOhost.

42. Ernest A. Dench, "Military Air Scouting by Motion Pictures," *Scientific American*, February 13, 1915, JSTOR; *New York City Telephone Directory; Brooklyn-Queens and Staten Island*, 1924, 166 (loc. 78 of 405), https://archive.org/details/newyorkcitytelep1924 newy/page/n77/mode/2up. Ernest Dench wrote articles on film and motion pictures for *Scientific American*, including a piece detailing the usage of film by the Imperial German Army for intelligence-gathering during the First World War. He also penned several books on the advertising and educational possibilities of film. He and his wife, Iva Dench, lived at 3052 Emmons Avenue, Brooklyn, New York.

43. Lovecraft to Clark, September 29, 1922, *Letters to Family*, 1:81.

44. Lovecraft to Clark, September 29, 1922, *Letters to Family*, 1:82.

45. Lovecraft to Morton, March 29, 1923, *Letters to Morton*, 33; Lovecraft to Morton, December [18], 1929, *Letters to Morton*, 207–10; Mara Kirk Hart and S. T. Joshi, "Everett McNeil," in *Lovecraft's New York Circle: The Kalem Club, 1924–1927*, ed. Mara Kirk Hart and S. T. Joshi (New York: Hippocampus Press, 2006), 201–2; "H. Everett M'Neil, Author, Dies in West," *New York Times*, December 15, 1929. Henry Everett McNeil (1862–1929) was born in Wisconsin and served in the Spanish-American War. After moving to New York City, he began publishing with E. P. Dutton and in boys' magazines. He also wrote screenplays during an indeterminate period early in the film industry. After learning about McNeil's death in December 1929, Lovecraft shared a warm reflection on his friend and his place in Lovecraft's own New York experience in a letter to James F. Morton.

46. Lovecraft to Clark, September 15, 1922, *Letters to Family*, 1:72.

47. "Mission & History," Morris-Jumel Mansion, accessed December 23, 2022, https://morrisjumel.org/about/; Jonathan Kuhn, "Morris-Jumel Mansion," in *The Encyclopedia of New York City*, ed. Kenneth T. Jackson, 2nd ed. (New Haven: Yale University Press; New York: New-York Historical Society, 2010), 854–55.

48. Lovecraft to Clark, September 13–16, 1922, *Letters to Family*, 1:65.

49. "History of the High Bridge," New York City Department of Parks & Recreation, accessed December 23, 2022, https://www.nycgovparks.org/park-features/highbridge-park /high-bridge-history; Kenneth T. Jackson, "High Bridge," in Jackson, *Encyclopedia of New York City*, 594–95; Lisa W. Foderaro, "High Bridge Reopens after More than 40 Years," *New York Times*, June 9, 2015. The High Bridge closed to the public in the 1970s. After a six-year, $61.8 million renovation, it reopened in 2015 as a park and pedestrian walkway.

50. Scott Peeples, *The Man of the Crowd: Edgar Allan Poe and the City*, photographs by Michelle Van Parys (Princeton: Princeton University Press, 2020), 156–57.

51. Lovecraft to Clark, September 13–16, 1922, *Letters to Family*, 1:66. Edgar Allan Poe wrote "Ulalume" in 1847 while living in the Bronx. Without supporting evidence, Lovecraft's statement concerning its precise location of composition (i.e., the High Bridge) is nothing more than speculation. Still, Lovecraft's anecdote does make a compelling story.

52. Lovecraft to Clark, September 13–16, 1922, *Letters to Family*, 1:66.

53. Lovecraft to Clark, September 23, 1922, *Letters to Family*, 1:72.

54. Center for Brooklyn History, "Flatbush Dutch Reformed Church," *Urban Archive*, January 14, 2019, https://www.urbanarchive.org/sites/ejZEYqkemFB/eFVPYog7QxA; Elizabeth Reich Rawson and John Manbeck, "Flatbush," in Jackson, *Encyclopedia of New York City*, 457–58. Although its name has changed throughout its long history, the church was known as the Flatbush Dutch Reformed Church during the period of Lovecraft's visit.

55. William A. Nardeley, "Dutch Reformed Cemetery," August 29, 1913, transcribed by Jane Devlin, http://dunhamwilcox.net/ny/flatbush_ny_cem.htm; Gertrude Lefferts Vanderbilt, *The Social History of Flatbush, and Manners and Customs of the Dutch Settlers in Kings County* (Brooklyn: Frederick Loeser, 1909; repr. Bowie, Md.: Heritage Books, 2003), 158–68.

56. Lovecraft to Clark, September 29, 1922, *Letters to Family*, 1:76.

57. Lovecraft to Clark, September 29, 1922, *Letters to Family*, 1:77.

58. Joshi, *I Am Providence*, 1:431–33.

59. Nardeley, "Dutch Reformed Cemetery," http://dunhamwilcox.net/ny/flatbush _ny_cem.htm; Vanderbilt, *Social History of Flatbush*, 158–68; Joshi, *I Am Providence*, 1:436–37, 2:592; H. P. Lovecraft, "The Lurking Fear," *Home Brew*, January–April 1923; H. P. Lovecraft, "The Lurking Fear," in *Tales* (New York: Library of America, 2005), 55–76. "The Lurking Fear" centers on a series of ghastly events in the Martense mansion, the former home of a Dutch family in the Catskill Mountains in New York. The Martense name appears on multiple tombstones in the cemetery. Martense Street is two blocks from the church complex. Flatbush, Brooklyn, is a setting in "The Horror at Red Hook," and Lovecraft utilized the Flatbush Dutch Reformed Church to add realistic and geographic detail to the story.

60. Lovecraft to Clark, September 29, 1922, *Letters to Family*, 1:81.

61. Lovecraft to Clark, September 29, 1922, *Letters to Family*, 1:81.

62. Christopher Inoa, "History of Streets: The Albemarle-Kenmore Terraces in Flatbush," *Untapped Cities*, May 7, 2015, https://untappedcities.com/2015/05/07/history -of-streets-the-ablemare-kenmore-terraces-in-flatbush/; Charles Lockwood, Patrick W. Ciccone, and Jonathan D. Taylor, *Bricks & Brownstones: The New York Row House*, foreword by New York Landmarks Conservancy, essay by Fran Leadon, photography by Dylan Chandler (New York: Rizzoli, 2019), 341–43. Slee & Bryson also designed the adjacent Kenmore Terrace and completed it in 1920. Kenmore Terrace's homes were built in the Colonial Revival and the Arts and Crafts styles. Both Albemarle and Kenmore Terraces gained New York City landmark status in 1978 and were placed on the National Register of Historic Places in 1983.

63. Lovecraft to Clark, September 29, 1922, *Letters to Family*, 1:81.

64. Rhode Island Historical Preservation Commission, *Historic and Architectural Resources of the East Side, Providence: A Preliminary Report* (Providence: Rhode Island Historical Preservation Commission, 1989), 15, https://preservation.ri.gov/sites/g/files /xkgbur406/files/pdfs_zips_downloads/survey_pdfs/prov_eastside.pdf.

65. Lovecraft to Clark, September 29, 1922, *Letters to Family*, 1:78.

66. James Bradley, comp. "Foreign-Born Population of New York City by Borough, in Absolute Numbers and as a Percentage of Total Population, 1900–2000," in Jackson, *Encyclopedia of New York City*, 642; Joseph J. Salvo and Arun Peter Lobo, "Population," in Jackson, *Encyclopedia of New York City*, 1,019. In 1920, 31,533 individuals, or 27 percent of Staten Island's total population of 116,531, were immigrants.

67. Museum of the City of New York, "Dutch Reformed Church," *Urban Archive*, April 24, 2018, https://www.urbanarchive.org/sites/i6gd1c8V3qW/6a3Pxatiu3T.

68. Lovecraft to Clark, September 29, 1922, *Letters to Family*, 1:78.

69. Lovecraft to Clark, September 29, 1922, *Letters to Family*, 1:78.

70. "An Overview of the Van Cortlandt House Museum," *Van Cortlandt House Museum*, accessed December 23, 2022, https://www.vchm.org/museum-overview.html. The Van Cortlandt family sold its mansion and land to the City of New York in the late nineteenth century for use as a public museum and park.

71. John Carini, Van Cortlandt House Museum, tour given to author, May 27, 2022; Collection inventory, VC.1988.11, Van Cortlandt Mansion, National Society of Colonial Dames.

72. Lovecraft to Clark, September 29, 1922, *Letters to Family*, 1:84.

73. "The Museum," Dyckman Farmhouse Museum Alliance, accessed December 23, 2022, https://dyckmanfarmhouse.org/about/history/the-museum/; "Dyckman House Museum," New York City Department of Parks & Recreation, accessed December 23, 2022, https://www.nycgovparks.org/parks/dyckman-house-museum/history; Elliot Willensky and Norval White, *AIA Guide to New York City*, 3rd ed. (San Diego: Harcourt Brace Jovanovic: 1988), 467; "Old Dyckman House Now City Museum," *New York Times*, July 12, 1916; Lovecraft to Clark, September 29, 1922, *Letters to Family*, 1:84; Lovecraft to Clark, November 4–6, 1924, *Letters to Family*, 1:194. The farmhouse remained in the Dyckman family until 1868 or 1871. By the early twentieth century, the farmhouse had changed hands several times, and it sat in general disrepair. Dyckman heirs and sisters Mary Alice Dyckman Dean and Fannie Fredericka Dyckman Welch bought the home in 1915. After restoring the farmhouse, the two women donated it to the City of New York in 1916 with the proviso that it would operate as a public museum.

74. Lovecraft to Clark, September 29, 1922, *Letters to Family*, 1:84–85; Henry Wadsworth Longfellow, "Evangeline: A Tale of Acadie," *Poets.org*, accessed April 22, 2023, https://poets.org/poem/evangeline-tale-acadie.

75. Lovecraft to Clark, September 29, 1922, *Letters to Family*, 1:85; "Inwood Hill Park," New York City Department of Parks & Recreation, accessed December 23, 2022, https://www.nycgovparks.org/parks/inwood-hill-park/history. Today, Inwood Hill Park contains the last old-growth forest and natural salt marsh in Manhattan. The city acquired the land in 1916. Inwood Hill Park officially opened in 1926—four years after Lovecraft's initial visit. Many of the trails were constructed by the Works Progress Administration during the Great Depression.

76. Andrew Beveridge, "Harlem's Shifting Population," *Gotham Gazette*, August 27, 2008, https://web.archive.org/web/20100212141227/http://gothamgazette.com/article//2008 0827/255/2635; Kathleen Benson et al., "Strivers' Row," in Jackson, *Encyclopedia of New York City*, 1,255; David Levering Lewis, *When Harlem Was Vogue* (New York: Penguin, 1997), 25–27. In 1910, Black residents consisted of roughly 10 percent of Central Harlem's population. That number grew to approximately 32 percent by 1920, and it reached 70 percent by 1930.

77. Lovecraft to Clark, September 13–16, 1922, Lovecraft Collection, https://repository .library.brown.edu/studio/item/bdr:425590/. The italicized word is underlined in the original manuscript letter.

78. Lovecraft to Clark, September 13–16, 1922, *Letters to Family*, 1:64.

79. T. J. English, *The Westies: Inside New York's Irish Mob* (New York: St. Martin's Griffin, 2006). Today, Hell's Kitchen is largely gentrified and more known for its dining scene and nightlife than its street crime.

80. Hart and Joshi, "Everett McNeil," in *Lovecraft's New York Circle*, 201; Lovecraft to Zealia Brown Reed, January 26, 1930, *Selected Letters*, 3:114–15.

81. Lovecraft to Clark, September 29, 1922, *Letters to Family*, 1:83.

82. Lovecraft to Clark, September 29, 1922, *Letters to Family*, 1:83.

83. Lovecraft to Gamwell, September 9–11, 1922, *Letters to Family*, 1:62.

84. Lovecraft to Gamwell, September 9–11, 1922, *Letters to Family*, 1:61.

85. Lovecraft to Clark, September 13–16, 1922, *Letters to Family*, 1:69.

86. Lovecraft to Moe, May 18, 1922, *Letters to Moe*, 86; Davis, *Private Life*, 11.

87. Joshi, *I Am Providence*, 1:429–30.

88. Lovecraft to Clark, September 29, 1922, *Letters to Family*, 1:76.

89. Lovecraft to Gamwell, September 9–11, 1922, *Letters to Family*, 1:59; Lovecraft to Clark, September 13–16, 1922, *Letters to Family*, 1:64, 69.

90. Lovecraft to Clark, September 13–16, 1922, *Letters to Family*, 1:70.

91. Davis, *Private Life*, 12.

92. Lovecraft to Clark, September 29, 1922, *Letters to Family*, 1:87; Lovecraft to Gamwell, October 3, 1922, *Letters to Family*, 1:89; Lovecraft et al. to Clark, October 12, 1922, *Letters to Family*, 1:94.

93. Lovecraft to Clark, October 7, 1922, *Letters to Family*, 1:93.

94. Davis, *Private Life*, 12.

4. "Brigham Young Annexing His 27th"

1. *The Official Guide of the Railways and Steam Navigation Lines of the United States, Puerto Rico, Canada, Mexico and Cuba*, July 1924, 77; H. P. Lovecraft to Lillian D. Clark, March 9, 1924, in *Letters to Family and Family Friends*, ed. S. T. Joshi and David E. Schultz, vol. 1, *1911–1925* (New York: Hippocampus Press), 104; S. T. Joshi and David E. Schultz, "Letters, Lovecraft's," in *An H. P. Lovecraft Encyclopedia* (Westport, Conn.: Greenwood Press, 2001), 147; Frank Belknap Long, *Howard Phillips Lovecraft: Dreamer on the Nightside* (Sauk City, Wisc.: Arkham House, 1975), 42. Many of Lovecraft's friends experienced his characteristic tardiness, and Lovecraft himself admitted to his own bad habit.

2. Lovecraft to Clark, March 9, 1924, *Letters to Family* 1:104; S. T. Joshi, *I Am Providence: The Life and Times of H. P. Lovecraft* (New York: Hippocampus Press, 2013), 1:498–99.

3. "To me all mankind seems too local & transitory an incident in the cosmos to take at all seriously. I am more interested in scenes—landscapes & architecture . . ."; H. P. Lovecraft to Clark Ashton Smith, January 25, 1924, in Lovecraft, *Selected Letters*, ed. August Derleth and Donald Wandrei, vol. 1, *1911–1924* (Sauk City, Wisc.: Arkham House, 1965), 285.

4. William McKensie Woodward, *PPS/AIAri Guide to Providence Architecture*, photography by Warren Jagger Photography, foreword by William Morgan (Providence: Providence Preservation Society; American Institute of Architects, Rhode Island Chapter, 2003), 104–5.

5. Woodward, *Guide to Providence Architecture*, 151–52; H. P. Lovecraft, "The Call of Cthulhu," in Lovecraft, *Tales* (New York: Library of America, 2005), 170. Lovecraft later incorporated the Fleur-de-Lys Studios into his short story "The Call of Cthulhu."

6. Lovecraft to Clark, March 9, 1924, *Letters to Family*, 1:106; Joshi, *I Am Providence*, 1:498–500; Harry Houdini [and H. P. Lovecraft], "Imprisoned with the Pharaohs," *Weird Tales*, April–May–June 1924; H. P. Lovecraft, "Under the Pyramids," in *Dagon and Other Macabre Tales*, selected by August Derleth, ed. S. T. Joshi, intro. T. E. D. Klein (Sauk City, Wisc.: Arkham House, 1987), 217–43; Duncan Norris, "Lovecraft and Egypt: A Closer Examination," *Lovecraft Annual*, no. 10 (2016): 22–27. The story in question was entitled "Under the Pyramids" in draft form and published as "Imprisoned with the Pharaohs." "Under the Pyramids" is now the canonical title. Duncan Norris discusses Ancient Egyptian art, culture, history, and mythology in the works of Lovecraft, including "Under the Pyramids."

7. "MANUSCRIPT, Lost," classified advertisement, *Providence Journal*, March 3, 1924.

8. Lovecraft to Clark, March 9, 1924, *Letters to Family*, 1:104. Lovecraft noted the exact time in a letter to his aunt Lillian Clark.

9. Lovecraft to Clark, March 9, 1924, *Letters to Family*, 1:104; Joshi, *I Am Providence*, 1:493.

10. Lovecraft to Clark, March 9, 1924, *Letters to Family*, 1:104.

11. *New York City Telephone Directory*, October 1923, microfilm, p. 802, reel 170; *Phillips' Standard Buyer and Business Directory of the Principal Cities of New York State* (New York: Phillips' Standard Buyer, 1926), 866, Ancestry.com; Lovecraft to Clark, March 9, 1924, *Letters to Family*, 1:104; Joshi, *I Am Providence*, 1:499. The October 1923 edition of the *New York City Telephone Directory* contains a listing for the Reading Lamp as a publisher at 437 Fifth Avenue. By 1926, Tucker appeared to have relocated her offices. The business address of Gertrude E. Tucker is listed as 45 West Thirty-Ninth Street in that year's edition of the *Phillips' Standard Buyer and Business Directory of the Principal Cities of New York State*.

12. Sonia H. Davis, *The Private Life of H. P. Lovecraft*, ed. S. T. Joshi (West Warwick, R.I.: Necronomicon Press, 1985), 11.

13. Lovecraft to Clark, March 9, 1924, *Letters to Family*, 1:104.

14. Lovecraft to Clark, March 9, 1924, *Letters to Family*, 1:105.

15. Davis, *Private Life*, 8. Sonia Greene legally changed her name to Sonia Lovecraft. To differentiate her clearly and simply from Lovecraft, her surname at the time of her meeting Lovecraft in 1921—that is, Greene—will be used throughout the remainder of this narrative. Additionally, Greene might have continued using this surname professionally after her marriage to Lovecraft.

16. Sonia H. Davis, "Lovecraft as I Knew Him," in *Lovecraft Remembered*, ed. Peter Cannon (Sauk City, Wisc.: Arkham House: 1998), 261; "Sarah Helen Whitman," *Poetry Foundation*, accessed December 21, 2022, https://www.poetryfoundation.org/poets/sarah-helen-whitman; Scott Peeples, *The Man of the Crowd: Edgar Allan Poe and the City*, photographs by Michelle Van Parys (Princeton: Princeton University Press, 2020), 163–67. Lovecraft enjoyed showing visitors to Providence the former home of Sarah Helen Whitman at 88 Benefit Street in the College Hill neighborhood and the nearby cemetery of St. John's Church (now, the Episcopal Cathedral of St. John), which according to legend was a favorite meeting spot for Poe and Whitman.

17. Lovecraft to Clark, March 9, 1924, *Letters to Family*, 1:105.

18. Davis, *Private Life*, 5.

19. Davis, *Private Life*, 5.

20. H. P. Lovecraft to Coryciani, July 14, 1936, in Lovecraft, *Lord of a Visible World: An Autobiography in Letters*, ed. S. T. Joshi and David E. Schultz (Athens: Ohio University Press, 2000), 339. Lovecraft remained steadfast in his disbelief throughout his life. When writing on his own possible death, Lovecraft approached it with a detached stoicism and perceived an overall meaningless to life.

21. Davis, *Private Life*, 13.

22. Lovecraft to Clark, March 9, 1924, *Letters to Family*, 1:105.

23. Lovecraft to Clark, March 9, 1924, *Letters to Family*, 1:105; William Montague Geer, comp., *Old St. Paul's Chapel, Trinity Parish, New York: Short History Published for the Celebration of the One Hundred and Fiftieth Anniversary of the Opening of the Chapel on October 30th, A. D. 1766* (New York: M. B. Brown, 1916), 13. St. Paul's Church (Boston) is now the Cathedral Church of St. Paul.

24. Lovecraft to Clark, March 9, 1924, *Letters to Family*, 1:105–6; H. P. Lovecraft to James F. Morton, March 12, 1924, in *Letters to James F. Morton*, ed. David E. Schultz and S. T. Joshi (New York: Hippocampus Press, 2011), 69; Howard Phillips Lovecraft and Sonia Haft Greene, marriage file, March 3, 1924, certificate no. 0006276, New York City Municipal Archives, https://a860-historicalvitalrecords.nyc.gov/view/9336063.

25. Lovecraft to Clark, March 9, 1924, *Letters to Family*, 1:106.

26. Lovecraft presented a similar justification to James F. Morton: "Don't you see the aesthetic impressiveness of investing a momentous decision with all the quaint & picturesque beauty of gesture & ritual that nearly two thousand years' practice has gently woven into the inmost texture of our civilisation! . . . Religion, my son, is a pleasing fiction associated inextricably with the artistic progress of our culture; & deserves just as much recognition as any other ornament"; Lovecraft to Morton, March 14, 1924, *Letters to Morton*, 74–75.

27. Lovecraft to Clark, March 9, 1924, *Letters to Family*, 1:101.

28. Lovecraft to Clark, March 9, 1924, *Letters to Family*, 1:106. For a readable history of the planning and construction of the former Pennsylvania Station, see Jill Jonnes, *Conquering Gotham: A Gilded Age Epic; The Construction of Penn Station and Its Tunnels* (New York: Viking, 2007).

29. *Official Guide of Railways*, July 1924, 358; Nathaniel Burt and Wallace E. Davies, "The Iron Age, 1876–1905," in *Philadelphia: A 300-Year History*, ed. Russell F. Weigley, Nicholas B. Wainwright, and Edwin Wolf II (New York: W. W. Norton, 1982), 474–76; Group for Environmental Education, *Philadelphia Architecture: A Guide to the City*, ed. John Andrew Gallery, 2nd ed. (Philadelphia: Foundation for Architecture, 1994), 98. Lovecraft and Greene likely rode the 4:00 P.M. (no. 241) train with a scheduled 6:00 P.M. arrival at Broad Street Station. Lovecraft logged their arrival as being that exact hour. The Wesley Building, also known as the Robert Morris Hotel, was built between 1914 and 1915 and later expanded between 1921 and 1922. It stands at 1701–1709 Arch Street in Center City (downtown) Philadelphia.

30. Lovecraft to Clark, March 9, 1924, *Letters to Family*, 1:106.

31. "New Hotel Vendig Opens," *Philadelphia Inquirer*, September 19, 1913; Marija Gudauskas, Free Library of Philadelphia, email to author, March 31, 2022.

32. Lovecraft to Clark, March 9, 1924, *Letters to Family*, 1:106.

33. Davis, *Private Life*, 6; Sonia H. Davis to August Derleth, October 6, 1965, August William Derleth Papers, Wisconsin Historical Society. Greene generously omits the fact that Lovecraft had already missed the deadline. Maybe she should have viewed this as a warning sign regarding Lovecraft's understanding of responsibility. Over four decades later, Greene still discussed this episode with happiness and pride. It clearly figured importantly in her understanding of her relationship and marriage with Lovecraft and her image of herself.

34. Lovecraft to Clark, March 18, 1924, *Letters to Family*, 1:117.

35. Lovecraft to Clark, March 18, 1924, *Letters to Family*, 1:119; Charlene Mires, *Independence Hall in American Memory* (Philadelphia: University of Pennsylvania Press, 2002) explores the place of the building as a symbol and structure in the American public imagination.

36. Lovecraft to Clark, March 9, 1924, *Letters to Family*, 1:107.

37. Lovecraft to Clark, March 18, 1924, *Letters to Family*, 1:119.

38. Lovecraft to Clark, March 18, 1924, *Letters to Family*, 1:120.

39. Lovecraft to Clark, March 18, 1924, *Letters to Family*, 1:120.

40. Lovecraft to Clark, March 18, 1924, *Letters to Family*, 1:120.

41. Lovecraft to Clark, March 18, 1924, *Letters to Family*, 1:121.

42. Lovecraft to Clark, March 18, 1924, *Letters to Family*, 1:121.

43. Lovecraft commented that Philadelphia seemed "dull to inhabit continuously," parroting a long-standing joke that Philadelphia was a boring city. Today, we might think of this as a meme. This joke possibly originated in a cartoon in *Life* magazine. Lovecraft's humor and awareness of his contemporary popular culture is often overlooked; Lovecraft to Clark, March 9, 1924, *Letters to Family*, 1:106; "And I Spent a Week in Philadelphia," cartoon, *Life,* April 2, 1908, 364; "I Spent a Week in Philadelphia One Sunday," *Quote Investigator*, December 26, 2011, https://quoteinvestigator.com/2011/12/26/week-in-philly/.

44. Lovecraft to Clark, March 18, 1924, *Letters to Family*, 1:121.

45. Lovecraft to Clark, March 9, 1924, *Letters to Family*, 1:107.

46. Lovecraft to Clark, March 9, 1924, *Letters to Family*, 1:107; Lovecraft to Morton, March 12, 1923, *Letters to Morton*, 71.

47. Davis, *Private Life*, 6.

48. Davis, "Memories of Lovecraft: I," in Cannon, *Lovecraft Remembered*, 275–76; Davis, *Private Life*, 9; Bobby Derie, *Sex and the Cthulhu Mythos* (New York: Hippocampus Press, 2014), 14–17, 19; R. Alain Everts, "Howard Phillips Lovecraft and Sex: Or the Sex Life of a Gentleman," *Nyctalops*, July 1974, 19.

49. Sonia H. Greene, "RE H. P. L.," Howard P. Lovecraft Collection, Brown Digital Repository, Brown University Library, https://repository.library.brown.edu/studio/item/bdr:417628/; W. Scott Poole, *In the Mountains of Madness: The Life and Extraordinary Afterlife of H. P. Lovecraft* (Berkeley, Calif.: Soft Skull Press, 2016), 139. W. Scott Poole might be the first scholar to have commented on this intriguing document.

50. Lovecraft to Clark, March 9, 1924, *Letters to Family*, 1:104.

51. Lovecraft to Clark, March 9, 1924, *Letters to Family*, 1:104; Davis, *Private Life*, 13.

52. Joshi, *I Am Providence*, 1:494–95.

53. Lovecraft to Clark, March 9, 1924, *Letters to Family*, 1:103.

54. Lovecraft to Clark, March 9, 1924, *Letters to Family*, 1:103.

55. Lovecraft to Clark, March 9, 1924, *Letters to Family*, 1:103.

56. Lovecraft to Clark, March 9, 1924, *Letters to Family*, 1:103.

57. Joshi, *I Am Providence*, 1:493–95.

58. Sidney and Florence Moseson to Sonia H. Davis, August 15, 1964, Sonia H. and Nathaniel Davis Papers, John Hay Library, Brown University; Davis, Autobiographical Writings, August 19, 1964, box 9, folder 1, Davis Papers. This man is referred to only as Kaufman or K. in Greene's unpublished autobiographical writings.

59. Muriel Eddy, "The Gentleman from Angell Street," in Cannon, *Lovecraft Remembered*, 57–58.

60. Eddy, "Gentleman from Angell Street," 58.

61. Eddy, "Gentleman from Angell Street," 58.

62. Lovecraft to Clark, March 9, 1924, *Letters to Family*, 1:101. Throughout his adult life, Lovecraft would allude to suicide out of world-weariness, boredom, or financial ruin. One wonders how seriously his friends and family took his proclamations.

63. Lovecraft to Clark, March 9, 1924, *Letters to Family*, 1:107.

64. Lovecraft to Clark, March 9, 1924, *Letters to Family*, 1:107. Lovecraft comes across as an overgrown child in listing Greene's careful attention to his health. He notes that Greene healed his cracked lips with Vaseline and nursed his shin skinned from slipping on stairs.

65. Eddy, "Gentleman from Angell Street," 56. Decades later, Muriel Eddy still expressed hurt and confusion over Lovecraft's secrecy. "And the strange part of it all was that he had not once mentioned his love affair to us . . . and we were his very good friends"; Eddy, "Gentleman from Angell Street," 58.

66. ". . . Like you, I don't know anyone who is at all congenial here; & I believe I shall migrate to New York in the end—perhaps when Loveman does." Interestingly, Lovecraft links his possible migration to New York to that of Samuel Loveman from Cleveland, Ohio. He fails to cite his romance with Greene as a driving factor; Lovecraft to Clark Ashton Smith, January 25, 1924, *Selected Letters*, 1:285; Lovecraft to Frank Belknap Long, February 1924, *Selected Letters*, 1:293–94; Joshi, *I Am Providence*, 1:494–95.

67. Lovecraft to Edwin Baird, February 3, 1924, *Selected Letters*, 1:298; Joshi, *I Am Providence*, 1:494.

68. Lovecraft to Baird, February 3, 1924, *Selected Letters*, 1:303.

69. Sonia H. Greene, "Amatory Aphorisms," *Rainbow*, May 1922. The *Rainbow* was largely a vanity project for Greene to showcase writings by Lovecraft and his amateur journalism friends.

70. Sonia H. Greene, "The Psychic Phenomenon of Love," Lovecraft Collection, https://repository.library.brown.edu/studio/item/bdr:417627/.

71. Greene, "Psychic Phenomenon of Love," Lovecraft Collection, https://repository .library.brown.edu/studio/item/bdr:417627/; Davis to Derleth, November 29, 1966, Derleth Papers. The document purportedly contains both sides of an epistolary exchange between Lovecraft and Greene. Its date is unknown. This is the only surviving letter from Lovecraft to Greene.

72. Davis, Autobiographical Writings, August 19, 1964, box 9, folder 1, Davis Papers; Davis, *Private Life*, 21.

73. Davis to [John E. Stanton], March 21, 1949, Derleth Papers.

74. Lovecraft to Morton, March 12, 1924, *Letters to Morton*, 69.

75. Lovecraft to Morton, March 12, 1924, *Letters to Morton*, 69.

76. Rheinhart Kleiner, "A Memoir of Lovecraft," in Cannon, *Lovecraft Remembered*, 198.

77. Rheinhart Kleiner, "Epistle to Mr. and Mrs. Lovecraft," *Brooklynite*, April 1924.

78. Lovecraft to Long, March 21, 1924, *Selected Letters*, 1:329.

79. Long, *Howard Phillips Lovecraft*, 16; Arthur S. Koki, "H. P. Lovecraft: An Introduction to His Life and Writings" (master's thesis, Columbia University, 1962), 89. In interviews with researcher Arthur Koki, both Frank Belknap Long and Samuel Loveman stated their belief that Lovecraft was somehow tricked into marrying Sonia H. Greene. Lovecraft's affection—albeit reserved—for his spouse is clear in his correspondence, casting absolute doubt on these assertions by his friends. Regardless of his foibles and oddities, Lovecraft appeared to love Greene.

80. Lovecraft to Morton, March 14, 1924, *Letters to Morton*, 75–76.

81. [H. P. Lovecraft], "News Notes," *United Amateur*, May 1924, 7; S. T. Joshi, *H. P. Lovecraft: A Comprehensive Bibliography* (Tampa, Fla.: Tampa University Press, 2009), 111. Lovecraft likely penned this notice himself. The "News Notes" column was unsigned, but it was generally written by the *United Amateur* editor. This was Lovecraft in March 1924.

82. "Blue Pencil Club Meets," *Brooklyn Daily Eagle*, April 2, 1924, Brooklyn Newsstand, Brooklyn Public Library; Club Chatter, *Brooklyn Citizen*, April 4, 1921, Brooklyn Newsstand, Brooklyn Public Library; "Blue Pencil Club Elects New Officers, *Chat* (Brooklyn), April 5, 1924, Brooklyn Newsstand, Brooklyn Public Library.

5. "The Somewhat Disastrous Collapse"

1. H. P. Lovecraft to Lillian D. Clark, March 9, 1924, in *Letters to Family and Family Friends*, ed. S. T. Joshi and David E. Schultz, vol. 1, *1911–1925* (New York: Hippocampus Press, 2020), 108–9.

2. Rheinhart Kleiner, "A Memoir of Lovecraft," in *Lovecraft Remembered*, ed. Peter Cannon (Sauk City, Wisc.: Arkham House, 1998), 201; S. T. Joshi, *I Am Providence: The Life and Times of H. P. Lovecraft* (New York: Hippocampus Press, 2013), 1:504.

3. H. P. Lovecraft, *Marginalia*, comp. August Derleth and Donald Wandrei (Sauk City, Wisc.: Arkham House, 1944), plates facing 215, 247.

4. Lovecraft to Clark, March 28, 1924, *Letters to Family*, 1:127.

5. Lovecraft to Clark, March 9, 1924, *Letters to Family*, 1:110; Lovecraft to Clark, March 10, 1924, *Letters to Family*, 1:110; Lovecraft to Clark, March 18, 1924, *Letters to Family*, 1:112–13.

6. Timothy S. Corlis, "Ho-Ho-Kus," in *The Encyclopedia of New Jersey*, ed. Maxine N. Lurie and Marc Mappen, maps by Michael Siegel (New Brunswick, Rutgers University Press, 2004), 380–81.

7. H. P. Lovecraft to James F. Morton, March 12, 1924, in *Letters to James F. Morton*, ed. David E. Schultz and S. T. Joshi (New York: Hippocampus Press, 2011), 70; Lovecraft to Clark, March 18, 1924, *Letters to Family*, 1:113–14; Lovecraft to Clark, March 19, 1924, *Letters to Family*, 1:126; Lovecraft to Clark, March 30, 1924, *Letters to Family*, 1:130–31. The exact dates of Annie Gamwell's stay in Ho-Ho-Kus and later Brooklyn cannot be discerned from the surviving correspondence.

8. H. P. Lovecraft to Frank Belknap Long, March 21, 1924, in *Selected Letters*, ed.

August Derleth and Donald Wandrei, vol. 1, *1911–1924* (Sauk City, Wisc.: Arkham House, 1965), 329.

9. Lovecraft to Frank Belknap Long, March 21, 1924, Howard P. Lovecraft Collection, Brown Digital Repository, Brown University Library, https://repository.library.brown.edu /studio/item/bdr:423624/.

10. Dennis E. Gale, *The Misunderstood History of Gentrification: People, Planning, Preservation, and Urban Renewal, 1915–2020* (Philadelphia: Temple University Press, 2021), 60–84. Gale characterizes this socioeconomic phenomenon subtly, yet significantly reshaping the demographics and built environment of Greenwich Village between the 1910s and the 1940s as "embryonic gentrification," a precursor to the institutional- and government-driven urban investment during the later decades of the twentieth century.

11. Lovecraft to Clark, March 18, 1924, *Letters to Family*, 1:122.

12. Lovecraft to Clark, March 18, 1924, *Letters to Family*, 1:122.

13. Lovecraft to Clark, March 18, 1924, *Letters to Family*, 1:122.

14. Lovecraft to Clark, March 18, 1924, *Letters to Family*, 1:122.

15. Lovecraft to Clark, March 18, 1924, *Letters to Family*, 1:122; "My Favorite Things: Washington Square North," *Off the Grid: Village Preservation Blog*, December 9, 2011, https://www.villagepreservation.org/2011/12/09/my-favorite-things-washington -square-north/. In fact, Henry James depicted the Gilded Age life and society centered on Washington Square and the surrounding neighborhood in his aptly entitled novel *Washington Square*.

16. New York Preservation Archive Project, "George McAneny and New York," *Urban Archive*, August 2, 2019, https://www.urbanarchive.org/stories/Qa4tY6ZwaMM; Gale, *Misunderstood History of Gentrification*, 69–70; Emily Kies Folpe, *It Happened on Washington Square* (Baltimore: Johns Hopkins University Press, 2002), 272–77. Washington Square served as the prime mover of the rehabilitation or "embryonic gentrification" of Greenwich Village.

17. Lovecraft to Clark, March 18, 1924, *Letters to Family*, 1:122.

18. Gale, *Misunderstood History of Gentrification*, 81; John Strausbaugh, *The Village: 400 Years of Beats and Bohemians, Radicals and Rogues; A History of Greenwich Village* (New York: Ecco, 2013), 149–50.

19. Lovecraft to Clark, March 18, 1924, *Letters to Family*, 1:122.

20. Strausbaugh, *Village*, 64.

21. Lovecraft to Clark, March 18, 1924, *Letters to Family*, 1:123.

22. Lovecraft to Clark, March 18, 1924, *Letters to Family*, 1:123.

23. Lovecraft to Clark, March 18, 1924, *Letters to Family*, 1:123.

24. Ben Wilson, *Metropolis: A History of the City, Humankind's Greatest Invention* (New York: Doubleday, 2020), 243–45; Lauren Elkin, *Flâneuse: Women Walk the City in Paris, New York, Tokyo, Venice, and London* (New York: Farrar, Straus and Giroux: 2018), 61.

25. Charles Baudelaire, "The Painter of Modern Life," in *The Painter of Modern Life and Other Essays*, trans., ed. Jonathan Mayne (New York: De Capo Press, 1986), 9.

26. Sonia H. Davis, *The Private Life of H. P. Lovecraft*, ed. S. T. Joshi (West Warwick, R.I.: Necronomicon Press, 1985), 4; Rutherford Platt, *The Manual of Occupations* (New York: G. P. Putnam's Sons, 1929), 197 (loc. 213 of 498), https://babel.hathitrust.org/cgi /pt?id=uc1.$b297640&view=1up&seq=213&q1=buyer. The sole source for this income figure is Sonia Greene's own autobiographical writings. This figure does seem inflated

when compared to available contemporaneous data and even factoring in the higher wages associated with salaried and professional positions in New York City. A buyer for a department store earned between $30 and $150 per week, or between $1,560 and $7,800 per year, in 1929.

27. Kathleen Drowne and Patrick Huber, *The 1920s* (Westport, Conn.: Greenwood Press, 2004), 294.

28. "Arriving Passenger and Crew Lists (including Castle Garden and Ellis, 1820–1957)," digital image s.v. "Sonia Lovecraft," Ancestry.com; "Lot #45119: [H. P. Lovecraft], Sonia Haft Greene Lovecraft Davis, Sonia Haft Greene Lovecraft's Passport," Heritage Auctions, last modified on April 6, 2016, https://historical.ha.com/itm/books/horror-and-supernatural/-h-p-lovecraft-sonia-haft-greene-lovecraft-davis-sonia-haft-greene-lovecraft-s-u-s-passport-dated-22-june-1932-total-4-/a/6155-45119.s; *New York City Telephone Directory*, October 1923, microfilm, p. 306, reel 170. This address was written on a label inserted into Greene's passport. The label reads, "Sonia Greene 25 West 57th St. New York." This item was sold at an auction in April 2016. (Many thanks for Bobby Derie for graciously providing this information.) However, the same address was listed as Greene's on the manifest of an ocean liner entering New York from Cherbourg, France, on August 27, 1932. The building at that address was likely a full commercial structure in that year, and, in fact, it did stand on the same block as Ferle Heller in the early 1920s. Thus, it is doubtful that Greene resided there. Ferle Heller operated in two locations, 9 East Forty-Sixth Street and 36 West Fifty-Seventh Street, between 1923 and 1924.

29. Sonia H. Davis, Autobiographical Writings: "I do not quite remember how and exactly when I had met James Ferdinand Morton . . ."; undated, box 9, folder 2, Sonia H. and Nathaniel Davis Papers, John Hay Library, Brown University; Wendy Gamber, "Hatting and Millinery," in *The Encyclopedia of New York City*, 2nd ed., ed. Kenneth T. Jackson (New Haven: Yale University Press; New York: New-York Historical Society, 2010), 583–84.

30. Sonia H. Greene to Lillian D. Clark, February 9, 1924, Arkham House Transcripts, quoted in Joshi, *I Am Providence*, 1:505, endnote 46.

31. Lovecraft to Clark, March 10, 1924, *Letters to Family*, 1:112; Lovecraft to Frank Belknap Long, March 21, 1924, *Selected Letters*, 1:330.

32. Lovecraft to Clark, March 30, 1924, *Letters to Family*, 1:131.

33. Joshi, *I Am Providence*, 1:506; Long to Lovecraft, December 20, 1928, Lovecraft Collection, https://repository.library.brown.edu/studio/item/bdr:418162/. Lovecraft penned a review of J. Arthur Thompson's *What Is Man?* (New York: G. P. Putnam's Sons, 1924) for an unknown periodical or the Reading Lamp house magazine.

34. Lovecraft to Clark, March 19, 1924, *Letters to Family*, 1:126; Robert Weinberg, *The Weird Tales Story* (West Linn, Ore.: FAX Collector's Library, 1977), 4. *Weird Tales* was owned by the Rural Publishing Corporation. The magazine's mailing address was in Indianapolis, Indiana, and it was officially based in that city. However, it appeared to maintain an editorial office in Chicago, Illinois.

35. Lovecraft to Long, March 21, 1924, *Selected Letters*, 1:332.

36. Lovecraft to Clark, March 18, 1924, *Letters to Family*, 1:116; Lovecraft to Long, March 21, 1924, *Selected Letters*, 1:332–33; Joshi, *I Am Providence*, 1:502.

37. Lovecraft to Clark, March 18, 1924, *Letters to Family*, 1:116; Lovecraft to Long, March 21, 1924, *Selected Letters*, 1:332.

38. Lovecraft to Long, February 7, 1924, *Selected Letters*, 1:304; Joshi, *I Am Providence*, 1:502; Weinberg, *Weird Tales Story*, 4. Henneberger was in debt for a minimum of $40,000 by the spring of 1924.

39. Lovecraft to Long, March 21, 1924, *Selected Letters*, 1:329.

40. Joshi, *I Am Providence*, 1:506; H. P. Lovecraft, "The Rats in the Walls," *Weird Tales*, March 1924; H. P. Lovecraft, "The White Ape," *Weird Tales*, April 1924; H. P. Lovecraft, "Hypnos," *Weird Tales*, May–June–July 1924; "Facts Concerning the Late Arthur Jermyn and His Family," in *Dagon and Other Macabre Tales*, selected by August Derleth, ed. S. T. Joshi, intro. T. E. D. Klein (Sauk City, Wisc.: Arkham House, 1987), 73–82. "Facts Concerning the Late Arthur Jermyn and His Family" was published as "The White Ape." The former is now the canonical title of the short story.

41. Lovecraft to Clark, March 18, 1924, *Letters to Family*, 1:115; Lovecraft to Clark, March 19, 1924, *Letters to Family*, 1:126.

42. Lovecraft to Clark, March 18, 1922, *Letters to Family*, 1:115.

43. "Harry Houdini Collection," Rare Book & Special Collections Reading Room, Library of Congress, https://www.loc.gov/rr/rarebook/coll/122.html?loclr=blogadm.

44. Joshi, *I Am Providence*, 2:650–51; Alison Flood, "Lost HP Lovecraft Work Commissioned by Houdini Escapes Shackles of History," *Guardian* (Manchester), March 16, 2016, https://www.theguardian.com/books/2016/mar/16/hp-lovecraft-harry -houdini-manuscript-cancer-superstition-memorabilia; Kenneth Silverman, *Houdini! The Career of Ehrich Weiss: American Self-Liberator, Europe's Eclipsing Sensation, World's Handcuff King & Prison Breaker* (New York: HarperCollins, 1996), 216–17, 227. The manuscript of *The Cancer of Superstition* was discovered in recent years after a private collector purchased memorabilia and papers from a former magic shop. This collection included material from Houdini's widow, Beatrice, and her manager, Edward Saint. Chicago-based Potter & Potter Auctions put the manuscript up for bids on April 9, 2016. Debate exists concerning the extent of Lovecraft's contributions to the unfinished piece.

45. "Congratulations," *Brooklynite*, April 1924, 1, 2.

46. "I am reduc'd to a state of the most compleat obedience; & never respond to a connubial admonition but by saying in the most domestick manner imaginable, 'Yes, My Dear!'"; Lovecraft to Edward Cole, July 21, 1924, Lovecraft Collection, https://repository .library.brown.edu/studio/item/bdr:423629/.

47. Lovecraft to Cole, July 21, 1924, Lovecraft Collection, https://repository.library .brown.edu/studio/item/bdr:423629/; Lovecraft to Arthur Harris, July 22, 1924, Lovecraft Collection, https://repository.library.brown.edu/studio/item/bdr:423630/. Arthur Harris also wrote under the pen name "Stanley Williams."

48. Rheinhart Kleiner, "Bards and Bibliophiles," in Cannon, *Lovecraft Remembered*, 190. Kleiner references Ernest Dench as belonging to or leading the Writers' Club. Dench hosted the Blue Pencil Club meetings at his home in Sheepshead Bay, Brooklyn. Thus, some connection likely existed between the two organizations.

49. Lovecraft to Lillian Clark, March 30, 1924, *Letters to Family*, 1:130; Robert V. Hudson, "Irwin, William Henry (1873–1948), Writer," in *American National Biography*, February 1, 2000, https://doi-org.avoserv2.library.fordham.edu/10.1093 /anb/9780198606697.article.1600831. William Henry Irwin (1873–1948) was a notable journalist, author, and editor. Over his career, he wrote for the *San Francisco Chronicle*, *New York Tribune*, *Collier's*, and the *Saturday Evening Post*. He served as a war

correspondent during the First World War and later penned a biography of his longtime friend President Herbert Hoover. In 1924, Irwin was giving lectures in the Chautauqua and Lyceum circuits.

50. Lovecraft to Morton, May 6, 1924, *Letters to Morton*, 78.

51. Lovecraft to Morton, May 6, 1924, *Letters to Morton*, 78.

52. Lovecraft to Morton, May 6, 1924, *Letters to Morton*, 78.

53. Joshi, *I Am Providence*, 1:506–7; "Builder of 400 Homes Here Would 'Circle' Manhattan," *Yonkers Statesman*, September 10, 1927, Newspapers.com; "Homeland Company Sells Plots," *New York Times*, January 6, 1927; Diane Mignault, Yonkers Public Library, telephone conversation, April 30, 2022.

54. Kenneth T. Jackson, *Crabgrass Frontier: The Suburbanization of the United States* (New York: Oxford University Press, 1985), 128–30; "Homeland Co. in Deal," *New York Times*, May 13, 1928; "Developer Takes Gramatan Hills," *New York Times*, June 14, 1925.

55. Lovecraft to Clark, May 28, 1924, *Letters to Family*, 1:132.

56. Lovecraft to Clark, August 1, 1924, *Letters to Family*, 1:143.

57. Martin H. Kopp, "Memories of Sonia H. Greene Davis," *Lovecraft Annual*, no. 1 (2007): 27–30. Racille Moseson anglicized her first name to "Rachel" at an indeterminate time.

58. Joshi, *I Am Providence*, 1:506.

59. Lovecraft to Clark, August 1, 1924, *Letters to Family*, 1:134; Lovecraft to Moe, June 15, 1925, in *Letters to Moe and Others*, ed. David E. Schultz and S. T. Joshi (New York: Hippocampus Press, 2018), 143.

60. Classified advertisement, *Brooklyn Daily Eagle*, April 20, 1924, Brooklyn Newsstand, Brooklyn Public Library.

61. Lovecraft to Clark, August 1, 1924, *Letters to Family*, 1:135.

62. Lovecraft to Clark, August 1, 1924, *Letters to Family*, 1:136.

63. Yeshiva University Museum, *A Perfect Fit: The Garment Industry and American Jewry, 1860–1960* (New York: Yeshiva University Museum, 2005), 17, 33. By the turn of the twentieth century, 75 percent of New York City's garment industry was Jewish-owned and operated.; 60 percent of employed Jewish New Yorkers worked in the garment trade in some capacity.

64. August Derleth and Donald Wandrei, "Preface," in *Selected Letters*, 1:xxvii–xxix; Kleiner, "A Memoir of Lovecraft," 201–2; Frank Belknap Long, *Howard Phillips Lovecraft: Dreamer on the Nightside* (Sauk City, Wisc.: Arkham House, 1975), 67. Derleth and Wandrei included the full business letter in their preface to the first volume of Lovecraft's letters.

65. "Writer and Reviser," Situations Wanted—Males, *New York Times*, August 10, 1924; Horace L. Lawson, H. P. Lovecraft, and Noah F. Whitaker, "Lovecraft, Howard P. to Unidentified," 1924, Lovecraft Collection, https://repository.library.brown.edu/studio/item/bdr:423632/.

66. "Originality Recognized and Rewarded: Two Women in a Premier Position in Six Years," *Illustrated Milliner*, January 1918, 25, https://babel.hathitrust.org/cgi/pt?id=nyp.33433031310323&view=1up&seq=31.

67. Silverman, *Houdini!*, 217–18; Jack Sanders, "Leopold and Sady Weiss: Why Houdini Wasn't Happy," *Wild About Harry*, September 4, 2018, https://www.wild abouthoudini.com/2018/09/guest-blog-leopold-and-sady-weiss-why.html; "Originality Recognized," *Illustrated Milliner*, January 1918, 25, https://babel.hathitrust.org/cgi/pt?id=

nyp.33433031310323&view=1up&seq=31. Houdini held a grudge toward his sister-in-law, Sadie (née Glantz) Weiss (also known as Sady Weiss) until his death in 1926. She divorced his brother Nathan and married his other brother, Leopold, a mere ten days later. Weiss opened Bruck-Weiss Millinery with her sister, Anna Bruck, in 1912. The firm eventually owned and operated out of an eleven-story building at 6–8 West Fifty-Seventh Street in Manhattan.

68. Lovecraft to Clark, August 1, 1924, *Letters to Family*, 1:137.

69. Lovecraft to Clark, August 1, 1924, *Letters to Family*, 1:137; Lovecraft to the Homeland Co., draft, July 29, 1924, Lovecraft Collection, https://repository.library.brown .edu/studio/item/bdr:423632/.

70. Lovecraft to Clark, August 1, 1924, *Letters to Family*, 1:137–38; Lovecraft to Cole, July 21, 1924, Lovecraft Collection, https://repository.library.brown.edu/studio/item/bdr: 423629/; Lovecraft to Arthur Harris, July 22, 1924, Lovecraft Collection, https://repository .library.brown.edu/studio/item/bdr:423630/. The letters to Edward Cole and Arthur Harris were written on Robert Morris Hotel stationery.

71. Lovecraft to Clark, August 1, 1924, *Letters to Family*, 1:138.

72. Lovecraft to Clark, August 1, 1924, *Letters to Family*, 1:141.

73. Lovecraft to Clark, August 1, 1924, *Letters to Family*, 1:141.

74. Lovecraft to Clark, August 20, 1924, *Letters to Family*, 1:148.

75. Lovecraft to Clark, August 20, 1924, *Letters to Family*, 1:151.

76. Lovecraft to Clark, August 20, 1924, *Letters to Family*, 1:149.

77. Lovecraft to Clark, August 20, 1924, *Letters to Family*, 1:150.

78. Lovecraft to Clark, August 20, 1924, *Letters to Family*, 1:150.

79. Lovecraft to Clark, August 20, 1924, *Letters to Family*, 1:151.

80. Lovecraft to Clark, August 20, 1924, *Letters to Family*, 1:151.

81. Lovecraft to Clark, August 20, 1924, *Letters to Family*, 1:151; Strausbaugh, *Village*, 72.

82. Lovecraft to Clark, August 20, 1924, *Letters to Family*, 1:151.

83. Lovecraft to Clark, August 20, 1924, *Letters to Family*, 1:151.

84. Lovecraft to Clark, August 20, 1924, *Letters to Family*, 1:151.

85. Christine Stansell, *American Moderns: Bohemian New York and the Creation of the New Century* (New York: Metropolitan Books, 2000), 90–92; David Koeppel, "A Bastion of Literature Is a Bulwark for Therapy: The Evolving Life of a Greenwich Village Street," *New York Times*, December 23, 2003.

86. Lovecraft to Clark, August 20, 1924, *Letters to Family*, 1:152; "Milligan Place," *Urban Archive*, May 15, 2017, https://www.urbanarchive.org/sites/9pBGnDxineZ/KMeo HwVDgNE. The four houses of Milligan Place were built in 1852 by Aaron Patchin. He also owned Patchin Place. The buildings at Milligan Place were converted into apartments in 1917. Both Milligan Place and Patchin Place received landmark status in 1969 as part of the Greenwich Village Historic District.

87. Lovecraft to Clark, August 20, 1924, *Letters to Family*, 1:152.

88. Lovecraft to Clark, August 20, 1924, *Letters to Family*, 1:152.

89. Lovecraft to Clark, August 20, 1924, *Letters to Family*, 1:152.

90. Lovecraft to Clark, August 20, 1924, *Letters to Family*, 1:152, 153.

91. Lovecraft to Clark, August 20, 1924, *Letters to Family*, 1:153.

92. "Cemeteries," Congregation Shearith Israel, accessed January 24, 2023, https:// www.shearithisrael.org/about/our-history/cemeteries/; "The Cemeteries of the

Spanish-Portuguese Synagogue Shearith Israel," *Off the Grid: Village Preservation Blog*, November 21, 2018, https://www.villagepreservation.org/2018/11/21/second-third -cemeteries-of-spanish-portuguese-synagogue-shearith-israel/. The original cemetery of Congregation Shearith Israel sits at 55–57 St. James Place near Manhattan's Chinatown. It is known as the First Shearith Israel Graveyard, or the Chatham Square Cemetery.

93. Lovecraft to Clark, August 20, 1924, *Letters to Family*, 1:153.

94. Lovecraft to Clark, August 20, 1924, *Letters to Family*, 1:153–54.

95. Lovecraft to Clark, August 20, 1924, *Letters to Family*, 1:153.

6. "A Maze of Poverty & Uncertainty"

1. H. P. Lovecraft to James F. Morton, March 29, 1923, in Lovecraft, *Letters to James F. Morton*, ed. David E. Schultz and S. T. Joshi (New York Hippocampus Press, 2011), 33.

2. Mara Kirk Hart and S. T. Joshi, "Arthur Leeds," in *Lovecraft's New York Circle: The Kalem Club, 1924–1927*, ed. Mara Kirk Hart and S. T. Joshi (New York: Hippocampus Press, 2006), 141; S. T. Joshi, *I Am Providence: The Life and Times of H. P. Lovecraft* (New York: Hippocampus Press, 2013), 1:519; S. T. Joshi and David E. Schultz, introduction to *Letters to Rheinhart Kleiner and Others*, by H. P. Lovecraft, ed. S. T. Joshi and David E. Schultz (New York: Hippocampus Press, 2020), 19–22; H. P. Lovecraft to Lillian D. Clark, October 24–27, 1925, in *Letters to Family and Family Friends*, ed. S. T. Joshi and David E. Schultz, vol. 1, *1911–1925* (New York: Hippocampus Press, 2020), 461; "U.S. Residents Serving in the British Expeditionary Forces, 1917–1919," digital image s.v. "Arthur Leeds," Ancestry.com; 1920 United States Census, Manhattan, New York County, New York, digital image s.v. "Arthur Leeds," Ancestry.com; Arthur Leeds, "The First Hundred Words Are the Hardest," *Writer's Digest*, October 1921, https://archive.org /details/sim_writers-digest_192110_1/page/12/mode/2up; J. Berg Esenwein and Arthur Leeds, *Writing the Photoplay* (Springfield, Mass.: Home Correspondence School, 1913). Arthur Leeds (1882–1952) never wrote a memoir about his relationship with Lovecraft, making him an anomaly among their shared circle. He immigrated to the United States in 1900. Among Lovecraft's close writer friends, Leeds appeared to experience the least success—no mean feat—and remains a murky figure.

3. Hart and Joshi, "George Kirk," in Hart and Joshi, *Lovecraft's New York Circle*, 119–20; Mara Kirk Hart, "Walkers in the City: George Willard Kirk and Howard Phillips Lovecraft in New York City, 1924–1926," in *Lovecraft Remembered*, ed. Peter Cannon (Sauk City, Wisc.: Arkham House, 1998), 221–22; Joshi, *I Am Providence*, 1:519. George Kirk (1898–1962) regularly wrote letters to his fiancée and later wife, Lucile Dvorak. In 1992, thirty years after Kirk's death, his daughters discovered a sealed box in their mother's home. Inside were hundreds of letters from Kirk to Dvorak dated between 1924 and 1927. Aside from Lovecraft's own letters, Kirk's correspondence offers the only contemporaneous primary documents of Lovecraft's life in New York City. Kirk's letters were published in 2006.

4. Lynne Farrington, Kislak Center for Special Collections, Rare Books and Manuscripts, University of Pennsylvania, email to author, April 1, 2021; Lovecraft to Clark, August 1, 1924, *Letters to Family*, 1:144; Lovecraft to Clark, September 29–30, 1924, *Letters to Family*, 1:167; Lovecraft to Clark, May 24–25, 1930, *Letters to Family*, 2:848–49; "Philadelphia's Centaur Book Shop and Press, 1921–1942," Free Library of Philadelphia, June 22, 2018, https://libwww.freelibrary.org/blog/post/3334; New York

Public Library, "110 Columbia Heights," *Urban Archive*, March 22, 2018, https://www
.urbanarchive.org/sites/Dvwnsrm2spT/1d5qi1vKWuV. Samuel Loveman arrived in New
York City on September 10, 1924. His monograph on Edgar Saltus was never published
by Centaur Press. The publisher listed a bibliography of Saltus's works as in preparation
in several issues of its catalogue. The building at 110 Columbia Heights was also known as
the Roebling House. Washington Roebling suffered from severe decompression sickness
(the bends) and resultingly weakened health during the construction of the Brooklyn
Bridge in 1872 and supervised the project from a room in the building with the assistance
of his wife, Emily Warren Roebling, until its completion in 1883. Lovecraft, Crane, and
Loveman were unaware of this detail in 1924. In fact, Loveman purportedly lived in the
very room where Roebling monitored the work on the bridge with a telescope.

5. "Because all of the last names of the permanent members of our club begin with K,
L or M, we plan to call it the Kalem Klybb"; George Kirk to Lucile Dvorak, February 5,
1925, in Hart and Joshi, *Lovecraft's New York Circle*, 44; "I don't know who thought
of it, but since the patronymics of members began with K, L, or M, why not call it the
Kalem Club? That was how the name came into being"; Rheinhart Kleiner, "Bards and
Bibliophiles," in Cannon, *Lovecraft Remembered*, 190. Although its members did not
adopt the name "Kalem Club" until February 1925, "Kalem Club" will be used for clarity
and consistency throughout the text.

6. Vrest Orton, "Recollections of H. P. Lovecraft," in Cannon, *Lovecraft Remembered*, 342.

7. A notable exception was a falling-out between Arthur Leeds and Everett McNeil.
This dispute originated because Leeds owed McNeil a small debt. This resulted in McNeil
hosting his own meetings in his Hell's Kitchen room with Lovecraft often as the sole guest.

8. Rheinhart Kleiner, "After a Decade and the Kalem Club," in Hart and Joshi,
Lovecraft's New York Circle, 219.

9. Kleiner, "After a Decade," 221.

10. Kleiner, "After a Decade," 221.

11. Christine Stansell, *American Moderns: Bohemian New York and the Creation of a
New Century* (New York: Metropolitan Books, 2000): 55–57. The limited formal education
of Lovecraft and other Kalem Club members contrasted with that of the bohemians of
Greenwich Village. Many of these men and women were college graduates.

12. Frank Belknap Long, *Howard Phillips Lovecraft: Dreamer on the Nightside* (Sauk
City, Wisc.: Arkham House, 1975), 157.

13. Rheinhart Kleiner, "A Memoir of Lovecraft," in Cannon, *Lovecraft Remembered*, 200.

14. Jane L. Smulyan, "Nedick's," in *Savoring Gotham: A Food Lover's Companion to
New York City*, ed. Andrew F. Smith (Oxford: Oxford University Press, 2015), Oxford
Reference; Andrew F. Smith, *New York City: A Food Biography* (Lanham, Md.: Rowan
& Littlefield, 2014), 79. Orange drinks and orange juice gained popularity in the 1920s
as a result of California and Florida citrus growers marketing the health properties of
orange juice. Lovecraft, Kirk, and Leeds likely patronized Nedick's, a New York City chain
specializing in orange drinks. The Nedick's Orange Juice Company operated 140 locations
by 1929.

15. Lovecraft to Clark, September 29–30, 1924, *Letters to Family*, 1:161.

16. Writer O. Henry set his 1907 short story "The Last Leaf" in Grove Court.
Interestingly, he wrote about the "the art people . . . prowling, hunting for north windows

and eighteenth-century gables and Dutch attics and low rents" in the building and Greenwich Village. That is, people like Lovecraft and Kirk; Lovecraft to Clark, September 29–30, 1924, *Letters to Family*, 1:162; O. Henry, "The Last Leaf," in *101 Stories*, ed. Ben Yagoda (New York: Library of America, 2021), 600; "Peeking into Grove Court," *Off the Grid: Village Preservation Blog*, October 5, 2011, https://www.villagepreservation.org/2011/10/05/peeking-into-grove-court/.

17. Lovecraft to Clark, September 29–30, 1924, *Letters to Family*, 1:162; Kirk to Dvorak, August 22, 1924, in Hart and Joshi, *Lovecraft's New York Circle*, 26. Kirk detailed the entire adventure in a letter to his fiancée, Lucile Dvorak, including a full description and sketch of Milligan Place and its inner, hidden courtyard.

18. Lovecraft to Clark, September 29–30, 1924, *Letters to Family*, 1:162.

19. Lovecraft to Clark, September 29–30, 1924, *Letters to Family*, 1:162.

20. Lovecraft to Clark, September 29–30, 1924, *Letters to Family*, 1:162.

21. Lovecraft to Clark, September 29–30, 1924, *Letters to Family*, 1:162; "The Lost James Monroe House—Prince and Lafayette Streets," *Daytonian in Manhattan*, May 2, 2016, https://daytoninmanhattan.blogspot.com/2016/05/the-lost-james-monroe-house-prince-and.html; New York Public Library, "63 Prince Street," *Urban Archive*, accessed January 13, 2022, https://www.urbanarchive.org/sites/U6bxgv5zy6c/3geftEhjX4a. The house was moved to 95 Crosby Street in 1926. In an early attempt at historic preservation in New York City, prominent individuals and organizations advocated for saving and restoring the building. It was demolished by 1928.

22. Kirk to Dvorak, August 22, 1924, in Hart and Joshi, *Lovecraft's New York Circle*, 27. This entire area bordering the northeastern side of the Brooklyn Bridge was razed in the 1950s to build the Governor Alfred E. Smith Houses, a public housing complex.

23. Lovecraft to Clark, September 29–30, 1924, *Letters to Family*, 1:163.

24. Lovecraft to Clark, September 29–30, 1924, *Letters to Family*, 1:163.

25. Kirk to Dvorak, August 22, 1924, in Hart and Joshi, *Lovecraft's New York Circle*, 24.

26. Sonia H. Davis, Autobiographical Writings: "I do not quite remember how and exactly when I had met James Ferdinand Morton . . ."; undated, box 9, folder 2, Sonia H. and Nathaniel Davis Papers, John Hay Library, Brown University.

27. Lovecraft to Clark, September 29–30, 1924, *Letters to Family*, 1:164.

28. Classified advertisement, *Brooklyn Daily Eagle*, April 20, 1924, Brooklyn Newsstand, Brooklyn Public Library; Kathleen Drowne and Patrick Huber, *The 1920s* (Westport, Conn.: Greenwood Press, 2004), 292. For comparison, a Steinway grand piano cost approximately $1,425 in the 1920s.

29. Lovecraft to Clark, September 29–30, 1924, *Letters to Family*, 1:164.

30. Lovecraft to Clark, September 29–30, 1924, *Letters to Family*, 1:164.

31. Lovecraft to Clark, September 29–30, 1924, *Letters to Family*, 1:165.

32. Lovecraft to Clark, September 29–30, 1924, *Letters to Family*, 1:165.

33. Lovecraft to Clark, September 29–30, 1924, *Letters to Family*, 1:165; Lovecraft to Clark, September 1, 1924, Howard P. Lovecraft Collection, Brown Digital Repository, Brown University Library, https://repository.library.brown.edu/studio/item/bdr:423638/; Joan Seguine-Levine, *Perth Amboy* (Dover, N.H.: Arcadia, 1996), 59.

34. Lovecraft to Clark, September 29–30, 1924, *Letters to Family*, 1:165; Lovecraft to Clark, September 1, 1924, *Letters to Family*, 1:154–55; Lovecraft to Clark, September 1,

1924, *Letters to Family*, 1:155; Lovecraft to Clark, September 2, 1924, *Letters to Family*, 1:155.

35. Lovecraft to Clark, September 29–30, 1924, *Letters to* Family, 1:166.

36. Lovecraft to Clark, September 18, 1924, *Letters to Family*, 1:157.

37. Joshi, *I Am Providence*, 1:510–11; Lovecraft to Clark, September 29–30, 1924, *Letters to Family*, 1:166, 169, 170; Lovecraft to Clark, September 18, 1924, *Letters to Family*, 1:157; Lovecraft to Clark, November 4–6, 1924, *Letters to Family*, 1:184–85.

38. Lovecraft to Clark, September 10, 1924, *Letters to Family*, 1:156.

39. Lovecraft to Clark, November 4–6, 1924, *Letters to Family*, 1:192; Lovecraft to Clark, September 29–30, 1924, *Letters to Family*, 1:178–79; Joshi, *I Am Providence*, 1:511; Directory of Newspaper Syndicate Features, *Editor & Publisher*, October 24, 1924, 11 (loc. 10 of 48), https://archive.org/details/sim_editor-publisher_1924-10-25_57_22/page/10/mode/2up.

40. Lovecraft to Clark, September 29–30, 1924, *Letters to Family*, 1:169; "Saks & Company Open New Store to Public To-day," *New York Herald, New York Tribune*, September 15, 1924, ProQuest.

41. Lovecraft to Clark, November 4–6, 1924, *Letters to Family*, 1:182.

42. Sonia H. Davis, *The Private Life of H. P. Lovecraft*, ed. S. T. Joshi (West Warwick, R.I.: Necronomicon Press, 1985), 5.

43. Lovecraft to Clark, September 29–30, 1924, *Letters to Family*, 1:179.

44. "Ann Arbor and Elizabeth," *New York Times*, October 5, 1924.

45. Lovecraft to Clark, October 10, 1924, *Letters to Family*, 1:181; "Ferry Routes of New York City," in *The Encyclopedia of New York City*, ed. Kenneth T. Jackson, 2nd ed. (New Haven: Yale University Press; New York: New-York Historical Society, 2010), 439.

46. Lovecraft to Clark, November 4–6, 1924, *Letters to Family*, 1:186; Arthur G. Adams, "Ferries," in *Encyclopedia of New York City*, 436.

47. Frank Bergen Kelley, comp., *Historic Elizabeth: 1664–1914*, ed. Warren R. Dix (Elizabeth, N.J.: *Elizabeth Daily Journal*, 1914); Lovecraft to Clark, November 4–6, 1924, *Letters to Family*, 1:186. Lovecraft acquired and used the 1914 historic guide published by the *Elizabeth Daily Journal*.

48. Lovecraft to Clark, November 4–6, 1924, *Letters to Family*, 1:186.

49. Lovecraft to Clark, November 4–6, 1924, *Letters to Family*, 1:187.

50. Lovecraft to Clark, November 4–6, 1924, *Letters to Family*, 1:187.

51. Dating from 1664, the First Presbyterian Church of Elizabeth is the oldest English-language congregation in New Jersey, and it has been known as "the Church of the Founding Fathers of New Jersey." Prominent early members included William Livingston, first governor of New Jersey and delegate to the Constitutional Convention, and Elias Boudinot, member of the Continental Congress and director of the United States Mint. The construction dates slightly differ in different sources, also being listed as between 1784 and 1792; "'Old First of Elizabeth,'" *National Register of Historic Places Inventory*, January 11, 1977, https://npgallery.nps.gov/NRHP/GetAsset/NRHP/77000914_text; Gulger, Kimball and Husted, *Architectural History: The First Presbyterian Church of Elizabeth, New Jersey* (Elizabeth: First Presbyterian Church Building Fund, 1947), 4, 7; Kelley, *Historic Elizabeth*, 21–25.

52. Lovecraft to Clark, November 4–6, 1924, *Letters to Family*, 1:187.

53. Lovecraft to Clark, November 4–6, 1924, *Letters to Family*, 1:188.

54. Kelley, *Historic Elizabeth*, 33, 35, 37.

55. Kelley, *Historic Elizabeth*, 18; Darren Tobia, "Elizabeth, a City Once Raided by the British, Now Under Siege by Time and Neglect, *Jersey Digs*, July 14, 2021, https://jerseydigs.com/elizabeth-a-city-once-raided-by-british-now-under-siege-by-time-and-neglect/. Lovecraft's chronicle of Elizabeth presents an argument for mining the deep veins of history in the city and other small and mid-sized municipalities in the greater New York region. If such riches are unappreciated by those with influence, they will simply disappear. This remains a concern for Elizabeth's artists, curators, and preservationists.

56. This "terrible old house" stood at 1099 Elizabeth Avenue at the southeast corner of the intersection of Elizabeth Avenue and Bridge Street. The Providence property at 135 Benefit Street clearly resembles the building described by Lovecraft in "The Shunned House"; Lovecraft to Clark, November 4–6, 1924, *Letters to Family*, 1:188; Steven J. Mariconda, "Lovecraft's Elizabethtown," in *On the Emergence of "Cthulhu" & Other Observations* (West Warwick, R.I.: Necronomicon Press, 1995), 58; Elizabeth Daily Journal, *The City of Elizabeth, New Jersey, Illustrated: Showing Its Leading Characteristics* [. . .] (Elizabeth: Elizabeth Daily Journal, 1889), 140.

57. Lovecraft to Clark, November 4–6, 1924, *Letters to Family*, 1:188.

58. Lovecraft to Clark, November 4–6, 1924, *Letters to Family*, 1:192.

59. S. T. Joshi and David E. Schultz, introduction to *From the Pest Zone: The New York Stories*, by H. P. Lovecraft, ed. S. T. Joshi and David E. Schultz (New York: Hippocampus Press, 2003), 13–14. Lovecraft submitted "The Shunned House" to both to *Detective Tales* and *Weird Tales*. Both publications rejected the story. W. Paul Cook, publisher of the *Vagrant* and the *Recluse*, printed the piece in 1928 with the intention of distributing it as a book. Cook never bound the pages. *Weird Tales* eventually published the story in October 1937—seven months after Lovecraft's death in March 1937.

60. Jean-Rae Turner and Richard T. Koles, *Elizabeth: The First Capital of New Jersey* (Charleston, S.C.: Arcadia, 2003), 100. Congregation B'nai Israel was formed in 1872. The synagogue seen by Lovecraft was dedicated in 1924 as a Reform Jewish congregation. It closed in 1992.

61. Lovecraft to Clark, November 4–6, 1924, *Letters to Family*, 1:189.

62. Lovecraft to Clark, November 4–6, 1924, *Letters to Family*, 1:189.

63. Lovecraft to Clark, November 4–6, 1924, *Letters to Family*, 1:189.

64. Turner and Koles, *Elizabeth*, 8, 111; Department of Commerce, *Statistical Abstract of the United States: 1921*, comp. Edward Whitney (Washington, D.C.: G. P. O., 1922), 55, https://www2.census.gov/prod2/statcomp/documents/1921-02.pdf#[33,{%22name%22:%22FitH%22},621]. Elizabeth's factories churned out trolley cars, automobiles, diners, metal typeface, and mostly famously Singer sewing machines. Jewish, Russian, Polish, Italian, Greek, Swedish, German, and Irish immigrants and their American descendants belonged to the city's population.

65. Lovecraft to Clark, November 4–6, 1924, *Letters to Family*, 1:190; Lovecraft to Clark, May 24–25, 1930, *Letters to Family*, 2:848–49. Years later, Lovecraft still remembered his first moment seeing the nighttime Manhattan skyline from Brooklyn.

66. Hart Crane to Grace Hart Crane and Elizabeth Belden Hart, September 14, 1924, in Hart Crane, *Letters of Hart Crane and His Family*, ed. Thomas S. W. Lewis (New York: Columbia University Press, 1974), 342; Crane to Grace Hart Crane and Elizabeth Belden Hart, October 14, 1924, *Letters of Hart Crane*, 354; Lovecraft to Clark, November 4–6, 1924, *Letters to Family*, 1:190; Joshi, *I Am Providence*, 1:525, 2:755–56.

67. Lovecraft to Clark, November 4–6, 1924, *Letters to Family*, 1:192.

68. Joshi, *I Am Providence*, 1:512–13. Brooklyn Hospital is now Brooklyn Hospital Center just off Fort Greene Park in downtown Brooklyn.

69. "Fort Greene Park," New York City Department of Parks & Recreation, accessed February 4, 2023, https://www.nycgovparks.org/parks/fort-greene-park/history.

70. Joshi, *I Am Providence*, 1:512; Lovecraft to Clark, November 4–6, 1924, *Letters to Family*, 1:193, 195–96; H. P. Lovecraft to Edgar J. Davis, May 12, 1925, in Lovecraft, *Selected Letters*, ed. August Derleth and Donald Wandrei, vol. 2, *1925–1929* (Sauk City, Wisc.: Arkham House, 1968), 7; H. P. Lovecraft to Maurice W. Moe, June 15, 1925, in Lovecraft, *Letters to Maurice W. Moe and Others*, ed. David E. Schultz and S. T. Joshi (New York: Hippocampus Press, 2018), 144.

71. "Mrs. Lovecraft went to the hospital the night before last because of another breakdown. Upon which my comment is that I make none. . . ." This elliptical remark by Kirk suggests that he knew more about Greene's mental health and the Lovecraft-Greene household than included in the surviving correspondence; Kirk to Dvorak, October 22, 1924, in Hart and Joshi, *Lovecraft's New York Circle*, 31.

72. Lovecraft to Davis, May 12, 1925, *Selected Letters*, 2:7.

73. Lovecraft to Moe, June 15, 1925, *Letters to Moe*, 144.

74. Lovecraft to Clark, November 4–6, 1924, *Letters to Family*, 1:195.

75. Lovecraft to Clark, November 4–6, 1924, *Letters to* Family, 1:196; Lovecraft to Moe, June 15, 1925, *Letters to Moe*, 144.

76. Lovecraft to Clark, [November 11, 1924], *Letters to Family*, 1:203.

77. Lovecraft only refers to the farm's owner as Mrs. R. A. Craig. The exact address and location of the Somerville-area rest home and the full name of its owner remain unknown. Lovecraft did not include either of those facts in his letters recounting this episode. These omissions prevent a detailed search through available public records.

78. Hazel Pratt Adams to H. P. Lovecraft, November 13, 1925, H. P. Lovecraft, "The Horror at Red Hook," manuscript, 1925, Manuscripts and Archives Division, New York Public Library; Erin Overby, "A New Yorker for Brooklynites," *New Yorker*, January 31, 2013, https://www.newyorker.com/books/double-take/a-new-yorker-for-brooklynites. Hazel Pratt Adams, founder of the Blue Pencil Club's magazine the *Brooklynite*, and a mutual friend of Greene and Lovecraft, wrote to Lovecraft and asked for his wife's temporary New Jersey address in November 1924. Lovecraft used the verso of the letter to compose the manuscript of "The Horror at Red Hook."

79. Lovecraft to Clark, [November 11, 1924], *Letters to Family*, 1:203.

80. Lovecraft to Clark, [November 11, 1924], *Letters to Family*, 1:203.

81. Lovecraft to Clark, [November 11, 1924], *Letters to Family*, 1:203.

82. Lovecraft to Clark, [November 11, 1924], *Letters to Family*, 1:203.

83. Lovecraft to Clark, [November 11, 1924], *Letters to Family*, 1:204; "Washington's Headquarters: Somerville, N.J.," postcard, Lovecraft Collection; "Somerset County Village Court House Green," *Historical Marker Database*, December 31, 2020, https://www.hmdb.org/m.asp?m=98263. His brief visit to Somerville must have deeply impressed Lovecraft. A blank postcard of the Wallace House was among Lovecraft's papers after his death. George Washington utilized the building as his headquarters when the Continental Army camped in Somerset County between 1778 and 1779.

84. "SH is coming back to NY in a week to help me break up . . ."; Lovecraft to Clark, November 10, 1924, *Letters to Family*, 1:201; "I took the 6:10 to Bound Brook . . . bidding

S H au revoir until Saturday, when she returns to 259 for a week to help in the packing up"; Lovecraft to Clark, [November 11, 1924], *Letters to Family*, 1:204. Although some accounts state that Lovecraft and Greene made this decision upon her return from Somerville and Lovecraft's from Philadelphia, the couple clearly planned to leave Parkside Avenue and search for smaller and cheaper housing before he left for Philadelphia on November 10, 1924.

85. Lovecraft to Moe, June 15, 1925, *Letters to Moe*, 145. Lovecraft's impressions and travelogues of Philadelphia and its surrounding region merit an extended study. Much like his New York experiences, these demonstrate his affair with the urban landscape, love of history, and hatred toward "the other."

86. Lovecraft to Clark, November 17–18, 1924, *Letters to Family*, 1:219.

87. Lovecraft to Clark, November 11, 1924, *Letters to Family*, 1:205; Lovecraft to Clark, November 11, 1924, *Letters to Family*, 1:206; Lovecraft to Clark, November 14, 1924, *Letters to Family*, 1:212; Lovecraft to Clark, November 14, 1924, *Letters to Family*, 1:213; Lovecraft to Clark, November 17–18, 1924, *Letters to Family*, 1:214–20.

88. Lovecraft to Lillian Clark, [November 11, 1924], *Letters to Family*, 1:204; Lovecraft to Clark, November 14, 1924, *Letters to Family*, 1:213.

89. H. P. Lovecraft to James F. Morton, June 9, 1926, *Letters to Morton*, 96. Lovecraft lost his detailed notes of his November 1924 Philadelphia trip. His June 9, 1926, letter to Morton is an extensive Philadelphia travelogue and an attempt to recreate them.

90. Lovecraft to Clark, November 17–18, 1924, *Letters to Family*, 1:219.

91. Lovecraft to Moe, June 15, 1925, *Letters to Moe*, 145.

92. Department of Commerce, *Statistical Abstract*, 56, https://www2.census.gov/prod2 /statcomp/documents/1921-02.pdf#[33,{%22name%22:%22FitH%22},621]; Lloyd M. Abernethy, "Progressivism, 1905–1919," in *Philadelphia: A 300-Year History*, ed. Russell F. Weigley, Nicholas B. Wainwright, and Edwin Wolf II (New York: W. W. Norton, 1982), 526–32; Arthur P. Dudden, "The City Embraces 'Normalcy,' 1919–1929," in Weigley, Wainwright, and Wolf, *Philadelphia*, 587–88, 589–91. Of Philadelphia's population of 1,823,779 residents, 989,398 individuals were foreign-born or the children of one or more foreign-born parents by 1920. This equaled approximately 54 percent of the city's total population. Black Americans numbered 135,599 of Philadelphia residents, or 7.4 percent of the total population.

93. Lovecraft to Clark, November 17–18, 1924, *Letters to Family*, 1:214.

94. Davis, *Private Life*, 5.

95. Lovecraft to Clark, November 17–18, 1924, *Letters to Family*, 1:221.

96. Lovecraft to Clark, November 17–18, 1924, Lovecraft Collection, https://repository .library.brown.edu/studio/item/bdr:423664/; Lovecraft to Clark, November 29, 1924, Lovecraft Collection, https://repository.library.brown.edu/studio/item/bdr:423667/.

97. James Warren Thomas, "Howard Phillips Lovecraft: A Self-Portrait" (master's thesis, Brown University, 1950), 59.

98. Lovecraft to Clark, November 17–18, 1924, *Letters to Family*, 1:222.

99. Lovecraft to Clark, November 29, 1924, *Letters to Family*, 1:233. This is a clear reference to Jewish immigrants and Jewish Americans. Again, Lovecraft offered no self-realization of the contradiction in writing such slurs while married to an immigrant of Jewish ancestry.

100. Lovecraft to Clark, [November 11, 1924], *Letters to Family*, 1:202.

101. Lovecraft to Morton, November 18, 1924, *Letters to Morton*, 79–80.

102. Lovecraft to Clark, November 29, 1924, *Letters to Family*, 1:231.

103. "Tate, [John Orley] Allen," in *Benét's Reader's Encyclopedia*, 4th ed., ed. Bruce Murphy (New York: HarperCollins, 1996), 1,009. John Orley Allen Tate (1889–1979) was a poet, critic, and man of letters. He was associated with the Southern Agrarians, a group of writers from the American South in the 1930s. Tate was the United States Poet Laureate between 1943 and 1944. The poem "Ode to the Confederate Dead" is his most well-known and anthologized work.

104. Davis, *Private Life*, 6; Joshi, *I Am Providence*, 1:533; Lovecraft to Moe, June 15, 1925, *Letters to Moe*, 146.

105. Lovecraft to Moe, June 15, 1925, *Letters to Moe*, 146.

106. Lovecraft to Bernard Austin Dwyer, March 26, 1927, *Letters to Moe*, 439. This was the former St. Ann's Church, an Episcopal house of worship, at 131 Clinton Street. The building is now part of the Packer Collegiate Institute, a private college preparatory school.

107. Lovecraft to Clark, December 31, 1924, Lovecraft Collection, https://repository.library.brown.edu/studio/item/bdr:423668/; Kirk to Dvorak, January 2, 1925, in Hart and Joshi, *Lovecraft's New York Circle*, 35.

7. "A Pleasing Hermitage"

1. H. P. Lovecraft to Maurice W. Moe, June 15, 1925, in Lovecraft, *Letters to Maurice W. Moe and Others*, ed. David E. Schultz and S. T. Joshi (New York: Hippocampus Press, 2018), 148.

2. Lovecraft to Moe, June 15, 1925, *Letters to Moe*, 148. Lovecraft's comparison of James F. Morton's apartment to his own indicates that Lovecraft's Brooklyn room was located on the building's second floor. He shared a description with his aunt Lillian Clark. "[Morton's] second-floor room . . . occupies the same relative place in the house that mine does in 169 Clinton." A later letter to Edward Cole confirms these details of Lovecraft's apartment; H. P. Lovecraft to Lillian D. Clark, September 1, 1925, in Lovecraft, *Letters to Family and Family Friends*, ed. S. T. Joshi and David E. Schultz, vol. 1, *1911–1925* (New York: Hippocampus Press, 2020), 372; Lovecraft to Edward Cole, February 24, 1925, Howard P. Lovecraft Collection, Brown Digital Repository, Brown University Library, https://repository.library.brown.edu/studio/item/bdr:423675/; Lovecraft to Bernard Austin Dwyer, March 26, 1927, *Letters to Moe*, 441.

3. Lovecraft, "Diary, 1925," Lovecraft Collection, https://repository.library.brown.edu/studio/item/bdr:425490/.

4. "Am in a twenty-five-room rooming house and I like it well"; George Kirk to Lucile Dvorak, February 17, 1925, in *Lovecraft's New York Circle: The Kalem Club, 1924–1927*, ed. Mara Kirk Hart and S. T. Joshi (New York: Hippocampus Press, 2006), 45; 1925 New York Census, Brooklyn, Kings County, New York, digital image, s.v. "Howard P. Lovecraft," Ancestry.com. Oddly enough, Lovecraft's occupation was listed as engineer in the state-level census.

5. Lovecraft to Moe, June 15, 1925, *Letters to Moe*, 146.

6. H. P. Lovecraft, "[Diary: 1925]," in Lovecraft, *Collected Essays*, ed. S. T. Joshi, vol. 5, *Philosophy; Autobiography and Miscellany* (New York: Hippocampus Press, 2006), 149.

7. Lovecraft to Moe, June 15, 1925, Lovecraft Collection, https://repository.library .brown.edu/studio/item/bdr:423681/. Lovecraft provided Moe with a detailed sketch of his new room at 169 Clinton Street.

8. Lovecraft, "[Diary: 1925]," in *Collected Essays*, 5:149.

9. Lovecraft to Moe, June 15, 1925, *Letters to Moe*, 148.

10. Lovecraft, "Diary, 1925," Lovecraft Collection, https://repository.library.brown.edu /studio/item/bdr:425490/.

11. Lovecraft to Clark, January 22, 1925, *Letters to Family*, 1:237; Lovecraft to Moe, June 15, 1925, *Letters to Moe*, 146. After helping Lovecraft find his new room in late December 1924, Clark remained in the New York area with friends in Mount Vernon, New York, until the middle of February. She appeared to have stayed in Lovecraft's room or rented her own at 169 Clinton Street for a period in January.

12. "Our Story," Green-Wood, accessed December 26, 2022, https://www.green-wood .com/about-history/; Alexandra Kathryn Mosca, *Green-Wood Cemetery* (Charleston, S.C.: Arcadia, 2008): 7, 12. Green-Wood Cemetery was founded in 1838 and today is a National Historic Landmark. Nearly 600,000 people permanently rest in its grounds, including prominent artists (Jean-Michel Basquiat), musicians (Leonard Bernstein), politicians (William "Boss" Tweed), publishers (Horace Greeley), and other figures in local, state, and national culture and history.

13. Lovecraft to Clark, January 22, 1925, *Letters to Family*, 1:237.

14. Rebecca Read Shanor, "Hippodrome," in *The Encyclopedia of New York City*, 2nd ed., ed. Kenneth T. Jackson (New Haven: Yale University Press; New York: New-York Historical Society, 2010), 597–98. The Hippodrome Theatre first opened in 1905 and hosted spectacles, musicals, and vaudeville acts and later movies and sporting events. Its exterior was built with red terra cotta brick in a Moorish style by Frederic Thompson and Elmer Dundy, the figures behind Luna Park in Coney Island. After struggling through the 1930s, the Hippodrome closed in 1939.

15. Lovecraft to Clark, January 22, 1925, *Letters to Family*, 1:238.

16. Anthony Slide, "Harry Houdini," in *The Encyclopedia of Vaudeville* (Jackson: University Press of Mississippi, 2012), 251; Olin Downes, "Music," *New York Times*, January 10, 1925; "Vaudeville Reviews: Hippodrome," *Variety*, January 21, 1925, Entertainment Industry Magazine Archive.

17. Lovecraft to Clark, January 22, 1925, *Letters to Family*, 1:239.

18. Lovecraft to Samuel Loveman, March 24, [1923], *Letters to Moe*, 493–94; Lovecraft to Clark, February 2, 1925, *Letters to Family*, 1:241. Greene's nasal condition predated her marriage to Lovecraft and their shared troubles.

19. Lovecraft to Clark, February 1925, Lovecraft Collection, https://repository.library .brown.edu/studio/item/bdr:423672/; Lovecraft to Annie E. P. Gamwell, February 10, 1925, *Letters to Family*, 1:243–44.

20. Lovecraft to Gamwell, February 10, 1925, *Letters to Family*, 1:243.

21. Lovecraft to Clark, February 16, 1925, *Letters to Family*, 1:253.

22. Lovecraft to Edward Cole, February 24, 1925, Lovecraft Collection, https:// repository.library.brown.edu/studio/item/bdr:423675/; Rheinhart Kleiner, "James Morton," in *Letters to James F. Morton*, by H. P. Lovecraft, ed. David E. Schultz and S. T. Joshi (New York: Hippocampus Press, 2011), 459; W. Paul Cook, "Jim Morton," *Letters to Morton*, 452. Lovecraft stated that Morton first learned of the civil service exam and the museum position through the sister of a librarian at the Paterson Free Public Library.

Members of the Blue Pencil Club rented a cottage at Echo Lake, New Jersey, from this unnamed woman for a Labor Day outing in 1924. According to W. Paul Cook, however, Morton and the Blue Pencil Club rented the cottage from the wife of the Paterson librarian, and Morton spoke with the librarian about the opening.

23. Lovecraft to Gamwell, February 10, 1925, *Letters to Family*, 1:245; Lovecraft to James F. Morton, February 16, 1925, *Letters to Morton*, 80–81.

24. Kirk to Dvorak, February 17, 1925, *Lovecraft's New York Circle*, 45; George Chauncey, *Gay New York: Gender, Urban Culture, and the Making of the Gay Male World, 1890–1940* (New York: Basic Books, 1994), 163–66; Jancee Dunn, "The Roosevelt Family Built a New York Coffee Chain 50 Years Before Starbucks, *Smithsonian Magazine*, December 2014, https://www.smithsonianmag.com/history/roosevelt-family-built-new-york -coffee-chain-50-years-starbucks-180953398/; Edward O'Reilly, "Meet Me at the Double R Coffee House," *From the Stacks: New-York Historical Society Library & Museum*, October 12, 2012, https://www.nyhistory.org/blogs/meet-me-at-the-double-r-coffee-house. The Double R Coffee House had multiple Manhattan locations: 112 West Forty-Fourth Street, 106 West Forty-Fifth Street, and 726 Lexington Avenue. The Forty-Fourth Street spot was the one favored by Lovecraft and his friends.

25. Lovecraft to Gamwell, February 10, 1925, *Letters to Family*, 1:247.

26. Lovecraft to Gamwell, February 10, 1925, Lovecraft Collection, https://repository .library.brown.edu/studio/item/bdr:423673/; Lovecraft to Clark, February 16, 1925, *Letters to Family*, 1:253.

27. Kirk to Dvorak, February 17, 1925, *Lovecraft's New York Circle*, 45.

28. Chauncey, *Gay New York*, 163–66.

29. Lovecraft to Moe, June 15, 1925, *Letters to Moe*, 148.

30. Lovecraft to Gamwell, February 26, 1925, *Letters to Family*, 1:254.

31. Lovecraft to Gamwell, February 26, 1925, *Letters to Family*, 1:254.

32. Lovecraft, "[Diary: 1925]," in *Collected Essays*, 5:152, 154.

33. Lovecraft to Gamwell, February 26, 1925, *Letters to Family*, 1:254.

34. Lovecraft to Gamwell, February 26, 1925, *Letters to Family*, 1:255.

35. H. P. Lovecraft, "To Xanthippe on Her Birthday—March 16, 1925," 1925, Lovecraft Collection, https://repository.library.brown.edu/studio/item/bdr:425460/; Sonia H. Davis, "Lovecraft as I Knew Him," in *Lovecraft Remembered*, ed. Peter Cannon (Sauk City, Wisc.: Arkham House, 1998), 261; Sonia H. Davis, *The Private Life of H. P. Lovecraft*, ed. S. T. Joshi (West Warwick, R.I.: Necronomicon Press, 1985), 22; C. C. W. Taylor, "Socrates," in *The Oxford Encyclopedia of Ancient Greece and Rome*, ed. Michael Gagarin (New York: Oxford University Press, 2010), Oxford Reference.

36. Lovecraft to Moe, June 15, 1925, *Letters to Moe*, 148.

37. Lovecraft to Clark, April 11, 1925, *Letters to Family*, 1:263.

38. Lovecraft to Clark, April 11, 1925, *Letters to Family*, 1:263.

39. H. P. Lovecraft to Rheinhart Kleiner, April 16, 1919, in Lovecraft, *Letters to Rheinhart Kleiner and Others*, ed. S. T. Joshi and David E. Schultz (New York: Hippocampus Press, 2020), 133.

40. "To [Lovecraft] a woman meant shelter, comfort, security—all without effort on his part; and, whether consciously or not, that is precisely what he expected of his marriage to Mrs. Greene"; James Warren Thomas, "Howard Phillips Lovecraft: A Self-Portrait" (master's thesis, Brown University, 1950), 44.

41. Lovecraft to Clark, April 11, 1925, *Letters to Family*, 1:262; Lovecraft to Clark,

April 2, 1925, *Letters to Family*, 1:259; Kathleen Drowne and Patrick Huber, *The 1920s* (Westport, Conn.: Greenwood Press, 2004), 293. A can of brand-name soup cost twelve cents and a loaf of bread twelve cents in the 1920s. This context underscores Lovecraft's impecunious food budget and meager diet.

42. Davis, *Private Life*, 7.

43. Rheinhart Kleiner, "A Memoir of Lovecraft," in Cannon, *Lovecraft Remembered*, 201.

44. Lovecraft to Clark, April 2, 1925, *Letters to Family*, 1:259; Lovecraft to Clark, April 11, 1925, *Letters to Family*, 1:262–63; Lovecraft to Moe, June 15, 1925, *Letters to Moe*, 148–49; Lovecraft, "Diary, 1925," Lovecraft Collection, https://repository.library .brown.edu/studio/item/bdr:425490/. Lovecraft lists his weight as 146 pounds in his June letter to Moe. In the personal information section of his diary, Lovecraft notes his height as five feet and eleven inches and his weight as 150 pounds.

45. Lovecraft to Moe, June 15, 1925, *Letters to Moe*, 149.

46. Lovecraft to Moe, June 15, 1925, *Letters to Moe*, 149.

47. Lovecraft to Moe, June 15, 1925, *Letters to Moe*, 149.

48. Lovecraft to Clark, April 11, 1925, *Letters to Family*, 1:264; Lovecraft to Moe, June 15, 1925, *Letters to Moe*, 149.

49. Lovecraft to Gamwell, February 10, 1925, *Letters to Family*, 1:243.

50. Lovecraft to Gamwell, February 26, 1925, *Letters to Family*, 1:256.

51. Lovecraft to Gamwell, February 26, 1925, *Letters to Family*, 1:256.

52. Lovecraft to Clark, April 2, 1925, *Letters to Family*, 1:259.

53. Lovecraft to Clark, April 21, 1925, *Letters to Family*, 1:268.

54. Lovecraft to Clark, April 21, 1925, *Letters to Family*, 1:268–69; Roger Straus III, *America's Great Railroad Stations*, text by Ed Breslin and Hugh Van Dusen (New York: Viking Press, 2011), 51–54.

55. Lovecraft to Clark, April 21, 1925, *Letters to Family*, 1:269, 275. Lovecraft refers to this individual as both "Miss Crist" and "Miss Dashiel." A full name has not been determined.

56. Lovecraft to Clark, April 21, 1925, *Letters to Family*, 1:268–69, 276; Scott W. Berg, *Grand Avenues: The Story of the French Visionary Who Designed Washington, D.C.* (New York: Pantheon Books, 2007), 102, 180–81.

57. Dennis E. Gale, *The Misunderstood History of Gentrification: People, Planning, Preservation, and Urban Renewal, 1915–2020* (Philadelphia: Temple University Press, 2021), 29–32.

58. Lovecraft to Clark, April 21, 1925, *Letters to Family*, 1:277.

59. Lovecraft to Clark, April 21, 1925, *Letters to Family*, 1:284.

60. Lovecraft to Clark, April 21, 1925, *Letters to Family*, 1:287; Lovecraft, "[Diary: 1925]," in *Collected Essays*, 5:156; Lovecraft to Gamwell, February 26, 1925, *Letters to Family*, 1:255; S. T. Joshi, *I Am Providence: The Life and Times of H. P. Lovecraft* (New York: Hippocampus Press, 2013), 2:583; Lovecraft to Jonathan Hoag, April 12, 1925, Lovecraft Collection, https://repository.library.brown.edu/studio/item/bdr:932200/; Lovecraft to Clark, April 21, 1925, Lovecraft Collection, https://repository.library .brown.edu/studio/item/bdr:423680/. Lovecraft ultimately chronicled every detail of his Washington, D.C., trip in a thirty-two-page typed letter—almost a short history of the region—to Lillian Clark.

61. Lovecraft, "[Diary: 1925]," in *Collected Essays*, 5:159.

62. "Big Gifts for Poor in Penfold's Will," *New York Times*, February 11, 1925. The mansion at 10 East Fortieth Street was the home of the late Edmund Penfold, a former director of the American Gas Company. He was a lifelong bachelor and the final descendant of an old New York family. If Lovecraft knew of Penfold's family history and social position, he likely felt some connection with the deceased and might have even seen in him a well-to-do version of himself. This would have made the experience at the estate sale especially traumatic for Lovecraft.

63. Kirk to Dvorak, June 10, 1925, *Lovecraft's New York Circle*, 54; Marvin Mondlin and Roy Meador, *Book Row: An Anecdotal and Pictorial History of the Antiquarian Book Trade*, foreword by Madeleine B. Stern (New York: Carroll & Graf, 2004), xiii–xiv.

64. By 1927, the entire building, "a typical mid-Victorian New York home" at 10 East Fortieth Street, had been demolished for the construction of a forty-four-story skyscraper once known as the Chase Tower; Lovecraft to Clark, May 20, 1925, *Letters to Family*, 1:288; Percy Loomis Sperr, *Manhattan: 40th Street (East)–Madison Avenue*, 1927, photograph, Irma and Paul Milstein Division of United States History, Local History and Genealogy, New York Public Library, https://digitalcollections.nypl.org/items/5ad54700 -c542-012f-c764-58d385a7bc34; Museum of the City of New York, "10 East 40th Street," *Urban Archive*, May 15, 2018, https://www.urbanarchive.org/sites/YF9tmEvGTqh /PXuH7taxrgC.

65. Lovecraft to Clark, May 20, 1925, *Letters to Family*, 1:288.

66. Lovecraft to Clark, May 20, 1925, *Letters to Family*, 1:288.

67. Lovecraft to Clark, May 20, 1925, *Letters to Family*, 1:290.

68. Lovecraft to Clark, May 20, 1925, *Letters to Family*, 1:290.

69. Lovecraft to Clark, May 20, 1925, *Letters to Family*, 1:289.

70. John's Spaghetti House was at 7 Willoughby Street near Brooklyn Borough Hall. Lovecraft wrote "my favourite restaurant" on the back of the eatery's business card; H. P. Lovecraft, "John's Spaghetti House," Lovecraft Collection, https://repository.library.brown .edu/studio/item/bdr:425871/.

71. Lovecraft to Clark, May 20, 1925, *Letters to Family*, 1:289.

72. Lovecraft to Clark, May 20, 1925, *Letters to Family*, 1:290.

73. Drowne and Huber, *1920s*, 294. A radio set averaged between $125 and $250 in the 1920s.

74. Lovecraft to Lillian Clark, May 25, 1925, *Letters to Family*, 1:292–93; Lovecraft, "[Diary: 1925]," in *Collected Essays*, 5:160.

75. Lovecraft to Clark, May 25, 1925, *Letters to Family*, 1:292; Lovecraft, "[Diary: 1925]," in *Collected Essays*, 5:160; Lovecraft to Moe, June 15, 1925, *Letters to Moe*, 149. Lovecraft noted himself retiring at different times in a letter (six o'clock in the morning) and his diary (seven o'clock in the morning). He dated the robbery as occurring on May 24, 1925, in a letter to Maurice W. Moe.

76. *Vault at Pfaffs: An Archive of Art and Literature by the Bohemians of Antebellum New York*, Lehigh University, s.v. "Edgar Fawcett," https://pfaffs.web.lehigh.edu/node /55233. A largely forgotten writer, Edgar Fawcett (1847–1904) was a New York City– born poet and novelist. Samuel Loveman had been collecting books by Fawcett for a prospective critical monograph.

77. Lovecraft to Clark, May 28, 1925, *Letters to Family*, 1:294.

78. Lovecraft to Clark, May 28, 1925, *Letters to Family*, 1:294.

79. Lovecraft to Clark, May 28, 1925, *Letters to Family*, 1:294.

80. Lovecraft to Clark, May 28, 1925, *Letters to Family*, 1:295.

81. Lovecraft to Clark, May 28, 1925, *Letters to Family*, 1:295.

82. Lovecraft to Clark, May 28, 1925, *Letters to Family*, 1:295.

83. Lovecraft to Clark, May 28, 1925, Lovecraft Collection, https://repository.library
.brown.edu/studio/item/bdr:932577/. A digital copy of the original letter provides the
highest-quality version of this image. Dr. Jessica Murphy discovered this reference to
"Yes! We Have No Bananas," which further displays Lovecraft's grasp of his contemporary
popular culture and his clever sense of humor.

84. H. P. Lovecraft, "Howard's Men's and Young Men's Clothes," Lovecraft Collection,
https://repository.library.brown.edu/studio/item/bdr:425870/; H. P. Lovecraft, "Franklin
Clothes," Lovecraft Collection, https://repository.library.brown.edu/studio/item/bdr:42
5869/.

85. Lovecraft to Clark, May 28, 1925, *Letters to Family*, 1:299; Lovecraft, "[Diary:
1925]," in *Collected Essays*, 5:160.

86. Joshi, *I Am Providence*, 2:574. Lovecraft might have earned a mere $250 in 1925:
$170 from his publications in *Weird Tales* and $74.16 from his share of mortgage payments
on a Providence-area rock quarry. This total would just cover half his rent at 169 Clinton
Street.

87. Lovecraft to Clark, May 28, 1925, *Letters to Family*, 1:297.

88. Lovecraft to Clark, May 28, 1925, *Letters to Family*, 1:299; Lovecraft, "[Diary:
1925]," in *Collected Essays*, 5:160.

89. Lovecraft to Clark, May 28, 1925, *Letters to Family*, 1:296–300; Lovecraft to Clark,
July 6, 1925, *Letters to Family*, 1:307, 309–10; Lovecraft to Clark, July 27, 1925, *Letters to
Family*, 1:320; Lovecraft, "[Diary: 1925]," in *Collected Essays*, 5:160, 162–63; Lovecraft,
"[Commercial Blurbs]," in *Collected Essays*, 5:180–85. The text of five advertising
articles written by Lovecraft is extant. None appear to have been published, including
the Alexander Hamilton Book Shop piece purportedly sold by Leeds. That business was
located at 22 Hamilton Street, Paterson, New Jersey.

8. "Circle of Aesthetic Dilettante"

1. H. P. Lovecraft to Maurice W. Moe, June 15, 1925, in Lovecraft, *Letters to
Maurice W. Moe*, ed. David E. Schultz and S. T. Joshi (New York: Hippocampus Press,
2018), 148.

2. Lovecraft to Moe, June 15, 1925, *Letters to Moe*, 148.

3. H. P. Lovecraft to Lillian D. Clark, May 28, 1925, in Lovecraft, *Letters to Family
and Family Friends*, ed. S. T. Joshi and David E. Schultz, vol. 1, *1911–1925* (New York:
Hippocampus Press, 2020), 296.

4. Lovecraft to Moe, June 15, 1925, *Letters to Moe*, 148; Lovecraft to Clark, May 28,
1925, *Letters to Family*, 1:300. His confession to Moe echoed that shared in an earlier
letter to his aunt, which utilized much more over-the-top language and imagery.

5. Lovecraft to Moe, June 15, 1925, *Letters to Moe*, 148; H. P. Lovecraft, "[Diary:
1925]," in Lovecraft, *Collected Essays*, ed. S. T. Joshi, vol. 5, *Philosophy; Autobiography
and Miscellany* (New York: Hippocampus Press, 2006), 161–64; S. T. Joshi, *I Am
Providence: The Life and Times of H. P. Lovecraft* (New York: Hippocampus Press, 2013),
2:570.

6. George Kirk to Lucile Dvorak, April 1925, in *Lovecraft's New York Circle: The*

Kalem Club, 1924–1927, ed. Mara Kirk Hart and S. T. Joshi (New York: Hippocampus Press, 2006), 52.

7. The original manuscript diary notes that Lovecraft visited Elizabeth, New Jersey, with "SH" (Sonia H. Greene) on June 13, 1925. This matches the details of the trip in his letter to Maurice W. Moe. The published diary notes "SL" in the entry for June 13, 1925; H. P. Lovecraft, "Diary, 1925," Howard P. Lovecraft Collection, Brown Digital Repository, Brown University Library, https://repository.library.brown.edu/studio/item/bdr:425490/; Lovecraft to Moe, June 15, 1925, *Letters to Moe*, 148; Lovecraft, "[Diary: 1925]," in *Collected Essays*, 5:161.

8. Lovecraft, "[Diary: 1925]," in *Collected Essays*, 5:162.

9. Lovecraft, "[Diary: 1925]," in *Collected Essays*, 5:162.

10. Lovecraft, "[Diary: 1925]," in *Collected Essays*, 5:162.

11. Lovecraft to Clark, July 6, 1925, *Letters to Family*, 1:306.

12. Lovecraft to Clark, July 6, 1925, *Letters to Family*, 1:306.

13. H. P. Lovecraft to Duane Rimel, September 12, 1934, in Lovecraft, *Selected Letters*, ed. August Derleth and James Turner, vol. 5, *1934–1937* (Sauk City, Wisc.: Arkham House, 1976), 34–35. Lovecraft patronized freak shows during his years in New York, including those located in Times Square and Coney Island. Arthur Leeds, his fellow Kalem Club member, had a past affiliation with circuses and carnivals, and he maintained relationships with performers at several New York establishments.

14. John S. Berman, *Coney Island* (New York: Barnes & Noble, 2003), 71–73; Michael Immerso, *Coney Island: The People's Playground* (New Brunswick, N.J.: Rutgers University Press, 2002), 139.

15. Lovecraft to Clark, July 6, 1925, Lovecraft Collection, https://repository.library.brown.edu/studio/item/bdr:423683/.

16. August Derleth, "Lovecraft's Sensitivity," in *Lovecraft Remembered*, ed. Peter Cannon (Sauk City, Wisc.: Arkham House, 1998), 32, 34; Winfield Townley Scott, Bookman's Galley, *Providence Sunday Journal*, September 19, 1948; Winfield Townley Scott, Bookman's Galley, *Providence Sunday Journal*, October 3, 1948.

17. Sonia H. Davis, *The Private Life of H. P. Lovecraft*, ed. S. T. Joshi (West Warwick, R.I.: Necronomicon Press, 1985), 2, 12.

18. Paul K. Longmore and Lauri Umansky, introduction to *The New Disability History: American Perspectives*, ed. Paul K. Longmore and Lauri Umansky (New York: NYU Press, 2001), 22; Bobby Derie, "Her Letters to Lovecraft: Elizabeth Toldridge," *Deep Cuts in a Lovecraftian Vein*, July 7, 2021, https://deepcuts.blog/2021/07/07/her-letters-to-lovecraft-elizabeth-toldridge/; Lovecraft to Clark, May 7, 1929, *Letters to Family*, 2:795. This empathy toward the disabled appeared again in Lovecraft's life. While traveling through Washington, D.C., in May 1929, he made a point to visit poet Elizabeth Toldridge (1861–1940). She suffered from an unspecified disability and was confined to her apartment. The limited evidence of Lovecraft's view of the disabled contrasted with the then dominant public perception of such individuals. In fact, medical, legal, and educational professionals collectively questioned if disabled people were fully competent to act as full citizens, and little thought was given to the disabled in public space and life at that time in America.

19. Eric K. Washington, "E. J. Perry, African-American Silhouette Cutter of America's Leisure Circuit," *Gotham: A Blog for Scholars of New York City History*, December 17, 2013, https://www.gothamcenter.org/blog/ej-perry-african-american-silhouette-cutter-of-americas-leisure-circuit. E. J. (Essaias James) Perry (c. 1879–1946) was working on the

Coney Island boardwalk as early as 1904. He plied his trade at world's fairs and expositions in the first decade of the twentieth century. By the 1910s, he was traveling between Manhattan and Coney Island to sell his silhouettes.

20. Lovecraft to Clark, July 6, 1925, *Letters to Family*, 1:309.

21. Lovecraft to Clark, July 6, 1925, *Letters to Family*, 1:309.

22. Lisa W. Foderaro, "How Big Is That Park? City Now Has an Answer," *New York Times*, May 31, 2013; Gary D. Hermalyn and Jonathan Kuhn, "Pelham Bay Park," in *The Encyclopedia of New York City*, ed. Kenneth T. Jackson, 2nd ed. (New Haven: Yale University Press; New York: New-York Historical Society, 2010), 986; Catherine Scott, "Rodman's Neck Estates: Gone but Not Forgotten," *Island Current* (Bronx), March 1990; Thomas X. Casey, East Bronx History Forum, email to author, February 18, 2022.

23. Lovecraft to Clark, July 6, 1925, *Letters to Family*, 1:310.

24. Lovecraft to Clark, July 6, 1925, Lovecraft Collection, https://repository.library .brown.edu/studio/item/bdr:423683/.The word "niggers" is underscored in the original letter.

25. Lovecraft to Clark, July 6, 1925, *Letters to Family*, 1:310.

26. Davis, *Private Life*, 22.

27. Lovecraft, "Diary, 1925," Lovecraft Collection, https://repository.library.brown.edu /studio/item/bdr:425490/.

28. Lovecraft to Clark, July 13, 1925, *Letters to Family*, 1:313.

29. The Luna Park currently operating on Coney Island modeled its main entrance after that of the historic and former Luna Park, the one patronized by Lovecraft and Greene in July 1925.

30. Lovecraft to Clark, July 27, 1925, *Letters to Family*, 1:320.

31. Lovecraft to Clark, July 27, 1925, Lovecraft Collection, https://repository.library .brown.edu/studio/item/bdr:423686/. Lovecraft's letter to Clark includes a sketch and diagram of the funhouse and its trick.

32. Lovecraft, "[Diary: 1925]," in *Collected Essays*, 5:163–64; Lovecraft to Clark, [July 20, 1925], *Letters to Family*, 1:318; Lovecraft to Clark, July 27, 1925, *Letters to Family*, 1:320–22.

33. Lovecraft to Clark, August 8, 1925, *Letters to Family*, 1:339.

34. Lovecraft to Clark, August 7, 1925, *Letters to Family*, 1:336.

35. Lovecraft to Clark, July 27, 1925, *Letters to Family*, 1:323.

36. Lovecraft to Clark, July 27, 1925, *Letters to Family*, 1:323; Sharon Seitz and Stuart Miller, *The Other Islands of New York City: A History and Guide*, 3rd ed. (Woodstock, Vt.: Countryman Press, 2011), 130–32.

37. Lovecraft to Clark, July 30–31, 1925, *Letters to Family*, 1:328.

38. Lovecraft to Clark, July 30–31, 1925, *Letters to Family*, 1:328.

39. Lovecraft to Clark, July 30–31, 1925, *Letters to Family*, 1:329; Lovecraft, "[Diary: 1925]," in *Collected Essays*, 5:164.

40. Lovecraft to Lillian Clark, August 7, 1925, *Letters to Family*, 1:335.

41. Lovecraft to Lillian Clark, August 7, 1925, *Letters to Family*, 1:335.

42. Lovecraft to Lillian Clark, August 7, 1925, *Letters to Family*, 1:335.

43. Lovecraft, "[Diary: 1925]," in *Collected Essays*, 5:164. "The Horror at Red Hook" was published in *Weird Tales*, January 1927, and later was included in two anthologies; Christine Campbell Thomson, ed., *You'll Need a Night Light* (London: Selwyn & Blount,

1927), and Herbert Asbury, ed., *Not at Night!* (New York: Macy-Masius, 1928), during Lovecraft's lifetime.

44. Lovecraft to Frank Belknap Long, August 2, 1925, *Selected Letters*, 2:20.

45. Brooklyn Historical Society, *Red Hook, Gowanus Neighborhood History Guide* (Brooklyn: Brooklyn Historical Society, 2000), 9–11. Before the construction of the Brooklyn-Queens Expressway, the borders and definition of Red Hook differed from those of the present day. For example, today's Carroll Gardens neighborhood was considered to be part of Red Hook.

46. H. P. Lovecraft, "The Horror at Red Hook," in *Tales* (New York: Library of America, 2005), 130.

47. Lovecraft, "Horror at Red Hook," 132, 137.

48. Lovecraft to Bernard Austin Dwyer, March 26, 1927, *Letters to Moe*, 438.

49. Lovecraft, "Horror at Red Hook," 127, 128.

50. Albert Johnson, foreword to *Immigration Restriction: A Study of the Opposition to and Regulation of Immigration into the United States*, by Roy L. Garis (New York: Macmillan, 1927), vii; John Higham, *Strangers in the Land: Patterns of American Nativism, 1860–1925*, 2nd ed. (New Brunswick, N.J.: Rutgers University Press, 1988), 324.

51. Brooks E. Hefner, "Weird Investigations and Nativist Semiotics in H. P. Lovecraft and Dashiell Hammett," *Modern Fiction Studies* 60, no. 4 (Winter 2014): 652.

52. F. Scott Fitzgerald, *The Great Gatsby*, notes and preface by Matthew J. Bruccoli (New York: Scribner, 2003), 17; Ian Frazier, "When W. E. B. Du Bois Made a Laughingstock of a White Supremacist," *New Yorker*, August 19, 2019, https://www.new yorker.com/magazine/2019/08/26/when-w-e-b-du-bois-made-a-laughingstock-of-a-white -supremacist. In *The Great Gatsby*, Tom Buchanan refers to "The Rise of the Colored Empires." This is an allusion by F. Scott Fitzgerald to Lothrop Stoddard, *The Rising Tide of Color against White World-Supremacy*, intro. Madison Grant (New York: Charles Scribner's Sons, 1920). The book was a well-reviewed bestseller.

53. Rheinhart Kleiner, "Bards and Bibliophiles," in Cannon, *Lovecraft Remembered*, 191–92.

54. J. Howard Suydam, *Hendrick Rycken, the Progenitor of the Suydam Family in America* (New York: Knickerbocker Press, 1898), 4, 32; James Riker Jr., *The Annals of Newtown, in Queens County, New York* [. . .] (New York: D. Fanshaw, 1852), 319–20, https://babel.hathitrust.org/cgi/pt?id=njp.32101072360546&view=1up&seq=11&skin= 2021; Walter Barrett, *Old Merchants of New York City*, 2nd ser. (New York: Carleton, 1863), 265–77; "Old Landmark Wiped Out by March of Improvement," *Brooklyn Daily Eagle*, May 10, 1911, Brooklyn Newsstand, Brooklyn Public Library.

55. Elizabeth Reich Rawson, "Gerritsen Beach," in *Encyclopedia of New York City*, 507; Thomas J. Campanella, *Brooklyn: The Once and Future City* (Princeton: Princeton University Press, 2019), 23–26, 312–14. The spelling of Gerritsen's name varies across sources; that used by Campanella is listed in this text.

56. Marc Beherec, "The Church That Inspired 'The Horror at Red Hook' and the Fall of the House of Suydam," *Lovecraft Annual*, no. 15 (2021): 128–66. Beherec catalogs each church in Red Hook and nearby neighborhoods that might have provided Lovecraft with creative fodder. The former and now demolished church building of the parish of the Sacred Hearts of Jesus and Mary Church at 35–39 President Street has long been cited as the inspiration for the cult's base in "The Horror at Red Hook." There is no direct evidence of this. The property on which the former church stood is now part of Mother

Cabrini Park. Beherec presents a compelling case that the former St. George's Syrian Catholic Church at 103 Washington Street in Manhattan was the primary architectural source for Lovecraft's writing. Ryneer Suydam originally commissioned this building sometime between 1812 and 1819. St. George's lived at 103 Washington Street between 1925 and 1982. These details buttress Beherec's hypothesis. However, Lovecraft's letters include no mention of this particular church.

57. Lovecraft to Dwyer, March 26, 1927, *Letters to Moe*, 436; Lovecraft to Wilfred Blanch Talman, January 15, 1929, *Selected Letters*, 2:258–59.

58. Ellen Fletcher, "Roosevelt Island," *Encyclopedia of New York City*, 1,122. Blackwell's Island was a prison infamous for overcrowding, crime, corruption, and harsh conditions.

59. Davis, *Private Life*, 6.

60. Lovecraft to Dwyer, March 26, 1927, *Letters to Moe*, 437; Lovecraft, "[Diary: 1925]," in *Collected Essays*, 5:153; Kleiner, "Bards and Bibliophiles," in Cannon, *Lovecraft Remembered*, 191–92.

61. Lovecraft to Dwyer, March 26, 1927, *Letters to Moe*, 437.

62. Lovecraft to Dwyer, March 26, 1927, *Letters to Moe*, 438.

63. Lovecraft to Dwyer, March 26, 1927, *Letters to Moe*, 438.

64. Lovecraft to Clark, August 13, 1925, *Letters to Family*, 1:344. The Chelsea neighborhood today contains three historic districts and holds several Greek Revival structures. These would have fascinated Lovecraft.

65. Lovecraft to Clark, August 13, 1925, *Letters to Family*, 1:344.

66. Lovecraft to Clark, August 13, 1925, *Letters to Family*, 1:345.

67. Lovecraft to Clark, August 13, 1925, *Letters to Family*, 1:345.

68. Lovecraft to Clark, August 13, 1925, *Letters to Family*, 1:345.

69. Lovecraft to Clark, August 13, 1925, *Letters to Family*, 1:346.

70. Lovecraft to Clark, August 13, 1925, *Letters to Family*, 1:346. The General Scott House was earlier known as Hampton Place.

71. Lovecraft to Clark, August 13, 1925, *Letters to Family*, 1:346.

72. Lovecraft to Clark, August 13, 1925, *Letters to Family*, 1:346.

73. Sonia H. Davis to [John Stanton], March 28, 1949, August William Derleth Papers, Wisconsin Historical Society. Lovecraft never showed "He" to Sonia Greene, possibly illustrating her diminishing place in his life or his reluctance to share the intensity of his loathing for New York. The story was first published by *Weird Tales* in its September 1926 issue.

74. H. P. Lovecraft, "He," in *Tales*, 147.

75. Lovecraft, "He," 147.

76. Lovecraft, "He," 147.

77. Lovecraft, "He," 148.

78. Lovecraft, "He," 149.

79. Lovecraft, "He," 154; Jay McRoy, "There Goes the Neighborhood: Chaotic Apocalypse and Monstrous Genesis in H. P. Lovecraft's 'The Street,' 'The Horror at Red Hook,' and 'He,'" *Journal of the Fantastic in the Arts* 13, no. 4 (2003): 345–46.

80. Lovecraft to Clark, August 20, 1924, *Letters to Family*, 1:152.

81. Lovecraft, "He," 150.

82. "The Warren-Van Nest Mansion—Bleecker and Charles Street," *Daytonian in Manhattan*, April 24, 2017, http://daytoninmanhattan.blogspot.com/2017/04/the-warren

-van-nest-mansion-bleecker.html#google_vignette; Elaine Schechter, *Perry Street: Then and Now*, illustrated by Carol Creutzbury (New York: n.p., 1972), 4–6; Andrew Gipe-Lazarou, "The 'Extreme Fantasy' of Delirious New York," *Lovecraft Annual*, no. 14 (2020): 130; S. T. Joshi and David E. Schultz, "He," in *An H. P. Lovecraft Encyclopedia* (Westport, Conn.: Greenwood Press: 2001), 108; Lovecraft to Clark, August 20, 1924, *Letters to Family*, 1:149; Frederick Clifton Pierce, *Field Genealogy* (Chicago: Hammond Press, 1901), 1:391–94. Pierce offers a full history and illustrated plates of the Warren-Van Nest Mansion.

83. Lovecraft to Clark, March 18, 1924, *Letters to Family*, 1:122; Lovecraft to Clark, August 20, 1924, *Letters to Family*, 1:149.

84. "Little Sketches About Town," *New York Evening Post*, August 29, 1924, microfilm, July 19–August 30, 1924.

85. Schechter, *Perry Street*, 4–6; Lovecraft to Clark, September 29–30, 1924, *Letters to Family*, 1:165.

86. Alexandra Bandon, "A Village in the City Hidden in Plain Sight," *New York Times*, October 20, 2002.

87. Lovecraft to Clark, August 13, 1925, *Letters to Family*, 1:347.

88. Lovecraft to Clark, August 13, 1925, *Letters to Family*, 1:347.

89. Lovecraft to Clark, August 13, 1925, *Letters to Family*, 1:347.

90. Lovecraft to Robert E. Howard, September 12, 1931, *Selected Letters*, 3:412–13; Lovecraft, "[Diary: 1925]," in *Collected Essays*, 5:153.

91. "Earth Tremor Shakes a Dozen States; New York Trembles with Rest of East; Shock Distinct but No Damage Done," *New York Times*, March 1, 1925; Jerry L. Coffman, Carl A. von Hake, and Carl W. Stover, eds., *Earthquake History of the United States* (Boulder, Colo.: U. S. Department of Commerce, National Oceanic and Atmospheric Administration; U. S. Department of the Interior, Geological Survey, 1982), 10–11, https://pubs.usgs.gov/unnumbered/70114182/report.pdf.

92. Lovecraft to Clark, August 13, 1925, *Letters to Family*, 1:347; Lovecraft, "[Diary: 1925]," in *Collected Essays*, 5:165.

93. Lovecraft to Clark, August 19–23, 1925, *Letters to Family*, 1:349.

94. Lovecraft to Clark, August 19–23, 1925, *Letters to Family*, 1:349; Lovecraft to Clark, August 27, 1925, *Letters to Family*, 1:367.

95. Marriage announcement, *Chicago Tribune*, September 14, 1924, Newspapers.com.

96. Lovecraft to Mrs. Alfred M. (Lillian) Galpin, August 16, 1925, Lovecraft Collection, https://repository.library.brown.edu/studio/item/bdr:423692/.

97. Lovecraft to Clark, August 19–23, 1925, *Letters to Family*, 1:354.

98. 1910 United States Census, Lowell, Middlesex County, Massachusetts, digital image s.v. "Lillian Galpin," Ancestry.com; 1920 United States Census, Chicago, Cook County, Illinois, digital image s.v. "Lillian Galpin," Ancestry.com; "Ireland, Select Births and Baptisms, 1620–11," s.v. "Maurice Roche," Ancestry.com. Additionally, Lillian Galpin (née Roche) has been mistakenly described as a native of France. This was likely a misreading of the fact that both she and Alfred Galpin, her husband, studied in Paris.

99. Lovecraft to Clark, August 19–23, 1925, *Letters to Family*, 1:356.

100. Anthony Ramirez, "Hotel Where Dodgers Celebrated a Title Is Up for Sale," *New York Times*, January 30, 2008.

101. Lovecraft to Clark, August 19–23, 1925, *Letters to Family*, 1:349, 352–58.

102. "New York, U.S., State and Federal Naturalization Records, 1794–1943," digital image s.v. "Sonia Greene," Ancestry.com; Lovecraft to Clark, August 19–23, 1925, *Letters to Family*, 1:356.

103. Lovecraft to Clark, August 19–23, 1925, *Letters to Family*, 1:358.

104. Lovecraft to Clark, September 1, 1925, *Letters to Family*, 1:370, 371, 370, 372. Lovecraft names the destination of the hike as Buttermilk Falls. One of the tallest waterfalls in New Jersey, Buttermilk Falls is in Sussex County, New Jersey, in the Delaware Water Gap National Recreation Area straddling the New Jersey–Pennsylvania border. However, Lovecraft's geographical (e.g., High Mountain) and geological (e.g., basalt outcrops) observations suggest that the location was, in fact, the present-day High Mountain Park Preserve, a 1,260-acre park in Wayne, New Jersey. The author confirmed these details on a visit to the park on July 1, 2022. Lovecraft's hike with the Paterson Rambling Club occurred on August 30, 1925. His September 1, 1925, letter to Lillian Clark contains a vivid travelogue of this outing and his overall impressions of Paterson.

105. Lovecraft to Clark, September 8, 1925, *Letters to Family*, 1:382.

106. Lovecraft to Clark, September 8, 1925, *Letters to Family*, 1:382. Lovecraft mistakenly notes this as a Saint Joseph festival. Saint Joseph's feast day is celebrated on March 19.

107. Lovecraft to Clark, September 8, 1925, *Letters to Family*, 1:382.

108. Lovecraft to Clark, September 12–13, 1925, *Letters to Family*, 1:387.

109. Lovecraft to Clark, September 23–24, 1925, *Letters to Family*, 1:405.

110. Lovecraft to Clark, September 23–24, 1925, *Letters to Family*, 1:405; Lovecraft to Clark, September 14, 1925, *Letters to Family*, 1:391–93.

111. Lovecraft to Clark, October 2, 1925, *Letters to Family*, 1:431; "About Our Church," South Bushwick Reformed Church, December 26, 2022, https://www.south bushwickchurch.org/our-story. The South Bushwick Reformed Church was organized in 1851, and construction began on its current building in 1852. The church was dedicated in 1853. It was designated as a historic landmark by the New York City Landmarks Preservation Commission in 1968, and it was added to the National Register of Historic Places in 1982. Because of the building's Greek Revival architecture, it is known as the "White Church."

112. Joshi, *I Am Providence*, 2:617. The Chelsea Book Shop had three successive locations: 317 West Fourteenth Street; 365 West Fifteenth Street; and 58 West Eighth Street.

113. Sonia H. Davis, Autobiographical Writings, August 25, 1964, box 9, folder 1, Sonia H. and Nathaniel Davis Papers, John Hay Library, Brown University.

114. Kirsten MacLeod, "What People Really Read in 1922: *If Winter Comes*, the Bestseller in *Annus Mirabilis* of Modernism," in *Transitions in Middlebrow Writing, 1880–1930*, ed. Kate Macdonald and Christopher Singer (New York: Palgrave Macmillan, 2015), 15–17. *If Winter Comes* was a huge sensation in the United Kingdom and the United States. It was adapted to both the stage and screen, and it inspired songs and advertisements.

115. Lovecraft to Clark, October 20, 1925, *Letters to Family*, 1:453.

116. Lovecraft to Clark, October 22, 1925, *Letters to Family*, 1:457.

117. Kirk to Dvorak, [Autumn 1925], in Hart and Joshi, *Lovecraft's New York Circle*, 65.

118. Lovecraft to Clark, October 19, 1925, *Letters to Family*, 1:450.

119. Robert H. Zieger, "Pennsylvania Coal and Politics: The Anthracite Strike of

1925–1926," *Pennsylvania Magazine of History and Biography* 93, no. 2 (April 1969): 244–62.

120. Both Lovecraft's friends and Sonia Greene attested to his negative reaction to cold weather. Lovecraft regularly commented about his need to maintain high indoor temperatures and his inability to physically function in the winter months. Since these symptoms were never medically diagnosed, it remains debatable whether this was a physical or psychological impairment or a symptom of an underlining health condition.

121. Lovecraft to Clark, November 7, 1925, *Letters to Family*, 1:476.

122. Lovecraft to Clark, October 20, 1925, *Letters to Family*, 1:453.

123. Lovecraft to Clark, November 7, 1925, *Letters to Family*, 1:474.

124. Lovecraft to Clark, November 14–19, 1925, *Letters to Family*, 1:485; Craig Radow, "The Coney Island of Canarsie," *New York Times*, July 1, 2007.

125. Lovecraft to Clark, November 14–19, 1925, *Letters to Family*, 1:486; Lovecraft, "[Diary: 1925]," in *Collected Essays*, 5:172.

126. Lovecraft to Clark, November 14–19, 1925, *Letters to Family*, 1:485, 486; Lovecraft, "[Diary: 1925]," in *Collected Essays*, 5:172.

127. "History," King Manor Museum, December 26, 2022, https://www.kingmanor.org/history; Jonathan Kuhn, "King Manor," *Encyclopedia of New York City*, 699.

128. Lovecraft to Clark, November 14–19, 1925, *Letters to Family*, 1:486.

129. Lovecraft to Clark, November 14–19, 1925, *Letters to Family*, 1:486; Vincent Seyfried, "Kew Gardens," *Encyclopedia of New York City*, 697–98.

130. Lovecraft to Clark, November 14–19, 1925, *Letters to Family*, 1:486.

131. Lovecraft to Clark, November 14–19, 1925, *Letters to Family*, 1:488; Queens Public Library, "129-11 Jamaica Avenue," *Urban Archive*, July 26, 2018, https://www.urbanarchive.org/sites/jpmNUKJuxUH/cD8MJRapK4R; Eugene L. Armbruster, *Douw Ditmars House*, 1923, photograph, Queens Public Library, http://digitalarchives.queenslibrary.org/browse/douw-ditmars-house2. This might have been the Douw Ditmars House at 129-11 (formerly 3915 or 39-15) Jamaica Avenue. Although documentary evidence suggests that it was demolished in 1922 or 1923, the sketch in Lovecraft's letters resembles the home in the photographs by Eugene L. Armbruster. Thus, the Douw Ditmars House might have been still standing in 1925.

132. Lovecraft to Clark, November 14–19, 1925, *Letters to Family*, 1:488. By 1925, the northern stretch of Flushing Creek was already a dumping ground operated by the politically connected Brooklyn Ash Removal Company. F. Scott Fitzgerald called this the "valley of ashes" in *The Great Gatsby*. In contrast, the virginal segments of the waterway remained inhabited by crabs and mussels; Fitzgerald, *Great Gatsby*, 28; Sergey Kadinsky, *Hidden Waters of New York City: A History and Guide to 101 Forgotten Lakes, Ponds, Creeks, and Streams in the Five Boroughs* (Woodstock, Vt.: Countryman Press, 2016), 98–99; Ted Steinberg, *Gotham Unbound: The Ecological History of Greater New York* (New York: Simon & Schuster, 2014), 211–12.

133. Lovecraft to Clark, December 22–23, 1925, *Letters to Family*, 1:516.

134. Lovecraft to Clark, December 22–23, 1925, *Letters to Family*, 1:517.

135. Excelsior Warehouse to Lovecraft, December 4, 1925, on verso of Lovecraft to James F. Morton, June 9, 1926, Lovecraft Collection, https://repository.library.brown.edu/studio/item/bdr:423763/.

136. Lovecraft to Clark, December 13, 1925, *Letters to Family*, 1:506.

137. Lovecraft to Clark, December 22–23, 1925, *Letters to Family*, 1:515.

138. Lovecraft to Clark, December 26, 1925, Lovecraft Collection, https://repository .library.brown.edu/studio/item/bdr:931925/.

9. "Long Live the State of Rhode-Island"

1. H. P. Lovecraft to Lillian D. Clark, January 11, 1926, in *Letters to Family and Family Friends*, ed. S. T. Joshi and David E. Schultz, vol. 2, *1926–1936* (New York: Hippocampus Press, 2020), 535.

2. Lovecraft to Clark, January 11, 1926, *Letters to Family*, 2:535.

3. Lovecraft to Clark, January 11, 1926, *Letters to Family*, 2:535.

4. Lovecraft to Clark, January 11, 1926, *Letters to Family*, 2:535.

5. Lovecraft to Clark, January 11, 1926, *Letters to Family*, 2:535.

6. Lovecraft to Clark, January 11, 1926, *Letters to Family*, 2:534, 535.

7. Lovecraft to Clark, January 11, 1926, *Letters to Family*, 2:535.

8. Lovecraft to Clark, January 11, 1926, *Letters to Family*, 2:535.

9. Lovecraft to Clark, January 11, 1926, *Letters to Family*, 2:535.

10. Lovecraft to Clark, January 11, 1926, *Letters to Family*, 2:536.

11. Lovecraft to Clark, January 11, 1926, *Letters to Family*, 2:536.

12. Lovecraft to Clark, January 11, 1926, *Letters to Family*, 2:536.

13. Lovecraft to Clark, January 11, 1926, *Letters to Family*, 2:536.

14. Lovecraft to Clark, January 11, 1926, *Letters to Family*, 2:536.

15. Lovecraft to Clark, January 11, 1926, *Letters to Family*, 2:536.

16. Lovecraft to Clark, January 11, 1926, *Letters to Family*, 2:536.

17. Lovecraft to Clark, January 11, 1926, *Letters to Family*, 2:537.

18. *Montague Branch*, photograph, 1947, 1949, 1953, Brooklyn Public Library, Center for Brooklyn History, https://www.bklynlibrary.org/digitalcollections/item/1fd1cb56-4b25 -4b2d-97ed-45cb96odab30; Center for Brooklyn History, "Montague Street Branch, Brooklyn Public Library," *Urban Archive*, May 19, 2017, https://www.urbanarchive.org /sites/F38f13pXS8N/FiZNodqzc3F. This would have been the Montague Street Branch at 197 Montague Street. Housed in a Romanesque Revival building, the library began its operations as the Brooklyn Mercantile Library Association of the City of Brooklyn in 1867 and became a branch of the Brooklyn Public Library in 1903. The branch closed and the building was demolished in 1962, three years before Brooklyn Heights was designated a historic district. Oddly enough, Lovecraft only signed up for a Brooklyn Public Library card on August 20, 1925—his thirty-fifth birthday and the same day Sonia Greene became a naturalized citizen.

19. H. P. Lovecraft, "Supernatural Horror in Literature," *Recluse*, August 1927; H. P. Lovecraft, *Supernatural Horror in Literature & Other Essays*, intro. Darrell Schweitzer (Rockville, Md.: Wildside Press, 2008), 15–112.

20. S. T. Joshi, *I Am Providence: The Life and Times of H. P. Lovecraft* (New York: Hippocampus Press, 2013), 2:609; S. T. Joshi and David E. Schultz, "Supernatural Horror in Literature, in *An H. P. Lovecraft Encyclopedia* (Westport, Conn.: Greenwood Press, 2001), 255–56.

21. T. O. Mabbott, "H. P. Lovecraft: An Appreciation," in *Lovecraft Remembered*, ed. Peter Cannon (Sauk City, Wisc.: Arkham House, 1998), 420, 421; "Thomas Mabbott, Poe Expert, Dies," *New York Times*, May 16, 1968.

22. Lovecraft to Clark, February 12, 1926, *Letters to Family*, 2:553.

23. Cynthia Tobar and Allen Thomas, *Guide to the Hall of Fame for Great Americans*

NOTES TO PAGES 157–58 · 241

Collection, 1894–2008 (Bronx: Archives and Special Collections, Bronx Community College, 2016), [3–4]; Bronx Community College, Brochure (Bronx: Bronx Community College, n.d); Cynthia Tobar, Twitter direct message to author, January 21, 2022; Remo Cosentino, email to author, January 22, 24, 2022. The Hall of Fame for Great Americans eventually grew to ninety-eight busts. In 2017, the statues of Confederate generals Robert E. Lee and Thomas Jonathan "Stonewall" Jackson were removed. This brought the current total to ninety-six busts. Many thanks to Cynthia Tobar, Bronx Community College archivist, and Remo Cosentino, Bronx Community College campus historian, for clarifying the details and history of the Hall of Fame for Great Americans.

24. Lovecraft to Clark, February 12, 1926, *Letters to Family*, 2:555.

25. Lovecraft to Clark, February 12, 1926, *Letters to Family*, 2:556. The chronology of events in this letter might lead to confusion regarding exact dates. Lovecraft mistakenly noted two separate days (Thursday and Saturday) as February 4, 1926. The first day was the correct one.

26. Lovecraft to Clark, January 26, 1926, *Letters to Family*, 2:541, 543, 546–46; Lovecraft to Clark, January 30, 1926, *Letters to Family*, 2:548–50; Lovecraft to Clark, February 12, 1926, *Letters to Family*, 2:552–56.

27. Lovecraft to Clark, February 12, 1926, *Letters to Family*, 2:557; Marvin Mondlin and Roy Meador, *Book Row: An Anecdotal and Pictorial History of the Antiquarian Book Trade*, foreword by Madeleine B. Stern (New York: Carroll & Graf, 2004), 39–46.

28. Lovecraft to Clark, February 26, 1926, *Letters to Family*, 2:566.

29. "Henry C. Brown, Historian, Dead," *New York Times*, July 14, 1961; Christopher Gray, "The Museum of the City of New York; Preserving the Past, Planning the Future," Streetscapes, *New York Times*, November 6, 2005; Mary Beth Betts, "Gracie Mansion," in *The Encyclopedia of New York City*, ed. Kenneth T. Jackson, 2nd ed. (New Haven: Yale University Press; New York: New-York Historical Society, 2010), 539–40; Claudia Keenan, "Henry Collins Brown and the Museum of the City of New York," in *Gotham: A Blog for Scholars of New York City History*, September 30, 2022, https://www.gothamcenter .org/blog/henry-collins-brown-and-the-museum-of-the-city-of-new-york. In addition to his museum work, Henry Collins Brown might be best known for overseeing the publication of several editions of the *Valentine's Manual of Old New York* and early historic preservation efforts in the city. The Museum of the City of New York was founded in 1923 and was housed in Gracie Mansion until 1932.

30. Lovecraft to Clark, February 26, 1926, *Letters to Family*, 2:566.

31. Lovecraft to Clark, February 26, 1926, *Letters to Family*, 2:566. "Our History," Brooklyn Public Library, Center for Brooklyn History, accessed January 27, 2023, https://www.bklynlibrary.org/cbh/about/history; Christopher Gray, "Brooklyn Historical Society; An 1881 Landmark in Red Brick and Terra Cotta," Streetscapes, *New York Times*, February 11, 2001; Deborah Tint, "Built for Brooklyn History: A Place with Many Names," *Brooklynology*, Brooklyn Public Library, February 15, 2022, https://www .bklynlibrary.org/blog/2022/02/15/built-for-brooklyn. The Center for Brooklyn History was founded as the Long Island Historical Society in 1863. Its building on Pierrepont Street was designed by architect George B. Post and completed in 1881. It changed its name to the Brooklyn Historical Society in 1985. After merging with the Brooklyn Public Library in 2020, it adopted its current name.

32. "Cool Air" was published in a minor pulp magazine, *Tales of Magic and Mystery*, in March 1928. The exact date of its composition is unknown. Lovecraft first mentions the story in a late February letter to artist and writer Clark Ashton Smith: "The other day

I ground out the enclosed new tale ["Cool Air"], which several readers have been good enough to mention quite kindly"; Lovecraft to Clark Ashton Smith, February 26, 1926, Howard P. Lovecraft Collection, Brown Digital Repository, Brown University Library, https://repository.library.brown.edu/studio/item/bdr:425670/.

33. H. P. Lovecraft, "Cool Air," in *Tales* (New York: Library of America, 2005), 158.
34. Lovecraft, "Cool Air," 160.
35. Lovecraft, "Cool Air," 160.
36. Lovecraft, "Cool Air," 161.
37. Lovecraft to Clark, August 19–23, 1925, *Letters to Family*, 1:360.
38. Lovecraft to Clark, August 19–23, 1925, *Letters to Family*, 1:360.
39. Lovecraft, "Cool Air," 160.
40. Lovecraft, "Cool Air," 158.
41. Lovecraft to Smith, February 26, 1926, Lovecraft Collection, https://repository.library.brown.edu/studio/item/bdr:425670/; H. P. Lovecraft to Henry Kuttner, July 29, 1936, in *Letters to C. L. Moore and Others*, ed. David E. Schultz and S. T. Joshi (New York: Hippocampus Press, 2017), 247–48.
42. George Kirk to Lucile Dvorak, March 3, 1926, in *Lovecraft's New York Circle: The Kalem Club, 1924–1927*, ed. Mara Kirk Hart and S. T. Joshi (New York: Hippocampus Press, 2006), 80.
43. Lovecraft, "Cool Air," 158.
44. Lovecraft, "Cool Air," 159.
45. Lovecraft, "Cool Air," 158.
46. Lovecraft to Clark, October 4, 1925, *Letters to Family*, 1:434.
47. Lovecraft, "Cool Air," 158.
48. Lovecraft, "Cool Air," 160.
49. H. P. Lovecraft to Bernard Austin Dwyer, March 26, 1927, in *Letters to Maurice W. Moe and Others*, ed. David E. Schultz and S. T. Joshi (New York: Hippocampus Press, 2018), 439–40.
50. Lovecraft, "Cool Air," 160.
51. Lovecraft, "Cool Air," 161.
52. Lovecraft, "Cool Air," 161.
53. Lovecraft to Clark, March 4, 1926, *Letters to Family*, 2:567.
54. Lovecraft to Clark, March 27, 1926, *Letters to Family*, 2:574. Revealing his fondness for eighteenth-century British spelling, punctuation, and language, Lovecraft incorporated the "long s" (ſ) in his writing of "Rhode Island" in the cited quotation. Thus, Lovecraft wrote "Rhode Iſland." This specific example of his archaic and quirky handwriting can be found in both archival and printed sources of this letter.
55. Lovecraft to Clark, March 27, 1926, *Letters to Family*, 2:576.
56. Lovecraft to Clark, March 27, 1926, *Letters to Family*, 2:576.
57. Lovecraft to Clark, March 27, 1926, *Letters to Family*, 2:577.
58. Lovecraft to Clark, March 29, 1926, *Letters to Family*, 2:583.
59. Winfield Townley Scott, "His Own Most Fantastic Creation: Howard Phillips Lovecraft," in Cannon, *Lovecraft Remembered*, 18.
60. Frank Belknap Long, *Howard Phillips Lovecraft: Dreamer of the Nightside* (Sauk City, Wisc.: Arkham House, 1975), 167.
61. Scott, "His Own Most Fantastic Creation," 18; Arthur S. Koki, "H. P. Lovecraft: An Introduction to His Life and Writings" (master's thesis, Columbia University, 1962),

159; Long, *Howard Phillips Lovecraft*, 167; Joshi, *I Am Providence*, 2:623. In his account shared with *Providence Journal* literary editor Winfield Townley Scott, Frank Belknap Long noted that he first contacted Lillian Clark about Lovecraft. Long later echoed this statement in an interview with researcher Arthur Koki. In his memoir published decades later, Long stated that his mother wrote to Clark. Long's mother and Clark had befriended one another during Clark's stay in New York during the winter of 1924–25.

62. Lovecraft to Clark, March 29, 1926, *Letters to Family*, 2:583.

63. Lovecraft to Clark, March 29, 1926, *Letters to Family*, 2:583.

64. *The Providence House Directory and Family Address Book: 1927–1928* [. . .] (Providence: Sampson & Murdock, 1927), 197, https://t93c12bb2a2098924.starter1ua .preservica.com/uncategorized/IO_cb7ac4a6-5ed8-4f24-bfaa-2ae35f38ae37/; Lovecraft to Frank Belknap Long, May 1, 1925, Lovecraft Collection, https://repository.library.brown .edu/studio/item/bdr:931814/. Lovecraft included a detailed description and sketch of the room in a letter to Frank Belknap Long.

65. Lovecraft to Clark, April 1, 1926, *Letters to Family*, 2:584–85.

66. Lovecraft to Clark, April 1, 1926, *Letters to Family*, 2:585

67. Lovecraft to Clark, April 1, 1926, *Letters to Family*, 2:585. Lillian Clark would later secure a room or an apartment for herself in the same building.

68. Lovecraft to Clark, April 1, 1926, Lovecraft Collection, https://repository.library .brown.edu/studio/item/bdr:423749/.

69. Lovecraft to Clark, April 1, 1926, *Letters to Family*, 2:585

70. Joshi, *I Am Providence*, 2:625; Sonia H. Davis, *The Private Life of H. P. Lovecraft*, ed. S. T. Joshi (West Warwick, R.I.: Necronomicon Press, 1985), 15. Greene's remembrance of the events leading to Lovecraft's return to Providence stand in contradiction to Lovecraft's letters written contemporaneously to his move. He made no mention of Greene first suggesting that he return to Providence with the plan for her eventually to follow him. However, the couple might have held such a discussion before the events of March–April 1926. Likewise, Greene could simply be misremembering the dates and the chain of the conversation, or Lovecraft might have misrepresented them to his aunts.

71. Lovecraft to Clark, April 6, 1926, *Letters to Family*, 2:586.

72. Lovecraft to Clark, April 12–13, 1926, *Letters to Family*, 2:595.

73. Lovecraft to Clark, April 12–13, 1926, *Letters to Family*, 2:595.

74. Lovecraft to Clark, April 12–13, 1926, *Letters to Family*, 2:595.

75. Lovecraft to Clark, April 12–13, 1926, *Letters to Family*, 2:595–96.

76. Lovecraft to Clark, April 12–13, 1926, *Letters to Family*, 2:596.

77. Lovecraft to Clark and Annie E. P. Gamwell, April 15, [1926], *Letters to Family*, 2:599.

78. D. Reynolds, "Farragut Theatre," *Cinema Treasures*, accessed December 27, 2022, http://cinematreasures.org/theaters/6266. The Farragut Theatre was at 1401 Flatbush Avenue; it operated between 1919 and 1959. Today, the Flatbush YMCA sits at this address. Architectural details of the former Farragut Theatre can still be seen on the building's second-story exterior.

79. Lovecraft to Clark and Gamwell, April 15, [1926], *Letters to Family*, 2:600; Kirk to Dvorak, April 19, 1926, Hart and Joshi, *Lovecraft's New York Circle*, 86.

80. Lovecraft to Clark and Gamwell, April 15, [1926], *Letters to Family*, 2:600.

81. Poe to Maria Clemm, April 7, [1844], in *The Letters of Edgar Allan Poe*, ed. John

Ward Ostrom (Cambridge, Mass.: Harvard University Press, 1948), 1:251; Arthur Hobson
Quinn, *Edgar Allan Poe: A Critical Biography*, new foreword by Shawn Rosenheim
(Baltimore: Johns Hopkins University Press, 1998), 408; Jaya Saxena, "Eating History: The
Haunting of the Planters Hotel," *First We Feast*, October 21, 2014, https://firstwefeast.com
/eat/2014/10/eating-history-the-haunting-of-the-planters-hotel; A. Everett Peterson, ed.,
Landmarks of New York: An Historical Guide to the Metropolis (New York: City History
Club of New York, 1923), 44; Federal Writers' Project, *The WPA Guide to New York
City: The Federal Writers' Project Guide to 1930s New York*, intro. by William H. Whyte
(New York: New Press, 1992), 77; Jell-O advertisement, *American Food Journal* 28, no. 11
(November 1923): 529. In a letter describing his arrival to New York, Poe mentioned
securing a room at a boarding house named Morrison on Greenwich Street. Since Planters
Hotel opened as early as 1833, Poe clearly stayed at a different establishment. Given the
expense associated with Planters, it seems unlikely that he could have even afforded its
rooms. However, Poe's association with the former hotel appears to have entered popular
lore by 1923. The proper name of the Planters Hotel and even its punctuation varied
across sources during its two respective lives.

 82. Lovecraft to Clark and Gamwell, April 15, [1926], *Letters to Family*, 2:600.

 83. Lovecraft to Clark and Gamwell, April 15, [1926], *Letters to Family*, 2:600.

 84. Lovecraft to Clark, [April 9, 1926], *Letters to Family*, 2:592; Lovecraft to Lillian
Clark, April 12–13, 1926, *Letters to Family*, 2:594; Lovecraft to Clark and Gamwell,
April 15, [1926], *Letters to Family*, 2:601.

 85. There remains some uncertainty whether Sonia Greene traveled with Lovecraft to
Providence on April 17, 1926, or whether she arrived on a later date. Lovecraft's letters
suggest that Greene, in fact, accompanied him. In his final letter to his aunts written in
New York, he discussed his travel plans and stated that Greene would arrive in Providence
with him. Recounting the journey in a later letter to Frank Belknap Long, he writes in
the first-person plural ("we") when describing the ride from Providence Union Station
to his new quarters at 10 Barnes Street. He continues to use the first-person plural in
detailing other activities, including a short trip to Boston that he certainly took with
Greene. However, L. Sprague de Camp writes in his biography of Lovecraft that Greene
was detained by a business meeting and traveled to Providence separately on a later date. I
suspect that he misread or misinterpreted a letter from April 15, 1926, in which Lovecraft
wrote that Greene had an "interview about a possible position in NY tomorrow." Lovecraft
was referring to April 16, 1926. He began this letter on April 15, 1926, and he finished it
on April 16, 1926. His meaning of "tomorrow" shifts during the course of the letter. That
is, "tomorrow" is "today" by the letter's conclusion. Immediately following Lovecraft's
move, Greene's address was listed as 10 Barnes Street in the *United Amateur* masthead.
Lovecraft to Clark and Gamwell, April 15, [1926], *Letters to Family*, 2:597, 598; H. P.
Lovecraft to Frank Belknap Long, May 1, 1926, in *Letters from New York*, ed. S. T. Joshi
and David E. Schultz (San Francisco: Night Shade Books, 2005), 311–12; L. Sprague de
Camp, *Lovecraft: A Biography* (Garden City, N.Y.: Doubleday, 1975), 259; Joshi, *I Am
Providence*, 2:634; Masthead, *United Amateur*, July 1926, 4.

 86. Lovecraft to Clark, April 12–13, 1926, *Letters to Family*, 2:594; *The Official Guide
of the Railways and Steam Navigation Lines of the United States, Puerto Rico, Canada,
Mexico and Cuba*, May 1926, microfilm, p. 75, April–May 1926. Two New York, New
Haven and Hartford Railroad departures would have met Lovecraft's desire: the 7:25 A.M.
(no. 8, Mayflower) and the 9:00 A.M. (no. 10, Bay State) trains.

 87. Lovecraft to Long, May 1, 1926, *Letters from New York*, 310.

Conclusion: "The Merest Vague Dream"

1. H. P. Lovecraft to Frank Belknap Long, May 1, 1926, in *Letters from New York*, ed. S. T. Joshi and David E. Schultz (San Francisco: Night Shade Books, 2005), 310.

2. Lovecraft to Long, May 1, 1926, *Letters from New York*, 310.

3. Lovecraft to Long, May 1, 1926, *Letters from New York*, 311.

4. Lovecraft to Long, May 1, 1926, *Letters from New York*, 311.

5. Lovecraft to Long, May 1, 1926, *Letters from New York*, 311.

6. Lovecraft to Long, May 1, 1926, *Letters from New York*, 311.

7. Lovecraft to Long, May 1, 1926, *Letters from New York*, 312.

8. Lovecraft to Long, May 1, 1926, *Letters from New York*, 315.

9. Lovecraft to Wilfred Blanch Talman, April 23, [1926], Howard P. Lovecraft Collection, Brown Digital Repository, Brown University Library, https://repository.library.brown.edu/studio/item/bdr:423757/; H. P. Lovecraft to Frank Belknap Long, April 23, 1926, in *Selected Letters*, ed. August Derleth and Donald Wandrei, vol. 2, *1925–1929* (Sauk City, Wisc.: Arkham House, 1968), 43, 44.

10. Lovecraft to Clark Ashton Smith, May 14, 1926, Lovecraft Collection, https://repository.library.brown.edu/studio/item/bdr:423762/.

11. Department of Commerce, *Statistical Abstract of the United States*, comp. Edward Whitney (Washington, D.C.: G. P. O., 1922), 56, 59, https://www2.census.gov/prod2/statcomp/documents/1921–02.pdf#[33,{%22name%22:%22FitH%22},621] .

12. H. P. Lovecraft to James Larkin Pearson, April 25, 1926, in *Letters to Rheinhart Kleiner and Others*, ed. S. T. Joshi and David E. Schultz (New York: Hippocampus Press, 2020), 323; David Brussat, *Lost Providence*, foreword by Andrés Duany (Charleston, S.C.: History Press, 2017), 25–26; Joseph A. Conforti, *Imagining New England: Explorations of Regional Identity from the Pilgrims to the Mid-Twentieth Century* (Chapel Hill: University of North Carolina Press, 2001), 7; John S. Gilkeson, *Middle-Class Providence: 1820–1940* (Princeton: Princeton University Press, 1986.), 7; Department of Commerce, *Statistical Abstract*, 39, 47, 54, https://www2.census.gov/prod2/statcomp/documents/1921-02.pdf#[33,{%22name%22:%22FitH%22},621]. In fact, Rhode Island was the most ethnically diverse state at the turn of the twentieth century. By 1920, nearly 70 percent of Rhode Island's population was comprised of immigrants or first-generation Americans, or 420,427 individuals within a total population of 604,397. Rhode Island became the first American state with a Catholic majority earlier in the twentieth century. Moreover, 97.5 percent of the state's population lived in an urban area.

13. Lovecraft to Long, May 1, 1926, *Letters from New York*, 314.

14. H. P. Lovecraft to James F. Morton, May 16, 1926, in *Letters to James F. Morton*, ed. David E. Schultz and S. T. Joshi (New York: Hippocampus Press, 2011), 93.

15. Lovecraft to Morton, May 16, 1926, *Letters to Morton*, 93; Lovecraft to Pearson, *Letters to Kleiner*, 323.

16. Lovecraft to Morton, May 16, 1926, *Letters to Morton*, 93.

17. H. P. Lovecraft to Lillian D. Clark, March 29, 1926, in *Letters to Family and Family Friends*, ed. S. T. Joshi and David E. Schultz, vol. 2, *1926–1936* (New York: Hippocampus Press, 2020), 583; Lovecraft to Morton, May 16, 1926, *Letters to Morton*, 93; L. Sprague de Camp, *Lovecraft: A Biography* (Garden City, N.Y.: Doubleday, 1975), 6.

18. S. T. Joshi, *I Am Providence: The Life and Times of H. P. Lovecraft* (New York: Hippocampus Press, 2013), 2:636.

19. Lovecraft to Clark Ashton Smith, October 15, 1927, *Selected Letters*, 2:176.

20. David E. Schultz, "From Microcosm to Macrocosm: The Growth of Lovecraft's Cosmic Fiction," in *An Epicure of the Terrible: A Centennial Anthology of Essays in Honor of H. P. Lovecraft*, ed. David E. Schultz and S. T. Joshi (Rutherford, N.J.: Fairleigh Dickinson University Press, 1991), 202–4; Joshi, *I Am Providence*, 2:636.

21. The term or classification of "great texts" refers to the stories and novellas collectively comprising Lovecraft's Cthulhu Mythos. French author Michel Houellebecq described these stories as Lovecraft's "great texts"; Houellebecq, *H. P. Lovecraft: Against the World, Against Life*, intro. by Stephen King, trans. Dorna Khazeni (New York: Cernunnos, 2019), 51.

22. W. Paul Cook, "In Memoriam: Howard Phillips Lovecraft; Recollections, Appreciations, Estimates," in *Lovecraft Remembered*, ed. Peter Cannon (Sauk City, Wisc.: Arkham House, 1998), 115.

23. Cook, "In Memoriam," 115.

24. Cook, "In Memoriam," 116.

25. Cook, "In Memoriam," 116.

26. Tyler L. Wolanin, "New Deal Politics in the Correspondence of H. P. Lovecraft," *Lovecraft Annual*, no. 7 (2013): 3–35. Wolanin's article surveys and comments upon references to the New Deal in Lovecraft's letters.

27. Schultz, "From Microcosm to Macrocosm," 202.

28. Lovecraft to Morton, June 12, 1933, *Letters to Morton*, 324.

29. Lovecraft to J. Vernon Shea, September 25, 1933, *Selected Letters*, 4:250.

30. Lovecraft to Natalie H. Wooley, November 22, 1934, *Selected Letters*, 5:78.

31. Lovecraft to F. Lee Baldwin, February 13, 1934, *Selected Letters*, 4:384; Lovecraft to Morton, [December 29, 1930], *Letters to Morton*, 251–52.

32. Teresa A. Carbone, "Body Language: Liberation and Restraint in Twenties Figuration," in *Youth and Beauty: Art of the American Twenties*, ed. Teresa A. Carbone (New York: Skira Rizzoli; Brooklyn: Brooklyn Museum, 2011), 87, 90; Thomas F. Gossett, *Race: The History of an Idea*, new ed. (New York: Oxford University Press, 1997), 418–26, 429–30; Lovecraft to Clark, September 29–30, 1924, *Letters to Family*, 1:163–64; W. Scott Poole, *In the Mountains of Madness: The Life and Extraordinary Afterlife of H. P. Lovecraft* (Berkeley, Calif.: Soft Skull Press, 2016), 65; Paul Roland, *The Curious Case of H. P. Lovecraft* (London: Plexus, 2014), 37; Margaret E. Wright-Cleveland, "Mentoring American Racial Identity: Sherwood Anderson's Lessons to Ernest Hemingway," *MidAmerica: The Yearbook of the Society for the Study of Midwestern Literature* 38 (2011): 28–40.

33. Sonia H. Davis, *The Private Life of H. P. Lovecraft*, ed. S. T. Joshi (West Warwick, R.I.: Necronomicon Press, 1985), 15.

34. Davis, *Private Life*, 15; Joshi, *I Am Providence*, 2:625. Joshi details the difficulties in ascertaining the exact date or approximate time of Sonia Greene's proposal of moving to Providence.

35. Davis, *Private Life*, 15.

36. Sonia H. Davis, Autobiographical Writings, undated, box 9, folder 1, Sonia H. and Nathaniel A. Davis Papers, John Hay Library, Brown University.

37. "Shopping with Susan," *Brooklyn Daily Eagle*, May 6, 1928, Brooklyn Newsstand, Brooklyn Public Library; *Brooklyn, Queens, Staten Island; New York City Telephone Directory*, Summer 1928, 421 (loc. 210 of 618), https://archive.org/details /brooklynqueensst1928newy/page/n209/mode/2up. Professionally, Sonia Greene resumed

using her previous last name (i.e., Greene) by 1928, possibly never having ceased doing so. Legally, she had taken Lovecraft's surname upon their marriage in 1924.

38. Davis, *Private Life*, 16.

39. Wilfred Blanch Talman [and H. P. Lovecraft], "Two Black Bottles," *Weird Tales*, August 1927; H. P. Lovecraft, "Some Dutch Footprints in New England," in *Collected Essays*, ed. S. T. Joshi, vol. 4, *Travel* (New York: Hippocampus Press, 2005), 253–55; Wilfred B. Talman, *The Normal Lovecraft* (Saddle River, N.J.: Gerry de la Ree, 1973); S. T. Joshi and David E. Schultz, "Talman, Wilfred Blanch," in *An H. P. Lovecraft Encyclopedia* (Westport, Conn.: Greenwood Press, 2001), 260–61. Wilfred Blanch Talman (1904–86) first began corresponding with Lovecraft while an undergraduate at Brown University. He solicited Lovecraft's editorial advice on a short story, "Two Black Bottles," in the summer of 1926. Lovecraft heavily revised the piece, and *Weird Tales* published it in 1927. In the early 1930s, Talman served as the editor of *De Halve Maen*, the journal of the Holland Society of New York, and solicited a piece from Lovecraft, "Some Dutch Footprints in New England." After Lovecraft's death, Talman wrote a memoir on the author, *The Normal Lovecraft*.

40. Lovecraft to Clark, April 29–30, 1928, *Letters to Family*, 2:637.

41. Lovecraft to Clark, April 29–30, 1928, *Letters to Family*, 2:628; Lovecraft to Clark, May 7, 1928, *Letters to Family*, 2:647.

42. Lovecraft to Clark, May 14, 1928, *Letters to Family*, 2:657.

43. Lovecraft to Clark, May 14, 1928, *Letters to Family*, 2:657; Legal Notice, *Herald Statesman* (Yonkers), February 14, 1934, Newspapers.com; "United States, New York Land Records, 1630–1975," digital image s.v. "Sonia Davis," Familysearch.org. Greene retained the one Yonkers property at least until 1937, when a property transfer was filed.

44. Lovecraft to Clark, July 5, 1928, *Letters to Family*, 2:708; Joshi, *I Am Providence*, 2:714.

45. J. Herbie DiFonzo and Ruth C. Stern, "Addicted to Fault: Why Divorce Reform Has Lagged in New York," *Pace Law Review* 27, no. 4 (Summer 2007): 559.

46. Sonia H. Davis to August Derleth, April 7, 1966, August William Derleth Papers, Wisconsin Historical Society; DiFonzo and Stern, "Addicted to Fault," 572. An estimated one-third of divorces involving New York residents were obtained in other states by 1922.

47. *Lovecraft v. Lovecraft*, No. 23118 (R. I. Super. Ct. Mar. 25, 1929). The author obtained all the pertinent records from the Rhode Island Supreme Court Judicial Records Center.

48. *Lovecraft v. Lovecraft*, No. 23118 (R. I. Super. Ct. Mar. 25, 1929). The initial divorce proceedings were scheduled to be held on the "First Monday of March 1929." This would have been March 4, 1929.

49. Muriel Eddy, "The Gentleman from Angell Street," in Cannon, *Lovecraft Remembered*, 61.

50. Andrew Smith, Rhode Island Supreme Court Judicial Records Center, email to author, January 21, 26, 27, 2022.

51. In his correspondence with Alfred Galpin in the early 1970s, Samuel Loveman discussed the rumor of Lovecraft and Greene's incomplete divorce; allegedly the former never signed or filed the final decree. Loveman emphatically stated that "Howard would not have permitted it and Sonia was a puritan." Considering that Loveman had disavowed his former friend because of Lovecraft's anti-Semitism, his support for Lovecraft on the matter of the legality of his divorce carried further weight; Samuel Loveman to Alfred

Galpin, April 1, 1971, Alfred Maurice Galpin Papers, Rare Book and Manuscript Library, Columbia University Library.

52. Lovecraft to August Derleth, January 16, 1931, *Selected Letters*, 3:262.

53. Davis, *Private Life*, 17–18; Lovecraft to J. Vernon Shea, March 24, 1933, *Selected Letters*, 4:159. This institution is now the Wadsworth Atheneum Museum of Art.

54. H. P. Lovecraft to Maurice W. Moe, [July 2], 1929, in *Letters to Maurice W. Moe and Others*, ed. David E. Schultz and S. T. Joshi (New York: Hippocampus Press, 2018), 206.

55. 1930 United States Census, Providence, Providence County, Rhode Island, digital image s.v. "Howard Lovecraft," Ancestry.com; 1935 Rhode Island State Census, Providence, Providence County, Rhode Island, digital image s.v. "Howard Lovecraft," Ancestry.com.

56. Davis to Derleth, May 29, 1966, Derleth Papers; Davis to Derleth, November 29, 1966, Derleth Papers.

57. Davis, *Private Life*, 9.

58. Sonia H. Davis, Autobiographical Writings, August 19, 1964, box 9, folder 1, Davis Papers; Davis, Autobiographical Writings: "When I held the very lucrative buyer and managership in N.Y.C . . . ," undated, box 9, folder 8, Davis Papers; "California, Los Angeles Passenger Lists, 1907–1948," digital image s.v. "Sonia Greene," Familysearch .org. Some sources cite Greene as having traveled to California in late December 1933. She dates this event as January 1934 in her unpublished autobiographical writings. A ship manifest from January 6, 1934, corroborates this fact.

59. Davis to August Derleth, October 6, 1965, Derleth Papers; Davis to Derleth, November 29, 1966, Derleth Papers; Davis, *Private Life*, 19; Bobby Derie, "Her Letters to H. P. Lovecraft: Sonia H. Greene," *Deep Cuts in a Lovecraftian Vein*, September 21, 2021, https://deepcuts.blog/2021/09/25/her-letters-to-lovecraft-sonia-h-greene/; Loveman to Galpin, April 1, 1971, Galpin Papers, Columbia University Library. In her published memoir, Greene claimed to have burned all of Lovecraft's letters before departing for California as a dramatic farewell to that chapter of her life. Author and scholar Bobby Derie speculated that Greene, however, destroyed the letters only after being threatened with legal action in 1947 and 1948 by Arkham House publisher August Derleth if she attempted to quote Lovecraft's letters in her memoirs. Erroneously or disingenuously, Derleth claimed to hold the copyright to all of Lovecraft's writings. The fact that Greene spontaneously decided to remain in California on a vacation in 1934 strengthens Derie's theory.

60. Arthur S. Koki, "H. P. Lovecraft: An Introduction to His Life and Writings" (master's thesis, Columbia University, 1962), 209–11; Davis to Derleth, March 2, 1961, Derleth Papers; Davis to Derleth, March 12, 1961, Derleth Papers; Christine D. Hathaway to Davis, August 29, 1968, Davis Papers; Derleth to Davis, October 7, 1968, Derleth Papers; L. Sprague de Camp to Alfred Galpin, November 28, 1972, Alfred Galpin Papers, John Hay Library, Brown University. It remains unclear exactly when Sonia Greene learned about the ambiguous status of both her divorce from H. P. Lovecraft and her marriage to Nathaniel Davis. Arthur Koki reviewed all the publicly available court and legal documents concerning Lovecraft and Greene's divorce during his research into the author and immediately reached the assumption that Lovecraft never had signed the final decree. Koki did not provide the legal context for this conclusion. Koki contacted Greene for his research in 1961, but she seemed to rebuff his attempts to gather information

from her. Koki might have told her what he had uncovered and what he suspected. R. Alain Everts (a.k.a. Randal Kirsch) obtained the court documents in 1968. Greene might have first heard these details from him. In his correspondence with Alfred Galpin in the early 1970s, Samuel Loveman noted that Everts/Kirsch was peddling this story and that he, Loveman, disbelieved it. Greene discussed the legal status of her divorce from Lovecraft in her correspondence with Arkham House publisher August Derleth and with Christine D. Hathaway, the special collections librarian at Brown University's John Hay Library, in 1968. Greene was certainly in possession of all the available facts by that time.

61. Lovecraft to Clark, April 12, 1929, *Letters to Family*, 2:750.

62. Lovecraft to Morton, [March 12, 1930], *Letters to Morton*, 223.

63. Lovecraft to Morton, [March 12, 1930], *Letters to Morton*, 224.

64. Lovecraft to Robert E. Howard, March 25–28–29, 1933, *Selected Letters*, 4:169.

65. Lovecraft to Howard, March 25–28–29, 1933, *Selected Letters*, 4:169.

66. H. P. Lovecraft, "[Diary—1937]," in *Collected Essays*, 5:241–42.

67. Lovecraft to Wilson Shepherd, February 17, 1937, Lovecraft Collection, https://repository.library.brown.edu/studio/item/bdr:425172/.

68. Lovecraft, "[Diary—1937]," in *Collected Essays*, 5:242; Joshi, *I Am Providence*, 2:1,006–8.

69. Harry K. Brobst to Robert H. Barlow, March 13, 1937, Lovecraft Collection, https://repository.library.brown.edu/studio/item/bdr:417379/; Joseph E. Garland, *To Meet the Wants: The Story of Rhode Island Hospital, 1863–1988*, 2nd ed. (Providence: Rhode Island Hospital, 1988), 68. The Jane Brown Memorial Hospital opened as the Jane Frances Brown Building for Private Patients, Rhode Island Hospital, in 1922.

70. Will Murray, "Autumn in Providence: Harry K. Brobst on Lovecraft," in Cannon, *Lovecraft Remembered*, 394.

71. Murray, "Autumn in Providence," in Cannon, *Lovecraft Remembered*, 394.

72. Lovecraft, "[Diary—1937]," in *Collected Essays*, 5:241–42; de Camp, *Lovecraft*, 427–28; "H. P. Lovecraft, Author, is Dead," *Providence Journal*, March 16, 1937; "Writer Charts Fatal Malady," *New York Times*, March 16, 1937; Death Notice: Lovecraft, *Providence Journal*, March 18, 1937.

73. Lovecraft to Morton, [December 1936?–February? 1937], *Letters to Morton*, 403, 404.

BIBLIOGRAPHY

Notes on sources: Through my research and writing, I relied heavily on the physical and digital archival collections of H. P. Lovecraft's writings and letters at the John Hay Library, Brown University, and at other institutions. To allow readers and researchers to easily access referenced material and to spare them the task of deciphering Lovecraft's handwriting, I cited published collections of his letters and other works when simultaneously available and not detrimental to an appreciation of their content.

Original Sources

ARCHIVES

Sonia H. and Nathaniel A. Davis Papers, John Hay Library, Brown University.

August William Derleth Papers, Wisconsin Historical Society.

Alfred Galpin Papers, John Hay Library, Brown University.

Alfred Maurice Galpin Papers, Rare Book and Manuscript Library, Columbia University Library.

Howard P. Lovecraft Collection, John Hay Library, Brown University, https://repository.library.brown.edu/studio/collections/bdr:jyhg75bu/.

H. P. Lovecraft, Letters to Richard Ely Morse, 1932–37, Manuscripts and Archives Division, New York Public Library.

H. P. Lovecraft, "The Horror at Red Hook," manuscript, 1925, Manuscripts and Archives Division, New York Public Library.

Sarah Susan Phillips Lovecraft, "Commonplace Book," 1889, John Hay Library, Brown University.

Carol Weld Papers, American Heritage Center, University of Wyoming.

NEWSPAPERS

Boston *Globe*
Boston *Post*
Brooklyn *Citizen*
Brooklyn *Daily Eagle*
Brooklyn *Daily Times*
Chat (Brooklyn)
Chicago *Tribune*
Chronicle *of Higher Education*
Cincinnati *Enquirer*
Cleveland *Plain Dealer*
Evening *Bulletin* (Providence)
Grape *Belt and Chautauqua Farmer*
Guardian (Manchester)
Herald *Statesman* (Yonkers)
Island *Current* (Bronx)
New *York Evening Post*
New *York Herald, New York Tribune*
New *York Post*
New *York Times*
Newport *Daily News*
Perth *Amboy Evening News*
Philadelphia *Inquirer*
Providence *Journal*
Yonkers *Statesman*

PERIODICALS

American *Art News*
Arkham *Sampler*
Atlantic
Brooklyn *Magazine*, first series
Brooklynite
Crisis
Cry *of the Cricket*
Editor *& Publisher*
Etchings *and Odysseys*
Haunted
Home *Brew*
Illustrated *Milliner*
Life
National *Tribune*
New *Republic*
New *Yorker*
Nyctalops
Rainbow
Recluse

Scientific *American*
Smithsonian *Magazine*
Tales *of Magic and Mystery*
United *Amateur*
Variety
Weird *N.J.*
Weird *Tales*
Wired
Writer's *Digest*
Zenith

Secondary Sources

Abernethy, Lloyd M. "Progressivism, 1905–1919." In Weigley, Wainwright, and Wolf, *Philadelphia*, 524–65.

Achebe, Chinua. "An Image of Africa: Racism in Conrad's 'Heart of Darkness.'" *Massachusetts Review* 57, no. 1 (Spring 2016): 14–27.

Adams, Bluford. *Old & New New Englanders: Immigration & Regional Identity in the Gilded Age*. Ann Arbor: University of Michigan Press, 2014.

Adams, Rachel. *Sideshow U. S. A.: Freaks and the American Cultural Imagination*. Chicago: University of Chicago Press, 2001.

Allen, Frederick Lewis. *Only Yesterday: An Informal History of the Nineteen-Twenties*. New York: Harper & Bros., 1931.

Armbruster, Eugene L. *Coney Island*. New York: Armbruster, 1924.

Asbury, Herbert, ed. *Not at Night!* New York: Macy-Masius, 1928.

Axelrod, Alan, ed. *The Colonial Revival in America*. New York: Norton, 1985.

Azar, Louis, II. *Downtown Providence*. Charlestown, S.C.: Arcadia, 2022.

Backscheider, Paula R. *Reflections on Biography*. Oxford: Oxford University Press, 1999.

Barr, Lockwood. *The Hunter-Desbrosses and Allied Families of New York City and Hunter's Island—Now Part of Pelham Bay Park of the City of New York: A Supplement to a Brief History of the Ancient Town of Pelham, Westchester County, New York*. Pelham Manor, N.Y.: n.p., 1945.

Barrett, Walter. *The Old Merchants of New York City*. 2nd ser. New York: Carleton, 1863.

Baudelaire, Charles. "The Painter of Modern Life." In *The Painter of Modern Life and Other Essays*, translated and edited by Jonathan Mayne, 1–40. New York: De Capo Press, 1986.

Beckwith, Henry L. P. *Lovecraft's Providence & Adjacent Parts*. West Kingston, R.I.: D. M. Grant, 1979.

Beherec, Marc. "The Church That Inspired 'The Horror at Red Hook' and the 'Fall of the House of Suydam.'" *Lovecraft Annual*, no. 15 (2021): 128–66.

Benjamin, Walter. *The Work of Art in the Age of Its Technological Reproducibility, and Other Writings on Media*. Edited by Michael W. Jennings, Brigid Doherty, and Thomas Y. Levin. Translated by Edmund Jephcott et al. Cambridge, Mass.: Belknap Press, 2008.

Berg, Scott W. *Grand Avenues: The Story of the French Visionary Who Designed Washington, D.C.* New York: Pantheon, 2007.

Berman, John S. *Coney Island*. New York: Barnes & Noble, 2003.

Blake, Angela M. "New York Is Not America: Immigrants and Tourists in New York After World War I, 1890–1924." In *How New York Became American*, 111–38. Baltimore: Johns Hopkins University Press, 2006.

Bolton, Reginald Pelham. "The Poe Cottage at Fordham." *Transactions of the Bronx Society of Arts, Sciences and History* 1, pt. 5 (1922): 1–14.

Bonner, Marian F. "Miscellaneous Impressions of H. P. L." In Cannon, *Lovecraft Remembered*, 28–29.

Botton, Sari, ed. *Goodbye to All That: Writers on Loving and Leaving New York*. Berkeley, Calif.: Seal Press, 2013.

Bowne House Historical Society. *The Bowne House: A National Shrine to Religious Freedom*. Flushing, N.Y.: Bowne House Historical Society, 1953.

Boyer, Paul S. *Urban Masses and Moral Order in America, 1820–1920*. Cambridge, Mass.: Harvard University Press, 1978.

Bromwich, David. "The Uses of Biography." *Yale Review* 73 (Winter 1984): 161–75.

Brooklyn Historical Society. *Red Hook, Gowanus Neighborhood History Guide*. Brooklyn: Brooklyn Historical Society, 2000.

Brown, Susan Jenkins. *Robber Rocks: Letters and Memories of Hart Crane, 1923–1932*. Middletown, Conn.: Wesleyan University Press, 1969.

Brussat, David. *Lost Providence*. Foreword by Andrés Duany. Charleston, S.C.: History Press, 2017.

Buchan, Perdita. *Utopia, New Jersey: Travels in the Nearest Eden*. New Brunswick, N.J.: Rivergate Books, 2007.

Buhle, Paul. "Dystopia as Utopia: Howard Phillips Lovecraft and the Unknown Content of American Horror Literature." *Minnesota Review*, no. 6 (Spring 1976): 118–31.

Burleson, Donald R. *Lovecraft: Disturbing the Universe*. Lexington: University Press of Kentucky, 1990.

Burt, Nathaniel, and Wallace E. Davies. "The Iron Age, 1876–1905." In Weigley, Wainwright, and Wolf, *Philadelphia*, 471–523.

Butler Hospital. *The Butler Hospital: Its Story; An Endowed Public Institution for the Treatment of Mental Illness*. Providence: Butler Hospital, 1926.

Campanella, Thomas J. *Brooklyn: The Once and Future City*. Princeton: Princeton University Press, 2019.

Cannon, Peter, ed. *Lovecraft Remembered*. Sauk City, Wisc.: Arkham House, 1998.

Carbone, Teresa A. "Body Language: Liberation and Restraint in Twenties Figuration." In *Youth and Beauty: Art of the American Twenties*, edited by Teresa A. Carbone, 15–111. New York: Skira Rizzoli; Brooklyn: Brooklyn Museum, 2011.

Carle, Sarah. "Cholecystitis and Cholangitis." In *Infectious Diseases Emergencies*, edited by Arjun S. Chanmugam et al., 181–86. New York: Oxford University Press, 2016. Oxford Academic.

Carter, Lin. *Lovecraft: A Look Behind the "Cthulhu Mythos."* St. Albans, UK: Panther Books, 1975.

Chauncey, George. *Gay New York: Gender, Urban Culture, and the Making of the Gay Male World, 1890–1940*. New York: Basic Books, 1994.

Clair, Jean. "Red October, Black October." In *The 1920s: Age of the Metropolis*, edited by Jean Clair, 17–42. Montreal: Montreal Museum of Art, 1991.

Cochran, Edwin A. *The Cathedral of Commerce: The Highest Building in the World*. New York: Broadway Park Place, 1916.

Coffman, Jerry L., Carl A. von Hake, and Carl W. Stover, eds. *Earthquake History of the United States*. Boulder, Colo.: U. S. Department of Commerce, National Oceanic and Atmospheric Administration; U. S. Department of the Interior, Geological Survey, 1982. https://pubs.usgs.gov/unnumbered/70114182/report.pdf.

Colonial *Architecture in New York City: Photographs*. Salem, Mass.: F. Cousins Art, 1913.

Conforti, Joseph A. *Imagining New England: Explorations of Regional Identity from the Pilgrims to the Mid-Twentieth Century*. Chapel Hill: University of North Carolina Press, 2001.

Cook, W. Paul. "In Memoriam: Howard Phillips Lovecraft; Recollections, Appreciations, Estimates." In Cannon, *Lovecraft Remembered*, 106–56.

———. "Jim Morton." In *Letters to James F. Morton*, by H. P. Lovecraft, edited by S. T. Joshi and David E. Schultz, 450–53. New York: Hippocampus Press, 2020.

Cowley, Malcolm. *Exile's Return: A Literary Odyssey of the 1920s*. New York: Viking, 1951.

Crane, Hart. *Letters of Hart Crane and His Family*. Edited by Thomas S. W. Lewis. New York: Columbia University Press, 1974.

Dana, Mary V. "A Glimpse of H. P. L." In Cannon, *Lovecraft Remembered*, 30–31.

Davenport-Hines, Richard. *Gothic: Four Hundred Years of Excess, Horror, Evil and Ruin*. New York: North Point Press, 1998.

Davis, Sonia H. "Lovecraft as I Knew Him." In Cannon, *Lovecraft Remembered*, 252–63.

———. "Memories of Lovecraft: I." In Cannon, *Lovecraft Remembered*, 275–76.

———. *The Private Life of H. P. Lovecraft*. Edited by S. T. Joshi. West Warwick, R.I.: Necronomicon Press, 1985.

Dean, Bashford, and Alexander McMillan Welch. *Dyckman House: Built Around 1783, Restored and Presented to the City of New York in MCMXVI*. 2nd ed. New York: Gillis Press, 1917.

de Camp, L. Sprague. *Lovecraft: A Biography*. Garden City, N.Y.: Doubleday, 1975.

de Certeau, Michel. *The Practice of Everyday Life*. Translated by Steven F. Rendall. Berkeley: University of California Press, 1984.

Department of Commerce. *Statistical Abstract of the United States: 1921*. Compiled by Edward Whitney. Washington, D.C.: G. P. O., 1922. https://www2.census.gov/prod2/statcomp/documents/1921-01.pdf.

Derie, Bobby. *Sex and the Cthulhu Mythos*. New York: Hippocampus Press, 2014.

Derleth, August. *H. P. L.: A Memoir*. New York: B. Abramson, 1945.

———. "Lovecraft's Sensitivity." In Cannon, *Lovecraft Remembered*, 32–37.

Derleth, August, and Donald Wandrei. "Preface." In *Selected Letters*, edited by August Derleth, and Donald Wandrei, 1:xxi–xxix. Sauk City, Wisc.: Arkham House, 1965.

Didion, Joan. "Goodbye to All That." In *Slouching Towards Bethlehem: Essays*, 331–51. New York: Picador Modern Classics, 2017.

DiFonzo, J. Herbie, and Ruth C. Stern. "Addicted to Fault: Why Divorce Law Has Lagged in New York." *Pace Law Review* 27, no. 4 (Summer 2007): 559–603.

Douglas, Ann. *Terrible Honesty: Mongrel Manhattan in the 1920s*. New York: Farrar, Straus and Giroux, 1995.

Drewer, Cecelia. "New York, Culture Shock, and a Glimpse of the Future in 'He.'" *Lovecraft Annual*, no. 11 (2017): 41–50.

Drowne, Kathleen, and Patrick Huber. *The 1920s*. Westport, Conn.: Greenwood Press, 2004.

Dudden, Arthur P. "The City Embraces 'Normalcy,' 1919–1929." In Weigley, Wainwright, and Wolf, *Philadelphia*, 566–600.

Dumenil, Lynn. *The Modern Temper: American Culture and Society in the 1920s*. New York: Hill and Wang, 1995.

Eberlein, Harold Donaldson. *The Architecture of Colonial America*. Illustrated from photographs by Mary H. Northend et al. Boston: Little Brown, 1915. Reprint, New York: Johnson Reprint, 1968.

Eddy, Muriel E. "The Gentleman from Angell Street." In Cannon, *Lovecraft Remembered*, 49–64.

———. *The Howard Phillips Lovecraft We Knew*. Providence: n.p., 1972.

Eddy, Muriel E., and C. M. Eddy, Jr. *The Gentleman from Angell Street: Memories of H. P. Lovecraft*. Edited by Jim Dyer. Narragansett, R.I.: Fenham, 2001.

Elizabeth Daily Journal. *The City of Elizabeth, New Jersey, Illustrated: Showing Its Leading Characteristics* [. . .]. Elizabeth, N.J.: Elizabeth Daily Journal, 1889.

Elkin, Lauren. *Flâneuse: Women Walk the City in Paris, New York, Tokyo, Venice, and London*. New York: Farrar, Straus and Giroux, 2018.

Ellis, Phillip A. "The Construction of Race in the Early Poetry of H. P. Lovecraft." *Lovecraft Annual*, no. 4 (2010): 124–35.

English, T. J. *The Westies: Inside New York's Irish Mob*. New York: St. Martin's Griffin, 2006.

Esenwein, J. Berg, and Arthur Leeds. *Writing the Photoplay*. Springfield, Mass.: Home Correspondence School, 1913.

Evans, Timothy H. "A Last Defense Against the Dark: Folklore, Horror, and the Uses of Tradition in the Works of H. P. Lovecraft." *Journal of Folklore Research* 42, no. 1 (January–April 2005): 99–135.

Everett, Justin, and Jeffrey H. Shanks, eds. *The Unique Legacy of Weird Tales: The Evolution of Modern Fantasy and Horror*. Lanham, Md.: Rowman & Littlefield, 2015.

Faig, Kenneth W., Jr. "Can You Direct Me to Ely Court? Some Notes on 66 College Street." *Lovecraft Annual*, no. 9 (2015): 54–69.

———. "Lovecraft's 1937 Diary." *Lovecraft Annual*, no. 6 (2012): 153–78.

———. "Lovecraft's Parental Heritage." *Books at Brown* 38–39 (1991–92): 43–66.

———. "The Parents of Howard Phillips Lovecraft." In *An Epicure in the Terrible: A Centennial Anthology of Essays in Honor of H. P. Lovecraft*, edited by David E. Schultz and S. T. Joshi, 45–77. Rutherford, N.J.: Farleigh Dickinson University Press, 1991.

———. "Whipple V. Phillips and the Owyhee Land and Irrigation Co." *Owhyee Outpost*, no. 19 (May 1988): 21–30.

Federal Writers' Project. *The WPA Guide to New York City: The Federal Writers' Project Guide to 1930s New York*. Introduction by William H. Whyte. New York: New Press, 1992.

Fenske, Gail. *The Skyscraper and the City: The Woolworth Building and the Making of Modern New York*. Chicago: University of Chicago Press, 2008.

Fisher, Clive. *Hart Crane: A Life*. New Haven: Yale University Press, 2002.

Fisher, Mark. *The Weird and the Eerie*. London: Repeater Books, 2016.

Fitzgerald, F. Scott. *The Great Gatsby*. Notes and preface by Matthew J. Bruccoli. New York: Scribner, 2003.

Flatness, James. "Mapping the World: Library Receives Hammond Archives." *Library of Congress Information Bulletin* 62, no. 5 (May 2003). https://loc.gov/loc/lcib/0305 /hammond.html.

Folpe, Emily Kies. *It Happened on Washington Square*. Baltimore: Johns Hopkins University Press, 2002.

France, Peter, and William St. Clair, ed. *Mapping Lives: The Uses of Biography*. Oxford: Oxford University Press, 2002.

Freind, Bill. "'Why Do You Want to Put Your Ideas in Order?': Re-Thinking the Politics of Ezra Pound." *Journal of Modern Literature* 23, no. 3–4 (Summer 2000): 545–63.

Gagarin, Michael, ed. *The Oxford Encyclopedia of Ancient Greece and Rome*. New York: Oxford University Press, 2010. Oxford Reference.

Gale, Dennis E. *The Misunderstood History of Gentrification: People, Planning, Preservation, and Urban Renewal, 1915–2020*. Philadelphia: Temple University Press, 2021.

Galpin, Alfred. "Memories of a Friendship." In Cannon, *Lovecraft Remembered*, 164–72.

Garis, Roy L. *Immigration Restriction: A Study of the Opposition to and Regulation of Immigration into the United States*. New York: Macmillan, 1927.

Garland, Joseph E. *To Meet the Wants: The Story of Rhode Island Hospital, 1863–1988*. 2nd ed. Providence: Rhode Island Hospital, 1988.

Gay, Peter. *Modernism: The Lure of Heresy; From Baudelaire to Beckett and Beyond*. New York: W. W. Norton, 2008.

Geer, William Montague, comp. *Old St. Paul's Chapel, Trinity Parish, New York: Short History Published for the Celebration of the One Hundred and Fiftieth Anniversary of the Opening of the Chapel on October 30th, A. D. 1776*. New York: M. B. Brown, 1916.

Gilkeson, John S. *Middle-Class Providence: 1820–1940*. Princeton: Princeton University Press, 1986.

Gipe-Lazarou, Andrew. "The 'Extreme Fantasy' of Delirious New York." *Lovecraft Annual*, no. 14 (2020): 109–37.

Gissing, George. *The Private Papers of Henry Ryecroft*. Introduction by John Stewart Collis. Bibliographic notes by Pierre Coustillas. Sussex, England: Harvester Press, 1982.

Goldberg, David J. *Discontented America: The United States in the 1920s*. Baltimore: Johns Hopkins University Press, 1999.

Gonzalez, Evelyn. *The Bronx*. New York: Columbia University Press, 2004.

Gordon, Linda. *The Second Coming of the KKK: The Ku Klux Klan of the 1920s and the American Political Tradition*. New York: Liveright, 2017.

Gossett, Thomas F. *Race: The History of an Idea in America*. New ed. New York: Oxford University Press, 1997.

Goudsward, David. *H. P. Lovecraft in the Merrimack Valley*. Foreword by Kenneth W. Faig Jr. New York: Hippocampus Press, 2013.

Grant, Donald M., and Thomas P. Hadley, eds. *Rhode Island on Lovecraft*. Providence: Grant-Hadley, 1945.

Group for Environmental Education. *Philadelphia Architecture: A Guide to the City*. Edited by John Andrew Gallery. 2nd ed. Philadelphia: Foundation for Architecture, 1994.

Gulger, Kimball and Husted. *Architectural History: The First Presbyterian Church of Elizabeth, New Jersey*. Elizabeth, N.J.: First Presbyterian Church Building Fund, 1947.

Haefele, John. "Chronological Listing of H. P. Lovecraft Photographs: Where Reproductions Have Been Published." In *James Van Hise Presents the Fantastic Worlds of H. P. Lovecraft*, edited by James Van Hise, 150–53. Yucca Valley, Calif.: James Van Hise, 1999.

Hamill, Pete. *Downtown: My Manhattan*. New York: Little, Brown, 2004.

Hapgood, Hutchins. *A Victorian in the Modern World*. Introduction by Robert Allen Skotheim. Seattle: University of Washington Press, 1972.

Harris, Luther S. *Around Washington Square: An Illustrated History of Greenwich Village*. Baltimore: Johns Hopkins University Press, 2003.

Harrison, John R. *The Reactionaries*. Preface by William Empson. London: Gollancz, 1966.

Hart, Mara Kirk. "Walkers in the City: George Willard Kirk and Howard Phillips Lovecraft in New York City, 1924–1926." In Cannon, *Lovecraft Remembered*, 221–47.

Hart, Mara Kirk, and S. T. Joshi. "Arthur Leeds." In Hart and Joshi, *Lovecraft's New York Circle*, 141.

———. "Everett McNeil." In Hart and Joshi, *Lovecraft's New York Circle*, 201–2.

———. "George Kirk." In Hart and Joshi, *Lovecraft's New York Circle*, 118–20.

———. "Rheinhart Kleiner." In Hart and Joshi, *Lovecraft's New York Circle*, 125–26.

———, eds. *Lovecraft's New York Circle: The Kalem Club, 1924–1927*. New York: Hippocampus Press, 2006.

Hefner, Brooks E. "Weird Investigations and Nativist Semiotics in H. P. Lovecraft and Dashiell Hammett." *Modern Fiction Studies* 60, no. 4 (Winter 2014): 651–76.

Heinze, Andrew R. "The Critical Period: Ethnic Emergence and Reaction, 1901–1929." In *The Columbia Documentary History of Race and Ethnicity in America*, edited by Ronald H. Bayor, 413–598. New York: Columbia University Press, 2004.

Hemp, William H. *New York Enclaves*. New York: C. N. Potter, 1975.

Henderson, Dylan. "Providence Lost: Natural and Urban Landscapes in H. P. Lovecraft's Fiction." Master's thesis, University of Arkansas, Fayetteville, 2020.

Hennessey, William J. *Walking Broadway: Thirteen Miles of Architecture and History*. New York: Monacelli Press, 2020.

Henry, O. "The Last Leaf." In *O. Henry: 101 Stories*, edited by Ben Yagoda, 600–605. New York: Library of America, 2021.

Hessel, Franz. *Walking in Berlin: A Flaneur in the Capital*. With an essay by Walter Benjamin. Translated by Amanda DeMarco. Cambridge, Mass.: MIT Press, 2017.

Higham, John. *Strangers in the Land: Patterns of American Nativism, 1860–1925*. 2nd ed. New Brunswick, N.J.: Rutgers University Press, 1988.

Houellebecq, Michel. *H. P. Lovecraft: Against the World, Against Life*. Introduction by Stephen King. Translated by Dorna Khazeni. New York: Cernunnos, 2019.

Houtain, George Julian. "Amateur Writings." In Cannon, *Lovecraft Remembered*, 86–89.

Hughes, Evan. *Literary Brooklyn: The Writers of Brooklyn and the Story of American City Life*. New York: Henry Holt, 2011.

Huxtable, Ada Louis. *Classic New York: Georgian Gentility to Greek Elegance*. Garden City, N.Y.: Anchor Books, 1964.

Immerso, Michael. *Coney Island: The People's Playground*. New Brunswick, N.J.: Rutgers University Press, 2002.

Jackson, Kenneth T. *Crabgrass Frontier: The Suburbanization of the United States*. New York: Oxford University Press, 1985.

————, ed. *The Encyclopedia of New York City*. 2nd ed. New Haven: Yale University Press; New York: New-York Historical Society, 2010.

Jacobson, Matthew Frye. *Whiteness of a Different Color: European Immigrants and the Alchemy of Race*. Cambridge, Mass.: Harvard University Press, 1998.

Jaher, Frederic Cople. *The Urban Establishment: Upper Strata in Boston, New York, Charleston, Chicago, and Los Angeles*. Urbana: University of Illinois Press, 1982.

Janicker, Rebecca. "New England Narratives: Space and Place in the Fiction of H. P. Lovecraft." *Extrapolation* 48, no. 1 (Spring 2007): 56–72.

Jemisin, N. K. *The City We Became*. New York: Orbit, 2020.

Johnson, Albert. Foreword. In *Immigration Restriction: A Study of the Opposition to and Regulation of Immigration into the United States*, by Roy L. Garis, vii–viii. New York: Macmillan, 1927.

Jonnes, Jill. *Conquering Gotham: A Gilded Age Epic; The Construction of Penn Station and Its Tunnels*. New York: Viking, 2007.

Joshi, S. T. *A Dreamer and a Visionary: H. P. Lovecraft in His Time*. Liverpool: Liverpool University Press, 2001.

————. *H. P. Lovecraft: A Comprehensive Bibliography*. Tampa, Fla.: Tampa University Press, 2009.

————. *I Am Providence: The Life and Times of H. P. Lovecraft*. 2 vols. New York: Hippocampus Press, 2013.

————. *An Index to the Selected Letters of H. P. Lovecraft*. 2nd rev. ed. West Warwick, R.I.: Necronomicon Press, 1991.

————, ed. "The Last Days of H. P. Lovecraft: Four Documents." *Lovecraft Studies*, no. 28 (Spring 1993): 36.

————. "A Look at Lovecraft's Letters." In *Lovecraft and a World in Transition: Collected Essays on H. P. Lovecraft*, 440–52. New York: Hippocampus Press, 2014.

————. *Lovecraft and a World in Transition: Collected Essays on H. P. Lovecraft*. New York: Hippocampus Press, 2014.

Joshi, S. T., and David E. Schultz. "He." In Joshi and Schultz, *An H. P. Lovecraft Encyclopedia*, 107–8.

————. *An H. P. Lovecraft Encyclopedia*. Westport, Conn.: Greenwood Press, 2001.

————. Introduction. In *Letters to Family and Family Friends*, by H. P. Lovecraft, edited by S. T. Joshi and David E. Schultz, 1:7–23. New York: Hippocampus Press, 2020.

————. Introduction. In *Letters to Rheinhart Kleiner and Others*, by H. P. Lovecraft, edited by S. T. Joshi and David E. Schultz, 9–32. New York: Hippocampus Press, 2020.

————. Introduction. In *Lord of a Visible World: An Autobiography in Letters*, by H. P. Lovecraft, edited by S. T. Joshi and David E. Schultz, vii–xix. Athens: Ohio University Press, 2000.

————. "Supernatural Horror in Literature." In Joshi and Schultz, *An H. P. Lovecraft Encyclopedia*, 255–56.

————. "Talman, Wilfred Blanch." In Joshi and Schultz, *An H. P. Lovecraft Encyclopedia*, 260–61.

Kadinsky, Sergey. *Hidden Waters of New York City: A History and Guide to 101 Forgotten Lakes, Ponds, Creeks, and Streams in the Five Boroughs*. Woodstock, Vt.: Countryman Press, 2016.

Kahn, Robert, ed. *New York City*. New York: Little Bookroom, 2002.

Kay, Jane Holtz. *Lost Boston*. Expanded and updated ed. Boston: Houghton Mifflin, 1999.

Kelley, Frank Bergen, comp. *Historic Elizabeth: 1664–1914.* Edited by Warren R. Dix. Elizabeth, N.J.: *Elizabeth Daily Journal,* 1914.

Kimball, Gertrude Selwyn. *Providence in Colonial Times.* Introduction by J. Franklin Jameson. Boston: Houghton Mifflin, 1912.

Kleiner, Rheinhart. "After a Decade and the Kalem Club." In Hart and Joshi, *Lovecraft's New York Circle,* 219–22.

———. "Bards and Bibliophiles." In Cannon, *Lovecraft Remembered,* 188–94.

———. "Discourse on H. P. Lovecraft." In Cannon, *Lovecraft Remembered,* 157–63.

———. "James Morton." In *Letters to James F. Morton,* by H. P. Lovecraft, edited by S. T. Joshi and David E. Schultz, 453–61. New York: Hippocampus Press, 2020.

———. "A Memoir of Lovecraft." In Cannon, *Lovecraft Remembered,* 195–203.

Koki, Arthur S. "H. P. Lovecraft: An Introduction to His Life and Writings." Master's thesis, Columbia University, 1962.

Kopp, Martin H. "Memories of Sonia H. Greene Davis." *Lovecraft Annual,* no. 1 (2007): 27–30.

Koritz, Amy. *Culture Makers: Urban Performance and Literature in the 1920s.* Urbana: University of Illinois Press, 2009.

Kraut, Alan M. *Silent Travelers: Germs, Genes, and the "Immigrant Menace."* New York: Basic Books, 1994.

Kyvig, David E. *Daily Life in the United States, 1920–1939: Decades of Promise and Pain.* Westport, Conn.: Greenwood Press, 2002.

Leazes, Francis J., Jr., and Mark T. Motte. *Providence, the Renaissance City.* Boston: Northeastern University Press, 2004.

La Farge, Paul. *The Night Ocean.* New York: Penguin, 2017.

LaValle, Victor. *The Ballad of Black Tom.* New York: Tom Doherty, 2016.

Law, Alma. "Nikita Balieff and the Chauve-Souris." In *Wandering Stars: Russian Emigré Theatre, 1905–1940,* edited by Laurence Senelick, 16–31. Iowa City: University of Iowa Press, 1992.

Leadon, Fran. *Broadway: A History of New York City in Thirteen Miles.* New York: W. W. Norton, 2018.

Lears, T. J. Jackson. *No Place of Grace: Antimodernism and the Transformation of American Culture, 1880–1920.* New York: Pantheon Books, 1981.

Lee, Hermione. *Biography: A Very Short Introduction.* Oxford: Oxford University Press, 2009.

Lee, O. Ivan. "Memorial of James F. Morton." *American Mineralogist* 27, no. 3 (March 1942): 200–202.

Leiber, Fritz. "My Correspondence with Lovecraft." In Cannon, *Lovecraft Remembered,* 299–302.

Levine, Philippa. *Eugenics: A Very Short Introduction.* New York: Oxford University Press, 2017.

Lévy, Maurice. *Lovecraft: A Study in the Fantastic.* Translated by S. T. Joshi. Detroit: Wayne State University Press, 1988.

Lewis, David Levering. *When Harlem Was Vogue.* New York: Penguin, 1997.

Lewis, Jane, ed. *Labour and Love: Women's Experience of Home and Family, 1850–1940.* Oxford: Basil Blackwell, 1986.

Ley, David. *The New Middle Class and the Remaking of the Central City.* Oxford: Oxford University Press, 1996.

Lippincott, Bertram. *Indians, Privateers, and High Society: A Rhode Island Sampler.* Philadelphia: J. B. Lippincott, 1961.

Little *Old New York: Illustrated.* Poughkeepsie, N.Y.: Oxford Pub., 1910.

Lockwood, Charles, Patrick W. Ciccone, and Jonathan D. Taylor. *Bricks & Brownstones: The New York Row House.* Foreword by New York Landmarks Conservancy. Essay by Fran Leadon. Photography by Dylan Chandler. New York: Rizzoli, 2019.

Long, Frank Belknap. *Howard Phillips Lovecraft: Dreamer on the Nightside.* Sauk City, Wisc.: Arkham House, 1975.

Longmore, Paul K., and Lauri Umansky. Introduction. In *The New Disability History: American Perspectives*, edited by Paul K. Longmore and Lauri Umansky, 1–29. New York: NYU Press, 2001.

Lovecraft, H. P. "The Call of Cthulhu." In Lovecraft, *Tales*, 167–96.

———. *Collected Essays.* Edited by S. T. Joshi. 5 vols. New York: Hippocampus Press, 2004–6.

———. "Cool Air." In Lovecraft, *Tales*, 158–66.

———. *Dagon and Other Macabre Tales.* Selected by August Derleth. Edited by S. T. Joshi. Introduction by T. E. D. Klein. Sauk City, Wisc.: Arkham House, 1987.

———. *Ec'h-pi-el Speaks: An Autobiographical Sketch.* Illustrated by Virgil Finlay. Saddle River, N.J.: Gerry de la Ree, 1972.

———. "'Facts Concerning the Late Arthur Jermyn and His Family." In *Dagon and Other Macabre Tales*, edited by S. T. Joshi, 73–82. Sauk City, Wisc.: Arkham House, 1987.

———. *From the Pest Zone: The New York Stories.* Edited by S. T. Joshi and David E. Schultz. New York: Hippocampus Press, 2003.

———. *Fungi from Yuggoth.* 3rd ed. West Warwick, R.I.: Necronomicon Press, 1990.

———. "He." In Lovecraft, *Tales*, 147–57.

———. "Homes and Shrines of Poe." In Joshi, *Collected Essays*, 4:255–59.

———. "The Horror at Red Hook." In Lovecaft, *Tales*, 125–46.

———. "The Horror at Martin's Beach." in Lovecraft, *The Horror in the Museum and Other Revisions*, edited by S. T. Joshi, 325–30. Sauk City, Wisc.: Arkham House, 1989.

———. *The Horror in the Museum and Other Revisions.* Edited by S. T. Joshi. Introduction by August Derleth. Sauk City, Wisc.: Arkham House, 1989.

———. *H. P. Lovecraft: Uncollected Letters.* West Warwick, R.I.: Necronomicon Press, 1986.

———. "In a Major Key." In Joshi, *Collected Essays*, 1:56–58.

———. *Letters from New York.* Edited by S. T. Joshi and David E. Schultz. San Francisco: Night Shade Books, 2005.

———. *Letters to C. L. Moore and Others.* Edited by David E. Schultz and S. T. Joshi. New York: Hippocampus Press, 2017.

———. *Letters to Elizabeth Toldridge and Anne Tillery Renshaw.* Edited by David E. Schultz and S. T. Joshi. New York: Hippocampus Press, 2014.

———. *Letters to Family and Family Friends.* Edited by S. T. Joshi and David E. Schultz. 2 vols. New York: Hippocampus Press, 2020.

———. *Letters to F. Lee Baldwin, Duane W. Rimel, and Nils Frome.* Edited by David E. Schultz and S. T. Joshi. New York: Hippocampus Press, 2016.

———. *Letters to James F. Morton.* Edited by David E. Schultz and S. T. Joshi. New York: Hippocampus Press, 2011.

———. *Letters to Maurice W. Moe and Others*. Edited by David E. Schultz and S. T. Joshi. New York: Hippocampus Press, 2018.

———. *Letters to Rheinhart Kleiner and Others*. Edited by S. T. Joshi and David E. Schultz. New York: Hippocampus Press, 2020.

———. *Lord of a Visible World: An Autobiography in Letters*. Edited by S. T. Joshi and David E. Schultz. Athens: Ohio University Press, 2000.

———. *Marginalia*. Collected by August Derleth and Donald Wandrei. Sauk City, Wisc.: Arkham House, 1944.

———. *The Occult Lovecraft*. With additional material and interpretations by Anthony Raven. Illustrated by Stephen E. Fabian. Saddle River, N.J.: Gerry de la Ree, 1975.

———. "The Rats in the Walls." In *Tales*, 77–96.

———. *Selected Letters*. Edited by August Derleth, James Turner, and Donald Wandrei. 5 vols. Sauk City, Wisc.: Arkham House, 1965–76.

———. "Some Dutch Footprints in New England." In Joshi, *Collected Essays*, 4:253–55.

———. *Supernatural Horror in Literature & Other Literary Essays*. Introduction by Darrell Schweitzer. Rockville, Md.: Wildside Press, 2008.

———. *Tales*. New York: Library of America, 2005.

———. "What Amateurdom and I Have Done for Each Other." In Joshi, *Collected Essays*, 1:271–74.

Lovecraft, H. P., and Willis Conover. *Lovecraft at Last*. With new introduction by S. T. Joshi. Foreword by Harold Taylor. New York: Cooper Square Press, 2002.

Lovecraft, H. P., et al. *The Dark Brotherhood and Other Pieces*. Sauk City, Wisc.: Arkham House, 1966.

Loveman, Samuel. "Of Gold and Sawdust." In *The Occult Lovecraft*, by H. P. Lovecraft, 21–22. Saddle River, N.J.: Gerry de la Ree, 1975.

———. "Howard Phillips Lovecraft." In Cannon, *Lovecraft Remembered*, 204–8.

———. "Lovecraft as a Conversationalist." In Cannon, *Lovecraft Remembered*, 209–11.

Low, Setha, Dana Taplin, and Suzanne Scheld. *Rethinking Urban Parks: Public Space & Cultural Diversity*. Austin: University of Texas Press, 2005.

Lurie, Maxine N., and Marc Mappen, eds. *The Encyclopedia of New Jersey*. Maps by Michael Siegel. New Brunswick, N.J.: Rutgers University Press, 2004.

MacLeod, Kirsten. "What People Really Read in 1922: *If Winter Comes*, the Bestseller in *Annus Mirabilis* of Modernism." In *Transitions in Middlebrow Writing, 1880–1930*, edited by Kate Macdonald and Christopher Singer, 14–34. New York: Palgrave Macmillan, 2015.

Mabbott, T. O. "H. P. Lovecraft: An Appreciation." In Cannon, *Lovecraft Remembered*, 420–22.

Manbeck, John B., ed. *The Neighborhoods of Brooklyn*. Introduction by Kenneth T. Jackson. 2nd ed. New York: Citizens Committee for New York City; New Haven: Yale University Press, 2004.

Mariconda, Steven J. "Lovecraft's Elizabethtown." In *On the Emergence of "Cthulhu" & Other Observations*, 56–58. West Warwick, R.I.: Necronomicon Press, 1995.

McCullough, David W. *Brooklyn . . . and How It Got That Way*. Photographs by Jim Kalett. New York: Dial Press, 1983.

McNamara, M. Eileen, annotator. "Medical Record of Winfield Scott Lovecraft." *Lovecraft Studies*, no. 24 (Spring 1991): 15–17.

————. "Winfield Scott Lovecraft's Final Illness." *Lovecraft Studies*, no. 24 (Spring 1991): 14.

McRoy, Jay. "There Goes the Neighborhood: Chaotic Apocalypse and Monstrous Genesis in H. P. Lovecraft's 'The Street,' 'The Horror at Red Hook,' and 'He.'" *Journal of the Fantastic in the Arts* 13, no. 4 (2003): 335–51.

Menegaldo, Gilles. "The City in H. P. Lovecraft's Work." Translated by S. T. Joshi. *Lovecraft Studies*, no. 4 (Spring 1981): 10–19.

Miller, Donald L. *Supreme City: How Jazz Age Manhattan Gave Birth to Modern America*. New York: Simon & Schuster, 2014.

Miller, Nathan. *New World Coming: The 1920s and the Making of Modern America*. New York: Scribner, 2003.

Miniter, Edith. "Amateur Writings." In Cannon, *Lovecraft Remembered*, 82–85.

Mires, Charlene. *Independence Hall in American Memory*. Philadelphia: University of Pennsylvania Press, 2002.

Mitgang, Herbert. *Once Upon a Time in New York: Jimmy Walker, Franklin Roosevelt, and the Last Great Battle of the Jazz Age*. New York: Free Press, 2000.

Moe, Maurice W. "Howard Phillips Lovecraft: The Sage of Providence." In Cannon, *Lovecraft Remembered*, 90–91.

Mondlin, Marvin, and Roy Meador. *Book Row: An Anecdotal and Pictorial History of the Antiquarian Book Trade*. Foreword by Madeleine B. Stern. New York: Carroll & Graf, 2004.

Moore, Lucy. *Anything Goes: A Biography of the Roaring Twenties*. New York: Overlook Press, 2010.

Moore, R. Laurence. "Insiders and Outsiders in American Historical Narrative and American History." *American Historical Review* 87, no. 2 (April 1982): 390–412.

Morton, James F., Jr. *The Curse of Race Prejudice*. New York: self-published, 1906.

Montague, Charlotte. *HP Lovecraft: The Mysterious Man Behind the Darkness*. New York: Chartwell, 2015.

Mordden, Ethan. *The Guest List: How Manhattan Defined American Sophistication— from the Algonquin Round Table to Truman Capote's Ball*. New York: St. Martin's Press, 2010.

Mosca, Alexandra Kathryn. *Green-Wood Cemetery*. Charleston, S.C.: Arcadia, 2008.

Murphy, Bruce, ed. *Benét's Reader's Encyclopedia*. 4th ed. New York: HarperCollins, 1996.

Murray, Will. "Autumn in Providence: Harry K. Brobst on Lovecraft." In Cannon, *Lovecraft Remembered*, 385–95.

Nelson, Gregg. "Architecture in the Fiction of H. P. Lovecraft." Master's thesis, University of Wisconsin–Eau Claire, 2002.

Nelson, Victoria. *The Secret Life of Puppets*. Cambridge, Mass.: Harvard University Press, 2001.

New York City Landmarks Preservation Commission. *Guide to New York City Landmarks*. 3rd ed. Text by Andrew S. Dolkart and Matthew A. Postal. Hoboken, N.J.: Wiley, 2004.

Norris, Duncan. "Lovecraft and Egypt: A Closer Examination." *Lovecraft Annual*, no. 10 (2016): 3–45.

Orton, Vrest. "Recollections of H. P. Lovecraft." In Cannon, *Lovecraft Remembered*, 339–46.

Osman, Suleiman. *The Invention of Brownstone Brooklyn: Gentrification and the Search for Authenticity in Postwar New York*. New York: Oxford University Press, 2011.

Owens, Patricia. "Racism in the Theory Canon: Hannah Arendt and 'the One Great Crime in Which America Was Never Involved.'" *Millennium* 45, no. 3 (2017): 403–24.

Panchyk, Richard. *Hidden History of Queens*. Charleston, S.C.: History Press, 2018.

Parascandola, Louis J., and John Parascandola, eds. *A Coney Island Reader: Through Dizzy Gates of Illusion*. New York: Columbia University Press, 2015.

Parrish, Michael E. *Anxious Decades: America in Prosperity and Depression, 1920–1941*. New York: W. W. Norton, 1992.

Parry, Albert. *Garrets and Pretenders: A History of Bohemianism in America*. New York: Dover, 1960.

Pavalko, Ronald M. "Racism and the New Immigration: A Reinterpretation of the Assimilation of White Ethnics in American Society." *Sociology and Social Research: An International Journal* 65, no. 1 (October 1980): 56–77.

Peeples, Scott. *The Man of the Crowd: Edgar Allan Poe and the City*. Photographs by Michelle Van Parys. Princeton: Princeton University Press, 2020.

Perrett, Geoffrey. *America in the Twenties: A History*. New York: Simon & Schuster, 1982.

Perry, Jeffrey B. *Hubert Harrison: The Struggle for Equality, 1918–1927*. New York: Columbia University Press, 2021. EBSCOhost.

———. *Hubert Harrison: The Voice of Harlem Radicalism, 1883–1918*. New York: Columbia University Press, 2009. EBSCOhost.

Peterson, A. Everett, ed. *Landmarks of New York: An Historical Guide to the Metropolis*. New York: City History Club of New York, 1923.

Pierce, Frederick Clifton. *Field Genealogy*. 2 vols. Chicago: Hammond Press, 1901.

Platt, Rutherford. *The Manual of Occupations*. New York: G. P. Putnam's Sons, 1929. https://babel.hathitrust.org/cgi/pt?id=uc1.$b297640&view=1up&seq=7&skin=2021.

Poe, Edgar Allan. *Doings of Gotham* [. . .]. Collected by Jacob E. Spannuth. With preface, introduction and comments by Thomas Ollive Mabbott. Pottsville, Pa.: Jacob E. Spannuth, 1929. https://www.eapoe.org/works/mabbott/spm29co0.htm.

Poe, Edgar Allan. *Letters of Edgar Allan Poe*. Edited by John Ward Ostrom. 2 vols. Cambridge, Mass.: Harvard University Press, 1948.

Poole, W. Scott. *In the Mountains of Madness: The Life and Extraordinary Afterlife of H. P. Lovecraft*. Berkeley, Calif.: Soft Skull Press, 2016.

Prendergast, Christopher. "Representing (Forgetting) the Past: Paul de Man, Fascism, and Deconstruction." In *The Triangle of Representation*, 63–81. New York: Columbia University Press, 2000.

The *Providence House Directory and Family Address Book: 1927–1928* [. . .]. Providence: Sampson & Murdock, 1927. https://t93c12bb2a2098924.starter1ua.preservica.com/uncategorized/IO_cb7ac4a6-5ed8-4f24-bfaa-2ae35f38ae37/.

Quinn, Arthur Hobson. *Edgar Allan Poe: A Critical Biography*. New foreword by Shawn Rosenheim. Baltimore: Johns Hopkins University Press, 1998.

Rhode Island Historical Preservation Commission. *Historic and Architectural Resources of the East Side, Providence: A Preliminary Report*. Providence: Rhode Island Historical Preservation Commission, 1989. https://preservation.ri.gov/sites/g/files/xkgbur406/files/pdfs_zips_downloads/survey_pdfs/prov_eastside.pdf.

Rider, Fremont, and Frederic Taber Cooper, comp. *Rider's New York City: A Guide-Book for Travelers, with 13 maps and 20 plans*. 2nd ed. New York: Henry Holt, 1923.

Riker, James, Jr. *The Annals of Newtown, in Queens County, New York* [. . .]. New York: D. Fanshaw, 1852. https://babel.hathitrust.org/cgi/pt?id=njp.32101072360546&view=1up &seq=11&skin=2021.

Roland, Paul. *The Curious Case of H. P. Lovecraft*. London: Plexus, 2014.

Ruff, Matt. *Lovecraft Country: A Novel*. New York: HarperPerennial, 2016.

Rybczynski, Witold. *A Clearing in the Distance: Frederick Law Olmsted and America in the 19th Century*. New York: Scribner, 1999.

Rydings, Joseph. *Country Walks in Many Fields: Being Certain Choice Annals of the Paterson Rambling Club*. Paterson, N.J.: Call, 1934.

Sanders, James. *Celluloid Skyline: New York and the Movies*. New York: Alfred A. Knopf, 2002.

Satariano, William A. "Immigration and the Popularization of Social Science, 1920 to 1930." *Journal of the History of Behavioral Sciences* 15, no. 4 (October 1979): 310–20.

Schechter, Elaine. *Perry Street: Then and Now*. Illustrated by Carol Creutzbury. New York: n.p., 1972.

Schmidt, Leah A. *Revere Beach*. Charleston, S.C.: Arcadia, 2002.

Schultz, David E. "From Microcosm to Macrocosm: The Growth of Lovecraft's Cosmic Fiction." In *An Epicure of the Terrible: A Centennial Anthology of Essays in Honor of H. P. Lovecraft*, edited by David E. Schultz and S. T. Joshi, 199–219. Rutherford, N.J.: Fairleigh Dickinson University Press, 1991.

———. "66 College Street." *Lovecraft Annual*, no. 9 (2015): 70–80.

Schultz, David E., and S. T. Joshi, eds. *An Epicure in the Terrible: A Centennial Anthology of Essays in Honor of H. P. Lovecraft*. Rutherford, N.J.: Farleigh Dickinson University Press, 1991.

Scott, Winfield Townley. "His Most Fantastic Creation." In Cannon, *Lovecraft Remembered*, 7–27.

Sederholm, Carl H., and Jeffrey Andrew Weinstock, eds. *The Age of Lovecraft*. Foreword by Ramsey Campbell. Commentary by China Miéville. Minneapolis: University of Minnesota Press, 2016.

———. "Lovecraft Rising." Introduction to Sederholm and Weinstock, *The Age of Lovecraft*, 1–42.

Seguine-LeVine, Joan. *Perth Amboy*. Dover, N.H.: Arcadia, 1996.

Seitz, Sharon, and Stuart Miller. *The Other Islands of New York City: A History and Guide*. 3rd ed. Woodstock, Vt.: Countryman Press, 2011.

Setiya, Kieran. "Correspondence: Revisiting H. P. Lovecraft." *Yale Review* 108, no. 3 (Fall 2020): 135–52.

Shaya, Gregory. "The *Flâneur*, the *Badaud*, and the Making of a Mass Public in France, circa 1860–1910." *American Historical Review* 109, no. 1 (February 2004): 41–77.

Silverman, Kenneth. *Edgar A. Poe: Mournful and Never-Ending Remembrance*. New York: HarperPerennial, 1992.

———. *Houdini! The Career of Ehrich Weiss: American Self-Liberator, Europe's Eclipsing Sensation, World's Handcuff King & Prison Breaker*. New York: HarperCollins, 1996.

Simmel, Georg. *The Art of the City: Rome, Florence, Venice*. Edited, translated and with an introduction by William Stone. London: Pushkin Press, 2018.

Slide, Anthony. *The Encyclopedia of Vaudeville*. Jackson: University Press of Mississippi, 2012.

Smith, Andrew F. *New York City: A Food Biography*. Lanham, Md.: Rowan & Littlefield, 2014.

———, ed. *Savoring Gotham: A Food Lover's Companion to New York City*. Oxford: Oxford University Press, 2015. Oxford Reference.

Smith-Rosenberg, Carroll. *Disorderly Conduct: Visions of Gender in Victorian America*. New York: Oxford University Press, 1985.

Sorensen, Leif. "A Weird Modernist Archive: Pulp Fiction, Pseudobiblia, H. P. Lovecraft." *Modernism/Modernity* 17, no. 3 (September 2010): 501–22.

Spencer, Truman Joseph. *The History of Amateur Journalism*. New York: Fossils, 1947.

Stansell, Christine. *American Moderns: Bohemian New York and the Creation of a New Century*. New York: Metropolitan Books, 2000.

St. Armand, Barton L. "Facts in the Case of H. P. Lovecraft." *Rhode Island History* 31, no. 1 (Winter 1972): 3–19.

Steinberg, Ted. *Gotham Unbound: The Ecological History of Greater New York*. New York: Simon & Schuster, 2014.

Stiles, Henry R., ed. *The Civil, Political, Professional and Ecclesiastical History, and Commercial and Industrial Record of the County of Kings and the City of Brooklyn, N.Y., from 1683 to 1884*. Assisted by L. B. Proctor and L. P. Brockett. 2 vols. New York: W. W. Munsell, 1884.

Stoddard, Lothrop. *The Rising Tide of Color against White World-Supremacy*. Introduction by Madison Grant. New York: Charles Scribner's Sons, 1920.

Straus, Roger, III. *America's Great Railroad Stations*. Text by Ed Breslin and Hugh Van Dusen. New York: Viking Studio, 2011.

Strausbaugh, John. *The Village: 400 Years of Beats and Bohemians, Radicals and Rogues; A History of Greenwich Village*. New York: Ecco, 2013.

Strohack, Matthew. "The City Under the Hill: Allegorical Tradition and H. P. Lovecraft's America." In *American Exceptionalisms: From Winthrop to Whitney*, edited by Sylvia Söderlind and James Taylor Carson, 223–42. Albany: State University of New York Press, 2011.

Suydam, J. Howard. *Hendrick Rycken, the Progenitor of the Suydam Family in America*. New York: Knickerbocker Press, 1898.

Talman, Wilfred Blanch. *The Normal Lovecraft*. Saddle River, N.J.: Gerry de la Ree, 1973.

Thomas, James Warren. "Howard Phillips Lovecraft: A Self-Portrait." Master's thesis, Brown University, 1950.

Thompson, J. Arthur. *What Is Man?* New York: G. P. Putnam's Sons, 1924.

Thomson, Christine Campbell, ed. *You'll Need a Night Light*. London: Selwyn & Blount, 1927.

Tobar, Cynthia, and Allen Thomas. *Guide to the Hall of Fame for Great Americans Collection, 1894–2008*. Bronx: Archives and Special Collections, Bronx Community College, 2016.

Torrey, Raymond H., Frank Place, Jr., and Robert L. Dickinson. *New York Walk Book* [. . .]. Pen sketches by Robert L. Dickinson. New York: American Geographical Society, 1923.

Turner, Jean-Rae, and Richard T. Koles. *Elizabeth: The First Capital of New Jersey*. Charleston, S.C.: Arcadia, 2003.

Tuttle, Lisa. *Encyclopedia of Feminism*. Harlow, UK: Longman, 1986.

Tyree, J. M. "Lovecraft at the Automat." *New England Review* 29, no. 1 (2008): 137–150.

Tyson, Donald. *The Dream World of H. P. Lovecraft: His Life, His Demons, His Universe.* Woodbury, Minn.: Llewellyn, 2010.

United States Department of Labor, Bureau of Labor Statistics. *Handbook of Labor Statistics.* 1936 ed. Washington, D.C.: G. P. O., 1936. https://fraser.stlouisfed.org/files/docs/publications/bls/bls_0616_1936.pdf.

Vanderbilt, Gertrude Lefferts. *The Social History of Flatbush, and Manners and Customs of the Dutch Settlers in Kings County.* Brooklyn: Frederick Loeser, 1909. Reprint, Bowie, Md.: Heritage, 2003.

Wallace, W. Stewart, comp. *A Dictionary of North American Authors Deceased Before 1950.* Toronto: Ryerson Press, 1951.

Wang, Peter H. "The Immigration Act of 1924 and the Problem of Assimilation." *Journal of Ethnic Studies* 2, no. 3 (Fall 1974): 72–75.

Walter, Dorothy C. *Lovecraft and Benefit Street.* North Montpelier, Vt.: Driftwind Press, 1943.

Warsh, Cheryl Krasnick. "The First Mrs. Rochester: Wrongful Confinement, Social Redundancy, and Commitment to the Private Asylum, 1883–1923." *Historical Papers/ Communications historiques* 23, no. 1 (1988): 145–167.

Watson, Steven. *Strange Bedfellows: The First American Avant-Garde.* New York: Abbeville Press, 1991.

Weigley, Russell F., Nicholas B. Wainwright, and Edwin Wolf II, eds. *Philadelphia: A 300-Year History.* New York: W. W. Norton, 1982.

Weinberg, Robert. *The Weird Tales Story.* West Linn, Ore.: FAX Collector's Edition, 1977.

Wells, Cornelius L. *Quarter Millennial Anniversary of the Reformed Dutch Church of Flatbush, New York.* Flatbush, N.Y.: Dutch Reformed Church, 1904.

Wetzel, George T., and R. Alain Everts. *Winifred Virginia Jackson: Lovecraft's Lost Romance.* Madison, Wisc.: Strange Co., [197?].

Wetzel, George T., ed. *Howard Phillips Lovecraft: Memoirs, Critiques & Bibliographies.* North Tonawanda, N.Y.: SSR, 1995.

Wetzsteon, Ross. *Republic of Dreams: Greenwich Village; The American Bohemia, 1910–1960.* New York: Simon & Schuster, 2002.

White, Edmund. *The Flâneur: A Stroll Through the Paradoxes of Paris.* New York: Bloomsbury, 2001.

Willensky, Elliot, and Norval White. *AIA Guide to New York City.* 3rd ed. San Diego: Harcourt Brace Jovanovich, 1988.

Williams, Raymond. *The Country and the City.* New York: Oxford University Press, 1973.

Wilson, Ben. *Metropolis: A History of the City, Humankind's Greatest Invention.* New York: Doubleday, 2020.

Wolanin, Tyler L. "New Deal Politics in the Correspondence of H. P. Lovecraft." *Lovecraft Annual*, no. 7 (2013): 3–35.

Woodward, William McKensie. *PPS/AIAri Guide to Providence Architecture.* Photography by Warren Jagger Photography. Foreword by William Morgan. Providence: Providence Preservation Society; American Institute of Architects, Rhode Island Chapter, 2003.

Wright-Cleveland, Margaret E. "Mentoring American Racial Identity: Sherwood Anderson's Lessons to Ernest Hemingway." *MidAmerica: The Yearbook of the Society for the Study of Midwestern Literature* 38 (2011): 28–40.

Yep, Laurence. "The Outsider in Fiction and Fantasy." *English Journal* 94, no. 3 (January 2005): 52–54.

Yeshiva University Museum. *A Perfect Fit: The Garment Industry and American Jewry, 1860–1960*. New York: Yeshiva University Museum, 2005.

Zieger, Robert H. "Pennsylvania Coal and Politics: The Anthracite Strike of 1925–1926." *Pennsylvania Magazine of History and Biography* 93, no. 2 (April 1969): 244–62.

INDEX

David J. Goodwin is the Assistant Director of the Center on Religion and Culture at Fordham University and was a Frederick Lewis Allen Room scholar at the New York Public Library from 2020 to 2023. He is a past commissioner and chairperson of the Jersey City Historic Preservation Commission and a former Jersey City Landmarks Conservancy board member. His first book, *Left Bank of the Hudson: Jersey City and the Artists of 111 1st Street*, received the J. Owen Grundy History Award in 2018. He blogs about cities, culture, and history at anothertownonthehudson.com.

Sharon Egretta Sutton, *When Ivory Towers Were Black: A Story about Race in America's Cities and Universities*

Britt Haas, *Fighting Authoritarianism: American Youth Activism in the 1930s*

David J. Goodwin, *Left Bank of the Hudson: Jersey City and the Artists of 111 1st Street*. Foreword by DW Gibson

Nandini Bagchee, *Counter Institution: Activist Estates of the Lower East Side*

Susan Celia Greenfield (ed.), *Sacred Shelter: Thirteen Journeys of Homelessness and Healing*

Susan Opotow and Zachary Baron Shemtob (eds.), *New York after 9/11*

Andrew Feffer, *Bad Faith: Teachers, Liberalism, and the Origins of McCarthyism*

Colin Davey with Thomas A. Lesser, *The American Museum of Natural History and How It Got That Way*. Forewords by Neil deGrasse Tyson and Kermit Roosevelt III

Wendy Jean Katz, *Humbug: The Politics of Art Criticism in New York City's Penny Press*

Lolita Buckner Inniss, *The Princeton Fugitive Slave: The Trials of James Collins Johnson*

Angel Garcia, *The Kingdom Began in Puerto Rico: Neil Connolly's Priesthood in the South Bronx*

Jim Mackin, *Notable New Yorkers of Manhattan's Upper West Side: Bloomingdale–Morningside Heights*

Matthew Spady, *The Neighborhood Manhattan Forgot: Audubon Park and the Families Who Shaped It*

Marilyn S. Greenwald and Yun Li, *Eunice Hunton Carter: A Lifelong Fight for Social Justice*

Jeffrey A. Kroessler, *Sunnyside Gardens: Planning and Preservation in a Historic Garden Suburb*

Elizabeth Macaulay-Lewis, *Antiquity in Gotham: The Ancient Architecture of New York City*

Ron Howell, *King Al: How Sharpton Took the Throne*

Phil Rosenzweig, *"12 Angry Men": Reginald Rose and the Making of an American Classic*

Jean Arrington with Cynthia S. LaValle, *From Factories to Palaces: Architect Charles B. J. Snyder and the New York City Public Schools*. Foreword by Peg Breen

Boukary Sawadogo, *Africans in Harlem: An Untold New York Story*

Alvin Eng, *Our Laundry, Our Town: My Chinese American Life from Flushing to the Downtown Stage and Beyond*

Stephanie Azzarone, *Heaven on the Hudson: Mansions, Monuments, and Marvels of Riverside Park*

Ron Goldberg, *Boy with the Bullhorn: A Memoir and History of ACT UP New York*. Foreword by Dan Barry

Peter Quinn, *Cross Bronx: A Writing Life*

Mark Bulik, *Ambush at Central Park: When the IRA Came to New York*

Matt Dallos, *In the Adirondacks: Dispatches from the Largest Park in the Lower 48*

Brandon Dean Lamson, *Caged: A Teacher's Journey Through Rikers, or How I Beheaded the Minotaur*

Raj Tawney, *Colorful Palate: Savored Stories from a Mixed Life*

Edward Cahill, *Disorderly Men*

Joseph Heathcott, *Global Queens: An Urban Mosaic*

Francis R. Kowsky with Lucille Gordon, *Hell on Color, Sweet on Song: Jacob Wrey Mould and the Artful Beauty of Central Park*

Jill Jonnes, *South Bronx Rising: The Rise, Fall, and Resurrection of an American City, Third Edition*

Barbara G. Mensch, *A Falling-Off Place: The Transformation of Lower Manhattan*

Felipe Luciano, *Flesh and Spirit: Confessions of a Young Lord*

Maximo G. Martinez, *Sojourners in the Capital of the World: Garifuna Immigrants*

For a complete list, visit www.fordhampress.com/empire-state-editions.